Sustainable Development and Human Security in Africa

Governance as the Missing Link

RECENTLY PUBLISHED BOOKS

Sustainable Development and Human Security in Africa: Governance as the Missing Link, Louis A. Picard, Terry F. Buss, Taylor B. Seybolt, and Macrina C. Lelei

Information and Communication Technologies in Public Administration: Innovations from Developed Countries, Christopher G. Reddick and Leonidas Anthopoulos

Creating Public Value in Practice: Advancing the Common Good in a Multi-Sector, Shared-Power, No-One-Wholly-in-Charge World, edited by John M. Bryson, Barbara C. Crosby, and Laura Bloomberg

Digital Divides: The New Challenges and Opportunities of e-Inclusion, Kim Andreasson

Living Legends and Full Agency: Implications of Repealing the Combat Exclusion Policy, G.L.A. Harris

Politics of Preference: India, United States, and South Africa, Krishna K. Tummala

Crisis and Emergency Management: Theory and Practice, Second Edition, Ali Farazmand

Labor Relations in the Public Sector, Fifth Edition, Richard C. Kearney and Patrice M. Mareschal

Democracy and Public Administration in Pakistan, Amna Imam and Eazaz A. Dar

The Economic Viability of Micropolitan America, Gerald L. Gordon

Personnel Management in Government: Politics and Process, Seventh Edition, Katherine C. Naff, Norma M. Riccucci, and Siegrun Fox Freyss

Public Administration in South Asia: India, Bangladesh, and Pakistan, edited by Meghna Sabharwal and Evan M. Berman

Making Multilevel Public Management Work: Stories of Success and Failure from Europe and North America, edited by Denita Cepiku, David K. Jesuit, and Ian Roberge

Available Electronically
PublicADMINISTRATION*netBASE*
http://www.crcnetbase.com/page/public_administration_ebooks

Sustainable Development and Human Security in Africa

Governance as the Missing Link

Edited by
Louis A. Picard • Terry F. Buss
Taylor B. Seybolt • Macrina C. Lelei

CRC Press
Taylor & Francis Group
Boca Raton London New York

CRC Press is an imprint of the
Taylor & Francis Group, an informa business

CRC Press
Taylor & Francis Group
6000 Broken Sound Parkway NW, Suite 300
Boca Raton, FL 33487-2742

Printed on acid-free paper
Version Date: 20150323

International Standard Book Number-13: 978-1-4822-5541-6 (Hardback)

Visit the Taylor & Francis Web site at
http://www.taylorandfrancis.com

and the CRC Press Web site at
http://www.crcpress.com

MIX
Paper from responsible sources
FSC® C013056
FSC www.fsc.org

Printed and bound in Great Britain by
TJ International Ltd, Padstow, Cornwall

Louis A. Picard dedicates this book to Pauline Greenlick and to the memory of his parents, Vincent and Katherine Picard.

Terry F. Buss dedicates this book to Dao Thi Thuy.

Taylor B. Seybolt dedicates this book to Willa M. Seybolt, Potter B. Seybolt, and Reed C. Seybolt.

Macrina C. Lelei dedicates this book to her wonderful parents who have always provided her with guidance, love, and support, and to her beloved children who give her reason to wake up and go to work each day. I love you all very much.

Contents

Preface

The chapters in this book, in part, stem from proceedings of an African sustainable development conference held at the University of Pittsburgh in March 2011 and hosted by the African Studies program and the Ford Institute for Human Security. In addition to Ford and African Studies, the two-day conference titled "Achieving Sustainable Development in Africa" was generously sponsored by the Office of the Provost and the University Center for International Studies (UCIS) with assistance from the Global Studies Center, the School of Education's Institute for International Studies in Education, and the Ridgeway Center of the Graduate School of Public and International Affairs.

The conference brought together practitioners, researchers, and scholars from the United States and Africa to discuss and debate challenges faced by Africa in achieving sustainable development within the context of improving economic conditions but continuing governance challenges.

The conference provided a forum to share knowledge and experiences that could inform conversations about sustainable development, human security, and governance. While many believe that sustainable development remains firmly in the environmental realm, this concept actually encompasses economic and sociopolitical concerns as well. As with many policies, the concept is also evolving as government agencies and individuals struggle to implement public policy. Priority areas of the conference included: health and environmental sustainability; gender equity; education; and governance, conflict mitigation, and development.

In planning the conference, organizers, under the leadership of Professor Joseph Adjaye, the director of African Studies, and Professor Louis A. Picard, the director of the Ford Institute for Human Security, agreed on the importance of looking at sustainable development from a holistic way, using a framework not only emphasizing the three pillars of sustainable development—economic, social, and environmental, but adding to these governance as a critical component. Governance became the central theme of the conference and this book.

The overarching argument of the book is that good governance is fundamental to achieving sustainable development and eradicating extreme poverty. Bad governance in African countries, since independence from colonial rule, produced social inequality, increased poverty, deprivation, political instability, political conflict, and poor policy-making.

African countries need improved governance structures and processes, especially strong institutions, to ensure sustainable economic growth and development that will significantly reduce poverty. Good governance is critical in bringing about prosperity through "smart" use of resources, mutually beneficial trade, effective economic management, productive citizen engagement, religious and ethnic harmony, conflict resolution, social service provision, regional cooperation, and rule of law, while reducing or eliminating reliance on foreign assistance and meddling by international organizations.

Acknowledgments

We have many individuals and institutional departments to thank for their support in this effort. Most importantly, we thank Professor Joseph Adjaye, then director of the African Studies program who developed the ideas and arguments discussed in this book. Louis A. Picard, director of the Ford Institute for Human Security was also instrumental in conceptualizing the idea for the conference, and submitting the proposal for funding to the Global Academic Partnership (GAP) Grant committee of the University Center for International Studies (UCIS). The GAP grant aims to strengthen interdisciplinary research and curriculum development on global themes at Pitt, while enhancing international scholarly ties at the University of Pittsburgh and raising the international profile of the Institution. It is an initiative of the Global Studies Program, and the Office of the Provost that generously provided a grant in the amount of $20,000 to support the conference. We express our sincere thanks to the Global Studies Program and the Office of the Program for their generous support.

Additional funding was provided by African Studies Program (ASP), Ford Institute for Human Security, Graduate School of Public and International Affairs (GSPIA), and University Honors College (UHC).

Macrina C. Lelei, the associate director of the African Studies Program and Diane Roth Cohen, administrator of the Ford Institute for Human Security provided invaluable assistance and administrative support throughout the conference planning, organizing, and implementation stages. Thanks to Kakwa K. McClain, at the time a master's student in Human Security at the Graduate School of Public and International Affairs and Hallie Powell, also at the time a master's student of International Development at the Graduate School of Public and International Affairs who actively participated in the organizing and mobilizing of student participants and student volunteers for the conference, as well as overseeing all the logistical issues.

Without the assistance of these individuals, the conference and book would not be possible: Sarah Kafui Amanfu, Abena Botwe-Asamoah, John Christie-Searles, Scott Crawford, Dr. Müge Kökten Finkel, Nitsa Bucritz Ford, Dr. Joshua B. Forrest, Dr. W. James Jacob, Andrew Juba, Zachary Karazsia, Kelly O'Rourke, Dr. Ravi K.

Sharma, Godfreyb Ssekajja, Kristin Huldah Walker, Dr. John C. Weidman II, Devani Whitehead, and Katherine Nami Yoon.

Our gratitude goes to the partnering units for the conference and the book project: the School of Education's Institute for International Studies in Education; and the Graduate School of Public and International Affairs Mathew B. Ridgeway Center for Security Studies, under their respective directors James Jacob and Phil Williams. Their support was invaluable and we are grateful to them, and the deans of the two schools.

We are indebted to all the authors without whose contributions this book would not have been written. Thanks also goes to the book editors who gave a lot of their time and worked tirelessly to ensure that the chapters were revised and edited accordingly and made ready for publication. Their editorial skills and valuable suggestions helped and guided the authors to complete their chapters and be ready for publication within the given deadlines. Above all, our gratitude goes to all the conference participants from within the United States and African institutions. Without their presence and participations there would not have been a successful conference resulting in this publication. Thank you to everyone!

Editors

Dr. Louis A. Picard is a professor and director of the Ford Institute for Human Security, Graduate School of Public and International Affairs at the University of Pittsburgh. He is also the former director of the International Development Division of the Graduate School of Public and International Affairs (GSPIA). He served as president of Public Administration Service from 2002 through 2005. His research and consulting specializations include international development, governance, development management, local government, civil society, and human resource development. His primary area of interest is Africa. Dr. Picard has served as a United Nations Development Programme and World Bank advisor and worked in more than 46 countries, 38 of which are in Africa and the Middle East. Dr. Picard has carried out research on regional and district administration in Tanzania as well as research on U.S. foreign aid, security, and diplomacy.

Dr. Terry F. Buss is a Fellow of the National Academy of Public Administration. Buss was past executive director and distinguished professor of public policy at Carnegie Mellon University (CMU), in Adelaide, Australia, from 2008 through 2014. Buss earned his doctorate in political science and mathematics at Ohio State University. Over the past 30 years, Buss has built his career in both academe and government. Before coming to CMU, he directed the program in International, Security and Defense Studies at the National Academy of Public Administration for five years. From 2000 through 2003, Buss served as dean of the School of Policy and Management at Florida International University (FIU) in Miami. In 2000, Buss worked as a senior policy advisor at the U.S. Department of Housing and Urban Development in Washington, DC. From 1997 through 2000, Buss chaired the Department of Public Management in the Sawyer School of Business at Suffolk University in Boston. While on leave from Suffolk, Buss spent one year at the World Bank as a full-time senior strategy advisor to the World Bank Institute and as the secretariat for the World Bank's Global Distance Learning Network (GDLN). From 1987 to 1997, Buss was director of the PhD program at and chair of the Department of Public Administration and Urban Studies at the University of Akron in Ohio and also director of research at the St. Elizabeth Hospital Medical Center/Northeast Ohio College of Medicine. During this period, Buss, while on leave from Akron, directed the U.S. Information Agency technical assistance program in Hungary for three years immediately following the fall of communism in Eastern Europe; he replicated this program in Russia from 1993 to 1996. Buss received the Most Honored Professor of the Russian Federation for his work in Russia. In addition, he worked on leave with the Council of Governors Policy Advisors, an affiliate of the National Governors Association as a senior advisor. He did so as an unprecedented two-time Fulbright scholar in Hungary, working with the Minister of the Interior. He also received two fellowships with the Congressional Research Service, where he authored policy studies mandated by Congress. From 1977 through 1987, Buss founded and directed the Public Service Institute—having five centers—at Youngstown State University and was professor of political science. Buss has published 12 books and nearly 350 professional articles on a variety of policy issues. Buss has won numerous awards for research and public service. Over the years, Buss has worked overseas on major projects in England, Wales, Italy, the Czech Republic, Slovakia, Hungary, Romania, Bulgaria, Ghana, Haiti, Canada, Colombia, Jamaica, the Bahamas, Singapore, Vietnam, and Australia. He also directed projects in Iraq, South Africa, Albania, Georgia, and Botswana from the United States. He has conducted executive education programs in Taiwan, Vietnam, Malaysia, Indonesia, Japan, Singapore, Australia, and the United States.

Dr. Taylor B. Seybolt joined Graduate School of Public and International Affairs at the University of Pittsburgh in 2008 after serving for six years as a senior program officer at the United States Institute of Peace (USIP) in Washington, DC. He has been a professorial lecturer at the Johns Hopkins School for Advanced International Studies and an adjunct professor in the Security Studies Program at Georgetown University. From 1999 through 2002, he was leader of the Conflicts and Peace Enforcement Project at the Stockholm International Peace Research Institute (SIPRI) in Sweden. Seybolt is the author of *Humanitarian Military Intervention: the Conditions for Success and Failure* (Oxford, 2007). He was also an advisor to the Genocide Prevention Task Force, co-chaired by Madeleine Albright and William Cohen.

Dr. Macrina C. Lelei is the interim director of the African Studies program (ASP), University Center for International Studies (UCIS), at the University of Pittsburgh. She is also an adjunct assistant professor in the Department of Administrative and Policy Studies, School of Education at the University of Pittsburgh. She received her PhD in social and comparative analysis in education and her master's degree in library science, both from the University of Pittsburgh. She received her bachelor's degree in education from Kenyatta University, Kenya. Her region of research and teaching focus is sub-Saharan Africa in the area of educational development with a specific emphasis on educational issues of access, opportunity, and equity especially gender equality, and the challenges faced by girls and women in accessing education. She has published four chapters in edited volumes and is completing her book manuscript on the challenges of education in rural Kenya.

Contributors

Dr. Isaac Addai is a professor of sociology at Lansing Community College Department of Social Science and Humanities. He obtained his doctoral degree in demography. His research interest focuses on fertility, religion, health, and well-being. He has published series of articles in a number of scholarly journals including: *Social Indicators Research, Journal of Happiness Studies, Social Biology, Biosocial Sciences, African Journal of Reproductive Health, Sociology of Religion, Review of Religious Research, Social Science, and Medicine, Review of Human Factor Studies, Journal of Comparative Family Studies,* and *International Journal of Contemporary Sociology.* Going beyond that, he has written four book chapters. He is an occasional manuscript reviewer for the following journals: *Social Science and Medicine, Ethnicity and Health, Social Biology, Sociology of Religion, Review of Religious Research, Canadian Journal of Sociology and Anthropology, Biosocial Sciences, Journal of Happiness Studies, Global Health, Family Planning Perspectives,* and the *Canadian Population Studies.*

Dr. Joseph K. Adjaye is a professor of history at the University of Ghana, Legon, and emeritus professor at the University of Pittsburgh, PA, USA, where, until his retirement in 2011, he was professor of Africana studies, history, and public and international affairs, and director of the African Studies Program from 2001. Prior to his appointment in Pittsburgh in 1987, he previously held academic and administrative appointments at the University of Illinois, Urbana-Champaign (1977–1980), and University of Wisconsin-Madison (1980–1987). Educated at the University of Ghana (BA), Binghamton University (MA), and Northwestern University (MA, PhD), Professor Adjaye specializes in African and Diaspora affairs, histories, and cultures. He is the author of five books, including the award-winning *Diplomacy and Diplomats in 19th Century Asante,* and *Language, Rhythm and Sound: Black Popular Cultures into the 21st Century,* and dozens of articles, review essays, and book chapters. A recipient of numerous awards and grants, including Ghana's Teacher Ambassador to the United States, Fulbright, and NEH, he has delivered over 400 invited lectures and presentations on campuses and in cities across the United States and around the world. Professor Adjaye developed the initial concept and conference ideas on sustainable development that generated most of the chapters in this volume.

Sarah Kafui Amanfu is a doctoral student at the University of Pittsburgh, School of Education, Department of Administrative and Policy Studies, in the area of social and comparative analysis in education with specialization in comparative and international education. She obtained her bachelor's degree majoring in chemistry from the Kwame Nkrumah University of Science and Technology in Ghana and her master's degree from the University of Pittsburgh, School of Education. Her research interests are: gender equality in education, health and economic development on which she is focusing her dissertation topic.

Dr. Barry Ames is the Andrew Mellon Professor of comparative politics at the University of Pittsburgh. He is also former chair of the Department of Political Science. He is the author of two major monographs, *Political Survival: Politicians and Public Policy in Latin America* and *The Deadlock of Democracy in Brazil* as well as many articles in political science journals. His early work focuses on institutions in Latin America, especially in Brazil; while more recent work concentrates on the relationship between social context and political behavior and on the study of state-level bureaucracies. He has also consulted extensively on governance and public management, particularly in Portuguese Africa.

Jeffrey W. Bassichis is now an operations research analyst at U.S. Transportation Command, Scott Air Force Base, Illinois. Prior to this assignment, he worked for AFRICOM.

Chris Belasco is the research and analysis coordinator on the USAID/West Africa Evaluation and Analytical Services project, for which he coordinates project assessments and conducts capacity development activities for organizations within the region. He serves as an instructor for the Department of Political Science at the University of Pittsburgh, where he teaches undergraduate courses on political development and international organizations. He is a doctoral candidate in the Graduate School of Public and International Affairs at the university and is completing a dissertation on comparative social policy in Latin America. His research interests include: political institutions, policy design, clientelism, and targeting of foreign aid and domestic social programs.

Miguel Cabrera is an assistant professor of political science at the University of California Santa Cruz and holds a PhD in Political Science from the University of Pittsburgh. He specializes in Latin American Politics.

N. Clark Capshaw is an operations research analyst at the Military Sealift Command in Washington, DC. Prior to this position, Capshaw worked for AFRICOM.

Carnegie Mellon University: Chapter 4 was completed by a group of graduate students in the Master of Public Policy and Management program at Carnegie

Mellon University—Australia. The project was completed in partial fulfillment of the requirements for the MSPPM degree, requiring a group capstone paper. Each student has graduated and gone on to work in government, consulting, and industry in Australia, Pakistan, Mongolia, and the United States. The students are: Peter Bucki, Simon Callaghan, Umair Khalid, Chris Morony, Jeremy Phillips, Ariunbilig Tsedendamba, and Ana Varela. Terry Buss served as faculty advisor on the project.

Dr. Joseph S. Chacha is a professor of chemistry at Maasai Mara University, Narok, Kenya. He received his PhD in electrochemistry from the University of Ottawa, Canada. He is a former acting deputy vice chancellor of academic affairs at Maasai Mara University. His current research interests are in environmental/analytical chemistry with a specific focus on determination of heavy metals and nutrients in water and soils. He also deals with determining the oxides of sulfur and nitrogen in ambient air using passive sampling techniques. Currently he is funded by the National Commission for Science, Technology and Innovation (NACOSTI) in the following projects: effects of tobacco growing on soil fertility and environmental degradation; development of nonporous ceramic membrane for domestic water filters; and biogas resource assessment, purification, and packaging for commercial use. He also has substantial interest in climate change, the conservation of water towers and rivers. He has published widely in reputable journals and attended and presented papers at local and international conferences.

Dr. John F. Clark is a professor and chair of the Department of International Relations at Florida International University. He is a leading scholar on politics and international relations in francophone Africa with particular regard to the Democratic Republic of the Congo (DRC-Kinshasa) and the Republic of the Congo (Brazzaville). He has carried out extensive field research for two decades in these two countries and elsewhere in eastern and central Africa. Clark has the unique distinction of publishing academic books on both Congos—a seminal study of Congo-Brazzaville (*The Failure of Democracy in the Republic of Congo*, Lynne Rienner Publishers 2008) and a widely praised analysis of the internationalization of war in the DRC (edited volume, *The African Stakes of the Congo War*, Palgrave, 2002). He has also authored more than 40 academic journal articles and book chapters on African politics. Clark holds a PhD in foreign affairs from the University of Virginia, and has served as Fulbright research scholar and lecturer at Makerere University, Uganda.

Dr. Joshua B. Forrest is an associate professor in the Department of History and Political Science at La Roche College. He is also the director of the Kerr Institute of African Studies. He attended the University of Wisconsin where he received his BA (French area studies), MA (political science), and PhD (political science and public administration). He received an award in 2002–2003 for research scholar, African policy studies, from the Graduate School of Public & International Affairs, University of Pittsburgh. His research focus is on the politics of local autonomy, subnationalism and Guinea-Bissauan history. His publications include: *Subnationalism in Africa* (2004), *Lineages of State Fragility: Rural Civil Society in Guinea-Bissau* (2003), and *Namibia's Post-Apartheid Regional Institutions* (1998).

Zachary A. Karazsia is a PhD student in political science at Florida International University. He serves as a graduate teaching assistant in the Department of Politics and International Relations, with a concentration in comparative politics and international relations coursework. He earned two bachelor of arts degrees in global studies and communication arts and sciences from the Pennsylvania State University and a master's in international development from the Graduate School of Public and International Affairs (GSPIA), University of Pittsburgh. His geographic specialization is sub-Saharan Africa with a concentration on reconciliation, disarmament, demobilization, repatriation, reinsertion, and reintegration (DDRRR), and post-conflict reconstruction programs aimed in achieving sustainable peace and security in societies following situations of genocide and mass trauma. Mr Karazsia has particular knowledge of Rwanda and the eastern Democratic Republic of Congo. His research includes the study of genocide and mass killing, ethnic conflict, security studies, and post conflict reconciliation through the lenses of comparative politics and international relations.

Kwesi Korboe has more than 27 years of considerable experience in designing and implementing agricultural projects funded by reputable multinational agencies. He has worked in the agribusiness sector in senior executive positions and also provided consulting services to numerous private sector firms. He is currently a senior technical/agribusiness advisor with ACDI/VOCA and country representative for its subsidiary Agribusiness Systems International (ASI) for project development and implementation with the private sector, the Government of Ghana, and other non-U.S. donor agencies. Kwesi also provided technical services to the USAID funded ADVANCE Project, which ended in February 2014 on value chains integration and studies and was the lead consultant in conducting three value chain studies in soya, maize, and rice value chains. Prior to this, he was the chief of party of the Southern Horticultural Zone Project of the Millennium Challenge Account (MCA) Compact Program for Ghana implemented by ACDI/VOCA and responsible for project administration, technical implementation, and budgets. He was the chief executive officer of Jei River Farms Ltd, a leading producer and exporter of fresh pineapples in Ghana with staff strength of 600. He served as a key member and agriculture team leader for the Ghanaian team that designed and negotiated the USD 547 MCA Compact Program for Ghana. Kwesi was the programme manager for the West Africa Fair Fruit Project which was linked fair-trade-certified farmers in Burkina Faso and Ghana to external markets. He was a financial/project analyst on the USAID Trade & Investment Reform Project (TIRP). He has worked with the private sector in various parts of the country and facilitated access to finance and linkages to various market initiatives. He provides technical support to clients, and currently serves on a number of boards of some key companies and technical team advisory committees to the Government of Ghana. He holds a master's degree in economics policy management, post graduate diploma in agriculture administration, and a bachelor's degree in agriculture, all from the University of Ghana, Legon.

Dr. William F. S. Miles is a professor of political science at Northeastern University in Boston, where he teaches courses on comparative politics, international development, religion, and politics. A former Peace Corps volunteer in Niger (1977–1979), Miles has also lived in Africa as a State Department intern (1980) and Fulbright scholar (1983, 1986, 1996–1997). His four books on Africa include, as editor and major contributor, *Political Islam in West Africa* (Lynne Rienner, 2007). Miles' Africanist articles have appeared in a wide span of major journals, including (among many others) *African Studies Review*, *Journal of Modern African Studies*, *Studies in Comparative International Development*, *Ethnic and Racial Studies*, *Comparative Politics*, and *the American Political Science Review*. Miles has consulted for USAID on the use of development projects in counterterrorism programming in Burkina Faso, Chad, and Mali. He holds a PhD in political science from the Fletcher School of Law and Diplomacy.

Dr. Thomas Mogale completed his BA with honors at the University of the North, South Africa, and his master's degree in science at the University of London's School of Oriental and African Studies. In 1995, Dr. Mogale obtained his doctorate from the University of Pittsburgh's Graduate School of Public and International Affairs (GSPIA) where he majored in various subjects covering economics, social development as well as urban and regional planning. Currently, he serves as a senior lecturer and program manager at the Witwatersrand Graduate School of Public & Development Management. He also currently sits on the board of an IT company and a development NGO as non-executive director and is a member of the National Anti-Corruption Forum.

Clive Mutunga is currently the Family Planning and Environment technical advisor at USAID, in Washington, DC. Prior to joining USAID, Mr. Mutunga led PAI's research team primarily working on population and climate change as well as on aid financing and effectiveness. He has several years of experience conducting public policy research and analysis on a broad range of socio-economic issues including the environment, population, and health. He had a long and rewarding stint at the Kenya Institute for Public Policy Research & Analysis (KIPPRA), a public think tank mandated to support the public policy process in Kenya by conducting policy research and analysis for the Government of Kenya and the private sector for policy formulation and implementation. Prior to joining PAI, he worked with Policy Planning and Evaluation Inc. (PP&E), a private consulting firm in Herndon, VA, conducting economic cost–benefit analysis of a proposed federal regulation for the Occupational Safety and Health Administration (OSHA) of the U.S. Department of Labor. He holds an MA (economics) from the University of Nairobi, Kenya, with a specialization in environmental and natural resource economics from the Centre for Environmental Economics Policy Research and Analysis in Africa (CEEPA) based at the University of Pretoria, South Africa; and a BA (economics and sociology) from the University of Nairobi. He delivered the opening keynote presentation at the sustainable development conference held at the University of Pittsburgh in March 2011. The topic of his paper was, "Population Dynamics, Climate Change and Sustainable Development in Africa."

Chris Opoku-Agyeman is a doctoral candidate (ABD) and adjunct faculty for research methods at the Department of Public Administration and Urban Studies at the University of Akron. His proposed dissertation is on the topic "Democratization, Civic/Citizens' Participation and Ghana's 4th Republic: Implications for Public Policy." He obtained his master's degree in public administration with a focus on strategic management and program evaluation from the University of Akron and his bachelor of arts degree (first class honors/dean's list) in political science with information from the University of Ghana, Legon. He has written book chapters and published in a number of academic journals including *Social Indicators Research*, *Journal of Happiness*, and *Africa Today*. He has received several awards which include The Most Distinguished Graduate Student for Leadership and Outstanding Contribution to the African community on Campus, African Student's Association, University of Akron, 2011 and was one of twenty-seven students selected from the University of Akron to visit Warren Buffett at Berkshire Hathaway's global headquarters for a day in Omaha, Nebraska, November 5–8, 2009.

Dr. Elke Zuern is an assistant professor of political science at Sarah Lawrence College and previously taught at Amherst College, where she was awarded a Mellon postdoctoral fellowship and a Loewenstein fellowship. She specializes in the study of community-level democratization; post-conflict reconciliation; poverty, inequality, and social movements in new democracies; collective memory and post-conflict reconciliation. Her field work has focused on South Africa and Namibia, and she is the author of the highly acclaimed *The Politics of Necessity: Community Organizing and Democracy in South Africa* (University of Wisconsin Press, 2011). She holds a PhD in political science from Columbia University.

OVERVIEW

I

Chapter 1

Achieving Sustainable Development in Africa

A Governance Perspective

Louis A. Picard and Macrina C. Lelei

Contents

Sustainable Development

The term "sustainable development" was used as early as 1972 at the United Nations (UN) Conference on the Human Environment in Stockholm, Sweden. However, it was not until 1987, with a UN report entitled *Our Common Future*, that the term was fully defined and translated into policy. Over the past decades, many new development initiatives have been introduced in Africa, each of which has been heralded as marking a new era in the continent's development, but most have failed to produce the much anticipated sustainability results due to numerous, interrelated challenges facing Africa.

Nowhere, until recently, has less growth and development taken place than in Africa, especially sub-Saharan Africa (SSA). The past decade, however, has seen dramatic growth in the economies of key African states. An analysis by *The Economist* (2011) observes that six of the world's ten fastest-growing economies are now in SSA, and in terms of raw economic growth, Africa has now topped the world. Yet, many African countries have lagged behind. Most of the human security crises worldwide are now in Africa. What accounts for the divergence between high-growth economies and human security crises? Are there factors that explain growth versus human security crisis? This is the focus of this book.

Key questions are: why has the economic growth performance of some countries been so disappointing, and why has human development progress in much of Africa continued to lag? UN documents have emphasized "human development," as improving people's lives measured by life expectancy, security against crime and physical violence, adult literacy, access to education, as well as people's average income, a necessary condition for freedom of choice.

In a broader sense, the notion of human development incorporates all aspects of an individuals' well-being, from their health status to their economic and political freedom. Unfortunately, despite the rapid growth of some countries, SSA lags behind in almost every indicator of human development, and therefore still has a long road ahead in achieving sustainable development. The broad approach to human development allows us to focus on its governance dimension and relationship between human insecurity on the one hand and sustainable development on the other.

The UN Report (1987) defined sustainable development as development that meets the needs of the present without compromising the future generation's ability to meet their own needs. It contains two key concepts: the essential needs of the world's poor to which overriding priority should be given, and, the idea of limitations imposed by the state of technology and social organization on the environment's ability to meet present and future needs (Our Common Future 1987, 43). Although sustainable development can be interpreted in many ways, at its core is an approach that looks to balance different, often competing, needs against an awareness of environmental, social, and economic limitations.

Sustainable development is about ensuring a strong, healthy, and just world that meets the diverse needs of all people now and in future communities, promoting personal well-being, social cohesion and inclusion, creating equal opportunity, and reducing poverty. To the authors of this book, a key to understanding sustainability is the role good governance plays.

The World Bank defines sustainability in terms of opportunities for future generations, using a governance framework of environmentally sustainable development (ESD) that encompasses equity and social objectives, including empowerment, participation, social mobility, and cultural identity for citizens. It includes the recognition that growth must be inclusive and environmentally sound to reduce poverty and build shared prosperity for today's populations and to continue to meet the needs of future generations.

Resources must be used efficiently and carefully planned to deliver immediate and long-term benefits for people, the planet, and prosperity (World Bank 1989). More recently, the international community's definition expanded to include a focus on human development, an emphasis on values and goals, such as increased life expectancy, education, equity, and opportunity. Human capital can be increased by investing in health care, education, and job training as necessary dimensions of sustainable development. The 1992 Rio Conference on Environment and Development conceptualized the pursuit of sustainable development within the framework of three "pillars"—environmental protection, economic development, and social development—that must go hand in hand (Figure 1.1). What is missing from this framework is the role that good governance plays in the true commitment to advancing the sustainable development agenda. There is a need to focus on strategies that emphasize strengthened governance within the context of institutional frameworks for sustainable development to promote a balanced integration of the economic, social, and environmental dimensions within the governance patterns, as well as strengthened partnerships with other players in the development field. It is through inclusive strategies, and decision-making based upon rules of the game that true sustainable development can be achieved.

From the African perspective as articulated by the New Partnership for Africa's Development (NEPAD), launched by the African heads of state in 2001, the sustainable development goal encompasses poverty reduction and the promotion of sustainable growth and development, and the empowerment of women through building genuine partnerships at country, regional, and global levels. NEPAD explicitly identified the governance issue as critical to sustainability (even if it often backs away from governance issues in practice).

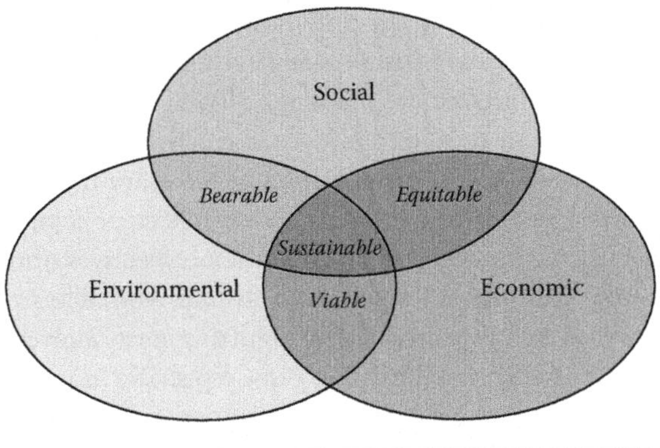

Figure 1.1 Scheme of sustainable development at the confluence of three pillars.

NEPAD provides unique opportunities for Africa to address critical challenges facing the continent, including the attainment of the Millennium Development Goals (MDGs) and other continental and international agreed-upon objectives. As specified by NEPAD (2001), Africa's challenge is to develop the capacity for sustained growth at all levels to achieve poverty reduction, generate major gains in national and per capita income, and produce noteworthy improvements in quality of life indices. Results will depend on factors such as infrastructure, capital accumulation, human capital, institutions, structural diversification, competitiveness, health, good stewardship of the environment, and most of all strong institutions of good governance. Among NEPAD's key principles is the recognition of good governance as a basic requirement for peace, human security, and sustainable political and socioeconomic development, its goal being sustainable improvement of the well-being and standard of living of current and future generations (NEPAD 2001).

Thus, the concept of sustainable development, broadly understood, implies a concern for present and future generations and for the long-term health and integrity of the physical, social, and cultural environment. It embraces a concern for the quality of life (not just income growth), for greater equity between people in the present (including prevention of poverty) and in the future, and for the social, ethical, and political dimensions of human welfare. It also implies that economic development can only take place as long as it is within the carrying capacity of natural and human social systems, suggests that human resource development (HRD) is a critical precondition to economic growth and sustainable development, and that HRD and sustainability are both closely linked to patterns of good governance.

However, such considerations cannot be appreciated if there is a lack of up-to-date information, knowledge, tools and skills, as well as institutions and appropriate structures to address the various concerns of sustainable development such as the fight against poverty, gender equality, human rights, education for all, health and environmental protection, population growth, and human security to realize a better quality of life for all, not only now, but also for generations to come. Frameworks aimed at advancing sustainable development and good governance in Africa have continued to face critical challenges: "Why are some African economies less sustainable today than they were 25 years ago while others are growing very rapidly?" The argument is that more attention is necessary in promoting conversations about the problems between academics, researchers, policymakers, and practitioners in the field. It is important to bring in the perspectives of practitioners who deal with day-to-day realities on the ground to find workable strategies that will advance sustainable development while recognizing past shortcomings in governance. The focus should be on identifying gaps, especially in participatory models, sound economic management and lower levels of corruption and other areas where further progress is required, and setting a series of pragmatic measures to address the challenges and avoid repeating the mistakes of the past.

Africa's Development Landscape since Independence

For many African countries, the years immediately following independence were filled with hope and high expectations for economic growth and development. Most people believed that rapid progress would be made in raising income and improving well-being. And indeed in the early years, many African countries successfully expanded basic infrastructure and social services and were economically successful. Overall economic growth in SSA averaged about 4% per year between 1961 and 1970 (World Bank 1989). Many newly independent countries used revenues generated from natural resources to build infrastructure, industry, education, and health systems while increasing employment. Much effort also went to consolidating fragile new nation states. After the initial period of growth, however, most African economies faltered, then went into decline. The sharp oil price increase in the 1970s erased many of the improvements that had been made. African countries borrowed massively to offset declining revenues and begun to live beyond their means—sowing the seeds of Africa's debt problems today. Also, heavy dependence on natural resources led to resource depletion and environmental degradation and worsened the exposure of weaker economies to external shocks, thereby increasing poverty and reversing social development in the continent. These events were tied to a series of changes in governance systems, one-party states, military regimes, and state failure.

Numerous and complex factors contributed to Africa's economic and political decline from the mid-1970s to the late 1990s. Key among them were falling world prices for commodities, high levels of violence, political instability, economic balkanization, and antitrade policies that sabotaged economic growth and reduced state capacities below the already low levels that had characterized colonial regimes, and the structural adjustment programs (SAPs). During this period, Africa lost half of its share of world markets to other developing countries simply because these countries were able to produce and deliver the same goods more cheaply (Calderisi 2006). Following the end of the cold war in the 1980s, the former eastern bloc markets were integrated with Western economies, releasing raw materials and other products onto the world market, to the detriment of the prices of these products, which included some of Africa's major exports. Further, the end of the cold war weakened Africa's position in the global economy and reduced its strategic significance (Van Der Veen 2004). Africa's governments had become fragile, soft, and at the same time predatory in their relationship to its citizenry.

By the 1980s, most African economies were in "freefall," both politically and economically, suffering from stagnation, contraction, and decline. Many economists have characterized the period as Africa's "lost decade," and also the transition decade that marked the beginning of the decline of "developmentalism" and rise of neo-liberalism, euphemistically called globalization (Shivji 2006).

Throughout the 1980s and early 1990s, African countries embarked upon SAPs enforced primarily by the IMF and the World Bank, with the support of Western nations. These SAPs were aimed at adapting African economies to the international economic environment and to globalization (Shivji 2006). African countries were required to achieve financial equilibrium before they could be integrated into the global economy. To receive development aid loans, African governments were required to meet specified conditions, including drastically cutting back on government expenditures, increasing exports of primary materials, privatization of industries, higher interest rates and trade liberalization, and reduced financial regulations, and to embark on market-based pricing and the devaluation of local currencies (Easterly 2003). Many critics of SAPs have argued that while these policies were an effort to root out the corruption and mismanagement of African economies, the budgetary austerity forced on the poor nations often led to the gutting of essential services such as agricultural extension, infrastructure, health, and education. SAPs ignored governance issues by focusing on financial reform.

SAPs have been and remain controversial. SAPs reversed the development successes of the 1960s and 1970s, with millions sliding into poverty every year (Easterly 2003). SAPs have proven economically disastrous, as all the 54 developing countries that implemented the programs have ended up poorer than they started (McGregor 2005). The World Bank has had to accept that SAPs have failed the poor, with a special burden falling on women and children (Nwankwo and Richards 2004). Yet, together with the IMF it still demanded that developing countries persist with SAPs.

Critics argue that Africa's problems were externally driven, caused by deteriorating terms of trade and a hostile environment in the global economy. The solution proposed lies in greater self-reliance and less prescriptions from the Washington consensus. Reflecting poor growth performance despite policy improvements, the real economic performance of countries that had recently adopted Washington consensus policies was disappointing (Krugman 1995). More autonomy should be given to African governments to map out their development agenda according to people's needs.

However, proponents of SAPs have taken the opposite view arguing that while external factors contributed to the continent's hardships, basic African problems were internal. Primary responsibility is placed on the African state for bad governance and lack of accountability, totally ignoring the role of globalization and the international economic system in both the exploitation of African resources and supporting of nondemocratic states when it suited their interests (Shivji 2006). Africa was living beyond its means, and was encumbered by poor policies, an overextended state, poor leadership, and little or no ownership of local development programs.

The process of structural adjustment went awry, in large part because of poor governance, and the way African governments were beholden to the donor community at the expense of the African people (Calderisi 2006). Most critics attribute the real problems of SAPs to Africa's high costs of production and distribution, and poor investment, and the West's failure to explain their strategy. But whoever is to blame, we need to look hard at the real reasons for Africa's development problems that are linked to governance issues—rule of law, equal opportunity, political freedom and pluralism, and civil liberties. Countries will not benefit from a sustainable increase in living standards and well-being that encompasses material consumption, education, health, and environmental protection without sustainable, and good governance.

With the experiences of SAPs and earlier development initiatives, there have been some useful lessons learned that have enabled Africa and its development partners to stem the economic decline and begin the slow process of recovery. Acceleration began in the early 2000s following the introduction of the Heavily Indebted Poor Countries (HIPC) initiative in 1995; MDGs in 2000; the establishment of NEPAD in 2000; the African Union (AU) in 2002; among other such programs, resulting in what has been dubbed by many as the new paradigm for Africa's development. The new shift places emphasis on poverty reduction, good governance, and accountability by all stakeholders. Development has to be approached from multiple dimensions in tackling climate change, food security, and inequality but above all, the issue of debt should be tackled with urgency.

HIPC Initiative

Starting in 1999, poverty reduction has become the prime objective of the programs and operations of international financial institutions (IFIs) in low-income countries. This marked a departure from an earlier emphasis on correcting macroeconomic imbalances and marked distortions through stabilization and SAPs. Following the failure of SAPs in poverty reduction, the World Bank and the IMF launched HIPC in 1995 to provide debt relief that was seen as key to poverty reduction. The initiative was also to ensure that no poor country faced a debt burden it could not manage. To qualify for debt relief, countries must meet certain criteria, commit to poverty reduction through policy changes, demonstrate a good track-record over time, and most importantly introduce political reforms that strengthened institutions of governance. The IMF and the World Bank provided interim debt relief in the initial stage, and when a country meets its commitments, full debt relief is provided. Debt relief is one part of a much larger effort, which also includes aid flows, to address the development needs of low-income countries, and make sure that debt sustainability is maintained over time. For debt reduction to have a tangible impact on poverty, additional money needs to be spent on programs that benefit the poor. As stated in the IMF factsheet (2014), before the HIPC initiative, eligible countries were, on average, spending slightly more on debt service than on health and education combined. But with the HIPC initiative, they have increased markedly their expenditures on health, education, and other social services. On average, such spending is about five times the amount of debt-service payments.

For the 36 countries receiving debt relief, debt service declined by 1.5% of GDP between 2001 and 2012 (IMF 2014). One of the four main conditions for a country to receive full debt relief is to prepare the Poverty Reduction Strategy Paper (PRSP) that has been widely accepted in the development community as the framework for low-income countries to accept loans from the IMF and the World Bank. As of June 2005, 49 countries had prepared a PRSP that has had a major impact on the overall policymaking that determines a country's development strategy. More than one-half of these HIPC countries are from Africa (UNDP 2005). Under a partnership principle, governments in collaboration with development partners plan, implement, and monitor the PRS to ensure that this partnership will increase the scale of operations, reduce government transaction costs, and improve accountability (UNDP 2005).

Many positive development activities are occurring all across Africa as countries race toward achieving the MDGs amidst a complex of challenges that include preserving peace and stability, and improving governance, delivery of basic services, and employment opportunities for youth. In the past decade, there has been a striking change in patterns of growth among countries that have followed the basic premises of MDG and its good governance principles.

Millennium Development Goals

MDGs developed over the course of the 1990s were unanimously ratified by all UN member countries in 2000 as part of the Millennium Declaration—committing nations to a new global partnership to reduce extreme poverty in its many dimensions—income poverty, hunger, disease, lack of adequate shelter, and exclusion, while promoting gender equality, education, and environmental sustainability. They are also basic human rights—the rights of each person on the planet to health, education, shelter, and security (see Table 1.1).

While sustainable governance was not an explicit MDG, it was central to the core approach to development. Africa, like other developing countries, has embraced MDGs as the basis for formulating its development and poverty reduction strategies and we are beginning to see positive trends in the continent's development. The *MDG Report* 2013 assessing progress in Africa toward the MDGs concludes that while Africa is the world's second fastest-growing region, its rate of poverty reduction is insufficient to reach the target of halving extreme poverty by 2015. The question remains, "Is Africa on track to achieving the MDGs?" In trying to answer this question, it is important to note that there are considerable variations in the prospects of individual African countries. Those that have implemented sound economic policies and improved their systems of governance have seen an acceleration in growth and poverty reduction and are likely to make significant headway in the future. There are, by contrast, other countries where policy improvements have yet to be secured, largely due to conflicts and poor governance, and where little

Table 1.1 United Nations Millennium Development Goals

MDG 1: Eradicate extreme hunger and poverty	Halve, between 1990 and 2015, the proportion of people whose income is less than $1 a day and the proportion of people who suffer from hunger
MDG 2: Achieve universal primary education	Ensure that, by 2015, children everywhere, boys and girls alike, will be able to complete a full course of primary schooling
MDG 3: Promote gender equality and empower women	Eliminate gender disparity in primary and secondary education, preferably by 2005, and in all levels of education no later than 2015
MDG 4: Reduce child mortality	Reduce by two-thirds, between 1990 and 2015, the under-five mortality rate
MDG 5: Improve maternal health	Reduce by three-quarters, between 1990 and 2015, the maternal mortality ratio
MDG 6: Combat HIV/AIDS, malaria, and other diseases	Halt and reverse by 2015 the spread of HIV/AIDS, incidence of malaria, and other major diseases
MDG 7: Ensure environmental sustainability	Integrate the principles of sustainable development into country policies and programs and reverse the loss of environmental resources Halve, by 2015, the proportion of people without sustainable access to safe drinking water and basic sanitation Have achieved by 2020 a significant improvement in the lives of at least 100 million slum dwellers
MDG 8: Develop a global partnership for development	Develop further an open, rule-based, predictable, nondiscriminatory trading and financial system (includes a commitment to good governance, development, and poverty reduction, both nationally and internationally) Address the special needs of the Least Developed Countries (includes tariff- and quota-free access for Least Developed Countries exports, enhanced program of debt relief for HIPCs and cancellation of official bilateral debt, and more generous official development assistance for countries committed to poverty reduction)

(*Continued*)

Table 1.1 (*Continued*) United Nations Millennium Development Goals

	Address the special needs of landlocked developing countries and small island developing states (through the Program of Action for the Sustainable Development of Small Island Developing States and 22nd General Assembly provisions)
	Deal comprehensively with the debt problems of developing countries through national and international measures in order to make debt sustainable in the long term
	In cooperation with developing countries, develop and implement strategies for decent and productive work for youth
	In cooperation with pharmaceutical companies, provide access to affordable essential drugs in developing countries
	In cooperation with the private sector, make available the benefits of new technologies, especially information and communications technologies

Source: Adapted from UNDP. 2005. *Investing in Development: A Practical Plan to Achieve the Millennium Development Goals. Overview.* New York: UNDP.

progress on MDGs is likely (African Development Bank 2002). But the biggest challenge for Africa lies in committing to inclusive, transformative development in both political and socioeconomic terms that reduces income poverty, creates decent jobs, enhances the quality of access to social services, reduces inequality, and promotes resilience to climate-related hazards. Achieving MDG governance objectives will invariably put Africa on a trajectory toward sustained and sustainable development. Africa must ensure intervention outcomes meet the litmus test of economic, social, and environmental sustainability, as well as good governance to ensure effective policies and equity.

Current Status of Africa's Development

After several decades of economic decline, and with many new initiatives to development, some countries in Africa are experiencing robust economic growth prospects reflected in strong GDP, 11% according to the *African Development Report* (2012). This strong economic growth has been dubbed by many as Africa's economic revolution, recording a decade of growth double that which it achieved in the late twentieth century. Analyses by the World Bank's *Africa's Pulse* (2013) show that six of the world's ten fastest-growing economies since 2002 are in SSA. Annual GDP growth has increased to a robust 5.3% in 2014 and is expected to rise to 5.5% in 2015 with some countries such as Ethiopia having growth as high as 8.1% and Rwanda having 7.9%. This growth rate according to the UN Report (2012) is more than twice the growth in the 1980s and 1990s when the continent was experiencing dismal economic performance with a GDP of about 2.5% or less.

But many challenges abound in achieving good governance, sustainable development, and MDGs in Africa. Economic growth has not translated into tangible change in the lives of many people in SSA. Governance in Africa remains spotty. The urgent priority for Africa is to reduce poverty through strong and sustained economic growth that benefits the poor, and through improved social services. According to the HDI (2012), Africa has the lowest levels of human development that has continued to be one of the major challenges facing the region. HRD is a critical factor in the fight to reduce poverty and reach MDGs and Africa needs to put more resources into the development of quality education in order to provide quality education at all levels, including improving secondary, tertiary, technical, and vocational education and education for orphans and other marginalized groups; addressing teacher and textbook shortages; and the interaction between HIV/AIDS and education.

Although remarkable progress has been made by some countries in Africa, the challenges of development often outweigh the positive gains. Even with the enforcement of PRSPs to address poverty issues and to help steer countries toward achieving MDGs, there is a strong argument to be made about the human development status across SSA. There is a need to approach the challenges of human development through multiple interventions rather than a single intervention of structural adjustment always initiated by the World Bank or the IMF. Focus, from the perspective of this book, should also be on the role of good governance in the process because some of the blame for Africa's poor performance has been attributed to flawed policies and weak political institutions.

Development experts need to think about the circumstances and opportunities—including a realistic development role of the state, dedication to improving human development (including supporting education and social welfare and addressing inequality), political diversity, and an openness to trade and innovation. It is also time to stop neglecting the poor and marginalized populations of Africa who happen to be the majority and start focusing on their needs in a realistic fashion. It will take a coordinated response across sectors and in particular building a strong capacity in public and private sectors and paying attention to institutional governance and conflict mitigation that are often the neglected components of a strategy of achieving sustainable development and human security in Africa. To achieve meaningful sustainable growth, governance should provide stability to allow people to engage in entrepreneurialism, creativity, and production. Authoritarianism, intra-ethnic and religious conflicts, border wars and social tensions, as well as the denial of basic human rights constrain efforts to promote sustainable development. A strong association has been found between high levels of conflict, human insecurity, and multidimensional poverty. It is the contention of this book that patterns of governance factor into the equation. Therefore, it is important to build human, organizational, political, and institutional capacity to mobilize development.

Governance

Governance is a broad concept covering all aspects of the way a country is governed, including its economic policies and regulatory framework, as well as adherence to the rule of law, acceptance of pluralism, and participatory models of leadership selection. Corruption—the abuse of public authority or trust for private benefit—is a closely linked factor: a poor governance environment offers greater incentives and more opportunities for corruption. Corruption undermines the public's trust in its government. It also threatens market integrity, distorts competition, and endangers economic development. There is a strong causal relationship from better governance to better development outcomes (Kaufmann et al. 1999). Four key African initiatives have emphasized the importance of strong political commitment and good governance in all African countries, to ensure that development does not destroy the resource base on which it is built (OAU 1985; UNECA and UNEP 1989; UNECA 1991, 1992). The central theme that emerged from these meetings was the recognition that sustainable development was essential, but would only be achieved if African countries had sufficient capacity in terms of viable institutions, appropriate and relevant technology, as well as adequate human and financial resources.

Significantly, achievement of this ideal required all sectors of society (government, civil society—or the lay public—and scientists or technology providers) to cooperate closely and share a common vision of the future. There has certainly been a growing awareness and need to promote good governance at all levels of government in all its dimensions. Additional impetus has been provided in that many African countries share similar visions and face comparable problems, while also sharing several geographic, historical, cultural, and linguistic ties that supersede political boundaries. This has prompted the formation of a variety of regional institutional structures such as SADC, and continental initiatives such as NEPAD. All these initiatives aim to improve the engagement of stakeholders from every sector of society in the decision-making processes that affect their livelihoods and well-being, and are a direct response to the growing demands from society for governments to be more accountable and transparent, and to respect human rights.

The UN, through the Commission for Global Governance defines governance as the sum of the many ways individuals and institutions, public and private, manage their common affairs. It is a continuing process through which conflicting or diverse interests may be accommodated and cooperative action may be taken. It includes formal institutions and regimes empowered to enforce compliance, as well as informal arrangements that people and institutions either have agreed to or perceive to be in their interests (Commission on Global Governance 1995). An ideal governance system needs to ensure that the participation of stakeholders is balanced and integrated so that the best and most sustainable outcomes can be agreed to and achieved.

Good Governance, Human Security, and Sustainable Development

Although there are diverse viewpoints on understanding the broad concept of good governance, no one contests its importance for the progress and prosperity of any nation. The former UN Secretary-General Kofi Annan while addressing a UNDP conference on "Governance for Sustainable Growth and Equity" in New York in July 1997, made a poignant remark about the interface between governance and sustainable development:

> Good governance and sustainable development are indivisible. Governance, especially when it assumes a normative dimension of being qualified as good, is generally believed to be a basis for the reconstruction of the state, society, and polity in Africa. It is a means through which the peoples' voices and expressions input into their life chances as it avows the principles of dialogue, consultation, consensus, and popular consent in decision-making and public policies. And without the people being the driving force of development, which (good) governance espouses, development can hardly take place and if it does, it cannot be sustainable (UNDP 1997, p. 19).

The Africa Progress Panel (2011) considers good governance both on the continent and across the globe as the key enabling factor for sustainable development. Leaders at the 2005 World Summit concluded that good governance is integral to economic growth, the eradication of poverty and hunger, and sustainable development. Views of all oppressed groups, including women, youth, and the poor, must be heard and considered by governing bodies because they will be the ones most negatively affected if good governance is not achieved. If Africa must attain sustainable development, good governance must be viewed from a more comprehensive lens rather than the narrow political and economic views that have overshadowed other important aspects of the lives of the African. Given our argument of promoting feasible and viable governance that benefits all within and outside Africa, we seek to define good governance in such a way as to provide protection for all Africans while not limiting its adherence to African governments, but to indulge the African people to adopt genuine expression of opinion, affection, and passion on matters relating to Africa. The implication is that, from an African background, good governance must extend to family, clan, ethnic, and general cultural values.

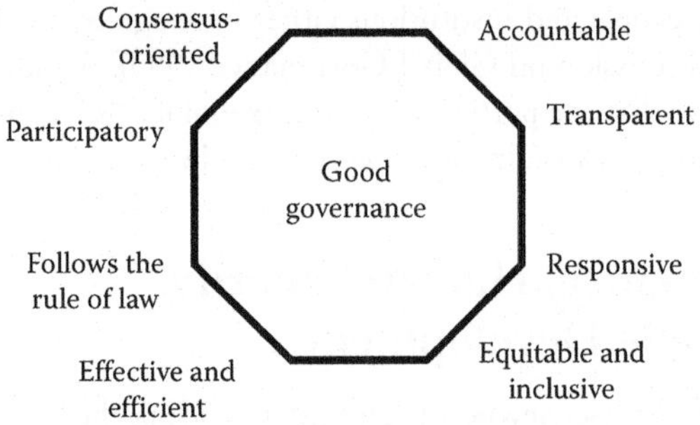

Figure 1.2 Characteristics of good governance. (From UNDP. 1997. *Governance for Sustainable Development Conference*. New York, July 28–30. New York: UNDP.)

Thus, the concept of good governance (illustrated in Figure 1.2) is participatory, consensus-oriented, accountable, transparent, responsive, effective and efficient, and equitable and inclusive, and follows the rule of law. It assures that corruption is minimized, the views of minorities are taken into account, and that the voices of the most vulnerable in society are heard in decision-making. It is also responsive to the present and future needs of society. Looking across SSA, how closely is good governance being practiced encompassing most or all of the characteristics?

Chapters in this book reflect multiple perspectives in the field of development and their relationship to good governance are presented addressing the various characteristics of good governance in respective African countries. We do not see a linear relationship between the two but suggest in the following chapters a richness of debate.

It is widely agreed from the various discussions that follow that good governance as an ideal is difficult to achieve in its totality. Many of the case studies illustrate the negative. Very few countries and societies have come close to achieving good governance in its totality. However, to ensure sustainable human development, actions must be taken to work toward this ideal with the aim of making it a reality. No society can claim to achieve sustainable development if it neglects the well-being of the majority of its populations.

About the Book

The chapters in this book seek to broaden the policy debate and provide conversations about the sustainable development challenges facing African countries from multiple viewpoints and interdisciplinary perspectives from academics, researchers, policymakers, and practitioners in the field. The focus is on the governance perspectives of practitioners who deal with day-to-day realities on the ground, especially as a means of finding sustainable strategies and solutions to the problems hindering the achievement of sustainable development in SSA. The goal is to use evidence-based information to enhance better understanding of the intricacies of Africa's development and governance challenges and make informed policies, programs, and strategies to move the continent toward achieving sustainable development.

Various dimensions of sustainable development are explored within the discourse on good governance and human security, what they mean, and how the various countries handle their development agenda. Chapters grew out of presentations that were delivered at the Sustainable Development in Africa Conference held at the University of Pittsburgh in the spring of 2012. The authors cover a wide range of sustainable development issues, especially what they view as the missing link in aspects of sustainability.

In Section II, "Foreign Aid, Goals and Practices," four chapters identify development issues as reflected in international policies and national-level experiences. Chapters 2 and 3, by Chris Belasco, Terry Buss, and Louis Picard, examine the relationship between human capacity and sustainable development. Chapter 4, by Peter Bucki et al., ask whether the much touted international development targets for 2015 set forth by the UN in its MDG program have been absorbed into the poverty reduction plans developed by countries under the World Bank's PRSP program. Chapter 5, by N. Clark Capshaw and Jeffrey W. Bassichis, highlights the AFRICOM assessment process, and describes how this ties in to U.S. national security and the U.S. role in Africa, to policy and budgetary planning priorities, and to AFRICOM's mission and plans. It shows how AFRICOM uses assessments to inform decisions to ensure plans, programs, and resources focused on achieving the U.S. security objectives.

Having examined human resource development and sustainability as a set of issues in the first five chapters, Section III, "Sustainable Development Challenges," examines policy and governance issues as a factor in changing perceptions of sustainability, and human security issues and human resource development as factors in sustainability. Clive Mutunga in Chapter 6 examines the issue of population from a climate change and sustainable development perspective. In Chapter 7, Joseph Chacha discusses local governance issues looking at the water sector. Joseph Adjaye and Kwesi Korboe in Chapter 8 look at irrigation from an environmental sustainability perspective.

The focus in Section IV, "Identity and Governance," is on problems and prospects for good governance in Africa given the problems of cultural subnationalism. Joshua Forrest in Chapter 9 discusses the spread of secessionism and large subnational and regional separatist movements in much of the African continent and their effects on the potential for social and economic development. The issue of ethnicity, conflict mitigation, and governance is the focus of John F. Clark in Chapter 10. William Miles adds the issue of religious groups into the mix in Chapter 11.

Section V of the book, "Governance and Development," examines selected case studies that explore the dynamics between conflict mitigation and governance on the one hand and efforts to promote human resource development and economic transformation on the other. In Chapter 12, Isaac Addai, Chris Opuku-Agyeman, and Sarah Kafui Amanfu look at the issue of subjective well-being as an indicator of governance patterns in Ghana. In Chapter 13, Zachary Karazsia hypothesizes a codependency of reconciliation, conflict mitigation, and economic development as part of achieving lasting sustainable peace in an ethnically fragmented collapsed state using Rwanda as a case study. In Chapter 14, Elke Zuern considers South Africa and the role that urban violence is playing in evolving governance problems.

In Chapter 15, Barry Ames, Louis Picard, and Miguel Carreras return to the issue raised in the first section of this book, the nature of international donor intervention in support of governance reform. The focus is on support given by international donors to political parties in Morocco as part of a broader reform process in Morocco. In Chapter 16, Thomas Mogale and Louis Picard examine fiscal management issues and sustainable local government financing in South Africa and conclude that even if there are evolving institutions of governance as is the case in South Africa, overambitious programs and unfunded mandates may have a corroding effect on perceptions of government and the concretization of local institutions. In the concluding Section VI, Chapter 17, Taylor Seybolt provides an overview of governance and development in Africa making the strong argument that good governance is necessary for sustainable development in Africa.

Conclusion

This introductory chapter has attempted to provide an overview of Africa's development challenges from a governance and a human security perspective. It highlights some of the strategies that have been instituted to address the challenges that have developed since the gaining of independence. Achieving sustainable development is discussed within the wider context of the MDGs, and NEPAD, that is the vision and strategic framework adapted by African leaders to address poverty and underdevelopment throughout the African continent. The achievement of the NEPAD vision is premised on concerted efforts to attain the MDGs—the world's time-bound and quantified targets for addressing extreme poverty in its many dimensions such as income poverty, hunger, disease, lack of adequate shelter, and exclusion, while promoting gender equality, education, and environmental sustainability.

There is a key consensus that has developed out of the first round of MDGs that better governance is a key element in promoting growth and development and in enabling African countries to achieve the MDGs. The goal here has been to highlight some key arguments in dealing with Africa's development challenges, preparing the reader for more detailed discussion and analysis of the issues raised and ways to ensure sustainability.

References

African Development Bank. 2002. *Global Poverty Report 2002: Achieving the Millennium Development Goals in Africa. Progress, Prospects, and Policy Implications.* Tunis: AFDB.

Calderisi, R. 2006. *The Trouble with Africa.* New York: Yale University Press.

Commission on Global Governance. 1995. *Our Global Neighborhood.* New York: Oxford University Press.

Easterly, W. 2003. IMF and World Bank structural adjustment programs and poverty. In *Managing Crisis in Emerging Markets.* Dooley, M., Frankel, J. (eds.). pp. 361–391. University of Chicago Press: Chicago.

IMF. 2014. *International Monetary Fund Factsheet: Debt Relief under the Heavily Indebted Poor Countries (HIPC) Initiative.* Washington, DC: IMF.

Kaufmann, D., Kraay, A., Zoido-Lobaton, P. 1999. *Aggregating Governance Indicators.* World Bank. Washington, DC: IMF.

Krugman, P. 1995. Globalization and the inequality of nations. *The Quarterly Journal of Economics* 110 (4) 857–880.

McGregor, S. 2005. Structural adjustment programmes and human well-being. *International Journal of Consumer Studies* 29 (3) 170–180.

NEPAD. 2001. *The New Partnership for Africa's Development.* Abuja, Nigeria: NEPAD.

Nwankwo, S., Richards, D. 2004. Institutional paradigm and the management of transition. *International Journal of Social Economics* 31 (1) 111–130.

Shivji, I. 2006. The silences in the NGO discourse: The role and future of NGOs in Africa. *Africa Development* 31 (4) 22–51. Council for the Development of Social Science Research in Africa (CORDESIA).

The Economist: Africa's impressive growth. The Economist Online, January 6, 2011. http://www.economist.com/blogs/dailychart/2011/01/daily_chart.

UN. 1987. *Report of the World Commission on Environment and Development: Our Common Future.* Oxford: Oxford University Press.

UN. 1992. *Sustainable Development: United Nations Conference on Environment & Development.* Rio de Janerio, Brazil, June 3–14, 1992. Agenda 21. http://sustainabledevelopment.un.org/content/documents/Agenda21.pdf.

UNDP. 1997. *Governance for Sustainable Development Conference.* New York, July 28–30. New York: UNDP.

UNDP. 2005. *Investing in Development: A Practical Plan to Achieve the Millennium Development Goals. Overview.* New York: UNDP.

UN ESCAP. 2009. What is good governance? UN Economic and Social Commission for Asia and the Pacific. Retrieved 4/28/2014 from http://www.unescap.org/resources/what-good-governance.

Van Der Veen, R. 2004. *What Went Wrong with Africa*? Amsterdam: KIT Publishers.

World Bank. 1989. *Sub-Saharan Africa: From Crisis to Sustainable Growth.* Washington, DC: World Bank.

World Bank. 1988. *Environment and Development: Exhaustive Resources.* Development Committee Pamphlet 17. Washington, DC: World Bank.

World Commission on Environment and Development (WCED). 1987. *Our Common Future.* Oxford: Oxford University Press ("The Brudtland Report").

II

FOREIGN AID GOALS AND PRACTICES

Chapter 2

Human Development and the Millennium Development Goals

Donors, Aid, and Sustainability

Chris Belasco, Terry F. Buss, and Louis A. Picard

Contents

Introduction

Although the UN Development Program (UNDP), and its human development (HD) initiative, called attention to human resource issues in the development (HD) context in the 1990s, HD concerns have already been a focus in post-1948 aid. Why do donors—bilateral, multilateral, and private—and developing country policymakers assign a high priority to HD policies? And, what is the relationship between HD and governance around Millennium Development Goal (MDG) target countries, particularly in Africa?

As is the case with so much in foreign aid policy, newer foci build barnacle-like on top of old programs. The goal in this book is to address and assess the perennial question: which comes first, HD or economic development, and within HD what are the priorities and how are these impacted by governance? These "chicken and egg" problems have been at the heart of the aid debate since its origins following World War II.

To contextualize these issues, we review the literature on trends in aid provision and donor support for HD over the past 50 years. The focus is on dominant themes, as well as the mix and priorities defining each era. We examine in the next few pages six somewhat overlapping phases that characterize aid prior to 1990.

A Historical Overview

Private and Humanitarian Influences Prior to 1948

Prior to 1945, countries that would later be categorized as less developed countries (LDCs) received little government-level support in health, education, or environmental sustainability. European and U.S. private sector and faith-based organizations provided only limited health, education, and training opportunities during which colonial states had little to offer beyond legal order and judicial procedures (Picard and Buss 2009).

British official aid began with the 1929 and 1940 British Colonial Development and Welfare Acts that funded social sectors in the British colonies. Aid was tied to the purchase of British goods and the provision of British experts, a pattern continuing into the postcolonial period. Meagre health and educational opportunities were available from missionary efforts. The values and assumptions of missionaries would have a long-term impact on aid.

France and other colonial powers expended miniscule amounts of development funds, although there were discussions about a hypothetical developmental future in the League of Nations and the other interwar international institutions such as the International Labour Organization (ILO). The 1929 stock market collapse, the 1930s worldwide depression, and World War II put such aspirations on hold until a system for international aid began to develop through Lend Lease from 1940 to 1941.

Expansion of the British Colonial Development Fund in the 1940s, though modest, focused on capital development and infrastructure (Jones 1977). In the 1950s, a period of economic and trade expansion saw a dramatic increase in support for health and education in Britain's African and Asian colonies. British aid at the end of the colonial period in the 1960s focused on the enlargement of "human capital stock" (Mosley 1987).

Similar, though less expansive, programs developed in Francophone countries and to a lesser extent in Dutch, Belgian, and Portuguese, and the other remnants of empire after 1945. More importantly, private organizations such as the Rockefeller, Carnegie, Ford, and Mellon foundations had discovered underdevelopment. By the 1950s, a number of American and European foundations were active in Africa, Asia, and Latin America.

Aid processes originated in World War II, beginning with Lend Lease, when the allied powers received weapons and nonmilitary commodity assistance, primarily from the United States. Food aid, commodities, and financial aid (in addition to military aid) were given to the allied countries of Europe and Asia through World War II (Mosley 1987; Ruttan 1996). This introduced processes based on "projects" delivered by nongovernmental organizations (NGOs) that focused on commodities, subsidies, and physical infrastructure development, rather than a more holistic approach (Ruttan 1996).

In 1947, aid institutions were largely multilateral: UN agencies and the World Bank assisted in the transition to peace. There was a small organization within the U.S. State Department that targeted Latin America and a few countries in Asia and Africa where the United States had interests. After 1948, bilateralism, initially through U.S. organizations, predominated as a result of the Cold War. The UN specialized agencies were sensitive to social development and HD. The World Bank initially focused on large infrastructure projects in the 1950s, paying scant attention to social issues such as health (Garrett 2007). By the late 1950s, some European countries had developed significant bilateral activities.

Assumptions of Economic Growth

The 1948 Marshall Plan set the stage for postwar aid in other parts of the world. Since trained professional and technical personnel were abundant in Europe, reconstruction assistance did not emphasize capacity building or social development. It did support technical assistance (TA) in engineering and finance. Experience from the Marshall Plan when transferred to LDC programs appears to have caused some development theorists and practitioners to neglect HD concerns (Ruttan 1996).

Given the success of the Marshall Plan, however, focus on aid to Asia and Latin America was on economic growth and capital investment, based on the Keynesian growth model (Ruttan 1996). The 1950s was the "decade" of aid, with the United States contributing 90% worldwide. However, by the end of the decade, European countries had begun to commit aid to former colonies.

In the 1950s, the focus of the U.S., and other bilateral and World Bank aid was on infrastructure, transportation, and capital investment in line with economics of the time (Lewis 1955; Rostow 1960). Aid involved direct government-to-government transactions.

There were debates over aggregate growth and sectoral growth (the importance of agriculture as a first stage of development) (Martinussen 1997). The scenario was one of aid-assisted countries in the pursuit of growth, where access to capital would lead to an economic "take off point." Provision was for access to investments, construction, and operational assistance, along with support for disease control and sanitation. An assumption was that governments had a role in managing markets.

In the United States, the 1949 Point Four policies of President Harry Truman identified health and education as HD concerns, though many development economists saw this funding as secondary and derivative of economic growth. The primary focus of aid for education was on elementary and secondary education and teacher training activities. Aid also funded university programs and nonprofit organizations to provide educational support. There was consensus that development aid had to be coordinated and long term. To ready a country for private investment, aid required health, education, agriculture, and infrastructure (Ruttan 1996). Point Four policies defined long-term aid, skills development, coordinated efforts, and rural investment as development objectives (Ruttan 1996).

There was much gap filling using operational experts and advisors. They provided temporary skills and knowledge, eventually replaced through education and training of indigenous professionals. Some support for university education and research, as well as in pursuit of TA objectives, was provided. Aid supported higher education and linkages between U.S. universities and those in LDCs (Picard and Smuckler 2008).

In the late 1950s, large foundations such as the Rockefeller, Carnegie, Ford, and MacArthur began to support higher education in Africa, Asia, and Latin America. Foundations would both fill in the gaps in professional training and step in when official aid declined. Private donors increasingly stimulated creative thinking on health, education, and development issues (Nielsen 1989).

European Donors, the Commonwealth, and Japan, 1960–1980s

A number of European countries established aid programs in the late 1950s that mirrored U.S. priorities in economic growth and Cold War competition, and HD. Initially, much of European aid focused on procurement advantages, commodities supplies, and infrastructure development (Brown and O'Connor 1996). By the 1960s, most European countries had created bilateral aid agencies. The European Union (EU) developed an aid program of its own. After 1990, it focused on Eastern Europe and became increasingly concerned with governance issues (Hook 1996; Lancaster 2007). Japanese, Canadian, Australian, and New Zealand aid also came on line in the 1960s.

Following independence, British aid sponsored the Colombo Plan supporting health and education, an expansion of programs begun during the colonial period (Mosley 1987). The British loaned former colonial officers to newly independent nations. As British aid evolved in the 1960s and 1970s, there followed an increased concern with education and capacity building, with significant support in the health and education sectors, in humanitarian and human security needs (Jones 1977).

France has long linked its aid to the promotion of trade in goods and services and to the protection and spread of the French language and culture (Brown and O'Connor 1996).

Primary recipients of French aid were former French colonies, especially those in Africa (Brown and O'Connor 1996; Minoiu and Reddy 2009). Close to 50% of French aid went to education, involving French contractors, operational experts, teachers, and nonprofit organizations.

German aid in the 1960s and early 1970s promoted commercial ties having two characteristics: (1) to cement relationships and fight the influence of East Germany, and (2) to have strong programs in parts of Africa that had been under German rule prior to World War I.

German aid became more redistributive and multilateral under the Social Democratic Party and the publication of the Brandt Commission advocating North/South redistribution. With the end of the Cold War, the German aid program followed those of the Scandinavian countries with a strong focus on social and equity issues. In the 1990s, environmental protection emerged as an issue (Lancaster 2007).

Scandinavian aid programs have long provided support to NGOs, including faith-based activities. Scandinavian countries targeted humanitarian aid, basic human needs, social welfare, health, and poverty reduction rather than economic growth. They emphasized rural development, and support for women's and children's rights. Basic literacy and numeracy rather than higher education were priorities (Hook 1996; Lancaster 2007). Scandinavia has long been known for its aid commitments.

The Scandinavian focus has been the most egalitarian among the donors. In the 1980s, they strongly supported efforts toward global redistribution—the new international economic order (NIEO). About 30% of aid passes through multilateral organizations, especially UN agencies. After initially focusing on their former colonies, Belgian and Dutch programs have come to resemble Scandinavian programs.

Japan initially linked aid to exports and trade, not social development (Lancaster 2007). While Southeast Asia remains its focus, Japan operates one of the largest aid programs worldwide (Rix 1996).

Formal Education and Skills Development

By the 1950s, European and North American universities had developed strong links with donors in their countries, often with attention to agriculture, schools of education, and public health. Health projects sought eradication of disease, beginning with polio (Butterfield 2004). There was continued support for primary and secondary education among donors into the 1960s (Brandt Commission).

Bilateral donors and foundations provided funding for higher education, educational institutional development, and research in agricultural development. The United States and European donors funded basic education, particularly in postcolonial Africa, that had fallen behind in basic literacy and numeracy. Education in Africa also included long-term professional training at the undergraduate and postgraduate level.

By the 1980s, given rigidities in aid provision, foundations took a more independent line, providing much innovation in HD, while official aid—bilateral and multilateral—supplied the bulk of financing. One estimate suggests that 70% of aid was bilateral during the Cold War while the remainder came from multilateral sources (Minoiu and Reddy 2009).

It was, for example, foundations that recognized basic education limitations: someone in power with only a basic education who fails to recognize technical or intellectual complexity. The Rockefeller Foundation called for aid to go first class with high quality support in education and research (Black et al. 1977). This model was successful in Asia and Latin America though much less so in Africa.

Thirty years after World War II, aid concentrated on professional education and research, including agricultural research (the Green Revolution), agricultural colleges, and later rural industrialization and micro-credit support (Picard and Smuckler 2008). Students were brought to the United States on scholarships. Most European aid programs also provided higher education and professional training. Overall, activities coalesced around the support of TA, higher education, and research and development (Butterfield 2004).

There was continued and increasing funding for higher education and skills development between 1962 and 1973 (Browne 1999). By 1975, however, friction had developed between the universities and the bilateral donors, especially in the United States. Critics of education programs also suggested that education quality remained poor despite technical and financial support. By the early 1970s, there was a loss of many skilled people from LDCs, often educated through aid programs, due to emigration.

The United States and others supported basic and advanced education from 1950 to 1975 but after that, except for basic skills, support for education declined until the 1990s. The decline in the support for long-term capacity development in the 1980s was, according to critics, caused by a search for "fast results" or "quick fixes" (Butterfield 2004). By that time, the short-term (3–5 year) projects had come to dominate aid.

By 1975, both bilateral and multilateral aid was increasingly based upon "low trust management" as donors feared fraud, corruption, and misuse of funds. This meant increasingly time-consuming and often humiliating supervisory procedures over host country managers. This changing pattern of aid included greater emphasis on project management focused on very narrow targets of delivery. A kind of donor fatigue had set in with a decline in living and productivity standards in a number of LDCs mainly in Africa.

Basic Needs, 1975–1983

The 1960s saw increased criticism of aid among development theorists. Structuralists pointed to the different physical, social, and geographical characteristics of production in temperate as opposed to tropical climates (Martinussen 1997). Economists at the Institute for Development Studies in Sussex called for a more redistributive approach to development theory (Chenery 1974). Dependency theorists focused on unequal economic power relationships. A more redistributive focus on aid was in the offing (Streeten et al. 1982).

In the 1980s, under the World Bank's "basic needs" approach, increasing attention was paid to basic education and adult literacy based on successful growth among the "Asian Tigers," emphasizing adult literacy, and numeracy in strong basic education systems (Martinussen 1997). There was also support for clean water, disease control, and rural development (Picard 1994). "Basic needs" was a precursor to the human development index (HDI) developed in the late 1980s.

This period (1975–1983) saw a rhetorical call for the devolution of decision making to LDCs with emphasis on popular participation. There was an increased use of NGOs and contractors as intermediaries between donors and social groups. The World Bank under Robert McNamara with support from UNDP called for a basic needs approach to development focusing on health, education, water, food and what came to be called integrated rural development—combining innovative agricultural techniques with the development of basic social service delivery systems.

Basic needs focused on inaccessible health systems, lack of basic education, access to food, and the problem of gastrointestinal disease. There were analyses of and focus on planning issues faced by donors as well (Butterfield 2004). Overall, by the mid-1980s, there was considerable evidence of the spread of basic literacy and numeracy worldwide.

In the late 1980s, there was increasing interest from the UN and the ILO in aggregate social indicators, especially in basic needs, health, and education. Even a number of the so-called aid sceptics supported education, and health systems and infrastructure development to support social development (Moyo 2009).

In the United States, as a result of the focus on rural development, strong linkages developed with Land Grant Universities continuing through the 1980s. In many European countries, rural development institutes and training centers were created to support research in agricultural production. Agriculture development, and particularly food production (rather than export agriculture), attracted bilateral donors (Butterfield 2004).

Emphasis on education shifted from tertiary to primary and secondary education assuming that literacy and numeracy should be spread widely both among children and adults. More broadly, donors turned away from urban development, infrastructure, and industrialization. The donor community reoriented its support toward rural development, food production, and integrated rural and community-based urban development.

Between 1975 and 1990, the roles of contractors and NGOs expanded in Europe and North America. There was a complementary shift to multilateral sources, and the use of technical advisors and international financial institutions. There was an increased use of short-term TA personnel, expatriate on-the-job training, and formal training and supervision skills.

By the end of the 1980s, U.S. aid had precipitously declined. Europe, Japan, and multilaterals outpaced the United States, providing 90% of aid. The World Bank became the largest donor overall (Butterfield 2004).

Structural Adjustment and Policy Reform

Between 1983 and 1995, as a result of policy reform and structural adjustment policy (SAP), bilaterals and multilaterals (though not UNDP) began to see excess labor capacity as destabilizing. There would be decreasing support, especially in the first decade of SAPs, for education, health, and skills development.

There was also decreased support for organizational development and institutional support activities that required long-term aid, no longer readily available. There was a tendency to terminate social development, as well as economic development activities, with an increased focus on financial management, national bank restructuring, currency reform, and economic deregulation. Multilateral donors, especially the World Bank, concentrated on capital management, debt, and policy reform.

Increasingly, some observers criticized structural adjustment programs as heartless, painful, and unconcerned with the poor. Despite the need for policy reform, SAPs imposed great social costs on countries and people where they were imposed. By the late 1980s, the so-called structural adjustment with a human face created social funds and other social support systems, including micro-credit to address declining community-based health and education (Cornea and Jolly 1987; UNICEF 1991). Debate focused on the extent to which the context of HD strategies was the definitive answer to aid (Killick 1989).

By 1990, the support for specialized professional development, long-term education, and designer training had either declined or virtually disappeared as priorities for donors, some Scandinavian and Benelux countries notwithstanding. Foundation support for higher education only partly filled this vacuum.

The UN supported HD efforts, specifically for women, children, and rural development through its specialized agencies. The UN supported the development of social funds under SAPs, including sectoral and meso-level programs that had been reduced due to policy reforms of the 1980s and 1990s. The UNDP HDI and the MDGs link attempts to adjust to the harshness of SAPs (Henry 2007).

End of the Cold War up to September 11

Whole of Government

In the aftermath of September 11, 2001, support in the United States increased significantly on the three Ds: defense, diplomacy, and development, within the context of the war on terror, failed states, and international crime (illegal drugs and human trafficking). Since 2001, many donors (including the United States, the United Kingdom, France, Australia, and Canada) have become increasingly committed to the management of crisis, fragile states, and civil conflict through what has come to be called the "whole of government" approach combining development aid with security aid and diplomatic action.

The war on terror fostered an increased militarization of aid on the part of the United States, the United Kingdom, and Australian donors, an increased role for humanitarian groups, and a renewed focus on basic needs (the NATO coalition in Afghanistan has labeled this "armed social work"). This has led some to fear that donors had become less enamored of growth and development concerns. Foundations target conflict resolution and human security, while returning to basic and community needs—food, water, and micro-enterprise development.

In the past decade, there has a been a high level of commitment to crisis and fragile states on the one hand and to high-performing states represented by the millennium challenge accounts (MCAs) and potentially emerging market countries on the other hand. The focus of traditional aid has narrowed to the underdeveloped heartland in Africa and the Middle East and other areas under threat from terrorist movements or drug cartels.

An ever larger number of "aid sceptics" doubt the utility of aid, suggesting that it is both destructive and subversive. Aid scepticism among opinion leaders has been increasingly widespread (Hancock 1989; Maren 1997; Moyo 2009).

There has been increased controversy over the role of aid in poverty reduction. Critics suggest that aid is not well suited to stimulate economic growth. At best, in line with Amartya Sen's thinking, the impact is indirect based on the provision of health and services, and support for social capital and critical infrastructure (Bauer 1972, 1981; Easterly 2001, 2006; Ferguson 2003, 2008; Moyo 2009). There is increasing evidence confirming that aid is not the best way to stimulate growth (Picard and Buss 2009).

In the post-September 11 period, the HD dilemma remains. Although there has been steady growth in the support for health facilities, disease prevention, and primary and secondary education, there has not been an accompanying reemphasis on holistic health systems or on professional and higher education and skills development. In emerging market countries, there is an increased role played by family and private support for higher education with accompanying increased social stratification.

Calls for the reform of technical cooperation emphasized support through budget systems (along the lines of the World Bank model) rather than through donor-driven processes. This in turn is dependent upon increasing donor confidence levels. Emphasis is on symmetrical as opposed to asymmetrical exchanges mainstreaming technical cooperation and normalizing professional exchanges.

LDC desires for greater symmetry have made the Fulbright program, the German Marshall Plan, and the South–North and South–South exchanges attractive. There was increased interest in interactive information systems that would be symmetrical.

Critics calling for reforms suggested a renewed role for foundations from 1990 and 2010. Bilateral aid program asymmetry (particularly in light of the resentment of trade discrimination and complaints to the World Trade Organization) remain sensitive issues. One key to this issue is that recipients as well as donors can reject aid relationships.

Development as HD?

Amartya Sen's perspective undergirds the UN's HD model. In *Development as Freedom* (2000), Sen cogently argued that advances in development arise as a result of increased individual freedom of choice that advance personal circumstances and society as a whole. Investments in health, education, and welfare expand and deepen the capacity of people to make the choices that will lead to the attainment of the goals they value. Good governance provides the process and opportunities to expand choice.

People in many developing countries are often "unfree" (in Sen's words) to choose, either because they do not have the capacity for or are prohibited from doing so. Sen also asserts that poor people do not have the requisite social networks and support—that is, social capital—to allow them not only to make choices but to also seize on opportunities. Sen refers to this as "functionings." Sen's so-called "capability approach" and "functionings approach" move development away from previous thinking that promoted free markets exclusively, measuring success based on improvements in economic growth and per capita income, to a focus on the human resource development necessary to stimulate development, in a more "ethical," balanced, less severe approach. Freedom is not separate from development, but is a necessary condition to realize it.

Bilateral and multilateral aid when assessed through Sen's lens can become a two-edged sword. If donors allocate aid in support of the free-market approach, then a developing country may not develop as fast or in the right direction, or this could even reverse development, because aid ignores HD concerns to its peril. Conversely, spending on HD, but not managing the economic side of development, can also be counterproductive. Effective development requires balance.

With the launch of the UNDP *Human Development Report* (HDR) initiative in 1990, UNDP developed the HDI to yield a single score that would summarize HD in a country. The score is a composite of life expectancy, education, including adult literacy and gross school enrolment, and GDP per capita. The HDI was a composite measure that would compel donors, developing country policymakers, and others to focus on the need to move away from narrow free-market approaches.

By 1990, a new thinking had coalesced around HD approaches, as reflected in the UN decision to publish its annual HDR. Following Sen, HD was finally seen as a precursor to growth and development (Dollar and Pritchett 1998). Social development, in turn, increasingly became linked to governance and citizen engagement and participation (see pp. 38–39). However, trends in aid support for many donors declined through the 1990s.

There was an increased role for NGOs, use of grants and subgrants, and private sector funding. In some bilateral programs, this included support for faith-based, political party-linked, and civil society organizations, often based on grants to international NGOs in the United Kingdom and the United States, which provided subgrants to indigenous groups. At least rhetorically, after 1993, "public–private partnerships" replaced that of structural adjustment and policy reform in states that have moved toward open governance (Brinkerhoff 2002).

During the 1990s, Europe and Japan were less likely to bypass governments in favor of NGOs. The International Monetary Fund (IMF), the World Bank, and the regional banks (African Development Bank) continued to focus on public sector reform and along with the UN, supported the creation of social funds, rural and urban (municipal) funds, and infrastructure.

Since 1990, there has been a fundamental shift from investment in growth and income-based policy to HD, social capital, governance, and institutional development, all in line with Sen's capability approach. Many economists had concluded that aid in the aggregate sense had little direct effect on growth and income (Mosley 1987). There remains considerable debate over direct support for industrialization and productivity through bilateral or multilateral aid processes though the growing consensus has been that there was a need to focus on HD as a prior condition to economic growth.

Aid is redistributive in that it expands and supports choice among poor people, directly promoting development. It has also become clear that aid often could not help the poorest of the poor, because they lack the freedom to choose. As thinking about HD evolved, the concern over how to define aid goals became an issue. Advocates talked of people-centered development, HD, social capital, and later human security (Lancaster 2007).

Understanding development as "a process of enlarging people's choices" involves placing importance on the capabilities created by education, health, and income (UNDP 1990). Aid takes into account the context of provision of public goods associated with health and education, as well as taking into account the contribution of economic development to HD. We will review various growth and capabilities approaches in the next chapters, describing and critiquing concepts and indicators for each.

Following Maslow (1954), there are stages to a framework for understanding HD. Humanitarian support and basic health programs targeting Maslow's basic (physical and security) needs are a first stage. Basic education (literacy and numeracy) operates at a second level of human operation (safety and income generation). Technical, professional, and intellectual development (higher education) operates at a third level (self-esteem and self-actualization). All three levels are part of an HD strategy.

The HD framework flowed from the basic needs literature of the late 1970s to the mid-1980s. Basic needs developed out of a period of increased attention to growth and inequality in the early 1970s particularly in the development economics literature. Basic needs drew attention to the failures of policy outcomes to improve incomes of the poor, provide them with critical social services, and offer developmental improvements (Streeten and Burki 1978; Stewart 1985). These viewpoints were rooted in definitions of poverty that are biological—how much subsistence people need and whether an individual is getting or not getting it—and policy oriented—how society feels responsible for deprivation (Sen 1981).

The HD framework builds on the basic needs indicator: physical quality of life index (PQLI), which measures quality of life according to literacy rate, infant mortality rate, and life expectancy (Morris 1979). The HDI broadens PQLI by including life expectancy (rather than infant mortality), adult literacy, gross educational enrollment, along with per capita GDP (purchasing power parity [PPP]), to accommodate growth (UNDP 2007). It evaluates the provision of public goods in terms of health and education and considers their impact.

HD sought to comprehend how to meet the needs of poor people as a means to permit more individuals to choose to do or to be what or who they value (Clark 2005; UNDP 1990; Nussbaum 2000; Sen 2000). Attempts are made to differentiate from the concept of income as an end, and to draw a broader distinction between this and how poverty involves the understanding of influences other than low income affect human capabilities. These authors criticized the instrumental relationship between low income and low capability as being variable between different communities, different families, and different individuals.

Sen (2000) argued for a focus on understanding the intrinsic importance of individual capability to undertake behaviors (which he called "functionings") within their daily life. He argues that the ability to achieve "functionings" depends not only on the commodities owned by the person in question but also in the availability of public goods. Achievements, such as being healthy, well nourished, and literate, depend on the public provision of health services, medical facilities, and educational arrangements (Sen 1988).

The HDI is a ranking system that compares countries using indicators, including life expectancy (health and longevity), education (knowledge, literacy, and formal education levels), and standard of living indicators. Our focus is on the way differences in a country's HDI can be explained by the different degrees or profiles of aid provided to them. Evidence shows that countries that have advanced significantly on the HDI and have done so because of improvements in education and health have been supported, at least in part, by aid.

An ongoing issue is the extent to which aid accounts for HD progress and the extent to which advances in education and health will account for a country's improvement on the HDI. There are alternative models of aid in support of HD and new models of HD that measure the impact of health on education, the need for sustained and relevant education and training, and the relationship between social and educational institutions and development.

A key to HD has been to get TA and cooperation right. There is a need to include psychological, social, and nongovernmental organizational factors, including social capital, private enterprise, and the capacity of societies as a whole. The goal has come to focus on social transformation (Browne 2002). The HDI is a tool to better understand how different approaches to social development impact upon human behavior.

HD and the Millennium Challenge Goals

The period between 1991 and 2001, constituted an interregnum period between the end of the Cold War and September 11, 2001 has been defined by MDGs. During this period, there continued to be a commitment to states in a policy reform mode, a policy that led to the creation of the MCA in 2002, designed to reward good governance and policy reform (Buss and Gardner 2008).

The goal was to bring these "reforming" states and emerging economies to a takeoff growth point. Concern for governance predominated, but HD received some emphasis. However, it has been the impact of thinking on HD as made operational by the MDGs that has defined a new paradigm for international development and aid.

Ten years later, the United Nations (UN) announced the *Millennium Declaration* (a radically new global effort to all but eliminate poverty) at a summit held at the UN headquarters from September 6 to 8, 2000. A framing document, encapsulating the new approach (UN General Assembly 2001), laid out eight MDGs to be attained by 2015:

1. Eradicating extreme poverty and hunger: To halve the proportion of people whose income is less than one dollar a day and halve the number of people who suffer from hunger
2. Achieving universal primary education: To ensure boys and girls have access to basic primary education and approach universal basic literacy and numeracy
3. Promoting gender equality and empowerment of women: To reduce and eventually eliminate disparity between male and female scholars at primary, secondary, and tertiary levels
4. Reducing child mortality: To reduce by two-thirds the child mortality level of children under 12 worldwide
5. Improving maternal health: To reduce by 75% the mortality of mothers

6. Combating HIV/AIDS, malaria, and other diseases: To stop the increase of HIV/AIDS infection, malaria infection, and other major diseases and to begin reducing the number of those infected
7. Ensuring environmental sustainability: To integrate the principles of sustainability into government policies and begin to reverse the loss of natural resources; to improve the lives of people worldwide living in rural and urban slum or substanding housing and halve the number of people without access to safe drinking water and basic sanitation
8. Developing a Global Partnership for Development: To ensure the rule of law, equal opportunity, and good governance, and to reduce poverty; to address the special needs of the poorest countries, those that are heavily indebted, landlocked, or are island nations, and to address the problems of inequitable trade restrictions

Debate about Balance

Central to the MDG debate and aid are balance issues, especially economic growth versus basic needs. The donor community does not have operational strategies to promote growth in the short to medium term in its tool kit (Easterly 2009). The evolving set of issues revolves around a renewed focus on basic needs, community development and community-based assessment of international aid, good governance, and civil society. This focus requires both qualitative and quantitative analysis. This debate over equity issues, access to health and education, and the concern for governance, property rights, free trade, and rule of law are in turn linked to the productivity versus HD approaches to aid (Easterly 2009). There are a number of components to this debate:

- Criticism of large scaling-up efforts in infrastructure, technology, and productivity (MCA) model—the macro–micro debate
- The extent and impact of the continued focus on policy reforms (structural adjustment) and their often perceived inconsistency with MDGs
- Scepticism about economic aid and productivity from community development advocates—the top-down versus bottom-up approach
- Debates about scaling entrepreneurial efforts (micro-credit, rural industrialization, and subsistence agriculture) with a need to develop productive and technical sectors that can impact upon macro-level GDP growth
- The aid versus trade debate and the failure to deal with structural (prices) and trade issues such as EU and U.S. tariffs on basic commodities (cotton and textiles), sugar, dairy products, and labor (wages)
- Entrepreneurialism versus cronyism and the line between innovation and corruption as an HD issue

Among those health priorities discussed within the MDGs, there are several choices that need to be made in terms of strategy and priority. Should priorities begin with prevention as opposed to treatment and if so, what strategy should define critical needs?

A significant health issue is that of targeting disease eradication (such as HIV/AIDS) as opposed to prevention and wellness promotion (maternal health and access to health care). The concern is that this can lead to a strategic choice focusing on short-term health and disease control with its potential for a quick fix rather than long-term wellness promotion and education, which are difficult, expensive, and not amenable to projectization. Critics of aid suggest that projectization of aid, conducive to targeting specific diseases, remains a problem to long-term institutional and organizational development, especially in the areas of health and education.

Where should the priority be in terms of levels of education: basic needs, technical education, or the postsecondary level? A related issue is the relationship between aid, health, and environmental sustainability. The focus on basic needs contained in the MDGs portends the potential neglect of higher-level education and professional skills development. Such higher-level skills development and professional diversification are likely to be necessary components of the whole strategic development schedule necessary to move developing states into the emerging country status.

The southern African country of Botswana provides a model for aid and development. From the 1960s through the 1980s, Botswana received significant amounts of aid from both official and private donors. Aid focused on HD, planning, and the pursuance of domestic marketing opportunities. As aid sceptic Dambisa Moyo has put it:

> Botswana's experience with aid ... is exactly what we would want to see: A country that began with a high ratio of aid to GDP uses the aid wisely to provide important public goods that help support good policies and sound governance that lays the foundation for robust growth. Over time, the ratio of aid to GDP would fall as a country develops. In this way, Botswana would seem like the poster-child for what aid can do in a well-managed country (Moyo 2009, p. 76).

There is the basic education versus higher education debate that needs to be addressed with regard to more specialized professional, technical, and skills development efforts within the context of the MDG agenda. With any decreased focus on long-term education and health programs, priority is given to short-term and narrowly targeted disease control, and targeted training concerns, sometimes referred to as "bridging training."

Bridging training and short-term capacity building, as well as narrow strategic health concerns, often result in the projectization of HD efforts when the need is for high volume aid on a long-term sustainable basis. Bridging training also raises the problem of bounded or limited knowledge among those with only a basic education. Basic education, on the long run, is not enough to move a country toward higher standards of social and economic development.

Long-term training and education and a systems approach to public health must address the need for unbounded knowledge and sophisticated and what are sometimes called unstructured skills in science, medicine, management, leadership, and problem-solving areas. The continued absence of high-quality professional programs and specialized skills development even on a regional basis, especially in Africa and parts of the Middle East, results in the continued dependence on international institutions in Europe and North America, though the tightening of immigration laws has meant that it is more difficult for potential students to get visas to study in Europe and North America.

Governance as the Interlocutor

The last item in the MDG list (the infamous number 8) has become a focal point for debate and discussion in the last 15 years. A recent paper, employing but one of many models, shows how complex the linkages between governance—essential in Sen's model—and HD—as measured by MDGs, HDI, and other indicators—can be (Cheema 2007). Most economists likely would find the relationships even more complex than this. No one has yet developed a framework, or "logic model," that effectively captures this complexity. Were we to add official and private aid to the model, it would become even more complex. Much more theoretical and practical work needs to be done to conceptualize the relationship originally hypothesized in Sen's work, and then study it empirically.

The MDGs capture HD from a variety of perspectives: three of the MDGs focus on health, another two on primary education (advanced education and skills development are not explicitly identified in terms of access other than concerns about discrimination), while three (reduction of child mortality, improvement of maternal health, and combating HIV/AIDS) relate to social policy concerns. The summit expressed an overall concern about the eradication of poverty, gender equality, and the issue of environmental sustainability as it relates to inequitable access to basic resources. These are wrapped up in the need for a global partnership between developed and developing countries, designed to address north–south trade, debt, geographical disadvantage, and governance issues.

Clearly, the MDGs central focus in development terms is on people rather than on economic growth (GDP) and per capita income, characteristic of past global initiatives. Focus on the individual from this perspective (confirmed in the *Barcelona Declaration*) sees the person within the context of his/her situational relationship with others and as a part of a social fabric (Kemp and Rendtorff 2007). MDGs assume that HD is a necessary precondition for economic growth, industrialization, and productivity, that there is interdependence between growth, poverty reduction, and sustainable development, and that progress in development depends upon the establishment of democratic governance, rule of law, human rights, and peace and security.

Complexities in theoretical models compound problems when they are tested empirically using common databases such as those in the HDR reports. Each developing country is unique with respect to its history, culture, economy, government, location, and people. As such, it is difficult to make sweeping statements about the developing world. Rather, analysis is forced to the country level. Nonetheless, there are some interesting overarching findings that apply in many LDCs and to the aid provided to them by donors.

When it became clear that progress in attaining MDGs in many developing countries had stalled, UNDP launched the *Call for Action* program in 2008 to get it back on track. It is, of course, too early to determine whether this renewed effort will have the desired impact. The global financial crisis of 2008 was especially devastating on developing countries, many of which had made much progress on their MDGs (World Bank Institute 2009), and individual countries (e.g., Haiti and Chile with their devastating earthquake of January 2010) continue to experience manmade and natural disasters.

Prior to the end of Cold War, the focus of donors was on alliance needs and support in the East–West rivalry. There were high levels of aid to states with no litmus test for good governance, human rights, or economic liberalism. The end of Cold War returned donors to a more objective view of the relationship between social development, economic growth, and HD. It is no accident that the HDI began in 1990.

The MDG initiative underpins a reengineered approach to HD that can significantly advance development thinking and policies in the last half decade of the MDG challenge. Of concern is the relationship between HD indicators, governance characteristics, economic growth, and, of course, official and private aid.

Concern is both with the human condition and the placing of individuals at the center of development. This book assumes that HD is crucial to managing social, economic, and environmental sustainability and that good governance is an important indicator of the environment needed to improve the human condition. It places individuals, families, and communities at the center of the generation of knowledge about development, arguing this is best achieved by understanding how societies, families, communities, and individuals conceptualize development practice and realize their potential for expanding choices and options and enjoying the freedom to lead lives they value (UNDP 2009).

Critics of international aid suggest there is a need for reassessment to determine how placing HD and good governance at the center of priorities can change the way in which we think about, formulate, implement, monitor, and evaluate development policies designed to promote empowerment, address inequality, and tackle sustainability. This becomes critical in addressing MDG impacts on donor and LDC behavior.

Of concern is the extent to which varying degrees of improvement among countries can be explained by different degrees or profiles of aid provided to them. The impacts of aid on HD will be examined within the context of aid for governance and rule of law, infrastructure development, micro and macro levels of economic entrepreneurialism, and community-based systems of economic production.

Limits of MDGs as Aid Development Tools

The Millennium Summit ended on September 8, 2000. One year later, the attack on the World Trade Center and the Pentagon, as well as the failed attack by a fourth set of highjackers over Pennsylvania, defined the first decade of MDGs. September 11, 2001 no doubt had a traumatizing impact on UN efforts to promote the MDG agenda.

In the wake of September 11, concerns for security and power relationships often ran up against commercial and humanitarian concerns all of which had a negative impact upon the goals for bilateral aid. Bilateral donors, subject to influences of domestic and international political pressures, are less able to focus strategically on a development agenda than was anticipated under MDG.

At issue is the extent to which MDGs and their recommended changes in aid priorities have had an impact on donors. An overarching issue is the extent to which MDGs have been incorporated into aid strategies and how the creation of MDGs may have changed the aid landscape (UNDP/HDRO 2009). Twenty years after its original declaration, the HD strategy articulated by UNDP demonstrates an enormous impact on development. After 10 years of the MDG paradigm, there is close to a consensus on an aid strategy as articulated in the Monterrey Consensus, including the following (UN 2003; Easterly unpublished; Rubey 2010):

1. The growth model based on public investment without preconditions based on increased human capacity (such as MDGs) is not realistic.
2. Conditionalities for development have to include some combination of free markets, sound economic policies, good governance, mechanisms to promote increased domestic savings and strong political institutions, and the rule of law.
3. Policy reform without social systems development (health, education, and social capital) does not work.
4. Aid, whether public or private, needs to be well thought out and of high quality.
5. Poorly thought out and badly implemented aid policies can impact negatively on patterns of good governance and the quality of LDC institutions.
6. Central to official aid should be long-term capacity building to achieve MDGs (nuanced by the need for choosing optimal strategies for health and educational achievements) managed by partnerships between LDC governments and international donor partners targeting fair trade and private investment.

An examination of MDGs suggests a strong focus on basic health, primary education, and environmental sustainability. The focus is on a basic, or lowest level, and goals appear more rhetorical and inspirational rather than operational. This lack of disaggregation of allocations suggests MDGs may be a blunt instrument particularly without taking account of the governance factor.

Conclusion

So, to what extent do MDGs promote changes in aid priorities? Have MDGs changed the composition of aid? To what extent do MDGs (with their focus on basic needs) impact upon aid and TA (governmental, international organizations, or private)? To what extent are critics correct when they suggest that MDGs have not significantly changed aid in the direction of basic needs?

Critics suggest MDGs have not significantly changed aid in the direction of basic needs operationally among aid and TA practitioners. There was a trend toward HD among all donors going back to the 1990s. Among European donors, there is focus on higher education and the basic needs as spelled out in the MDGs as opposed to the continued concern of the United States with disease control, public sector reform, privatization, and security needs.

Some observers see the basic needs goals of the MDGs as partly, and in some cases, largely rhetorical. Following from this are debates over the role of the government sector in social and environmental development (health, education, and sustainable rural development) that are part of a European (and Japanese)–U.S. split in the debate about international aid. Among most donors (with the exception of the Scandinavians), there is a degree of disjuncture between the current patterns of aid with the perceived need for aid and the current understanding of development needs as loosely defined by MDGs.

Many see the MDG program as coordinating bilateral programs to be inconsistent with multilateral and bilateral development aid to fragile and war-torn states, where terrorism is likely to fester. Many donors have come to believe that fragile and war-torn states require a different development aid model than developing countries, especially in contrast to the so-called middle-income countries. Yet, MDGs do not take this into account directly, especially in monitoring and evaluation (M&E), and reporting.

For the past 10 years, a number of bilateral donors have become preoccupied with counterterrorism and several have engaged in what one observer has called "armed social work." Central to the debate is a concern about the militarization of aid. For many observers of aid, the MDGs represent little more than symbolic statements.

UNDP and the international donor community and developing countries were correct to be concerned about the uneven progress in attaining the worthy, if somewhat vague, MDG goals in spite of the limits of global efforts in their *Call for Action* as of 2010. Calls to reengineer the program before its termination in 2015 abound. Many of the recommendations seem appropriate, while others do not. We offer the following observations that might inform the program policymakers, both in the donor community and within developing countries, as it moves to completion.

Many critics complain that MDGs are variously too narrow or too broad, too generic or too specific, too few or too many, or not quite the right ones, or mostly the wrong ones, or largely unattainable, or are not actionable. As such, it is not particularly surprising that some argue that the performance indicators of MDGs measure the wrong things or are not measurable, are exacerbated by poor quality or unavailable data, and are concerned mostly with inputs (e.g., numbers of doctors in a health-care system) versus outcomes (e.g., whether aid improved the health status of poor people). There is some truth to each of these criticisms, but they fail to take into account that highly developed countries themselves do not have monitoring and evaluation systems that satisfy these criteria. Why should developing countries be any different?

In the United States, for example, the publicly funded Medicare program, expending hundreds of billions of dollars annually on millions of elderly people, has the same M & E limitations as those in developing countries. One of the few outcome measures for the program that encompasses 7% of the U.S. economy is "the number and percentage of elderly people who received a flu shot." These criticisms also fail to take into account that there is often little agreement within developed countries about how to measure performance and what performance goals are appropriate.

Every time European and North American governments change hands, entire performance management systems get reengineered. In the United States, for example, just in the past two decades, the country went from minimal performance measures under George H. W. Bush, to a comprehensive national performance review under Bill Clinton, to a parallel performance system under George W. Bush, to a reconfigured system under President Barack Obama. Experiences in the United States replicate those in Canada, Australia, New Zealand, and the United Kingdom (Buss et al. 2010). It was unlikely that the MDG program would satisfy everyone and not surprising that there would be calls for change over a 15-year period. For years, the Controller General at the Government Accountability Office (GAO) tried to develop a national indicators project for the United States—not unlike the MDG in many ways—but was unable to do so, political will and lack of resources being major barriers (GAO 2007).

The MDG program will never have the right measures necessary to satisfy the majority of critics. Moreover, were MDGs to include every possible HD measure necessary to satisfy critics, the program would attract new critics, who would claim that too much funding was expended on data gathering, reporting, and monitoring at the expense of programs for poor people. Nonetheless, the authors in this book see the need to articulate a link between human resource development and good governance as a framework for sustainable economic development in the twenty-first century.

So, proponents and opponents alike might agree to disagree, and proceed with the MDGs as they are, even though the resources may be meagre. The goals focus attention on major issues and they provide policymakers and observers enough information to assess progress and hold governments and donors accountable. All would agree that they have served one of their major purposes: to get developed and developing countries alike to focus on poverty reduction in a much more serious way. Aid impacts (to date) on health and education indicators are testimony to the wisdom of the MDG efforts.

References

Bauer, P. 1972. *Dissent on Development.* London: Weidenfeld and Nicolson.

Bauer, P. 1981. *Equality, the Third World and Economic Delusion.* London: Methuen.

Black, J., Coleman, J., Stifel, L. (eds.). 1977. *Education and Training for Public Sector Management in the Developing Countries.* New York: Rockefeller Foundation.

Brandt Commission (Independent Commission on International Development Issues). 1980. *North-South: A Programme for Survival.* London: Pan Books.

Brinkerhoff, J. 2002. *Partnership for International Development: Rhetoric or Results?* Boulder, CO: Lynne Rienner Publishers.

Brown, M., O'Connor, J. 1996. Cross-pressures in western European foreign aid. In: S. Hook (ed.). *Foreign Aid: Toward the Millennium.* Boulder, CO: Lynne Rienner.

Browne, S. 1999. *Beyond Aid: From Patronage to Partnership.* Aldershot, UK: Ashgate.

Browne, S. (ed.). 2002. *Development Capacity through Technical Cooperation: Country Experiences.* London: Earthscan and UNDP.

Buss, T., Buss, N., Hill, E. 2010. Performance management in comparative perspective. In: A. Shillabeer, T. Buss, and D. Rousseau (eds.). *Evidence Based Public Management.* Armonk, NY: ME Sharpe.

Buss, T., Gardner, A. 2008. The millennium challenge account: An early appraisal. In: L. Picard, R. Goelsema, and T. Buss (eds.). *Foreign Aid and Foreign Policy: Lessons for the Next Half Century.* Armonk, NY: ME Sharpe, pp. 329–356.

Butterfield, S. 2004. *U.S. Development Aid—An Historic First-Achievements and Failures in the Twentieth Century.* Westport, CN: Praeger.

Cheema, S. 2007. *Governance and MDGs.* New York: UN Department of Economic and Social Affairs.

Chenery, H. 1974. *Redistribution with Growth.* London: Oxford University Press.

Clark, D. 2005. Capability approach: Its development, critiques, and recent advances. Global Poverty Research Group WPS-32. Available at http://www.gprg.org/pubs/workingpapers/pdfs/gprg-wps-032.pdf. Accessed 8/8/14.

Cornea G., Jolly, R. 1987. *Adjustment with a Human Face* (Two Volumes). Oxford: Clarendon Press.

Dollar D., Pritchett, L. 1998. *What Works, What Doesn't and Why.* Washington, DC: World Bank.

Easterly, W. 2001. *The Elusive Quest for Growth: Economists' Adventures and Misadventures in the Tropics.* Cambridge, MA: MIT Press.

Easterly, W. 2006. *The White Man's Burden: Why the West's Efforts to Aid the Rest Have Done So Much Ill and So Little Good.* New York: Penguin Press HC.

Easterly, W. 2009. The Indomitable in Pursuit of the Inexplicable: The World Development Reports' Failure to Comprehend Economic Growth Despite Determined Attempts, 1978–2008. NYU College of Arts and Sciences Lecture, DRI Working Paper 39, October 6.

Easterly, W. *Was Development Assistance a Mistake.* Unpublished Paper. New York.

Ferguson, N. 2003. *Empire: The Rise and Demise of the British World Order and the Lessons for Global Power.* New York: Basic Books.

Ferguson, N. 2008. *The Ascent of Money: A Financial History of the World.* New York: Penguin Press.
Garrett, L. 2007. The Challenge of Global Health, *Foreign Affairs.* January/February. http://www.foreignaffairs.com/articles/622268/laurie-garrett/the-challenge-of-global-health. Accessed 8/8/14.
Government Accountability Office (GAO). 2007. *National Indicators.* Washington, DC: GAO, 07-1069CG.
Hancock, G. 1989. *Lords of Poverty: The Power, Prestige and Corruption of the International Aid Business.* New York: Atlantic Monthly Press.
Henry, C. 2007. *What Are the Elements of the 'Washington Consensus' and How Is This Different from 'Adjustment with a Human Face'.* Unpublished Paper. Mona: University of the West Indies.
Hook, S. (ed.). 1996. *Foreign Aid: Toward the Millennium.* Boulder, CO: Lynne Rienner.
Jones, D. 1977. *Aid and Development in Southern Africa.* London: Croon Helm.
Kemp, P., Rendtorff, J. 2007. The Barcelona declaration: Towards an integrated approach to basic ethical principles. *Synthesis Philiosophica* 46, 239–251.
Killick, T. 1989. *A Reaction Too Far: An Economic Theory and Role of the State in Developing Countries.* London: Overseas Development Institute.
Lancaster, C. 2007. *Foreign Aid: Diplomacy, Development, Domestic Politics.* Chicago, IL: University of Chicago Press.
Lewis, A. 1955. *The Theory of Economic Growth.* London: Allen and Unwin.
Maren, M. 1997. *The Road to Hell: The Ravaging Effects of Foreign Aid and International Charity.* New York: The Free Press.
Martinussen, J. 1997. *Society, State and Market: A Guide to Competing Theories of Development.* London: Zed Press.
Maslow, A. 1954. *Motivation and Personality.* New York: Harper.
Minoiu, M., Reddy, S. 2009. *Development Aid and Economic Growth: A Positive Long-Run Relation.* IMF Working Paper. Washington, DC: IMF.
Morris, D. 1979. *Measuring the Condition of the World's Poor: The Physical Quality of Life Index.* New York: Pergamon.
Mosley, P. 1987. *Overseas Aid: Its Defence and Reform.* Brighton, UK: Wheatsheaf Books.
Moyo, D. 2009. *Dead Aid: Why Aid Is Not Working and How There Is a Better Way for Africa.* New York: Farrar, Straus and Giroux.
Nielsen, W. 1989. *The Golden Donors: A New Anatomy of the Great Foundations.* New York: E.L. Dutton.
Nussbaum, M. 2000. *Women and Human Development: The Capabilities Approach.* Cambridge, MA: Cambridge.
Picard, L. 1994. The challenge of structural adjustment, In: L. Picard and M. Garrity (Eds.), *Policy Reform for Sustainable Development in Africa: The Institutional Imperative.* Boulder, CO: Lynne Rienner.
Picard, L., Buss, T. 2009. *A Fragile Balance: Re-examining the History of Foreign Aid, Security and Diplomacy.* Sterling, VA: Kumarian Press.
Picard, L., Smuckler, R. 2008. Higher education capacity building and aid: Lessons learned, In: L. Picard, R. Groelsema, and T. Buss (eds.). *Foreign Aid and Foreign Policy: Lessons for the Next Half-Century.* Armonk, NY: ME Sharpe, pp. 302–314.
Rix, A. 1996. Japan's emergence as a foreign aid superpower. In: S. Hook (ed.). *Foreign Aid: Toward the Millenium* Boulder, CO: Lynne Rienner.
Rostow, W. 1960. *The Stages of Economic Growth.* Cambridge, MA: Cambridge University.

Rubey, L. 2010. *Why the Global Food Security Initiative Risks Failure (And What We Can Do To Succeed.* Unpublished Paper. Washington, DC: USAID.
Ruttan, V. 1996. *United States Development Assistance Policy: The Domestic Politics of Foreign Aid.* Baltimore, MD: Johns Hopkins University Press.
Sen, A. 1981. *Poverty and Famines.* Oxford: Clarendon Press.
Sen, A. 1988. The concept of development. In: H. Chenery and T. N. Srinivasan (eds.). *Handbook of Development Economics.* Amsterdam: North-Holland.
Sen, A. 2000. *Development as Freedom.* Oxford, UK: Oxford University Press.
Stewart, F. 1985. *Basic Needs in Developing Countries.* Baltimore, MD: Johns Hopkins.
Streeten, P., Burki, S. 1978. Basic needs: Some issues. *World Development* 6(3) 411–421.
Streeten, P. et al. 1982. *First Things First: Meeting Basic Human Needs in Developing Countries.* London: Oxford University Press (Published for the World Bank).
UN. 2003. Financing for Development: Monterrey Consensus of the International Conference on Financing for Development. Monterrey, Mexico, March 18–22.
UN Childrens Fund (UNICEF). 1991. *Structural Adjustment with a Human Face.* Paris: United Nations.
UN Development Program (UNDP). 1990. *Human Development Report.* New York: Palgrave.
UN Development Program (UNDP). 2007. *Human Development Report 2007–2008: Fighting Climate Change: Human Solidarity in a Divided World.* New York: Palgrave.
UN Development Program (UNDP). 2009. The effectiveness of aid and the MDGs in advancing human development. Typescript.
UNDP/HDRO. 2009. The 2010 Human Development Report: Rethinking Human Development Brussels: Joint European Commission-UNDP/HDRO Consultation on Human Development and Development Cooperation, European and Economic Social Committee, November 12.
UN General Assembly. 2001. *A Roadmap towards Implementation of the UN Millennium Declaration.* New York: United Nations, September.
World Bank Institute. 2009. Growing out of crisis. *Development Outreach*, December (entire issue).

Chapter 3

Aid, Institutions, and Human Development

Chris Belasco, Terry F. Buss, and Louis A. Picard

Contents

How do governance and aid affect human development (HD)? Which factors contribute most to determining HD? Scholars of sustainable development in developing countries seek a balance between too much aid and too little, and whether results have an effect on countries with poor governance track records, or if innovative methods will be necessary. If governance serves as a conditioning variable, then donors must know under what conditions success in HD occurs. From this, donors can examine what conditions can be reproduced to sustainably contribute to development, and when results could be damaging.

This study examines the literature on aid, institutions, and HD, drawing on studies of public service delivery, then develops and tests hypotheses on the conditional nature of governance and aid and how they affect HD. To evaluate the hypotheses, results of six cross-country regression models are reported to assess the relationship between health aid and education aid interacted with governance measures. This sectoral approach allows for the examination of factors expected to affect the Human Development Index (HDI), measured over the immediate term, and over the medium run. It finds relationships between health aid and public participation in governance as measured by Freedom House and the Worldwide Governance Indicators (WGI) measure of Voice and Accountability, showing positive effects on HDI.

We compare marginal effects plots to analyze conditional relationships. Most of the evidence supports the hypothesis that governance conditions the relationship between aid and HDI, where health aid negatively affects HDI in countries with poor governance and positively affects HDI in countries with improved governance. Some evidence also supports the hypothesis that poor governance hinders HDI change in countries with little health aid. Unlike the support for health aid, we found no relationships between education aid and HDI.

Analytical Challenges

Governance, aid, and HDI have separate histories in the literature, and this is true even for annual reports produced by United Nations Development Programme (UNDP). The relationship between governance and HDI was the subject of the *2002 Human Development Report (HDR)*, which argued for effectiveness, plurality, and independence in institutions, while the 2005 and 2011 *HDR*s argued for reform in aid in light of the Millennium Development Goals (MDGs) discussed in Chapter 2.

Critics of aid practices such as Bauer (1972, 1981), Easterly (2001, 2006, 2007), Ferguson (2003, 2008), Moyo (2009), and Picard and Buss (2009) see limited effectiveness of aid in the economic aspects of HD. These viewpoints are in contrast to cross-country and panel evidence that shows a positive long-run relationship (Minoiu and Reddy 2009). This evidence supports others who argue aid assists with economic growth (Burnside and Dollar 2000; Guillaumont and Chauvet 2001; Hansen and Tarp 2001; Collier and Dollar 2001; Clemens et al. 2004; Dalgaard et al. 2004). More generally, Sachs et al. (2004), Sachs (2005) championed aid as a way to escape poverty traps and generate development.

In focusing on the economic outcome of aid, these debates do not match the concept of HD used in the HDI. In a comparison of 40 years of HDI values, Gray and Purser (2010) find a near-zero correlation with the income and nonincome (health, education) aspects of HDI. Service delivery relates to government finance, but differences in how components of HDI—measurement of income and how health and education outcomes of service provision are met—suggest that HDI relates to governance and aid more broadly than just as a factor of income. Service delivery matters, and is dependent on governance to achieve objectives in the education and health sectors. Public service delivery literature yields additional perspective on the relationship between sectoral aid, governance, and HDI.

Recent literature links governance to effective spending in achieving education and health outcomes (Rajkumar and Swaroop 2002, 2008). Wolf (2007) draws on this to analyze the interactive effect of governance and aid on health, education, and water and sanitation service delivery. For scholars of politics, the finding is intuitive: aid and improved governance go hand in hand in generating better outcomes. Better governance permits the allocation and administration of resources to achieve improvements in HDI.

Governance and aid have an interactive effect on each other: the effects of aid can be amplified or minimized by the quality of governance and good institutions can be improved and weak institutions diminished by the aid received. Our null hypothesis is:

H0: There is no relationship between aid, good governance, and HDI.

The above null hypothesis states that no relationship exists between the interactive effect of aid and governance and HDI. This is possible if either aid is ineffective or quality of governance does not create conditions to improve HDI within the country sample.

H1: Aid weakens governance in determining the level of HDI.

An alternative hypothesis is aid makes governance less effective in attaining HDI. This will be revealed in a negative relationship, where aid can worsen a poorly governed country, and little aid can make a well-governed country less well-off than could be achieved with more aid.

H2: Governance strengthens aid in determining the level of HDI.

Another hypothesis is governance makes aid effective in achieving HDI. This happens when a positive relationship as better governance yields improved aid effectiveness in determining HDI.

H3: Governance and aid jointly condition the level of HDI.

A third hypothesis is that the conditions of governance and the amount of aid reinforce each other, resulting in improved levels of HDI. A positive relationship between both dimensions of the interaction and dependent variable would reveal this.

Data, Model, and Methods

This study draws data from a sample of 150 developing countries* across Africa, Eastern Europe, Latin America, Asia, the Middle East, and North Africa. Data sources and transformations are listed in Table 3.1. HDI was compiled from various years of UNDP data. Aid measures were compiled from Organisation for Economic Cooperation and Development (OECD) Development Assistance Council (OECD DAC 2014). WGI were gathered over various years (Kaufmann et al. 2004–2009). Freedom in the World indices were compiled from various years of Freedom House data (Freedom House 2014). Primary education and health expenditures were compiled from UNESCO and from The Millennium Challenge Corporation "Country Scorecard–Time Series Data" (Millennium Challenge Corporation [MCC] 2010). Data on covariates were compiled from the World Development Indicators and the Database on Political Institutions (World Bank).

Model: Our model is

$$\begin{aligned}\text{Ln(Human development}_{it}) = {} & A_{it-1} + \alpha \text{ governance} * \beta \ln(\text{aid to sector/aid})_{it-1} + \\ & \alpha \text{ governance}_{it-1} + \beta \ln(\text{aid to sector/aid})_{it-1} + \gamma \ln \\ & (\text{public expenditure per capita})_{it-1} + \delta \ln(\text{aid/GNI})_{it-1} + \\ & \Theta \ln(\text{covariates}_{it-1}) + \varepsilon\end{aligned}$$

* Afghanistan; Albania; Algeria; Andorra; Angola; Antigua and Barbuda; Argentina; Armenia; Azerbaijan; Bahamas; Bahrain; Bangladesh; Barbados; Belarus; Belize; Benin; Bhutan; Bolivia; Bosnia and Herzegovina; Botswana; Brazil; Brunei Darussalam; Burkina Faso; Burundi; Cambodia; Cameroon; Cape Verde; Central African Republic; Chad; Chile; China; Colombia; Comoros; Congo, Dem. Rep.; Congo, Rep.; Costa Rica; Cote d'Ivoire; Croatia; Cuba; Cyprus; Djibouti; Dominica; Dominican Republic; Ecuador; Egypt; Arab Rep.; El Salvador; Equatorial Guinea; Eritrea; Ethiopia; Fiji; Gabon; Gambia; Georgia; Ghana; Grenada; Guatemala; Guinea; Guinea-Bissau; Guyana; Haiti; Honduras; India; Indonesia; Iran; Islamic Rep.; Iraq; Israel; Jamaica; Jordan; Kazakhstan; Kenya; Kiribati; Korea, Dem. Rep.; Korea, Rep.; Kuwait; Kyrgyz Republic; Lao PDR; Lebanon; Lesotho; Liberia; Libya; Madagascar; Malawi; Malaysia; Maldives; Mali; Malta; Marshall Islands; Mauritania; Mauritius; Mexico; Micronesia, Fed. Sts.; Moldova; Mongolia; Morocco; Mozambique; Myanmar; Namibia; Nepal; Nicaragua; Niger; Nigeria; Oman; Pakistan; Palau; Panama; Papua New Guinea; Paraguay; Peru; Philippines; Qatar; Rwanda; Samoa; Sao Tome and Principe; Saudi Arabia; Senegal; Seychelles; Sierra Leone; Singapore; Slovenia; Solomon Islands; Somalia; South Africa; Sri Lanka; St. Kitts and Nevis; St. Lucia; St. Vincent and the Grenadines; Sudan; Suriname; Swaziland; Syrian Arab Republic; Tajikistan; Tanzania; Thailand; Togo; Tonga; Trinidad and Tobago; Tunisia; Turkey; Turkmenistan; Uganda; Ukraine; United Arab Emirates; Uruguay; Uzbekistan; Vanuatu; Venezuela, RB; Vietnam; Yemen, Rep.; Zambia; Zimbabwe.

Table 3.1 Data Sources and Transformations

Variable	*Data Source*	*Transformation*
Log HDI average 2005–2007	UNDP	Log; 3-year average
Change in HDI 2005–2012	UNDP	Change $t_1 - t_0$
Rule of law 1995–2004	World Bank	10-year average
Voice and accountability 1995–2004	World Bank	10-year average
Freedom House inverted 1995–2004	Freedom House	Average of political rights and civil liberties, subtracted from 7 to invert directionally
Rule of law 1995–2004[a] education aid 1995–2004 interaction	World Bank WGI; DAC	Log primary education aid as a share of total aid multiplicative interaction with rule of law
Rule of law 1995–2004[a] health aid 1995–2004 interaction	World Bank WGI; DAC	Log health aid as a share of total aid multiplicative interaction with rule of law
Freedom House 1995–2004[a] education aid 1995–2004 interaction	Freedom House Freedom in the World; DAC	Log primary education aid as a share of total aid multiplicative interaction with Freedom House inverted
Freedom House 1995–2004[a] health aid 1995–2004 interaction	Freedom House Freedom in the World; DAC	Log health aid as a share of total aid multiplicative interaction with Freedom House inverted
Voice and accountability 1995–2004[a] education aid 1995–2004 interaction	World Bank WGI; DAC	Log primary education aid as a share of total aid multiplicative interaction with voice and accountability

(*Continued*)

Table 3.1 (*Continued*) Data Sources and Transformations

Variable	*Data Source*	*Transformation*
Voice and accountability 1995–2004[a] health aid 1995–2004 interaction	World Bank WGI; DAC	Log health aid as a share of total aid multiplicative interaction with voice and accountability
Log foreign assistance as a share of GNI 1995–2004	DAC	Log; share of GNI
Log primary education aid as a share of total aid 1995–2004	DAC	Log; share of total aid
Log health aid as a share of total aid 1995–2004	DAC	Log; share of total aid
Log health expenditure per capita 1995–2004	MCC country scorecard	Log taken
Log primary education expenditure per capita 1995–2004	MCC country scorecard (compiled UNESCO data)	Log taken
Log fertility rate 1995–2004	World Bank, World Development Indicators	Log taken
Log share access to water 1995–2004	World Bank, World Development Indicators	Log taken
Log population	World Bank, World Development Indicators	Log taken
Log literacy 1995–2004	World Bank, World Development Indicators	Log taken
Log HIV/AIDS incidence	World Bank, World Development Indicators	Log taken
Federalism dummy	Database of Political Institutions, World Bank	
Sub-Saharan Africa	World Bank, World Development Indicators	

[a] Separate efforts to examine aid and rule of law utilizing the RST 2SLS model were made as background research for the *2010 Human Development Report* by the authors (Picard et al. 2010). It found a positive relationship for aid on HDI but not one for rule of law. No interactions were taken at that time, but the comparison would be fruitful for future analysis.

where for every *i*th country, A is a constant; α represents the parameter estimate of governance; β represents the parameter estimate of the amount of aid; γ represents the parameter estimate of public expenditure per capita for the items of interest (health, education); δ represents the parameter estimate of aid as a share of GNI; Θ represents parameter estimates of the covariates: fertility rate, share access to water, population density, literacy, HIV/AIDS incidence, and categorical variables for federalism and sub-Saharan Africa; and ε represents the error term.

This is an ordinary least squares (OLS) model with HDI outcomes lagged to reduce problems with endogeneity. It diverges from Gray, Molina, and Purser, which adapted Rodrik et al. (2004) to examine the effect of rule of law on HDI, which compared OLS and two-stage least squares (2SLS). Their work found a positive result for rule of law among OLS specifications, but not among 2SLS specifications. The models below find no significant effect for rule of law. Others find similar results for rule of law in 2SLS specifications, but inclusion of aid revealed positive effect on HDI, life expectancy, and literacy.

Dependent Variable: HDI

HDI is a composite measure, and one can expect that on the aggregate, improvements in health, education, and social capacity will be associated with increased aid, provided quality of governance is good. While Wolf's indicators of service delivery outcomes include primary completion rate, youth literacy, infant mortality, and under-5 mortality, utilizing the HDI to examine delivery outcomes allows for comparison of the interactive effect of governance and both education and health aid on HD (Wolf 2007, pp. 666–668). The model enables analysis of aid to health and education sectors at once, comparing effects of aid on HDI. It is possible to make inferences about the effect of the sectoral distribution of aid on HDI. HDI is calculated as a 3-year average (2005–2007) to smooth distortions in a given year and then the change in HDI is taken for the years (2005–2012) to gauge the medium-term effect of aid and institutions on HD.

Independent Variables

Independent variables are governance and aid. They are expected to have an interactive effect on each other. These are drawn from measurements taken from WGI, and will also include a summary measure from Freedom House.

We assess governance using WGI's rule of law and voice and accountability, and an average of the Freedom House Freedom in the World Civil Liberties and Political Rights indices. Wolf incorporated WGI's control of corruption and press freedom into models for the outcomes of service delivery, and systematically assessed only control of corruption across the models (Wolf 2007). Aspects of governance captured by WGI such as respect for rule of law and the degree to which voice and accountability affects were not examined, nor were any summary measures included such as the Freedom House Freedom in the World index. These elements are central to the discussion of governance, and aim to capture elements not discussed in the previous study.

Sectoral aid, both education and health, will be measured as a share of total aid, excluding military aid. This will allow for the examination of the amount of aid distributed in each recipient country economy. A limitation of the OECD DAC is that commitment data is not as accurate as disbursement data, only reported by donors. This has a tendency to inflate the measurement versus the total amount of aid distributed and reflects a limitation of the use of OECD DAC data. Though disbursements and commitments differ, Hudson notes that many commitments are actually disbursed over time, though there are lags in the time period between when commitments are made and funds are disbursed (Hudson 2013, p. 114). Delays may occur due to procedural issues, political uncertainty, and bureaucratic issues among donors (Hudson 2013, p. 110). Overall commitments reflect between 87% and 94% of disbursements from 1994 through 2005 in the DAC, meaning that the inflation effect can range from 13% to 28%. Comparing sectoral data from 2002 through 2010, Hudson finds that health commitments are actually disbursed at lower share (89% disbursed) than education commitments (96% disbursed) (Hudson 2013, p. 114).* However, based on estimating more recent data, Hudson adds an important conclusion: many commitments are actually disbursed over longer time horizons, rather than what is examined in year-to-year measurements. Greater time periods (such as the 9-year panel in Hudson and the 10-year average taken here) allow for commitments to actually be disbursed (Hudson 2013).

For the interaction term, each model will consider one governance measure interacted with health and education aid to examine conditional effects the institutional measure and aid measure have on each other. This allows for comparison of governance and aid effects on HDI.

Covariates

Our model replicates covariate choices of Rajkumar and Swaroop (2002, 2008), and Wolf (2007):

- Public expenditure per capita (for health) or per student (for education) serves as a measurement of spending that controls for the share of population expected to receive the service (Rajkumar and Swaroop 2002; Wolf 2007).

* Utilizing recent data, Hudson (2013) finds that the average ratio of disbursements to commitments for all nonmilitary aid over 2002–2010 is 89.4%, meaning that much, but not all, of the aid committed is actually disbursed.

More education and health expenditures per capita (or per student) would have a positive relationship with HDI outcomes.

- Aid as a share of gross national income is included, as aid may increase fungibility between spending choices by enlarging the range of choices available to governments (Rajkumar and Swaroop 2002; Wolf 2007). This would have a positive effect on HDI.
- Fertility rate is expected to have negative effects on education and health service provision costs, as more service users would raise the cost of schooling, and the cost of health care for more women and children (Rajkumar and Swaroop 2002; Wolf 2007).
- Share of access to water is expected to have positive effects on health service provision, but also for education since fewer children would be expected to obtain clean water (Rajkumar and Swaroop 2002; Wolf 2007).
- Population density is expected to result in lower costs of service provision, given the proximity of population and costs to transport goods and travel to services. This should be positively associated with HDI outcomes (Rajkumar and Swaroop 2002; Wolf 2007).
- Literacy is expected to result in positive HDI outcomes as more literate populations would be expected to send their children to school (Rajkumar and Swaroop 2002; Wolf 2007).
- HIV/AIDS incidence is expected to result in negative effects on HDI outcomes as the costs of health care are expected to increase and infants and children are put at risk of death due to infection (Rajkumar and Swaroop 2002; Wolf 2007).
- Federalism dummy is expected to improve HDI outcomes as needs are better articulated and met at the local level (Wolf 2007; Bardhan 2002).
- Sub-Saharan African dummy is expected to have a negative relationship with HDI as the area of the continent is a major focus area of goals to improve delivery of the key services under examination here (Rajkumar and Swaroop 2002; Wolf 2007).

Endogeneity

To minimize endogeneity, this study lags the dependent variable to reflect the period after aid and institutional effects. Aid, institutions, and covariates are examined as an average of the 10-year period 1995–2004, and the two measurements of the independent variable occur in the period afterward: for the average measurement, the dependent variable measures the period 2005–2007, and for the change rate measurement, the dependent variable measures the period 2005–2012. Conditions present in 2004 in a country's institutions, demographics, and so on are likely to still be present in 2005, but the likelihood of the conditions of HDI serving as a cause for the prior period should be minimized by dividing the data diachronically.

Interactive Effects

Berry et al. (2012) have raised questions about the interpretation of independent variables that condition each other. Too frequently, one of the interactive variables are treated as "conditioning" the other in analysis, rather than acknowledging the effect each has on the other (Berry et al. 2012). When variables are treated as interactive, their effects on the dependent variable are symmetric—meaning that both aid (conditioned by governance) and governance (conditioned by aid) could be expected to affect HDI. The interactive effects of select significant variables will be examined via marginal effects plot analysis. This analysis probes conditional effects on HDI to assess relationships between aid and institutions on HD. Providing this analytical rigor will improve assessments of aid effects and governance on HDI as it will enable us to examine whether aid or governance serve as driving influences of HD (Table 3.2).

Results

Findings include a positive effect for Voice and Accountability and Freedom House interactions with health aid on the 2005–2007 average HDI and change in HDI from 2005 through 2012. Results of education aid interactions neither serve as HDI predictors in any model, nor were any interactions with rule of law predictors of HDI. This contradicts the findings of OLS models of Gray and Purser (2010), but is consistent with the 2SLS findings of their work and ours.

Average HDI 2005–2007

Table 3.3 presents the results of the models used to predict the 2005–2007 average HDI value. Several trends emerge among independent variables: positive effect of interactions of health aid with measures of governance, absence of a significant effect of the interactions of education aid with all measures of governance, and absence of a significant effect of rule of law in either interaction. Another trend is the positive effect of education expenditures per capita on HDI.

In Models 1 and 2, the interaction of health aid and Freedom House and the interaction of health aid and voice and accountability each show a positive and significant relationship with HDI ($\alpha = 0.05$). Interaction of education aid and the two governance measures do not show the same result. This presents a counterintuitive result: expectations that increasing levels of foreign assistance in education should yield a positive change in HDI are not found but the amount of education expenditures per capita positively affects HDI. Results suggest a stronger relationship with HDI among health aid and institutions than among education aid and institutions.

Results for Model 3 and the Federalism variable (in Models 1 and 2) may be commonly linked to age of representative institutions. In Model 3, neither the interaction of education aid and rule of law nor health aid with rule of law shows a significant relationship with HDI outcomes. The federalism variable shows a

Table 3.2 Summary Statistics

Variable	*Obs*	*Mean*	*Std. Dev.*	*Min*	*Max*
Log HDI average 2005–2007	130	−0.4161621	0.2738308	−1.087672	−0.0502412
Change in HDI 2005–2012	136	−0.0554338	0.0415478	−0.296	0.164
Rule of law 1995–2004	150	−0.3638519	0.7755313	−2.134183	1.583451
Voice and accountability 1995–2004	150	−0.339365	0.8793686	−2.097657	1.491059
Freedom House inverted 1995–2004	150	2.990333	1.826425	0	6
Rule of law 1995–2004[a] education aid 1995–2004 interaction	134	0.9417163	1.381539	−3.001907	4.67962
Rule of law 1995–2004[a] health aid 1995–2004 interaction	123	0.202923	1.417416	−3.19701	6.14449
Freedom House 1995–2004[a] education aid 1995–2004 interaction	134	−5.46002	4.018667	−19.26189	0
Freedom House 1995–2004[a] health aid 1995–2004 interaction	123	−1.97917	5.24447	−26.11402	15.32524
Voice and accountability 1995–2004[a] education aid 1995–2004 interaction	134	0.6637531	1.603282	−3.18072	4.189516
Voice and accountability 1995–2004[a] health aid 1995–2004 interaction	123	0.3999506	1.817927	−4.672002	7.093193

(*Continued*)

Table 3.2 (*Continued*) Summary Statistics

Variable	*Obs*	*Mean*	*Std. Dev.*	*Min*	*Max*
Log foreign assistance as a share of GNI 1995–2004	141	−3.67319	1.993639	−9.315701	−0.8308473
Log primary education aid as a share of total aid 1995–2004	134	−1.805967	0.6698922	−3.606583	−0.3744935
Log health aid as a share of total aid 1995–2004	123	−0.7765977	1.659981	−5.193057	3.354763
Log health expenditure per capita 1995–2004	142	7.822218	1.698415	3.032332	11.24732
Log primary education expenditure per capita 1995–2004	99	7.52377	1.490558	2.408404	10.56385
Log fertility rate 1995–2004	150	1.218357	0.4688396	0.1906204	2.044022
Log share access to water 1995–2004	145	−0.3052926	0.3262354	−1.560648	0
Log population	150	4.019071	1.394424	0.4310545	8.675672
Log literacy 1995–2004	122	−0.3347133	0.3952121	−2.365383	−0.0020113
Log HIV/AIDS incidence	104	−0.2176366	1.606652	−2.302585	3.256172
Federalism dummy	150	0.0463576	0.2109581	0	1
Sub-Saharan Africa	150	0.2847682	0.4528058	0	1

[a] Separate efforts to examine aid and rule of law utilizing the RST 2SLS model were made as background research for the *2010 Human Development Report* by the authors (Picard et al. 2010). It found a positive relationship for aid on HDI but not one for rule of law. No interactions were taken at that time, but the comparison would be fruitful for future analysis.

Table 3.3 Average HDI 2005–2007

Variables	*(1)* *Log HDI 2005–2007 (Average)*	*(2)* *Log HDI 2005–2007 (Average)*	*(3)* *Log HDI 2005–2007 (Average)*
Education aid[a] Freedom House interaction	−0.00388 (0.0418)		
Education aid[a] voice and accountability interaction		−0.0248 (0.0937)	
Education aid[a] rule of law interaction			−0.177 (0.160)
Health aid[a] Freedom House interaction	0.0249** (0.00869)		
Health aid[a] voice and accountability interaction		0.0617** (0.0178)	
Health aid[a] rule of law interaction			0.0517 (0.0636)
Freedom House (inverted)	0.0682 (0.0751)		
Voice and accountability		0.109 (0.169)	
Rule of law			−0.422 (0.327)
Education aid (share of total aid)	0.0594 (0.148)	0.0199 (0.104)	−0.0783 (0.123)
Health aid (share of total aid)	−0.0396 (0.0332)	0.0569† (0.0322)	0.0424 (0.0482)
ODA share of GNI	0.0195 (0.0264)	0.0246 (0.0289)	0.0390 (0.0298)
Health expenditures per capita (Log)	−0.104# (0.0652)	−0.0971 (0.0697)	−0.0594 (0.0640)
Education expenditures per capita (Log)	0.111† (0.0568)	0.109# (0.0655)	0.150* (0.0651)

(*Continued*)

Table 3.3 (*Continued*) Average HDI 2005–2007

	(1)	(2)	(3)
Variables	*Log HDI 2005–2007 (Average)*	*Log HDI 2005–2007 (Average)*	*Log HDI 2005–2007 (Average)*
Fertility (Log)	0.175	0.163	−0.0573
	(0.166)	(0.171)	(0.162)
Population density (Log)	0.0222	0.0280	0.0414
	(0.0318)	(0.0324)	(0.0359)
Literacy (Log)	0.168[#]	0.163	0.0805
	(0.114)	(0.116)	(0.113)
HIV/AIDS prevalence (Log)	−0.0109	−0.0105	−0.0201
	(0.0312)	(0.0309)	(0.0316)
Federalism	−0.318*	−0.340*	−0.237
	(0.146)	(0.159)	(0.183)
Sub-Saharan Africa	0.115	0.122	0.226†
	(0.122)	(0.130)	(0.128)
Constant	−0.737	−0.553	−1.163*
	(0.553)	(0.514)	(0.469)
Observations	55	55	55
R-squared	0.333	0.323	0.308

Note: Robust standard errors in parentheses.

[a] Separate efforts to examine aid and rule of law utilizing the RST 2SLS model were made as background research for the *2010 Human Development Report* by the authors (Picard et al. 2010). It found a positive relationship for aid on HDI but not one for rule of law. No interactions were taken at that time, but the comparison would be fruitful for future analysis.

*** $p < 0.001$, ** $p < 0.01$, * $p < 0.05$, † $p < 0.1$, # $p < 0.15$.

negative and significant relationship with HDI. Democracies (and their bureaucracies in particular) benefit from the respect for the rule of law in managing corruption and efficiently distributing resources. Equally, they benefit from decentralized decision making about resources and other aspects of governance. However, young democracies (and young federal ones too) struggle with the distribution of resources among their populations as they seek to maintain credible authority in the face of clientelism (Keefer 2007). Younger democracies face these challenges more than older ones; HDI results may reflect this.

The interactive effect of health aid and better institutions (measured by voice and accountability and Freedom House) have more predictive strength for HDI than do the interaction of education aid and better institutions. The sections below will examine what conditioning effect do health aid and governance have on HD.

Model 1: Freedom House Freedom in the World Average

Figure 3.1 presents the marginal effect of Freedom House measurements on HDI over the entire range of health aid.* For Model 1, there is no statistically significant effect of Freedom House ratings on HDI over values of health aid.

Figure 3.2 presents marginal effects of health aid on HDI over the entire range of Freedom House measurements. Marginal effect plots use parameter estimates of Model 1. Results show that, at greater levels of governance, health aid enhances HDI. When Freedom House ratings are lower, health aid has a reductive effect on HDI. This

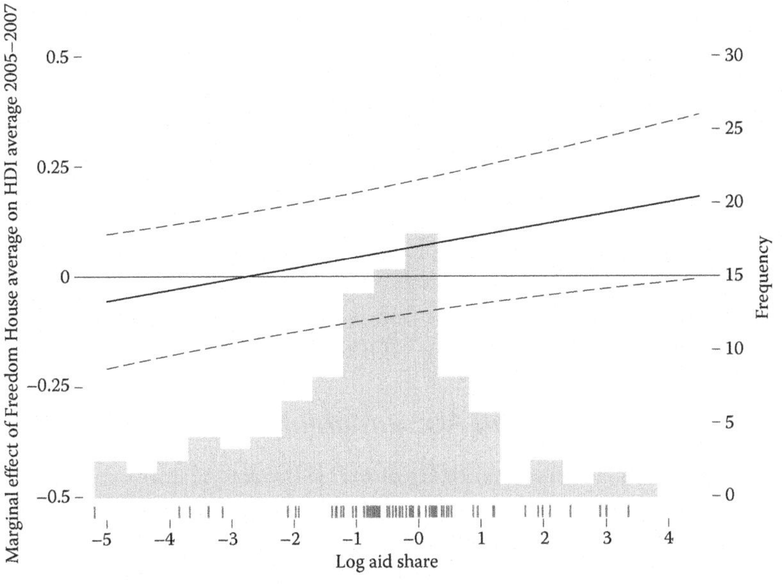

Figure 3.1 Marginal effect of Freedom House ratings on HDI over health aid values.

* The marginal effect plots are constructed using the parameter estimates of Model 1. The vertical axes on the right indicate the magnitude of the marginal effect. The vertical axes on the right are for the histogram, which depicts the distribution of observations in the sample on the variable health aid, depicted on the horizontal axis. The dashed lines represent 95% confidence intervals of the plot of the marginal effect of Freedom House on HDI over the range of health aid. Interpreting the significance of the marginal effects plot involves examining whether there is an effect of Freedom House ratings on HDI over the entire observed range of health aid, at points where both 95% confidence interval lines are above (positive effect) or below (negative effect).

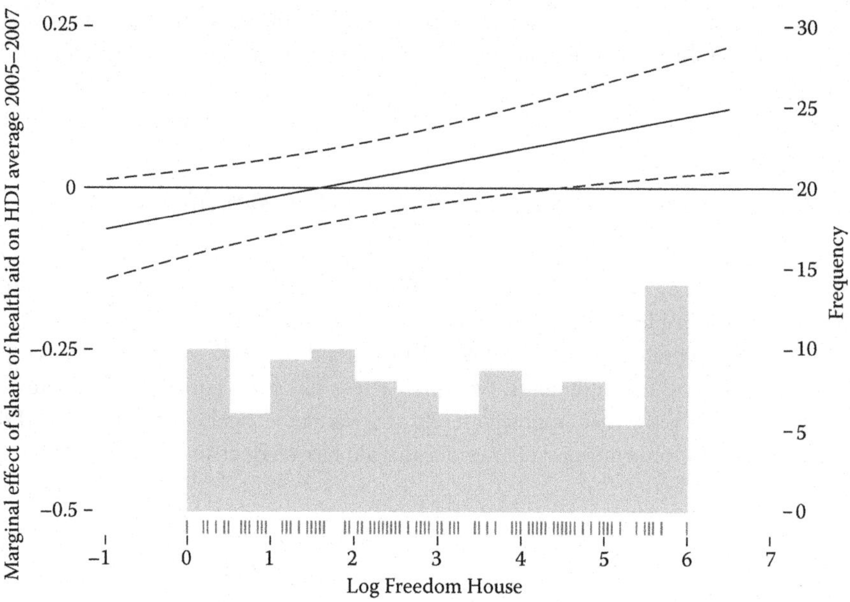

Figure 3.2 Marginal effect of health aid on HDI over Freedom House ratings.

reductive effect decreases as Freedom House ratings increase, though the effect is only statistically significant at the highest levels of Freedom House ratings (>4.5). At values of governance beginning with the upper measurements of "Partly Free," health aid has a positive effect on HDI, enhancing the HDI score.

Model 2: WGI Voice and Accountability

Figure 3.3 presents the marginal effect of on HDI over the entire range of health aid values using the parameter estimates of Model 2. There is no statistically significant effect of voice and accountability on HDI over values of health aid.

Figure 3.4 presents the marginal effect of health aid over the entire range of Freedom House ratings using the parameter estimates of Model 2. At greater levels of governance, health aid enhances HDI. When voice and accountability ratings are lower than −1.75, health aid has a reductive effect on HDI. This reductive effect decreases as voice and accountability ratings increase to a score of 0, when it has a positive effect on HDI, which improves over greater ratings of governance. A small share of the sample falls within the region of significance on the negative ratings, but for the positive ratings, roughly one-third of the sample falls within the range of significance. For the upper half of voice and accountability ratings, health aid has a positive, significant effect on HDI. Only one-third of the observations in the model are rated in the upper half of the voice and accountability measure.

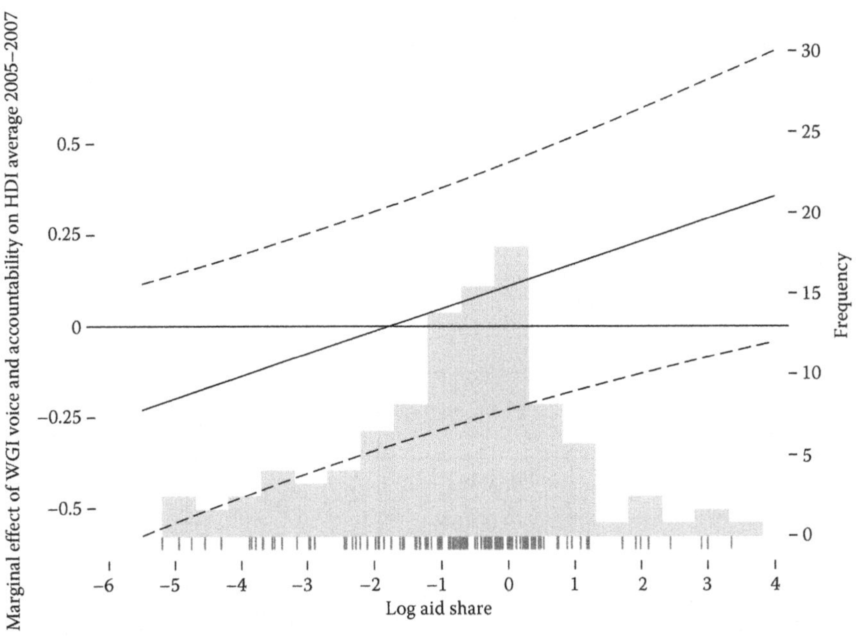

Figure 3.3 Marginal effect of voice and accountability ratings on HDI over health aid values.

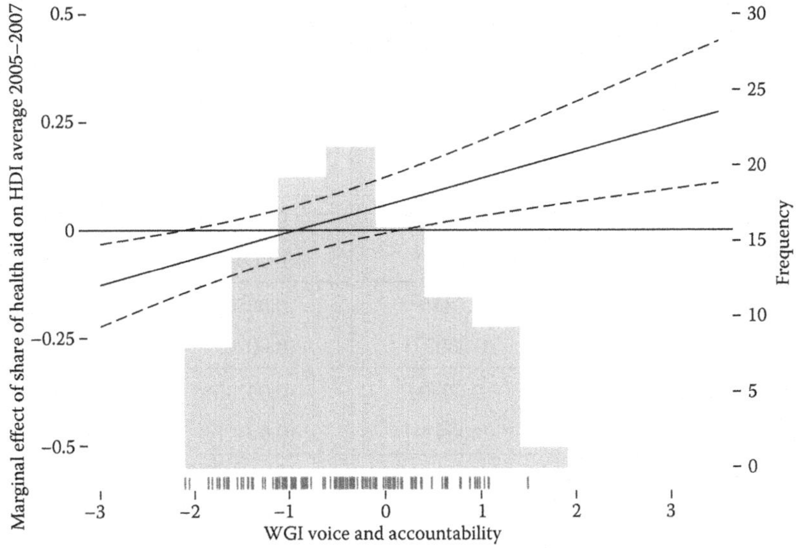

Figure 3.4 Marginal effect of health aid on HDI over voice and accountability ratings.

Table 3.4 Change in HDI 2005–2012

Variables	(4) Change in HDI 2005–2012	(5) Change in HDI 2005–2012	(6) Change in HDI 2005–2012
Education aid[a] Freedom House interaction	0.00116 (0.00558)		
Education aid[a] voice and accountability interaction		0.00226 (0.0124)	
Education aid[a] rule of law interaction			0.00226 (0.0124)
Health aid[a] Freedom House interaction	0.00483** (0.00164)		
Health aid[a] voice and accountability interaction		0.0101** (0.00372)	
Health aid[a] rule of law interaction			0.00964 (0.00794)
Freedom House (inverted)	0.00591 (0.00967)		
Voice and accountability		0.0151 (0.0217)	
Rule of law			0.0244 (0.0457)
Education aid (share of total aid)	0.000180 (0.0239)	0.00473 (0.00844)	0.0100 (0.0106)
Health aid (share of total aid)	−0.0119† (0.00627)	0.00581* (0.00227)	0.00503 (0.00355)
ODA share of GNI	−0.00704† (0.00414)	−0.00745† (0.00417)	−0.00902* (0.00414)
Health expenditures per capita (Log)	−0.00240 (0.00790)	−0.00276 (0.00786)	−0.00392 (0.00842)
Education expenditures per capita (Log)	−0.0202* (0.00858)	−0.0204* (0.00828)	−0.0178* (0.00770)

Table 3.4 (*Continued*) Change in HDI 2005–2012

Variables	*(4)* *Change in HDI 2005–2012*	*(5)* *Change in HDI 2005–2012*	*(6)* *Change in HDI 2005–2012*
Fertility (Log)	−0.0370*	−0.0338†	−0.0365#
	(0.0163)	(0.0171)	(0.0234)
Population density (Log)	−0.00102	−0.00105	−0.00177
	(0.00344)	(0.00349)	(0.00368)
Literacy (Log)	0.0183	0.0187	0.0184
	(0.0217)	(0.0217)	(0.0207)
HIV/AIDS prevalence (Log)	−0.00680#	−0.00704#	−0.00656#
	(0.00438)	(0.00440)	(0.00442)
Federalism	−0.0188	−0.0242	−0.0165
	(0.0192)	(0.0209)	(0.0243)
Sub-Saharan Africa	0.0711***	0.0685***	0.0669***
	(0.0168)	(0.0165)	(0.0184)
Constant	0.104	0.128	0.126
	(0.119)	(0.100)	(0.0919)
Observations	63	63	63
R-squared	0.543	0.535	0.491

Note: Robust standard errors in parentheses.

[a] Separate efforts to examine aid and rule of law utilizing the RST 2SLS model were made as background research for the *2010 Human Development Report* by the authors (Picard et al. 2010). It found a positive relationship for aid on HDI but not one for rule of law. No interactions were taken at that time, but the comparison would be fruitful for future analysis.

$^{***}p < 0.001$, $^{**}p < 0.01$, $^{*}p < 0.05$, $^{\dagger}p < 0.1$, $^{\#}p < 0.15$.

HDI Change Rates 2005–2012

Table 3.4 presents the results of the models used to predict the 2005–2012 change in HDI. Several key trends repeat from the previous models: the positive effect of the health aid and governance interactions, the absence of a significant effect of education aid interactions in the models, and the absence of a significant effect of rule of law in either interaction.

In Models 4 and 5, the interaction of health aid and Freedom House and the interaction of health aid and voice and accountability each show a positive and significant relationship with HDI ($\alpha = 0.05$). In both models, the interaction of education aid and the two governance measures are not significant predictors of HDI, providing confirming evidence of the results in the previous models. Interestingly, the amount of education expenditures per capita negatively affects the change in HDI. Further analysis should seek to disentangle this relationship, as it may be supported by an unobserved relationship in the model.

Another unexpected relationship among the covariates is the sub-Saharan African dummy, which shows a significant positive relationship with the change in HDI. The region has made considerable improvements in the past decade (and has plenty left to make), and these consistent results are a positive for the region (UNDP 2011). Expected relationships among the covariates fungibility of aid (ODA as a share of GNI) has a negative effect on HDI, and fertility and HIV/AIDS prevalence each show an expected negative relationship with HDI.

Change over time in HDI confirms the point estimate regressions above. Over the medium term, the interactive effect of health aid and better institutions (measured by voice and accountability and Freedom House) and health have more predictive strength than those of education aid and better institutions. The next subsection will again examine the dynamics of the interactive relationship of health aid and governance.

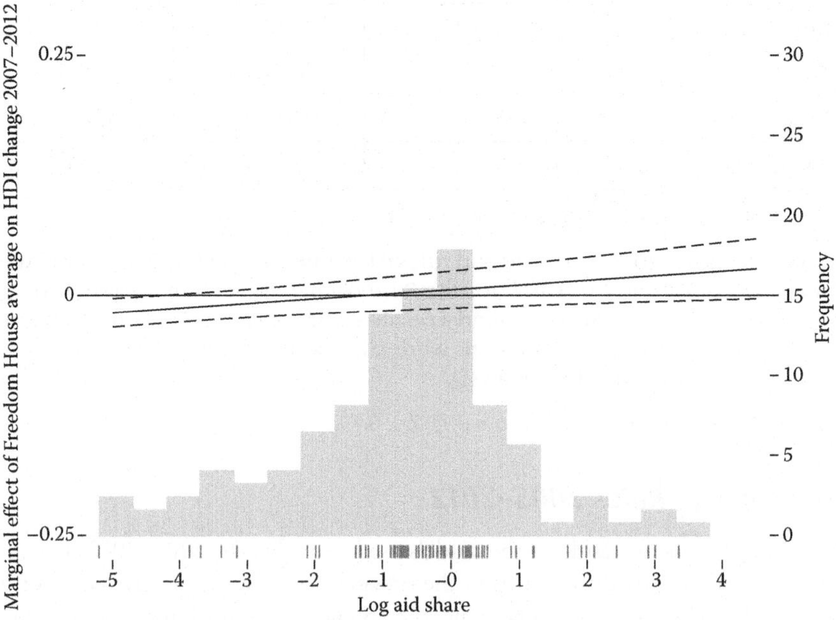

Figure 3.5 Marginal effect of Freedom House ratings on HDI over health aid values.

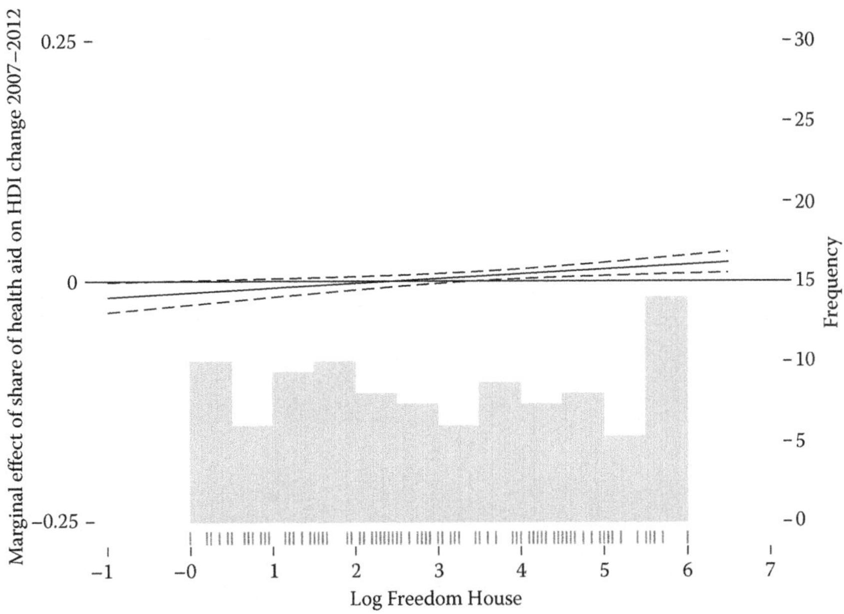

Figure 3.6 Marginal effect of health aid on HDI over Freedom House ratings.

Model 4: Freedom House Freedom in the World Average

Figure 3.5 presents marginal effects of Freedom House on HDI change over the range of health aid values using parameter estimates of Model 4. When health aid is a smaller share of the economy, poor Freedom House ratings have a reductive effect on the change in HDI. This reductive effect decreases as more aid is extended into the economy, though the effect is only significant at the lowest levels of health aid where few observations support the relationship.

Figure 3.6 presents the marginal effect of health aid on HDI change over the entire range of Freedom House values using the parameter estimates of Model 4. Aid can have a negative effect on the change in HDI at the lowest ratings of governance, and a positive effect at higher ratings. When Freedom House ratings are lower than 1, health aid has a reductive effect on the change in HDI. This reductive effect decreases as rule of law ratings increase to a score of 1. A positive effect on the change in HDI occurs at Freedom House values of 3.5 (Partly Free).* This strong result of health aid on the change in HDI for countries that are at least rated Partly Free shows how aid's benefit is conditioned on governance.

* A smaller share of the sample falls within the region of significance on the negative ratings, but for the positive ratings, a little under half of the observations fall within the range of significance.

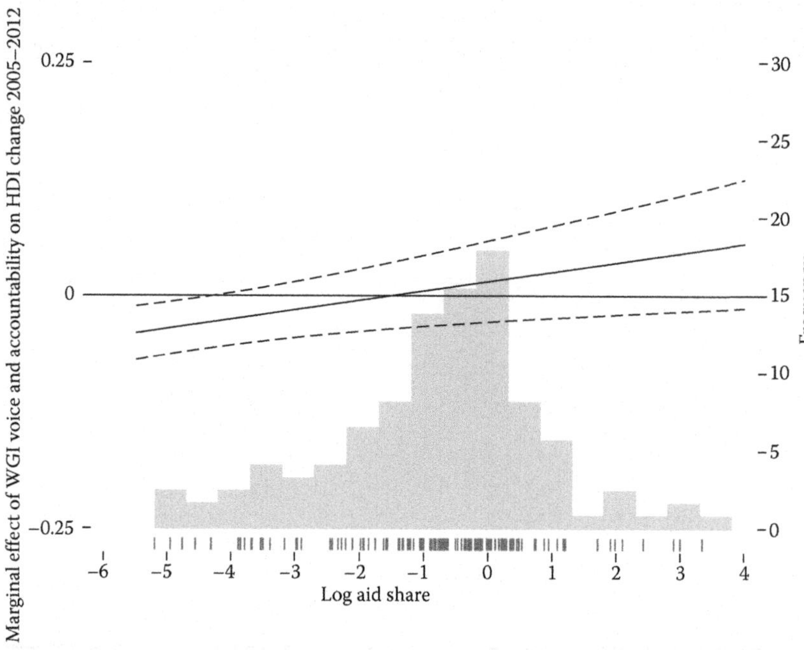

Figure 3.7 Marginal effect of voice and accountability ratings on HDI over health aid values.

Model 5: WGI Voice and Accountability

Figure 3.7 presents the marginal effect of Freedom House on HDI change over the entire range of health aid values using the parameter estimates of Model 5. When health aid is lower, poor voice and accountability ratings have a reductive effect on HDI. This reductive effect decreases as more aid is extended into the economy, though the effect is only significant at the lowest levels of health aid, where there are few observations to support the relationship.

Figure 3.8 presents the marginal effect of health aid on HDI change over the entire range of Freedom House values using the parameter estimates of Model 5. Figure 3.8 corroborates Figure 3.6: aid can hurt HDI in countries with very poorly rated governance, and improve it in countries with better governance. When voice and accountability is rated lower than −1.5 by the World Bank (very poor governance), health aid has a reductive effect on change in HDI. This reductive effect decreases as voice and accountability ratings increase to a score of −0.25, when it has a positive effect on HDI over better ratings of voice and accountability (over all positive ratings).*

* A smaller share of the sample falls within the region of significance on the negative ratings, but for the positive ratings, a little under half of the sample falls within the range of significance, suggesting strength of the positive effect of health aid on HDI in cases of better governance.

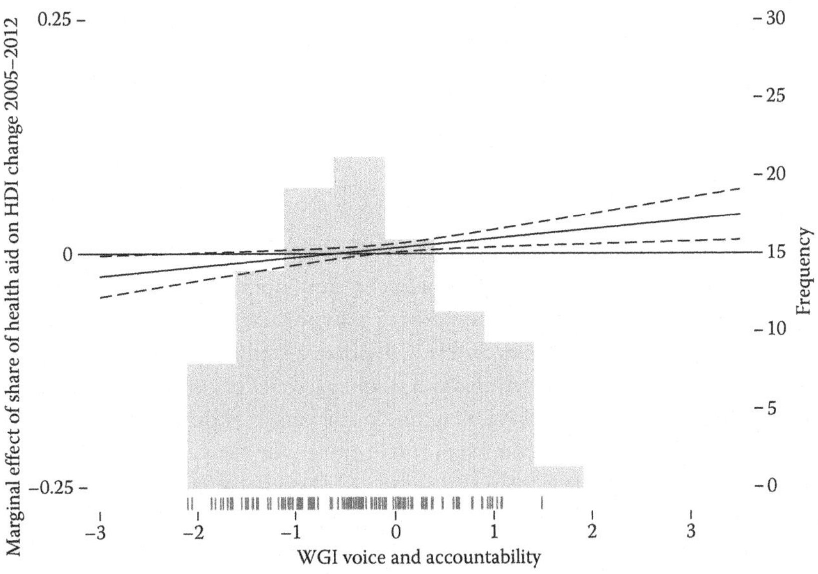

Figure 3.8 Marginal effect health aid on HDI over voice and accountability ratings.

Discussion

This section reviews the evidence in light of the hypotheses. The conditional effect of institutions on health aid is shown in the examination of marginal effects plots on HDI and change in the measure. For all the measures of poor governance we tested, health aid has a negative effect on HDI, while across all our measures of good governance, the effect is positive. The abundance of evidence supports hypothesis H2: that governance conditions aid in determining HD levels. In the models that predict change in HDI (Models 4 and 5), there is limited but consistent evidence in support of H3: that in addition to governance conditioning aid, aid also conditions governance: very poor scores of Freedom House and voice and accountability in cases of low health aid negatively affect the change in HDI. Aid and governance affect HDI. However, the most consistent result is that health aid affects HDI negatively in cases of poor governance, and positively in cases of good governance. This intuitive result supports those advocating sectoral approaches, particularly for health aid.

The nonintuitive result is that when evaluated alongside health aid as a determinant, education aid does not affect HDI. For education aid, the null hypothesis is supported: there is no statistically significant relationship between education aid, governance, and HDI. Education aid did not have any effect on the six models examined here. Models isolating education aid from health aid (not reported here) did not capture changes in HDI. This surprising result suggests a deeper examination of the degree to which HDI captures interventions undertaken by the aid community. The positive results shown by Wolf's model on particular education outcomes may reveal that the HDI has limits as a composite measure. If HDI is adequately capturing education aid interventions, concerns exist about the ability to move the measure in developing countries.

Conclusion

This study examines the relationship between development aid, institutions, and HD. Utilizing the HDI, it finds support for hypotheses relating to the interactive effect of aid and institutions on HDI. Evidence supported the hypothesis that institutions condition aid, meaning aid has a negative effect on HDI in conditions of poor governance, and a positive effect in conditions of good governance, though evidence showed aid can also condition institutions (very low amounts in very poor governance countries). These relationships were found between health aid and governance, but we found no evidence of a relationship with HDI or governance for education aid. This evidence supports the sectoral approach, particularly for those aiding health.

Acknowledgment

Excellent research assistance was provided by Katherine Yoon of the University of Pittsburgh Graduate School of Public and International Affairs. Errors are the authors' own.

References

Bauer, P. 1972. *Dissent on Development.* London: Weidenfeld and Nicolson.

Bauer, P. 1981. *Equality, the Third World and Economic Delusion.* London: Methuen.

Berry, W., Golder, M., Milton, D. 2012. Improving tests of theories positing interaction. *The Journal of Politics* 74(03): 653–671.

Burnside, C., Dollar, D. 2000. Aid, policies and growth. *American Economic Review* 90(4): 847–869.

Clemens, M., Radelet, S., Bhavnani, R. 2004. Counting chickens when they hatch: The short-term effect of aid on growth. Working Paper No. 44. Washington, DC: Center for Global Development.

Collier, P., Dollar, D. 2001. Can the world cut poverty in half? How policy reform and effective aid can meet MDGs. *World Development* 29(11): 1787–1802.

Dalgaard, C., Hansen, H., Tarp, H. 2004. On the empirics of foreign aid and growth. *Economic Journal* 114(496): 191–216.

Easterly, W. 2001. *The Elusive Quest for Growth: Economists' Adventures and Misadventures in the Tropics.* Cambridge, MA: MIT Press.

Easterly, W. 2006. *The White Man's Burden*. New York: Penguin.
Easterly, W. 2007. Was development assistance a mistake? *American Economic Review Papers and Proceedings* 97(2): 328–332.
Ferguson, N. 2003. *Empire*. New York: Basic Books.
Ferguson, N. 2008. *The Ascent of Money: A Financial History of the World*. New York: Penguin Press.
Freedom House. 2014. *Freedom in the World*. Available at: http://www.freedomhouse.org/sites/default/files/Country%20Ratings%20and%20Status%2C%201973-2014%20%28FINAL%29.xls. Accessed 8/8/14.
Gray, M., Purser, M. 2010. Human development trends since 1970. Human Development Research Paper 2010/02. Available at: http://hdr.undp.org/sites/default/files/hdrp_2010_02.pdf. Accessed 8/8/14.
Guillaumont, P., Chauvet, L. 2001. Aid and performance: A reassessment. *Journal of Development Studies* 37(6): 66–92.
Hansen, H., Tarp, F. 2001. Aid and growth regressions. *Journal of Development Economics* 64(2): 547–570.
Hudson, J. 2013. Promises kept, promises broken? The relationship between aid commitments and disbursements. *Review of Development Finance* 3(3): 109–120.
Kaufmann, D., Kraay, A., Mastruzzi, M. 2004–2009. Various years. *Governance Matters*. Washington, DC: World Bank.
Keefer, P. 2007. Clientelism, credibility, and the policy choices of young democracies. *American Journal of Political Science* 51(4): 804–821.
Millennium Challenge Corporation (MCC). 2010. *Country Scorecard/Timeseries Data*. Available at: http://www.mcc.gov/mcc/bm.doc/score-fy10-timeseriesdata.xls. Accessed 8/8/14.
Minoiu, M., Reddy, S. 2009. Development aid and economic growth: A positive long-run relation. IMF Working Paper. Washington, DC: International Monetary Fund.
Moyo, D. 2009. *Dead Aid*. New York: Farrar, Straus and Giroux.
Organisation for Economic Cooperation and Development. DAC Database (OECD DAC). 2014. Available at: http://stats.oecd.org/qwids/. Accessed 8/8/14.
Picard, L., Buss, T. 2009. *A Fragile Balance*. Sterling, VA: Kumarian Press.
Picard, L., Buss, T., Belasco, C. 2010. The effectiveness of aid and MDGs in advancing human development, 1990 to 2010. UNDP Working Paper.
Rajkumar, A., Swaroop, V. 2002. Public spending and outcomes: Does governance matter. World Bank Policy Research Working Paper 2840. Washington, DC: World Bank.
Rajkumar, A., Swaroop, V. 2008. Public spending and outcomes: Does governance matter?. *Journal of Development Economics* 86(1): 96–111.
Rodrik, D., Subramanian, A., Trebbi, F. 2004. Institutions rule: The primacy of institutions over geography and integration in economic development. *Journal of Economic Growth* 9(1): 131–165.
Sachs, J., McArthur, J., Schimdt-Traub, G., Kruk, M., Bahadur, C. Faye, M., McCord, G. 2004. Ending Africa's poverty trap. *Brookings Papers on Economic Activity* 1: 117–240.
Sachs, J. D. 2005. *The End of Poverty*. New York: Penguin.
United Nations Development Program (UNDP). 2011. *Human Development Report*. New York: Palgrave.
Wolf, S. 2007. Does aid improve public service delivery? *Review of World Economics* 143 (4): 650–672.
World Bank. Various years. *World Development Indicators*. Washington, DC: World Bank.

Chapter 4

Millennium Development Goals and Poverty Reduction Strategies

Peter Bucki, Simon Callaghan, Umair Khalid, Chris Morony, Jeremy Phillips, Ariunbilig Tsedendamba, Ana Varela, and Terry F. Buss

Contents

Introduction

In this chapter, we ask whether the much touted international development targets for 2015 set forth by the United Nations (UN) in its Millennium Development

Goals (MDG) program,* have been absorbed into the poverty reduction plans developed by countries under the World Bank's Poverty Reduction Strategy Papers (PRSP) program.† We analyze the factors that might explain absorption rates for countries and their targets: (1) factors in the PRSP development process, (2) geographical region, (3) development level, (4) governance competency, and (5) income.

Why is this important? Policymakers believed that if MDGs were embedded in country development strategies, they would have a better chance of being achieved: PRSPs are a major mechanism for justifying and requesting foreign aid. So, this chapter tries to account for why some countries succeeded and why others did not.

In September 2000, at the UN Millennium Summit, world leaders agreed to eight specific and measurable development goals that center on halving poverty and improving welfare of the world's poorest, to be achieved by 2015.

The first seven MDG goals focus on eradicating extreme poverty and hunger; achieving universal primary education; promoting gender equality and empowering women; reducing child mortality; improving maternal health; combating HIV/AIDS, malaria, and other diseases; and ensuring environmental sustainability. The eighth goal focuses on effective international support for low-income countries and the enabling of an international economic and trade environment for development. Each goal has between one and five targets, associated with a series of measurable indicators.

A major document laying out a country's planned action for reducing poverty and meeting the UN's MDGs is the country PRSP initiated by the World Bank in 1999. PRSPs coordinate national public policies, programs and strategies, donor support, and development performance outcomes, and are seen as being critical in attaining MDGs.

Countries prepare PRSPs through a participatory process involving domestic stakeholders as well as bilateral and multilateral development partners. Nominally updated every 3 years with annual progress reports, PRSPs describe the country's macroeconomic, structural, and social policies and programs, and risk assessments over a 3-year or longer horizon to promote broad-based growth and reduce poverty, as well as associated external financing needs and major sources of financing.

We believe that a decade of action on MDGs and PSRPs would constitute a good time frame to see how the two initiatives were progressing. We were guided on the study by the UN *Millennium Development Goals 2010 Report*, presenting a decade-long set of annual assessments of global progress toward MDG attainment. As of 2014, the initiative has yielded mixed results.

---

* http://www.undp.org/content/undp/en/home/mdgoverview.html

† http://www.imf.org/external/np/prsp/prsp.aspx

Methodology

Fifty-nine countries have prepared PRSPs since the program's inception in 2000 through 2010. Each PRSP was coded and analyzed using widely accepted social science standards to improve validity and reliability.*

We looked at 15 individual targets representing the first seven MDGs (see Table 4.1); we excluded the eighth goal pertaining to provision of international support to other countries as it was not relevant. We scored each target according to the criteria in Table 4.2.

Next, we developed an overall compliance score for each country using a weighted average of the sum of occurrences of each score across the 15 targets:

$$\text{Compliance score} = (\Sigma 4*1) + (\Sigma 3*0.33) + (\Sigma 2*1) + (\Sigma 1*0.66) + (\Sigma 0*0)$$

The highest possible score is 15. Table 4.3 breaks down individual compliance scores by country and year of PSRP against weighted MDG targets.

We looked at four variables capturing the PRSP development process, the geographical region a country belongs to, two variables related to the level of a country's national development, five variables associated with a country's national governance structure, and three indicators of a country's level of income to determine contributing factors to levels of absorption.

To determine whether factors in a PRSP's development process had an effect on a country's absorption of MDGs, we looked at the year in which the country published the PRSP to determine whether more recently published PRSPs had greater absorption of MDGs than those published earlier in the decade. Presumably, countries having an earlier start in attaining MDG goals would perform better. Alternatively, countries preparing PRSPs at a later time might have learned from the experience of their peers. We looked for a relationship between the PRSP's number of pages and MDG absorption. There are no page requirements for PSRPs. As they are complex, comprehensive documents, we expected that those who took the exercise seriously would have a lot more to report than those who did not. Similarly, we looked for a relationship between the number of PRSPs as well as the total number of pages in PRSP documents (Interim PRSPs, PRSPs, and PRSP Progress Reports) prepared by participating countries to determine whether PRSPs "matured" over time, leading to increased alignment with MDGs. If countries were taking PRSPs seriously, this should become increasingly reflected in their strategies.

We looked for relationships between the geographical region a country belongs to and the absorption level of MDGs into its PRSP, as well as at the absorption of individual targets by region to determine whether there was a regional focus on particular MDGs.

* A detailed overview of the study methodology is available from the authors upon request. The complete methodology was not included here to save space.

Table 4.1 MDG Targets by Goal

Target 1A: Halve, between 1990 and 2015, the proportion of people whose income is less than 1$ a day.
Target 1B: Achieve full and productive employment and decent work for all, including women and young people.
Target 1C: Halve, between 1990 and 2015, the proportion of people who suffer from hunger.
Target 2A: Ensure that, by 2015, children everywhere, boys and girls alike, will be able to complete a full course of primary schooling.
Target 3A: Eliminate gender disparity in primary and secondary education, preferably by 2005, and in all levels of education no later than 2015.
Target 4A: Reduce by two-thirds, between 1990 and 2015, the under-five mortality rate.
Target 5A: Reduce by three-quarters, between 1990 and 2015, the maternal mortality ratio.
Target 5B: Achieve, by 2015, universal access to reproductive health.
Target 6A: Have halted by 2015 and begun to reverse the spread of HIV/AIDS.
Target 6B: Achieve, by 2010, universal access to treatment for HIV/AIDS for all those who need it.
Target 6C: Have halted by 2015 and begun to reverse the incidence of malaria and other major diseases.
Target 7A: Integrate the principles of sustainable development into country policies and programs and reverse the loss of environmental resources.
Target 7B: Reduce biodiversity loss, achieving, by 2010, a significant reduction in the rate of loss.
Target 7C: Halve, by 2015, the proportion of people without sustainable access to safe drinking water and basic sanitation.
Target 7D: By 2020, have achieved a significant improvement in the lives of at least 100 million slum dwellers.

We examined a variety of indicators, including relative poverty using the 2007 UN Human Poverty Index (HPI), and level of national development using the 2009 UN Human Development Index (HDI).*

We included five variables characterizing type of government and country governance. Government type—full democracies, flawed democracies, hybrid regimes, and authoritarian regimes—was measured by *The Economist* 2008 Democracy

* http://hdr.undp.org/en

Table 4.2 Coding Criteria

Score	*Criteria*	*Assessment*	*Weight*
0	MDG target not identified in PRSP	Target not absorbed	0
1	PRSP states a lower target and references MDG	Target significantly absorbed	0.66
2	PRSP states and references the exact MDG target	Target fully absorbed	1.00
3	PRSP states a lower target without mention of MDG	Target somewhat absorbed	0.33
4	PRSP states the exact target without mention of MDG	Target fully absorbed	1.00

Index.* There were no full democracies among our countries. We measured governance using World Bank indicators for effectiveness, political stability, and control of corruption.†

We considered eligibility for the U.S. Millennium Challenge Corporation (MCC)‡ funding as an indicator of effective governance. The MCC only extends membership to countries it deems as having effective governance and encourages countries to define their own development priorities and solutions, rather than having foreign aid agencies define them externally. Achieving MCC status means hundreds of millions in aid for some countries.

The percentage of women in parliament is another aspect of a nation's governance. For bicameral parliaments, this represents the number of women in each house added together and divided by the total number of members in both houses, multiplied by 100%.

We included Gross Domestic Product (GDP) per capita to represent the wealth of a nation, and Official Development Assistance (ODA) per capita as published by World Bank in 2008. We created an ODA/GDP ratio to standardize ODA as a percentage of GDP for all participating countries.

As our analyses covered all countries publishing PRSPs, we did not analyze results for statistical significance.

Findings

We observed that MDG absorption into PRSPs occurred more often than not, as evidenced in Figure 4.1. There were 41 countries with compliance scores between

* http://graphics.eiu.com/PDF/Democracy%20Index%202008.pdf

† http://papers.ssrn.com/sol3/papers.cfm?abstract_id=1424591

‡ http://www.mcc.gov/

Table 4.3 Country Compliance Scores

Compliance Score				
0–3	*4–6*	*7–9*	*10–12*	*13–15*
2001	2003	2002	2001	2003
Bolivia	Georgia	Guyana	Honduras	Mongolia
2003	2005	Sao Tome and Principe	2002	2004
Azerbaijan	Burkina Faso	2003	Sri Lanka	Serbia
2005	2006	Benin	Timor-Leste	2006
Ghana	Mauritania	Chad	2003	Zambia
2006	Vietnam	Nepal	Cameroon	2008
Lesotho	2007	2004	Pakistan	Liberia
2007	Congo, Democratic Republic of the	Bosnia and Herzogovina	2004	Rwanda
Central African Republic	2008	2005	Kenya	2009
2008	Afghanistan	Bangladesh	2005	Bhutan
Moldova	Armenia	Cambodia	Nigeria	
		Tanzania	2006	
		2006	Dominica	
		Ethiopia	Mozambique	
		Malawi	2007	
		Mali	Burundi	
		Albania	Gambia	
		Kyrgyzstan	Niger	
		Madagascar	Tajikistan	
		Senegal	2008	
		2008	Cape Verde	
		Guinea	Haiti	

(*Continued*)

Table 4.3 (*Continued*) Country Compliance Scores

Compliance Score				
0–3	*4–6*	*7–9*	*10–12*	*13–15*
		Sierra Leone	Laos	
		2009	Maldives	
		Nicaragua	Uzbekistan	
			2009	
			Cote d'Ivoire	
			Djibouti	
			2010	
			Uganda	

8 and 14. The number of countries increased as did the compliance score. Average overall compliance score by countries was 9.12.

Is Absorption of MDGs Related to the Process of Developing PRSPs?

Examining compliance scores of PRSPs by their publication date indicated a general trend toward increasing absorption of MDGs over time: 5.49 in 2001, 7.90 in 2005, and 12.63 in 2010 (see Table 4.4). We observed two distinct periods of increasing absorption from 2001 through 2004 and 2006 through 2010.

Analysis of the number of iterations of national PRSP documents indicated that countries with only one or two PRSP documents had a higher average compliance

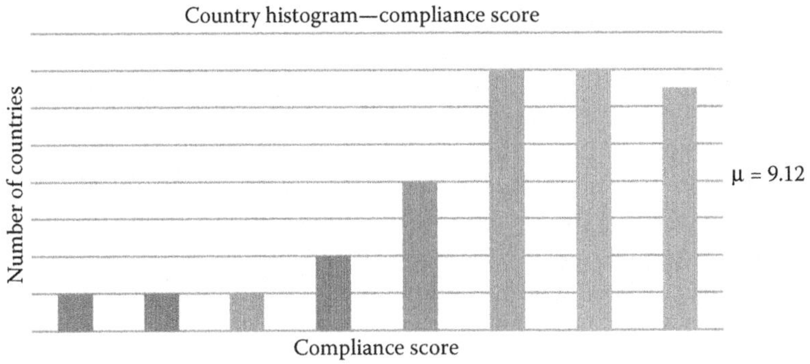

Figure 4.1 MDG absorption into PRSPs occurred more often than not.

Table 4.4 Overall Average Compliance Scores Increased over Time

PRSP Publication Date	*Number of Countries*	*Average Compliance Score (by Year)*	*Average Compliance Score (Total)*	*Deviation from Mean*
2001	2	5.49	9.12	–3.63
2002	3	9.51	9.12	0.39
2003	7	8.41	9.12	–0.71
2004	6	10.75	9.12	1.62
2005	5	7.90	9.12	–1.22
2006	9	8.22	9.12	–0.90
2007	10	8.53	9.12	–0.60
2008	12	9.78	9.12	0.66
2009	4	11.65	9.12	2.53
2010	1	12.63	9.12	3.51

Note: Deviation expresses difference between total average compliance score for all countries and average compliance score by date of PRSP publication.

score (11.90 for one PRSP/Progress Reports and 10.73 for two PRSP/Progress Reports) compared to those countries with 3–6 PRSP documents and average compliance score ranges from 7.05 through 9.00 (see Table 4.5). We found no relationship between the length of a PRSP and the absorption of MDG goals.

Does a Country's Geographical Region Affect How MDGs Are Absorbed?

African countries had the highest overall absorption of MDGs, with an average score of 9.31. Asian, Latin American, and European countries had scores below the overall average of 9.12 (see Table 4.6). However, overall MDG absorption into countries' PRSPs was not uniform across regions.

Asian countries had greater absorption across individual MDG targets with an average of 11 targets absorbed. They were followed by the African countries with an average of eight, Latin American countries with an average of four, and European countries with average absorption of two targets.

Asian countries fell below average absorption rates only on HIV/AIDS, sustainable environment, and biodiversity (see Table 4.7). Africa, by contrast, fell below the average on nearly half of the targets, including poverty, employment, hunger, infant

Table 4.5 Greater Numbers of PRSPs Did Not Equate to Higher MDG Absorption

Number of PRSPs and Progress Reports	*Number of Countries*	*Average Score per Number of PRSP and Progress Report*	*Overall Average*	*Deviation from the Mean*
1	4	11.90	9.12	2.77
2	11	10.73	9.12	1.61
3	9	7.05	9.12	–2.07
4	12	8.85	9.12	–0.27
5	9	8.48	9.12	–0.65
6	12	9.00	9.12	–0.12
7	1	11.66	9.12	2.54
8	0	–	9.12	–
9	1	6.97	9.12	–2.15

Note: Deviation expresses difference between total average compliance score for all countries and average compliance score by date of PRSP publication.

mortality, maternal mortality, reproductive health, and biodiversity. Latin America fared less well, but on different targets, while Europe fell below on all but two targets.

Does Level of Development or Relative Poverty Influence MDG Absorption?

Examination of national development levels (measured by HDI) showed that countries with higher human development demonstrated greater absorption of MDGs overall than countries with medium and low human development.

Table 4.6 Average Compliance Score Varied by Region

Region	*Number of Countries*	*Average Compliance Score*
Africa	29	9.31
Asia	18	9.08
Latin America	8	8.81
Europe	4	8.56
Total	59	9.12

Table 4.7 Different Absorption Patterns Were Evidenced by Region

	Target														
Region	*1A: Absolute Poverty*	*1B: Full Employment*	*1C: Hunger Reduction*	*2A: Universal Primary Education*	*3A: Gender Equality*	*4A: Infant Mortality*	*5A: Maternal Mortality*	*5B: Reproductive Health*	*6A: Halt Spread of HIV/AIDS*	*6B: Access to HIV/AIDS Treatment*	*6C: Halt Spread of Malaria/Other Diseases*	*7A: Sustainable Development*	*7B: Biodiversity Loss*	*7C: Water/Sanitation*	*7D: Slum Dwellers' Living Standards*
Africa				■	■				■	■	■	■		■	■
Asia	■	■	■	■	■	■	■	■		■	■			■	■
L/America	■	■			■	■		■						■	
Europe		■										■			

■ *Greater than average absorption.*

Compliance score was highest for most developed countries with an average score of 10.40 (see Table 4.8). High human development countries included three countries from Europe and one from Latin America. Average compliance score for low human development countries (9.60) was higher than medium human development countries (8.68).

Table 4.8 Most and Least Developed Countries Showed above Average Absorption of MDGs

HDI Rank	*Number of Countries*	*Average Compliance Score (by Year)*	*Average Compliance Score (Total)*	*Deviation from the Mean*
High	4	10.40	9.12	1.27
Medium	34	8.68	9.12	–0.45
Low	21	9.60	9.12	0.48

Note: Deviation expresses difference between total average compliance score for all countries and average compliance score by date of PRSP publication.

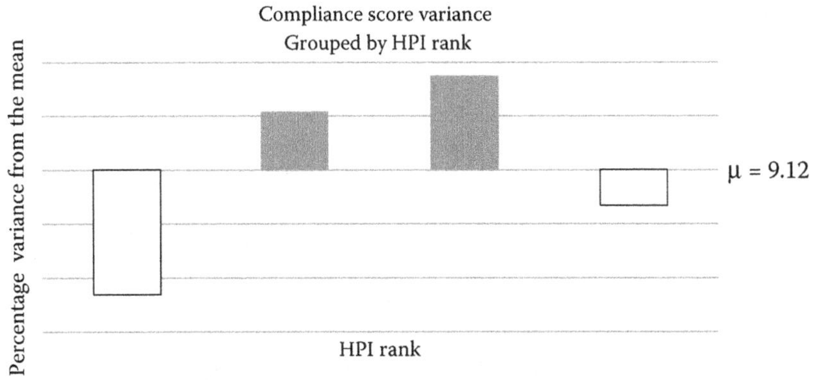

Figure 4.2 Countries in highest and lowest HPI quartiles showed lowest MDG absorption.

Countries in the second (ranking 119–95) and third HPI quartile (ranking 94–58) had a higher than average absorption (9.12) (see Figure 4.2). The poorest countries according to the HPI displayed the least absorption.

Higher or lower human development did not consistently predict increased or decreased absorption across all targets.

Goals were increasingly absorbed as countries' HDIs rating decreased—hunger reduction (1C) moves from nearly 25% below average to almost 12% above; access to HIV/AIDS treatment (6B) moves from 100% below average to more than 50% above; sustainable development (7A) moves from 19% below average to nearly 11% above; and slum dwellers' living standards (7D) moves from 5% below average to nearly 30% above (see Table 4.9).

Table 4.9 Country Development Was Related to Increasing Absorption of Some MDGs

	HDI Rank	2	3	4
MDG Target		*Increasing Absorption* →		
1C	Hunger reduction	–24.8%	–4.4%	11.8%
6B	Access to HIV/AIDS treatment	–100.0%	–19.8%	51.1%
7A	Sustainable development	–19.0%	–4.5%	10.9%
7D	Slum dwellers' living standards	–5.0%	–17.9%	29.9%

Note: Percentages express deviation between average compliance score by target and average compliance score for that target by country's HDI rating.

Table 4.10 Country Development Is Related to Decreasing Absorption of Some MDGs

	HDI Rank	*2*	*3*	*4*
MDG Target		*Increasing Absorption* ←		
1A	Absolute poverty	12.8%	1.5%	−4.9%
1B	Full employment	76.8%	5.7%	−23.8%
5B	Reproductive health	53.7%	−0.9%	−8.8%
7B	Biodiversity loss	56.2%	4.1%	−17.4%

Note: Percentages express deviation between average compliance score by target and average compliance score for that target by country's democracy index: see note for Table 9.

Goals were increasingly absorbed as HDIs increased—absolute poverty (1A) moved from nearly 5% below average to almost 13% above; full employment (1B) moved from nearly 24% below average to nearly 77% above; reproductive health (5B) moved from almost 9% below average to nearly 54% above; and biodiversity loss (7B) moved from more than 17% below average to nearly 57% above (see Table 4.10).

Five of 15 goals were increasingly absorbed as countries' poverty increased (see Table 4.11). Those targets were full employment (1B), universal primary education (2A), reproductive health (5B), sustainable development (7A), and biodiversity loss

Table 4.11 Greater Relative Poverty Was Related to Decreasing Absorption of Some MDGs

	HPI Quartiles	*1*	*2*	*3*	*4*
MDG Target		*Increasing Absorption* ←			
1B	Full employment	−18.7%	32.9%	−8.5%	−3.9%
2A	Universal primary education	−21.4%	19.3%	13.4%	−8.6%
5B	Reproductive health	−18.3%	20.5%	14.9%	−13.9%
7A	Sustainable development	−20.7%	19.9%	16.1%	−12.1%
7B	Biodiversity loss	−21.3%	24.1%	4.1%	−4.6%

Note: Percentages express deviation between average compliance score by target and average compliance score for that target by country's HDI rating.

Table 4.12 Lower Relative Poverty Was Related to Increasing Absorption of Some MDGs

	HPI Quartiles	*1*	*2*	*3*	*4*
MDG Target		*Increasing Absorption* →			
1A	Absolute poverty	–20.1%	10.9%	14.2%	–3.2%
3A	Gender equality of education	–22.7%	6.1%	22.9%	–4.1%
5A	Maternal health	–5.7%	–2.3%	21.7%	–11.6%
6B	Universal HIV/AIDS treatment	–41.7%	–6.5%	64.2%	–11.4%
6C	Halt spread of malaria and other diseases	–18.6%	6.3%	21.5%	–7.0%
7C	Water/sanitation	–16.6%	–1.2%	15.1%	3.4%
7D	Slum dwellers' living standards	–6.9%	–0.3%	8.8%	–1.0%

Note: Percentages express deviation between average compliance score by target and average compliance score for that target by country's HDI rating.

(7B). However, countries in the highest poverty quartile showed lower absorption of these goals.

Seven of 15 goals were increasingly absorbed as countries' poverty decreases (see Table 4.12). These were absolute poverty (1A), gender equality of education (3A), maternal health (5A), universal HIV/AIDS treatment (6B), halting spread of malaria and other diseases (6C), water/sanitation (7C), and slum dwellers' living standards (7D). Countries in the lowest poverty quartile show lower absorption of these goals.

Does Better National Governance Result in Greater Absorption of MDGs?

Analysis showed a decreasing trend in overall absorption of MDGs as government effectiveness increased and no observable trend for control of corruption and political stability. Countries with government effectiveness scores of between –1.6 and –0.98 were above the mean (9.12) compliance score whereas more effective governments with scores between –0.3 and 0.7 were below the mean compliance (see Figure 4.3).

In looking at the number of targets absorbed type of government regime, we found hybrid regimes had the highest absorption (see Figure 4.4). Our PSRPs consisted of 12 flawed democracies, 26 hybrid regimes, and 18 authoritarian regimes

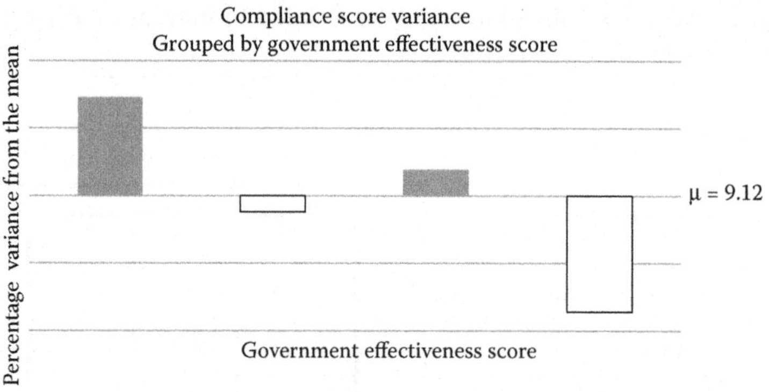

Figure 4.3 As government effectiveness improved, MDG absorption decreased.

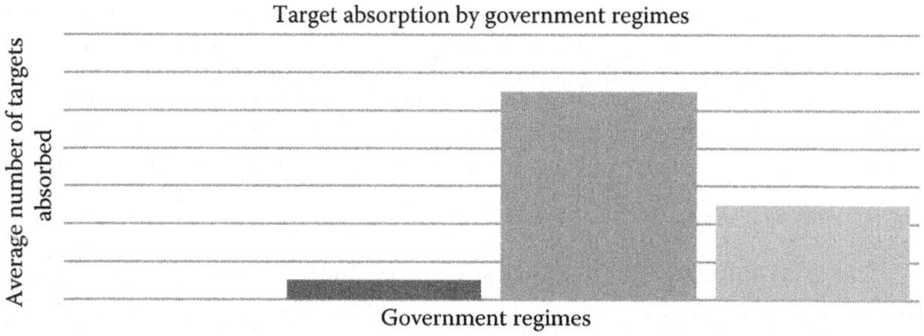

Figure 4.4 MDGs were least absorbed by countries described as flawed democracies.

as determined by the 2008 Democracy Index. No countries in the population were defined as full democracies.

Flawed democracies (considered the most democratic in the survey population) showed lower than average absorption across all goals except that relating to biodiversity loss (7B). The margin was quite large (10%–40% lower) for goals relating to full employment (1B), hunger reduction (1C), primary education (2A), gender equality in education (3A), maternal mortality (5A), reproductive health (5B), HIV/AIDS treatment (6B), halting the spread of malaria and other diseases (6C), and slum dwellers' living standards (7D) (see Table 4.13).

Hybrid regimes showed above average absorption in 11 of 15 goals. Goals relating to halting the spread of HIV/AIDS (6A), sustainable development (7A), biodiversity loss (7B), and slum dwellers' living standards (7D) were lower than the average.

Authoritarian regimes reflected below average absorption in 10 of 15 goals. Those relating to full employment (1B), reproductive health (5B), halting the spread

Table 4.13 Different National Government Types Absorbed Different MDGs (%)

	1A	*1B*	*1C*	*2A*	*3A*	*4A*	*5A*	*5B*	*6A*	*6B*	*6C*	*7A*	*7B*	*7C*	*7D*
Flawed (*n* = 12)	–4.1	–20.0	–39.9	–11.9	–18.7	–7.0	–17.5	–10.8	–5.1	–17.8	–24.7	–5.3	15.6	–3.1	–20.8
Hybrid (*n* = 26)	7.7	13.5	22.8	8.0	7.2	10.0	8.9	3.1	–0.5	9.2	12.5	–0.1	–3.9	4.8	–4.8
Authoritarian (*n* = 18)	–13.9	6.9	–16.4	–5.1	–1.9	–13.1	–5.5	2.2	3.5	–3.1	–2.6	2.3	–3.5	–5.6	26.9

Note: Percentages express deviation between average compliance score by target and average compliance score for that target by country's democracy index.

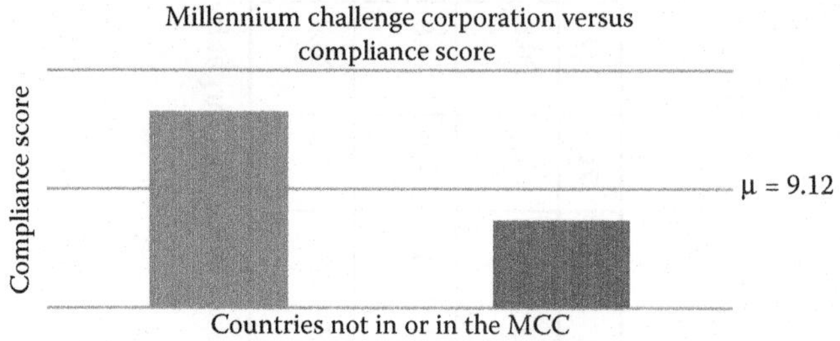

Figure 4.5 MCC countries had a lower overall absorption of MDGs.

Table 4.14 Fewer MDGs Were Absorbed by MCC Countries (below Average Absorption)

	n	*1A*	*1B*	*1C*	*2A*	*3A*	*4A*	*5A*	*5B*	*6A*	*6B*	*6C*	*7A*	*7B*	*7C*	*7D*
MCC member	59															
Yes	26															
No	33															

of HIV/AIDS (6A), sustainable development (7A), and slum dwellers' living standards (7D) were higher than the average.

Interestingly, 26 MCC countries showed lower overall absorption of the MDGs with an average compliance score below the mean of 9.12 (Figure 4.5).

Twenty-six MCC countries exhibited a common bias in absorption of particular goals. Priority targets for MCC countries included full employment (1B), hunger poverty (1C), primary education (2A), gender equality of education (3A), maternal health (5A), reducing the spread of HIV/AIDS treat (6A), halting the spread of malaria and other diseases (6C), and slum dwellers' living standards (7D) (Table 4.14).

Is the Absorption of MDGs Related to National Income (GDP per Capita)?

Unlike the measures of development and poverty, there was no discernible pattern of target absorption related to national GDP per capita (see Figure 4.6). Countries with lowest GDP per capita of $114–$458 scored slightly above the mean (9.12) on compliance, second lowest GDP/capita ($458–$791) countries had lowest absorption, second highest GDP/capita ($889–$1513) countries had the highest

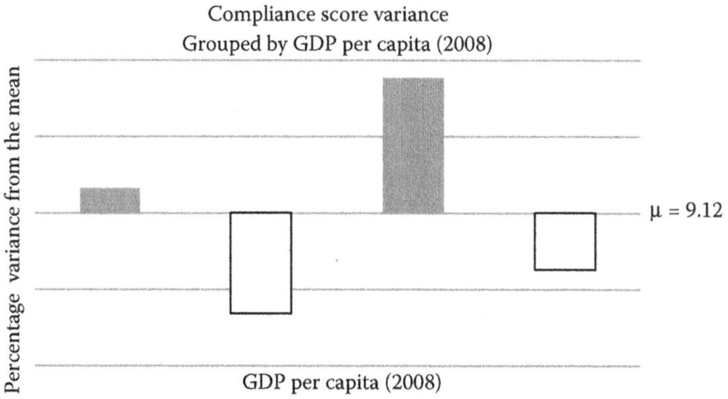

Figure 4.6 GDP per capita had no bearing on MDG absorption.

absorption, and highest income ($1693–$6810) countries were below mean compliance score.

MDG absorption was highest with highest aid dependence. Countries with highest aid dependence (>12.8%) had highest MDG absorption (9.30) and countries with the lowest aid dependence had the lowest MDG absorption (8.86) (see Table 4.15). The general trend, despite a dip in the third quartile, was that as ODA increased as a proportion of GDP absorption of the MDGs increased as well. It was at least done so more than the countries that were least dependent upon aid.

Table 4.15 As National Dependence on Development Assistance as a Proportion of GDP Increased, Average Absorption of MDGs Increased

ODA over GDP	*Number of Countries*	*Average Compliance Score (Quartile)*	*Average Compliance Score (Total)*	*Difference from Average*
First quartile (<4%)	14	8.86	9.12	–0.27
Second quartile (4%–7.89%)	15	9.20	9.12	0.08
Third quartile (7.9%–12.79%)	15	9.12	9.12	0.00
Fourth quartile (>12.8%)	15	9.30	9.12	0.18

Conclusion

The overall conclusion of the study is that analysis failed to expose a set of explanatory factors that might help countries and policymakers improve MDG goal attainment using PRSPs as a vehicle. Rather, data reveal that individual countries are unique for the most part, and that if there is a strategy for attaining MDGs, it will likely need to be customized. Individual countries may have to find their own way to success with support of international and bilateral donors. Having said this, there were some intriguing findings.

International development targets for 2015 set forth by the UN in its MDG program have been absorbed into the poverty reduction plans developed by the countries in the World Bank's PSRP program. There were relationships between a country absorbing MDGs into their PRSPs and the process by which it develops the PRSP, the level of human development of the country, and governance effectiveness.

Analysis of the development process of PRSPs showed MDGs are better absorbed into PRSPs over time. We observed no pattern in the length of a PRSP as indicated by the number of pages and an analysis of the number of iterations of PRSPs and PRSP documents was inconsistent.

Examination of the level of national development showed that high human development countries had a higher overall absorption of MDGs than medium and low human development ones. The level of human development affected MDG absorption. Analyses of the effect of human development and relative poverty on the absorption of individual targets showed no consistent trend across the individual targets. Our investigation into level of income and development assistance showed no effect on MDG absorption.

Government effectiveness is the only World Bank governance measure with any noticeable relationship to MDG absorption, showing a lower level of absorption by flawed democracies. This finding was contrary to our original expectation that countries with flawed democracies would score higher in MDG absorption into their PRSPs. International organizations stress the significance of democracy in alleviating poverty, but our findings show that governance is not a factor in MDG absorption.

We have identified three areas for further study, trends in MDG absorption over time, relative regional absorption of individual targets and the development process used for individual PRSPs. Looking into the impact of conflicts and reconstruction projects on international financial and aid organizations resourcing priorities may explain the trends in MDG absorption.

We identified a difference in the absorption of individual targets between MCC countries and non-MCC countries. Identifying the parties involved in the development of a PRSP could further explain some of the trends for the absorption of individual targets that we have identified.

It is possible that the MCC may be a "competing paradigm" to UN sponsored MDGs. The MCC "requires selected countries to identify their priorities for achieving sustainable economic growth and poverty reduction. Countries develop their MCC proposals in broad consultation within their society. MCC teams then work in close partnership to help countries refine a program."

Chapter 5

How U.S. Africa Command Conducts Assessments

N. Clark Capshaw and Jeffrey W. Bassichis

Contents

Military and Its Influence on Social Cohesion

As Capshaw (2005) argued, governments, in particular the armed elements of those governments (i.e., military and police), have an outsized influence on the ability of those nations to survive and thrive. However, the role and influence of armed elements is not limited to repelling invaders or checking internal violence and criminal activity. Its influence is perhaps more strongly determined by the behavior that these armed elements display toward the people of a country and its governing officials. The "social cohesion" role of governments is undermined by those elements that are corrupt, separatist, unjust, or capricious in the use of power.

Many African countries have struggled with governance from their independence. Whether one attributes this to the legacy of colonialism, to the seemingly arbitrary borders drawn by the colonial powers, or to the greed and authoritarianism of the African strongmen who emerged shortly after independence to lead weakly cohesive societies, it remains a challenge for African peoples to govern themselves. One of the instruments of national power—the military—which should be a force for stability, often becomes part of the problem—leading coups d'état or other rebellions that lead to greater instability, further violence, and the lack of national cohesion. When militaries use power capriciously, or engage in corruption, they undermine the idea of justice, which also causes society to become less cohesive.

One part of the solution to this is to create military organizations in African societies that are professional, trustworthy, representative of the people, and controlled by civilian institutions. This is one of the main missions of the U.S. Africa Command (AFRICOM). It engages in military training, joint exercises and operations, peacekeeping, and crisis response interventions that are intended to help Africa's military organizations to attain these objectives. However, this raises the question, "how does AFRICOM know when it is being effective in its efforts to professionalize Africa's military sector?" This is the focus of this chapter.

This chapter highlights the AFRICOM assessment process, and describes how this ties in to U.S. national security and the U.S. role in Africa, to policy and budgetary planning priorities, and to AFRICOM's mission and plans. It shows how AFRICOM uses assessments to inform decisions to ensure plans, programs, and resources are focused on achieving U.S. security objectives. A positive assessment result means not only that AFRICOM is doing its job, but also that Africa's military forces are becoming a positive force for cohesion in their societies.

What Is Assessment?

"How'm I doing?" In the 1980s, this simple question was made famous by Mayor Ed Koch, asking the New York public for feedback about his performance as mayor. Although Koch doubtlessly elicited some colorful replies to his question, the question's lack of specificity probably made it difficult for him to use many of those responses in an effort to improve his leadership of the city. As an approach to assessment, whatever Mayor Koch may have gained in political folksiness he lost in precision.

In contrast to Mayor Koch, AFRICOM has developed a rigorous process to answer that question, with answers that help AFRICOM's leadership know if its policies are having their intended effects, or whether leadership needs to adjust course in order to achieve its objectives.

AFRICOM and the Role of Strategic Assessments

AFRICOM was created in 2008 to centralize and coordinate military relations with African nations, the African Union, and African regional security organizations. Although its mission is fundamentally tied to U.S. national security interests and the achievement of U.S. goals for the African region, those goals have a significant intersection with the development goals of *sustainable development, human security, and stable, democratic governance for African nations.* Hence, there is a strong basis for partnership with both governmental and nongovernmental entities that are equally committed to these goals for Africa.

The AFRICOM Mission Statement spells out the nature of this partnership:

> United States Africa Command, in concert with interagency and international partners, builds defense capabilities, responds to crisis, and deters and defeats transnational threats in order to advance U.S. national interests and promote regional security, stability, and prosperity ... Our core mission of assisting African states and regional organizations to strengthen their defense capabilities better enables Africans to address their security threats and reduces threats to U.S. interests. We concentrate our efforts on contributing to the development of capable and professional militaries that respect human rights, adhere to the rule of law, and more effectively contribute to stability in Africa. (US [United States] Africa Command, 2014)

Specific efforts focus on combating terrorism, narcotics, and piracy, and on helping African countries build strong defense institutions that respect the rule of law, are subordinate to civilian control, and are capable of responding to humanitarian crises in other African countries, and on conducting peacekeeping operations.

AFRICOM conducts training, exercises, and joint military operations with African nations in order to help advance these objectives.

The authors' organization is responsible for performing the strategic assessments that measure the extent to which these objectives are being met. This chapter outlines that process in terms of six focus areas (Lines of Effort), addresses assessment from a strategic, operational, and tactical level, and shows how assessments feed back to the overall planning process.

AFRICOM's Strategic Objectives Are Guided by the U.S. National Security Strategy

The 2010 U.S. National Security Strategy (United States of America 2010) focuses on four primary pillars: security, prosperity, values, and international order. Although some parts of these pillars are domestically focused, many aspects of this strategy are outwardly focused. In addition to defeating al-Qaida and its affiliates, the National Security Strategy aims to "promote democracy and human rights abroad … [and] promote dignity by meeting basic needs" (pp. 37–39) as part of the *Values* pillar, and to "ensure strong alliances … build cooperation … strengthen institutions and mechanisms for cooperation … [and] sustain broad cooperation on key global challenges" (pp. 41–47) as part of the *International Order* pillar. This National Security Strategy then flows down to become a part of the U.S. National Military Strategy, the Department of State's Global Development Policy and Policy for Africa, and the U.S. Agency for International Development Strategy for Democracy, Human Rights, and Governance, all addressed below.

National Military Strategy, Global Development Policy, and Policy for Africa

Flowing from the National Security Strategy are substrategies related to the U.S. policy toward Africa and African development. Four of the most prominent of these are the U.S. Global Development Policy (State Department), the National Military Strategy (Department of Defense [DoD]), the U.S. Strategy toward Sub-Saharan Africa (State Department), and the U.S. AID Strategy of Democracy, Human Rights, and Governance (USAID). Each substrategy has its own particular focus that impacts the work that AFRICOM does.

"[The U.S. Global Development Policy] … calls for the elevation of development as a core pillar of American power and charts a course for development, diplomacy, and defense (3Ds) to mutually reinforce and complement one another in an integrated comprehensive approach to national security" (The White House 2010).

The 2011 U.S. National Military Strategy (U.S. Department of Defense 2011) echoes the language of the National Security Strategy with its focus on (1) Countering Violent Extremism, (2) Deterring and Defeating Aggression, (3) Strengthening International and Regional Security, and (4) Shaping the Future Force (pp. 5–16).

The U.S. Strategy toward Sub-Saharan Africa (United States of America 2012) consists of four pillars:

1. Strengthening democratic institutions
2. Spurring economic growth, trade, and investment
3. Advancing peace and security
4. Promoting opportunity and development

The U.S. AID Strategy of Democracy, Human Rights, and Governance (DRG) (U.S. Agency for International Development 2013) also rests on four pillars:

1. Promote participatory, representative, and inclusive political processes and government institutions
2. Foster greater accountability of institutions and leaders to citizens and to the law
3. Protect and promote universally recognized human rights
4. Improve development outcomes through the integration of DRG principles and practices across USAID's development portfolio (p. 14)

Each of these substrategies has an impact on the work done by AFRICOM, and, even though AFRICOM is a military organization, a major part of its activities relates to functions that are not traditionally associated with military missions.

Now, let us look more closely at the mission of the Africa Command, and how its elements flow down from the U.S. National Security Strategy and the other documents mentioned above.

AFRICOM's Mission and the Role of Assessment

The AFRICOM Mission is supported by six Lines of Effort, addressed below. Only numbers 1 and 5 are traditionally thought of as military missions. The others are often thought of either as development missions, humanitarian missions, or police functions:

1. Counter violent extremist organizations (CVEO)
2. Strengthen African defense institutions (SADI)
3. Support the development of crisis response/peacekeeping capabilities in African countries (CRPK)
4. Counter illicit trafficking and narcotics (CITN)

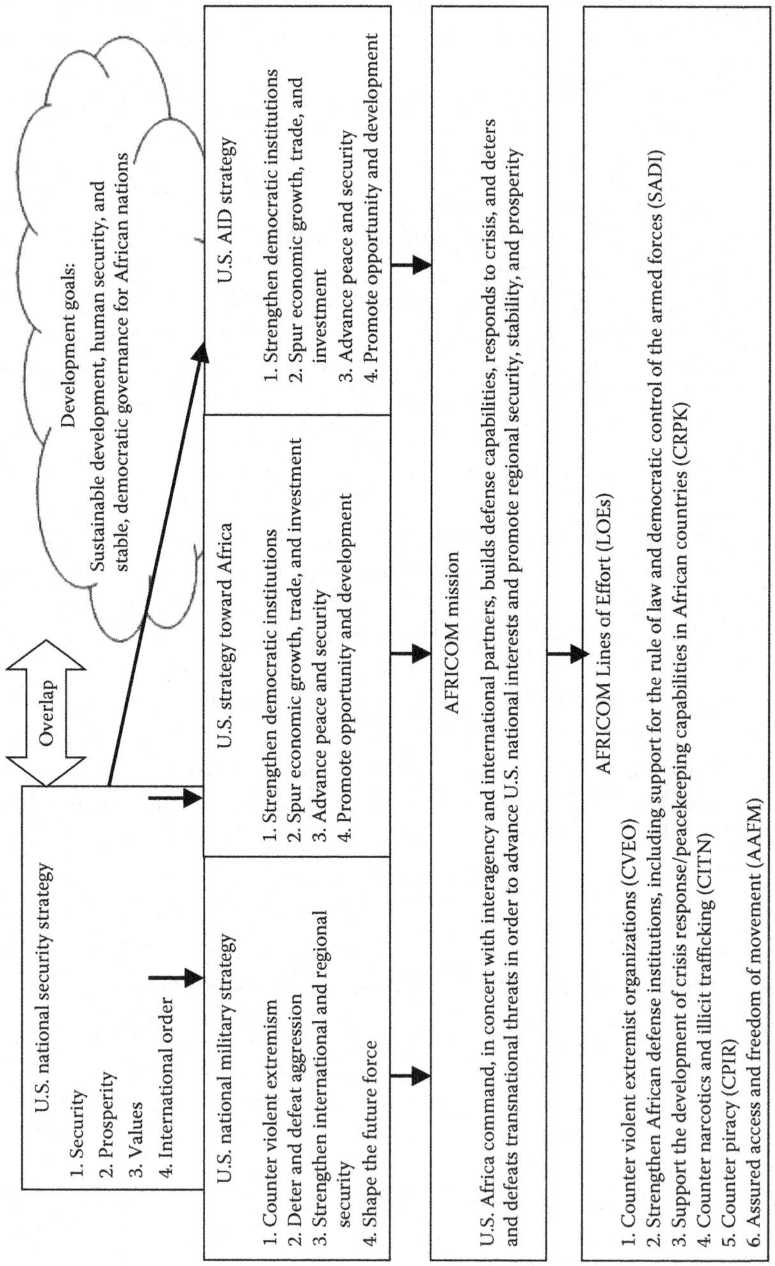
U.S. national security strategy
1. Security
2. Prosperity
3. Values
4. International order
Overlap
Development goals:
Sustainable development, human security, and stable, democratic governance for African nations
U.S. national military strategy
1. Counter violent extremism
2. Deter and defeat aggression
3. Strengthen international and regional security
4. Shape the future force
U.S. strategy toward Africa
1. Strengthen democratic institutions
2. Spur economic growth, trade, and investment
3. Advance peace and security
4. Promote opportunity and development
U.S. AID strategy
1. Strengthen democratic institutions
2. Spur economic growth, trade, and investment
3. Advance peace and security
4. Promote opportunity and development
AFRICOM mission
U.S. Africa command, in concert with interagency and international partners, builds defense capabilities, responds to crisis, and deters and defeats transnational threats in order to advance U.S. national interests and promote regional security, stability, and prosperity
AFRICOM Lines of Effort (LOEs)
1. Counter violent extremist organizations (CVEO)
2. Strengthen African defense institutions, including support for the rule of law and democratic control of the armed forces (SADI)
3. Support the development of crisis response/peacekeeping capabilities in African countries (CRPK)
4. Counter narcotics and illicit trafficking (CITN)
5. Counter piracy (CPIR)
6. Assured access and freedom of movement (AAFM)

Figure 5.1 AFRICOM's mission flows from U.S. National Security Objectives and is operationalized through six Lines of Effort.

5. Counter piracy (CPIR)
6. Assure access and freedom of movement (AAFM)

Figure 5.1 is a depiction of how the National Security Strategy flows down through the various plans, and are fully realized in the mission and Lines of Effort at AFRICOM.

A Hierarchy for Assessment: Objectives, Effects, Measures, Indicators

Assessments are likewise driven by strategic concerns. U.S. DoD guidance directs campaign assessments to be done to ensure *strategic objectives* are being met. Beyond that, combatant commands (COCOMs) are given substantial latitude in how to conduct those assessments. Nevertheless, most COCOMs conduct assessments within a hierarchical flow down of campaign objectives. Known by the acronym OEMI, strategic *objectives* flow down into specific *effects* that we want to accomplish. *Effects* are more detailed than *objectives*, and they are gauged by *measures of effectiveness*. These *measures* are, more often than not, compilations of smaller pieces of data called *indicators*. Assessments are designed by breaking the mission *objectives* into these smaller parts that can be answered. Assessments are conducted by answering the lower level *indicators*, and then compiling them to answer the strategic questions at the top of the design.

Indicators, then, are the heart of the assessment. They are the precise "How-are-we-doing?" questions, whose answers provide the data that are used to score the accomplishment of objectives, or to measure the progress of African countries (or regions) over time in a certain capability—such as a country's ability to combat terrorism or respond to humanitarian crises. As a core part of its mission, AFRICOM aims to assist African countries to improve their capabilities in these areas. Doing so accomplishes the dual objective of helping African nations' governments and military forces become more professional and responsible, and reduces the need for American troops in such circumstances. Assessing their progress is therefore also an essential part of AFRICOM's mission, and helps us to know if we are doing the right things in the right countries.

Structure of AFRICOM's Assessment Working Groups

As the newest of nine COCOMs, AFRICOM has learned from networking with the others such that more can be done when we work together. One of the practices adopted is the use of multi-organizational working groups to do the strategic thinking that benefits the entire command. These working groups provide multiple perspectives, provide for multiple feedback loops, and are task focused.

Multi-Organizational = Different Perspectives

Early on, AFRICOM adopted a multi-organizational working group structure for assessments. We did this because we recognized that AFRICOM's planning organizations needed assessment products that would help them to refine their plans. We also recognized that valuable expertise resided in the different AFRICOM directorates and components, and we would gain valuable input and feedback by including the other organizations. Therefore, we chartered AWGs that include leadership and representation from each of the eight AFRICOM Directorates, other AFRICOM components, and the Combined Joint Task Force, Horn of Africa (CJTF-HOA), headquartered in Djibouti. In addition to this, we included AFRICOM's interagency personnel (e.g., Departments of State, Justice, Homeland Security, and Treasury) as part of the teams. At present, most of the AWGs have members from these organizations, providing this valuable perspective.

Multiple Feedback Loops = Checks and Balances

Another thing that multi-organizational working groups do is provide multiple feedback loops—a valuable cross-check. Assessments provide feedback to campaign and military exercise planning and vice versa. Interagency personnel bring a different perspective and information from their departments to DoD.

Enduring Teams with "Ad Hoc" Purposes

Frequently chaired by a Colonel-level (O-6) military officer and led by his or her deputy, AWGs meetings are intended to serve focused "ad hoc" purposes—either to develop *indicators* at the beginning of the assessment process or to review the assessment results and develop actionable recommendations at the end of that process. Each of these goals has a timeline associated with it, and this drives the agenda of the meetings. AWGs endure because the assessment process is cyclic. There is often a time of intense activity during the *indicator* development stage, with a break while the assessment is being completed, followed by the review/assessment period. This "cyclic" nature makes the AWG teams enduring, and gives the members time to develop some institutional knowledge and memory (Figure 5.2).

Working Groups and Products

Each AFRICOM Line of Effort has a separate AWG. Figure 5.3 illustrates how these teams are integrated with the AFRICOM mission, the planning cycle, and ultimately how assessment results are fed back into the planning cycle.

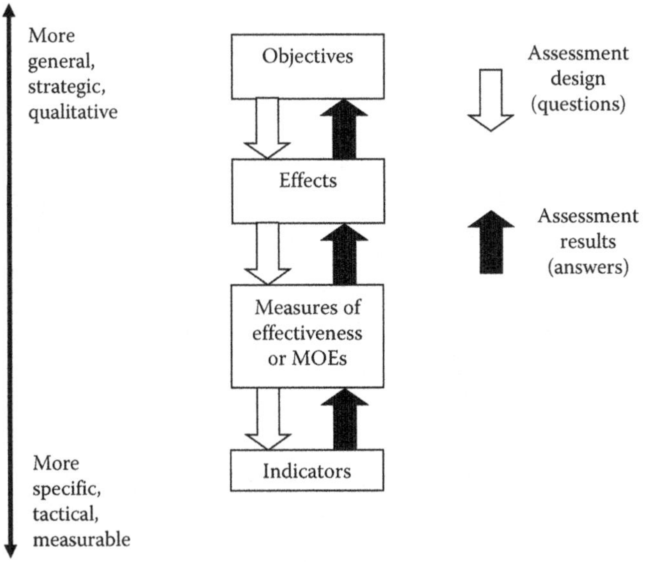

Figure 5.2 OEMI—how objectives flow down to indicators.

Three Types of Assessment Indicators

In the AFRICOM assessment process, three types of numeric indicators are used: *objective, subjective,* and *perceptive.* Each of these indicators is different, and each is important in telling the complete story. All indicators, regardless of type, are used to measure the percentage of some effect or objective to be achieved.

Objective indicators are those that can be answered directly with a number. For example, Africa's military forces are increasingly being called upon to assist in peacekeeping operations in other African countries. In assessing peacekeeping operations, it may be necessary to determine how many troops are available in a particular country to conduct these kinds of operations. In such a case, an appropriate objective indicator might be:

EXAMPLE

How many of the country's battalions have been trained in peacekeeping operations?

If carefully constructed, such an indicator facilitates scoring along a normalized (100 point) scale, and is useful to AFRICOM's leadership in planning further joint training exercises with African military forces to ensure they meet the standard.

Many objective indicators useful for assessment are available via open sources. The World Bank, Transparency International, the United Nations, and the African Union compile many objective indicators that are useful in assessments.

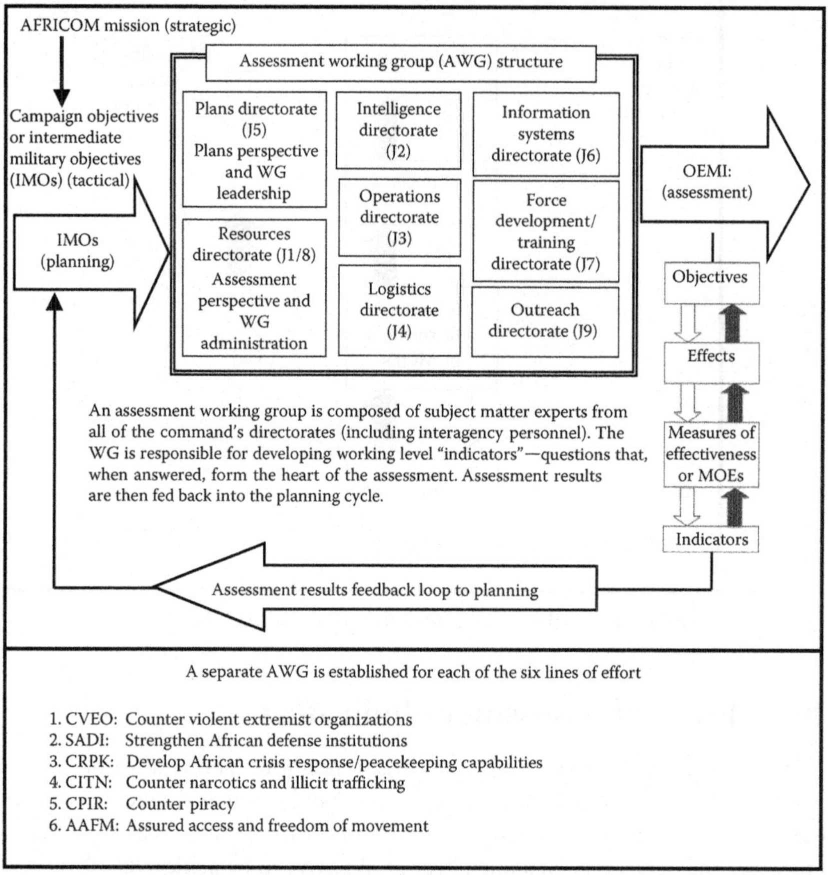

Figure 5.3 AWG process and feedback loops.

Subjective indicators are those that solicit an expert's opinion (e.g., a Country Desk Officer, Defense Attaché, or an academic expert), but the answers are framed with descriptive scoring criteria.

EXAMPLE

On a scale of 0–100, what is the degree to which human rights norms are embodied in military and security force training?

Different experts score differently. To ensure consistency, it is necessary to define scoring criteria for subjective indicators, such as the following:

- 80–100: All military and security force personnel (officers and enlisted) receive annual human rights training.
- 60–79: All military and security force personnel (officers and enlisted) receive human rights training at least every 3 years.

- 40–59: Most military and security force personnel (officers and enlisted) receive human rights training, but only during their initial enlistment or commissioning training.
- 20–39: Human-rights training is only conducted occasionally with select units (military police, detention authorities and guards, etc.).
- 0–19: Human-rights training is not provided to military and security force personnel.

Although the scoring criteria shown above provide for some subjectivity in the response, the definitions associated with the scoring bins minimize that subjectivity. Refining these scoring criteria is a continuing task of the assessment analysts.

Perceptive indicators are based on the U.S. Department of State polling data of local African country populations, thus providing an idea of how the country's population perceives the situation, particularly in regard to the professionalism and readiness of the country's military force.

EXAMPLE

What percentage of the civilian population believes their country's military keeps them safe from threats from other countries?

Complete Assessment Picture

In forming an answer to a question about a capability or a situation of an African country, a more complete picture often emerges when objective, subjective, and perceptive indicators are combined to complete the puzzle (see Figure 5.4). For example, in trying to determine if an African country's military is respectful of human rights, it may be useful to combine objective indicators (such as the number

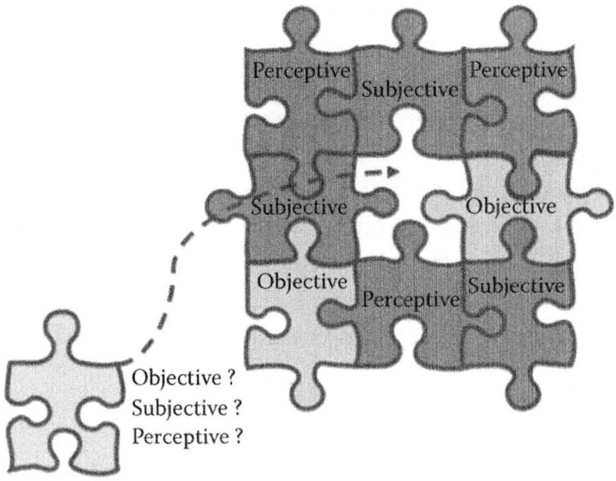

Figure 5.4 What indicator helps complete the picture?

of units trained in human rights), subjective indicators (e.g., the U.S. Defense Attaché's assessment of the country's military), and perceptive indicators (such as the country population's perception that the military is respectful of such rights).

Objective numerical indicators are useful in determining the degree to which an objective is being met, and are useful when it is important to measure progress over time. Subjective and perceptive indicators are frequently more useful in giving greater confidence to the numerical data. A high score on an objective indicator and a low score on a subjective or perceptive indicator may create doubt as to the reliability of the score on the objective indicator. Subjective and perceptive indicators are also more likely to be based on what anthropologist Clifford Geertz (1973) calls "thick description," leading an assessment expert to probe more deeply in a certain area where those indicators are perplexing, unexpected, or in opposition to one another.

Weighting: Determining What Is Most Important

Team members may initially be reluctant to assign weights for assessments, but neglecting to assign weights means that you have already made a tacit decision to weigh everything equally. To avoid such an eventuality, it is important to discuss the relative weight of information, indicators, effects, and countries within the AFRICOM region, and to do so with stakeholders from all AFRICOM directorates. Some African countries are more important to the AFRICOM mission (perhaps due to population size, economy, or potential political instability), and some effects (e.g., counterterrorism) are more important. They deserve higher weight in the assessment.

Weighting Countries

Africa has more than 50 countries, varying in population from less than 250,000 in São Tomé e Principe to nearly 150 million in Nigeria. Some are failed or failing states with terrorist havens, whereas others are models of stability and democracy, such as Cape Verde and Ghana. Some are budding economic powerhouses, while others are mineral or oil-rich, but internal conflict has made it difficult for the population to reap the benefits. With such diversity, AFRICOM cannot realistically place equal emphasis on every country. We must prioritize; weighting enables us to do so. Weights of countries may also shift over time when crises unfold in a particular country or region. Although the existence of a crisis in one particular country does not automatically propel it to the top priority, such crises do usually result in a reevaluation of weighting.

Weighting Indicators and Effects

Not only do we weight individual countries by objective, we also weight the indicators and effects that we wish to measure. Peacekeeping or humanitarian operations

Indicator weighting			Category weighting		
Background data:	Number	Weight	Background data:	Number	Weight
Number of band one countries	2	0.3214	Number of band one countries	3	0.2647
Number of band two countries	3	0.1071	Number of band two countries	2	0.0882
Number of band three countries	1	0.0357	Number of band three countries	1	0.0294
Total countries	6	1.0000	Total countries	6	1.0000

Figure 5.5 Weighting by indicator and by country.

may matter more to the command in one region, whereas combating piracy or terrorism may occupy the top position in another region of this vast continent. We are able to reflect the command's priorities by appropriately weighting our effects and indicators (Figure 5.5).

Reporting Results: Standardized Presentation

Once indicators are developed and weights are chosen, then the data are collected and compiled to produce an assessment report. Assessment reports provide four things: (1) a numerical assessment of progress measured as a percentage of an effect or objective, (2) whether that measure is trending up or down, (3) the analyst's certainty (high, medium, low) of that conclusion, and (4) actionable recommendations that can be inferred from the data.

Presentation of assessment results in this way has become standard practice at AFRICOM. With results presented in this manner, AFRICOM's leadership can quickly see, at a glance, how well we are performing on each objective, whether we are moving forward or regressing, and how much confidence we have in the assessment results. Once the numerical results are tallied, the working groups reconvene to review those results. Hence, "actionable recommendations" represent the consensus of the AWG (Figure 5.6)

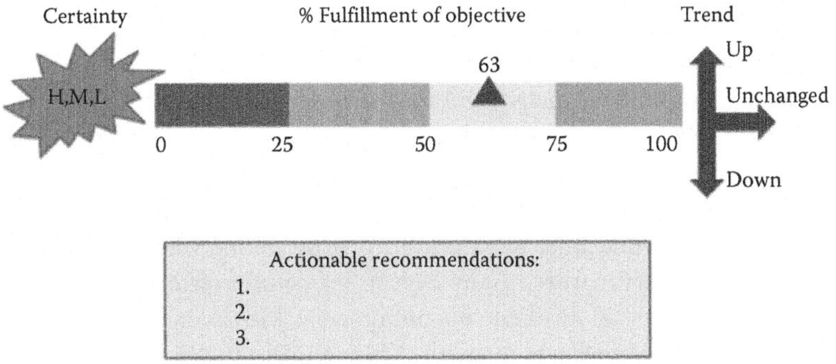

Figure 5.6 Assessment results—standardized presentation.

Where Do We Go from Here?

AFRICOM's assessment capability continues to improve as assessment personnel gain more experience and as we reap the benefits of the work done to date. There is a long-range plan to improve several areas of the assessment process, from indicator development, to refinement of the AWGs process, to accessibility, manipulation, and presentation of the data. Some of those efforts are highlighted here.

Correlation analysis. Right now we are expanding work on correlation analysis. We have conducted analyses to determine the correlation between inputs to achieve our objectives in the region (events, dollars, personnel, man-days), and the achievement of those objectives (more professional African militaries, public health improvements, reduced incidents of piracy, or terrorism). As a result, for example, we found that improvement in African military health capability is highly correlated with the number of AFRICOM personnel sent on health-related training activities or exercises. This result may indicate that it makes more sense to send a larger medical team to conduct fewer events than try to parcel out smaller teams for a larger number of events. Such information is a valuable input to an organization that needs to use its limited resources in the most effective and efficient manner.

Cultivating additional data sources. We already use data from other non-DoD organizations, such as the World Bank, the UN, and Transparency International. The use of these sources as a "check-and-balance" helps the command ensure that its assessments are not biased by its desired outcomes. The assessment team continues to search for other sources to complement existing sources. One challenge is how to factor purely qualitative, narrative/historical, or anecdotal information into assessment products. Another challenge is to find experts outside the command who can add their input to assessments.

Sharing lessons learned. We have begun to share our assessment lessons learned with others through forums such as the Military Operations Research Society (MORS) and other conferences. We recently held an assessment lessons learned conference and compared methods with the U.S. European Command, and have quarterly Assessment Community of Interest meetings via teleconference. We share lessons with other COCOMs through these conferences and other engagements.

Being more transparent. Owing to National Security concerns, some aspects of AFRICOM's work must remain hidden from public view, but certainly not all. By their very nature, many aspects of counterterrorism operations are classified, hence not available for public view. However, many other aspects of AFRICOM's engagement with Africa's military forces demonstrate the development of a strong spirit of partnership, and, as such, should be shared. A true partnership can be forged between AFRICOM and African countries, their leaders, and their military forces. AFRICOM wants to be a positive force for that change.

A final word. The U.S. Africa Command has some lofty goals—both in terms of U.S. security and in terms of helping Africa's military forces become more professional and be able to address the many future challenges on the continent. A robust assessment process helps to ensure that these objectives can be met—so ultimately we can go forward together. This way of thinking goes hand-in-hand with the AFRICOM motto, taken from an African proverb:

If you want to go quickly, go alone.
If you want to go far, go together.
We choose to go far.
We choose to go together (Ham 2011, p. 2).

References

Capshaw, N. C. 2005. The social cohesion role of the public sector. *Peabody Journal of Education* 80(4) 53–77.

Geertz, C. 1973. *The Interpretation of Cultures*. New York: Basic Books.

Ham, C. 2011. Commander's Intent. *U.S. Africa Command* (August 2011). Retrieved August 3, 2012 from http://www.africom.mil/pdfFiles/2011%20Commander's%20 Intent.pdf.

The White House, 2010. Office of the Press Secretary. *Fact Sheet: U.S. Global Development Policy.* Retrieved February 24, 2014 from http://www.whitehouse.gov/the-press-office/ 2010/09/22/fact-sheet-us-global-development-policy.

United States of America. 2010. *National Security Strategy.* Retrieved February 24, 2014 from http://www.whitehouse.gov/sites/default/files/rss_viewer/national_security_strategy.pdf.

United States of America. 2012. *U.S. Strategy toward Sub-Saharan Africa.* Retrieved February 24, 2014 from http://www.whitehouse.gov/sites/default/files/docs/africa_strategy_2.pdf.

US Agency for International Development. 2013. *USAID Strategy on Democracy, Human Rights, and Governance.* Retrieved February 24, 2014 from http://www.usaid.gov/sites/ default/files/documents/1866/USAID%20DRG_%20final%20final%206–24%20 3%20(1).pdf.

US Department of Defense. 2011. *The National Military Strategy of the United States of America: Redefining America's Military Leadership.* Retrieved February 24, 2014 from http://www.army.mil/info/references/docs/NMS%20FEB%202011.pdf.

US (United States) Africa Command. 2014. *About the Command; What We Do.* Retrieved February 24, 2014 from http://www.africom.mil/about-the-command.

III

SUSTAINABLE DEVELOPMENT CHALLENGES

Chapter 6

Why Population Dynamics Matter for Climate Change and Sustainable Development in Africa

Clive Mutunga

Contents

Introduction

Size, composition, and spatial distribution of human populations must be at the core of any analysis of the challenges and opportunities for sustainable development. The linkage between population dynamics and sustainable development, including the environment and climate change, is particularly critical for Africa. Africa is the only continent whose population is projected to continue to grow beyond 2100 (UN DESA 2010), and Africa has the weakest technical capacity to effectively adapt to the consequences of climate change. A large percentage of the African population lives in areas susceptible to climate variation and extreme weather events. Population growth is occurring most rapidly in Africa on an average, increasing the scale of vulnerability to the projected impacts of climate change. Recent United Nations (UN) projections show that Africa's population will grow from 1 billion in 2010 to 2.1 billion by 2050, and that this growth is driven exclusively by countries in sub-Saharan Africa (SSA) where the population will increase from 0.8 billion to 1.9 billion by 2050 (UNPD 2010). Thirty-one of the 51 countries in SSA are projected to at least double in population by 2050.

Rapid population growth has resulted from the imbalance between persistent high fertility and a substantial decline in overall mortality over the past four decades. High fertility can be addressed by making family planning and reproductive health universally accessible. Yet, only 16% of married women in SSA used modern contraception as of 2009, compared to a global average of 56% (UN DESA 2011). Levels of unmet need for family planning in SSA are high with about 30% (47 million) of those who want to avoid pregnancy not using an effective contraception method. Meeting family planning needs can reduce 76% of unintended pregnancies (Singh et al. 2009).

Despite the link between population and climate change and their direct implications on sustainable development, there is limited commitment, investment, and programming to address both issues. In cases where population and climate change challenges are being addressed, they are tackled in isolation, limiting synergistic benefits.

The 1987 Brundtland Commission's report, *Our Common Future*, defines sustainable development as "development that meets the needs of the present without compromising the ability of future generations to meet their own needs." Using this definition, the UN built a sustainable development framework with three pillars: economic, environmental, and social factors. Population falls under the social pillar. However, population size, growth, distribution, density, and age structure, as well as migration and urbanization, matter for all three pillars. The intergenerational focus of sustainable development reinforces the centrality of population to the UN framework.

A country's population growth affects the prospects for economic growth and poverty reduction. A rapidly increasing population may create greater demands on an economy and constrain economic growth. When women have fewer children, it reduces the number of dependents in a household and provides opportunities for increasing productivity, savings, and future economic growth. Children are healthier and more likely to attend school. Women themselves are healthier and able to earn an income and participate in their communities. Slowing population growth also reduces pressure on the environment and natural resources.

These links were emphasized in the International Conference on Population and Development (ICPD) Program of Action (United Nations 1994) and the Rio Declaration on Environment and Development (United Nations 1992). Agenda 21 discusses reproductive health programs, including family planning, as approaches that promote changes in demographic trends and sustainability. These linkages were reaffirmed at the UN Conference on Sustainable Development, Rio +20, held in Rio de Janeiro, Brazil, in 2012.

Linking Population to Climate Change Strategies

Population issues are important for both the challenges and solutions associated with climate change and climate compatible development efforts. There is strong evidence that demographic change does impact greenhouse gas emissions, and that population dynamics can play a key role in adapting to and mitigating climate change efforts.

Mitigation

Although there is much debate on the relative contribution of population vis-à-vis consumption to greenhouse gas emissions, there is evidence that higher population growth means more greenhouse gas emissions (Jiang and Hardee 2009, O'Neill et al. 2010). On the basis of population projections produced by integrated models, higher population growth is associated with higher emissions in future decades. Other demographic factors such as changes in population composition, urban–rural residence, and household structure have significant effects on emissions responsible for climate change (Jiang and Hardee 2009). Following a slower population growth path could reduce fossil fuel emissions significantly.

The contribution of least developed countries (LDCs), including those in SSA, to global warming will increase due to rapid population growth and socioeconomic development. Estimates indicate that even at current consumption levels, population growth in the LDCs will significantly contribute to global warming. However, the more immediate concern in developing countries and especially in SSA is the role of rapid population growth in exacerbating vulnerability to the negative consequences of climate change.

Adaptation

For climate change adaptation, there is growing evidence that population dynamics are critical in building resilience and as adaptation strategies (UNFPA 2009, IIED 2009).

In fact, several developing countries explicitly link population and family planning/reproductive health (FP/RH) within their national adaptation plans. Analysis of National Adaptation Program of Actions (NAPA) to explore how they describe population dynamics and climate change has shown that most NAPAs identify population and health issues as relevant for climate change adaptation strategies. Twenty-six of 31 NAPAs submitted by African LDCs explicitly make linkages between climate change and population and identify rapid population growth as a problem that either aggravates vulnerability or reduces population resilience in dealing with the effects of climate change. Although different NAPAs have diverse concerns, effects of rapid population growth have been linked with climate change through five factors: food insecurity, natural resource depletion/degradation, water resource scarcity, poor human health, and migration and urbanization (Mutunga and Hardee 2010).

Key Population Dynamics in SSA

SSA, one of the poorest regions in the world, is undergoing critical demographic transformation. SSA is home to around 900 million people, a number projected to grow to 1.2 billion by 2025, and to almost 2 billion by 2100 (UNPD 2010). With an average population growth rate of more than 2% for most countries, the region has the fastest growing population in the world. Of the 2.4 billion people projected to be added to the world by 2050, about half will be born in SSA. Thirty-one countries out of the region's 51 are projected to at least double their population by 2050, according to recent projections (UNPD 2010).

Africa's high population growth rate is driven largely by high total fertility. Although the region's population growth rate has slowed, fertility rates remain high at approximately 5 children per woman on average (compared to a world average of 2.5), with very few countries averaging a TFR below four (UNPD 2010).

High fertility countries overlap with those experiencing the most youthful age structures. The median age of the population in SSA is around 18 years, but it is as low as 15 years in some countries like Niger. The population aged below 15 years grew by 150% in the region as a whole between 1970 and 2005, and by over 200% in Niger (Das Gupta et al. 2011), and 43% of the total population is below 15 years old (PRB 2011). Such young age structures harbor high inbuilt momentum for the population to continue growing for many years even after attaining replacement level fertility (AFIDEP and Venture Strategies).

Urbanization

Most of the expected population growth in SSA will be absorbed in urban areas. While the urbanization process has stabilized in most developed countries with about 75% of the population living in urban areas, most African countries are transitioning from being predominantly rural to urban (UN-HABITAT 2010).

In 2010, SSA was mainly rural with 37% living in urban areas, compared to 50% of the global urban population. However, with a high projected urban growth rate, the total urban population in SSA will increase from 319 million in 2010 to about 1.2 billion in 2050, representing a share of 45% and 60% of the total population in 2050, respectively (WPP 2010).

In general, urbanization has been accompanied by social and economic development. If properly managed, such an increase in the absolute number of urban inhabitants in SSA could propel social and economic growth, part of a phenomenon called the "demographic dividend." However, given the current development pace in the region, most countries might not be able to harness this urban dividend. The scale of urban growth being experienced in SSA, and in Africa as a whole, overwhelms the capacity of governments to provide basic services such as education, health services, housing, potable water, electricity, and waste disposal. As such, most urban dwellers in SSA cities live in overcrowded informal settlements—slums. In Lagos, the second largest city in Africa, about 62% of the urban dwellers live in this condition. While countries like Mali, Senegal, Ghana, and Benin have achieved considerable decline (up to 30%) in the proportion of urban slum dwellers between 1990 and 2010, countries like Kenya and Namibia remained stagnant with about 55% and 34% urban slum dwellers, respectively. Worse still, countries like Mozambique, Malawi, and the Central African Republic have experienced between 4% and 9% increase in the proportion of urban slum dwellers (UN-HABITAT 2010). The effect of rapid population growth in urban areas on poverty is demonstrated by the fact that while the proportion of urban residents living in slums has declined from 70% to 62% in Africa between 1990 and 2010, the actual number of people living in slum settlements had almost doubled from 103 million to 200 million over the same period (UN-HABITAT 2010).

Climate change further compounds the challenges associated with the rapid rate of urbanization in SSA by increasing the vulnerabilities of urbanites. Two-fifths of the West African population currently lives in coastal cities, and it is expected that three coastal megacities (Cairo, Lagos, and Kinshasa) of at least eight million inhabitants will be located in Africa by 2015 (Klein et al. 2002). Since most of the big cities in SSA are concentrated along the coast, the rising sea level resulting from changing climatic conditions will threaten these settlements because of the increased likelihood of flood and storm surges exacerbated by sea level rise (Satterthwaite 2008). Recent projections suggest that the number of people at risk of coastal floods in Africa will increase from one million in 1990 to 70 million in 2080 (Intergovernmental Panel on Climate Change [IPCC] 2007), and most of these people will be residing in cities. Owing to increased levels of rainfall, poor urban residents even in noncoastal cities like Nairobi also face increased risks of flooding because many slum settlements are often located along river banks and other fragile pieces of land that were not designed for human occupation (Zulu et al. 2011).

The links between climate change and urbanization are recognized by a number of NAPAs submitted by African LDCS. NAPAs mention that climate change will have a significant impact on urban settlements, especially in the face of increasing population and continual urban migration. In Djibouti, the NAPA notes, unfavorable climatic conditions have led to migration from rural areas to "new urban areas" where previously nomadic populations are being forced to settle around water points established by the state. Rapid urbanization in Gambia is "paralleled by clearing of forests and woodlands, expansion of cultivated area, over-fishing of particular species and severe coastal erosion." In São Tomé e Principe, the relocation of the population at risk of food insecurity and landslides in Malanza, Santa Catarina, and Sundy was identified as a priority adaptation activity (Mutunga and Hardee 2010).

Growth, Climate Change, and Sustainable Development

This analysis highlights the implications of population growth and its likely impacts on key development challenges, namely, agricultural production and water, in the face of climate change.

Population Growth and Agricultural Food Production

SSA populations are projected to grow as agricultural production declines. Most people in SSA depend on agriculture for livelihoods, with the sector employing 65% of the labor force and generating 32% of GDP growth. Despite this, agricultural food production per capita in the region was stagnant during 1960–2005 in terms of both overall production and cereal yield (Das Gupta et al. 2011). Pressure on agricultural crop land is growing mostly due to population growth. Almost a quarter of rural households in Ethiopia, Kenya, Mozambique, Rwanda, and Zambia were virtually landless and had little nonfarm income to supplement their livelihood (Jayne et al. 2003). SSA is one of the regions projected to be most severely affected by drought and temperature rises as the effects of climate change add up. Extreme food insecurity episodes, such as those that have affected the Horn of Africa, will become more common. Even in the relatively short term, between 1990 and 2020, every country on the continent except Zambia is projected to experience a decline in agricultural production, mostly in the range of less than 5%. The dual challenges of population growth and climate change are likely to compound the challenge of food insecurity.

The linkages between population growth and food security have been captured by several climate adaptation plans in SSA. Thirty-six NAPAs submitted by African countries link population growth to food insecurity. According to these documents, population pressure contributes to food insecurity by increasing a country's vulnerability to food shortages through two main channels. The first is a result of direct losses and damages in the event of occurrences such as droughts and floods. The second is by increasing demand for food and putting additional pressure on the food supply system and already diminishing food resources, for example, fish stocks, as reported in Gambia. Population pressure is more pronounced in certain areas that are more susceptible to events such as droughts and floods. For instance, NAPAs recognize high populations residing on scarce arable land (Central Sudan along the Nile River, Uganda) (Mutunga and Hardee 2010).

Population Growth and Water Resources

Population growth increases demand and competition for water resources and compounds water scarcity (PAI 2011). SSA is projected to be severely impacted by water scarcity, as a result of climate change effects. Fifteen countries in SSA, which are home to about 400 million people, are suffering from water scarcity or water stress. The number is projected to double to over 800 million by 2050 as more countries join the water scarce or stressed category. Djibouti, Cape Verde, Kenya, and Burkina Faso are the most severely affected by water scarcity with less than 800 cubic meters of water available per person per year. The water-stressed and water-scarce countries all have high population growth rates, with Eritrea's population growing at a very high rate of 3.2% per year. Combined with anticipated changes in climate, water shortages in these areas are likely to become even more acute, particularly in areas where economic and political factors impede access to freshwater. The path of future population growth will impact water stress and scarcity.

The linkages between population pressures and water scarcity as they relate to climate change are well articulated in the NAPAs of African LDCs. In general, population pressure is deemed to increase the demand for water and further reduce its future availability. In Sudan, for example, the NAPA states that "unfavorable weather conditions combined with population growth have rendered the Setaite River incapable of sustaining the town of Gedarif." Population increases in urban centers have put pressure on groundwater, as noted by Zambia's NAPA.

Population Growth and Climate Change Vulnerability

Climate change continues to pose a major threat to development and to the achievement of the UN Millennium Development Goals in SSA. The region, which has contributed the least to climate change, is the least resilient and highly vulnerable to its effects (Potts and Marsh 2010).

The vulnerability and resilience of countries to climate change can be measured in many ways. One method is the Vulnerability-Resilience Indicators Model (VRIM). The VRIM has an index, which combines 17 physical, social, and economic indicators that assess the resilience of a society to anticipated climate change impacts. The index measures countries' abilities to recover from occurrences of climate change according to indicators of current sensitivity (e.g., food security, human health, water resources) and adaptive capacity (economic, human and civic resources, environment) for the year 2000. Countries for which data are available are grouped into four categories (most, more, less, and least resilient) based on their sensitivity to the future effects of climate change and their adaptive capacity to address and adjust to those effects. In 2000, most of the countries in Africa were rated as least resilient to climate change. According to the analysis of Population Action International (PAI), the countries that are least resilient to climate change are also experiencing rapid population growth. Thirty-four countries in SSA are considered as having a high population growth rate.

Population and Climate Change Hotspots

High rates of population growth are already intersecting with the negative consequences of climate change in many countries in Africa. Some countries are currently experiencing high rates of population growth and high projected declines in agricultural production, and demonstrate low resilience to climate change. Such countries can be considered "hotspots" of population and climate change. Fifteen hotspot countries are in SSA and four—Burkina Faso, Djibouti, Malawi, and Somalia—are also currently experiencing water stress or scarcity.

Many of the hotspot countries already face widespread poverty, low levels of education, limited access to health services, and high levels of gender inequality. The impacts of climate change are magnifying these challenges. These conditions will likely extend to even more countries as population grows and limited natural and environmental resources are stretched.

Most of the hotspot countries have high levels of unmet needs for family planning, indicating that fertility is very high partly because of the inability of women and their partners to access and use contraception. Investing in voluntary health programs that meet family planning needs could, therefore, slow population growth and reduce vulnerability to climate change impacts. This is especially important because women, especially those who live in poverty, are likely to be most affected by the negative effects of climate change and also bear the disproportionate burden of having unplanned children due to lack of contraception.

Policy Considerations

1. Integrate policies and programs to address climate change and mainstream this across development sectors. This should include setting up strong coordination and governance systems. Supervision is needed to make sure various sectors work together to avoid duplicating efforts and wasting resources.

2. Prioritize population in national climate change and development plans, with adequate resources for effective implementation of programs. In particular, climate change plans and programs should include expanding access to family planning. This will boost resilience to climate change.
3. Prioritize meeting women and their partners' needs for family planning as it will yield a "triple win" in the UN sustainable development framework. Universal access to family planning would reduce fertility rates and slow population growth, which would help (1) reduce poverty by improving and expanding health, schooling, and economic opportunities, (2) protect and manage natural resources for economic and social development, and (3) reduce inequality and create greater opportunities for all through social development.
4. Improve technical capacity in program design, research, and application of research to decision-making processes. Decision makers engaged in climate change policy, planning, and implementation at all levels should have access to research on population trends, climate change, and development. It is important to strengthen the technical capacity of local experts to design and carry out integrated programs, and to monitor and evaluate these programs.
5. Incorporate population, reproductive health, and family planning into global and regional institutions and frameworks for sustainable development. Such institutions include the African Union and the UN Economic Commission for Africa. The frameworks include the post-2015 millennium development goal (MDG), the International Conference on Population and Development (ICPD), and the post-Rio +20 agendas.

References

Das Gupta, M., J. Bongaarts, J. Cleland. 2011. *Population, Poverty, and Sustainable Development: A Review of the Evidence.* Policy Research Working Paper # 5719. Washington, DC: The World Bank.

Intergovernmental Panel on Climate Change (IPCC). 2007. *Climate Change 2007: Synthesis Report. Contributions of Working Groups I, II, and III to the Fourth Assessment Report of the Intergovernmental Panel on Climate Change.* Geneva: IPCC.

International Institute for Environment and Development (IIED). 2009. Annual Report 2008/2009, UK.

Jayne, T.S., T. Yamano, M. Weber, D. Tschirley, R. Benfica, A. Chapoto, B. Zulu. 2003. Smallholder income and land distribution in Africa: Implications for poverty reduction strategies. *Food Policy* 28 253–275.

Jiang, L., K. Hardee. 2009. *How Do Recent Population Trends Matter to Climate Change?* Washington, DC: PAI.

Klein, R., R. Nicholls, F. Thomalla. 2002. The resilience of coastal megacities to weather-related hazards: A review. In: Kreimer A., M. Arnold, A. Carlin (eds.). *Building Safer Cities: The Future of Disaster Risk.* Washington, DC: World Bank, pp. 101–117.

Mutunga, C., K. Hardee. 2010. Population and reproductive health in National Adaptation Program of Action (NAPAs) for climate change in Africa. *African Journal of Reproductive Health* 14 (4) 133–145.

O'Neill, B., M. Dalton, R. Fuchs, L. Jiang, S. Pachauri, K. Zigova. 2010. Global demographic trends and future carbon emissions. *Proceedings of the National Academy of Sciences* 107 (41) 17521–17526.

Population Action International (PAI). 2011. *Why Population Matters.* Washington, DC: PAI.

Population Reference Bureau (PRB). 2011. World Population Data Sheet. Available at http://www.prb.org/pdf11/2011population-data-sheet_eng.pdf.

Potts, M., L. Marsh. 2010. *The Population Factor: How Does It Relate to Climate Change?* Berkeley: Bixby Center for Population, Health and Sustainability, University of California.

Satterthwaite, D. 2008. Climate change and urbanization: Effects and implications for urban governance. Presented at the United Nations Expert Group Meeting on Population Distribution, Urbanization, Internal Migration and Development, Population Division, Department of Economic and Social Affairs, United Nations Secretariat, New York, pp. 21–23. http://www.un.org/esa/population/meetings/EGM_PopDist/P16_Satterthwaite.pdf. Accessed March 1, 2012.

Singh, S., J. Darroch, L. Ashford, M. Vlasoff. 2009. *Adding It Up: The Costs and Benefits of Investing in Family Planning and Maternal and Newborn Health.* New York: Guttmacher Institute and United Nations Population Fund.

The United Nations Human Settlements Program (UN-HABITAT). 2010. The State of African Cities 2010: Governance, Inequality and Urban Land Markets. Nairobi: UN-HABITAT. http://www.unhabitat.org/pmss/listItemDetails.aspx?publicationID=3034. Accessed February 28, 2012.

United Nations, 1992. Agenda 21: Programme of Action for Sustainable Development. *United Nations Conference on Environment and Development.* Rio de Janeiro, Brazil, June 3–14.

United Nations, 1994. Report of the International Conference on Population and Development. Cairo, September 5–13.

United Nations Department of Economic and Social Affairs (UN DESA). 2011. World Contraceptive Use 2010. New York: UN DESA. http://www.un.org/esa/population/publications/wcu2010/WCP_2010/Data.html. Accessed February 7, 2012.

United Nations, Department of Economic and Social Affairs, Population Division. 2011. *World Population Prospects: The 2010 Revision, Volume I: Comprehensive Tables.* ST/ESA/SER.A/313. New York.

United Nations Population Fund (UNFPA). 2009. *State of World Population 2009: Facing a Changing World: Women, Population and Climate.* New York, NY: UNFPA.

United Nations (UNPD), 2010. Department of Economic and Social Affairs, Population Division (DESA, UNPD). *World Urbanization Prospects: The 2009 Revision.* New York: DESA, UNPD. Retrieved from http://esa.un.org/unpd/wup/index.htm. Accessed February 10.

Zulu, E., D. Beguy, A. Ezeh, P. Bocquier, N. Madise, J. Cleland, J. Falkingham. 2011. Overview of migration, poverty and health dynamics in Nairobi City's slum settlements. *Journal of Urban Health* 88 (Suppl 2) 185–199.

Chapter 7

Building Local Capacity and Creating Awareness in Conserving the Mau Forest and Water Resources

Joseph S. Chacha

Contents

Introduction

Kenya faces critical declines in forest and water resources—faced nowhere more acutely than in the Mau Forest complex and its dependent river basins. The Mau, a once densely forested land in southern Kenya, west of the Great Rift Valley, is the source of numerous rivers feeding the Rift Valley lakes and Lake Victoria.

According to the Joint Enforcement Unit (2010), the Kenya government goals for 2012 include increasing forest cover from less than 3% at present to 4% and lessening by half all environment-related diseases.

The Mau forest complex in Kenya's Rift Valley covers over 400,000 ha, and is the largest of the five "water towers" of Kenya (GoK and UNEP 2008). Its montane forests are an important part of water-flow regulation, flood mitigation, water storage, groundwater recharge, water purification, microclimate regulation, and reduced soil erosion and siltation. The forest is one of the major water towers and catchments in Kenya recognized in Vision 2030 and at least 12 rivers spring from the Mau and flow to different corners of the country (Reconnaissance Flight 2008).

Besides, the lakes support water transportation, community livelihoods, and international trade since they are a popular source of fish in the country. Some of the rivers whose catchments are in the Mau are also transboundary, serving and recharging important water bodies in the region. Without the Mau, water flow in the Nile River system will be drastically affected. According to a report by The Secretariat Convention on Biological Diversity (CBD) (2009), it is important to address the conservation and sustainable use of forest biodiversity through a comprehensive program of work as stipulated in its revised framework in 2008.

Conflict in the Mau Water Catchment

The CBD (2009) reports that more than 1.6 billion people depend to varying degrees on forests for their livelihoods, for example, fuel wood, medicinal plants, and forest foods. Approximately 300 million depend on forests directly for their survival, including about 6 million people of indigenous and ethnic groups, who are almost wholly dependent on forests.

The critical role of the Mau is in the water it provides to urban centers and some of the most densely populated regions of Kenya supporting livelihoods and economic development. Africa is facing an unprecedented water crisis: about 25%

of Africa's population lives in water stressed areas and this figure will rise dramatically to an estimated 500 million people by 2050. This situation is exacerbated by climate change; Africa is going to be hit the most (IPCC 2002). While some of this will be caused by climate change in arid and semiarid lands, water stress in the Mau is the result of land degradation and deforestation whose effects are widespread and are to be felt far beyond the Mau.

Kenya's forests are declining due to pressure from increased population and other land uses. Kenya is classified among the countries with low forest cover of less than 3% of the total land area. Dwindling forest cover has a severe effect on the climate, wildlife, streams, and the human population, especially forest dwellers.

Recently, however, there have been alarming reports that the Mau ecosystem is undergoing a relentless onslaught from illegal loggers and land-grabbing farmers, including large and small recipients of political patronage. The result is a devastating fragmentation of what environmentalists call an ecological utility whose services stretch from watering Kenya's tea estates to feeding the rivers powering its hydroelectric plants, and regulating temperature and rainfall throughout an often arid land. Kenya has ignored warnings over the importance of conserving the Mau, despite being home to the UN Environment Program headquarters.

The Mara River, famous for its crossing by the massive Serengeti wildebeest migration between Tanzania and Kenya, is threatened by upstream land use change in the Mau and the uncertain impacts of climate change. These land use changes cause diverse, often violent, conflicts generated by access to land, forest, and water resources as well as interethnic political strife. Recognizing the cross-sectoral importance of reversing these trends, the Kenyan Prime Minister's office took charge of coordinating the Mau restoration.

In addition, an estimated 43,700 ha have been encroached in the remaining protected forests of the Mau. Such extensive and ongoing destruction of natural assets is a matter of national emergency. It presents significant environmental and economic threats.

Historically, the Mau was overlooked when the forest was intact and when land pressure was low. The tourist potential of the Mau has never been exploited despite its proximity to the world famous wildlife areas of the Maasai Mara National Reserve and adjoining Serengeti National Park in Tanzania. As land pressure increased, the forest was viewed as an untapped area with high potential agricultural value. This scenario coupled with the lack of a strict institutional framework in the past led to the destruction of vast areas of forest in the Mau complex.

The veteran Kenyan green campaigner and Nobel laureate, the late Wangari Maathai believed that the destruction of the Mau and other forests is possibly more damaging to the region than climate change. "Life is unsustainable in East Africa without these environmental services from forests," she once said. It could also seriously affect the Serengeti leading to the loss of the tourism dollar. There is scientific agreement on the importance of restoring the Mau for both Kenya's economy and environment, but vested interests have managed to block better protection.

Critical Role of Conservation Measures

The importance of the Mau is related to the ecosystem services it provides, such as river flow regulation, flood mitigation, water storage, water purification, recharge of groundwater, reduced soil erosion and siltation, protection of biodiversity, carbon sequestration, carbon reservoir, and regulation of microclimate, which provides favorable conditions for optimum crop production.

Command-and-control efficiency in developing countries is often restricted by weak institutions and poor governance, especially on the agricultural front (Wunder 2008). This was a likely result of a moral imperative by past political systems not to have strict prohibitions hurt poor farmers, who traditionally occupy productively marginal yet environmentally fragile lands.

However, for the Mau forest to survive in perpetuity, some of the key issues that needed to be resolved include among others a backlog in planting and clear felling, the lack of incentives for local communities to participate in protecting the ecosystem, delinking management of the forest from political interference, the lack of equipment to facilitate effective forest management and protection, the lack of resources by the Kenya Forest Service (KFS) to deal effectively with management of the forest, and having clear forest boundaries from settlement areas. The public forum recognized the need to empower communities to participate in the management of the forest. It also recognized the need to maintain a high level of professionalism among forest staff working in the area, political will, and effective application of existing legislations such as the Forests Act 2005, as well as the development of forest management guidelines within the ecosystem.

The total value of the Mau would include timber, firewood, fodder, and medicinal plants. In addition to these, it contributes to climate stabilization, water supply and filtration, and wilderness, including plants whose value may not yet even be known.

The Mau helps secure the provision of water supply to urban areas and supports the livelihood of millions of people living in rural areas. It is the home of a minority group of indigenous forest dwellers, the Ogiek. Many communities also live in the immediate surroundings of the forest, and depend extensively on the forest goods and services. Despite its critical importance to future economic development, the Mau has been impacted by extensive irregular and ill-planned settlement, as well as illegal forest resource extraction.

Conservation Efforts

No universal solutions exist to solve the problem of unsustainability in tropical forests. Approaches must be nation, site, and context specific, based on a detailed knowledge of hunting patterns and the ecology of the hunted species, and be tailored to local cultural, socioeconomic, and political conditions (Nasi et al. 2008).

Forestry management has evolved considerably in the past decades, demonstrating significant positive impacts for biodiversity conservation, while also delivering social and economic benefits to host communities (CBD 2009, p. 13).

There have been many changes in forest management and thinking in Africa and globally, as well as an increase in forest products and services consumption, which justify the rekindling of interest in dry forests. However, water resources, specifically the Mau, require management planning in which biodiversity conservation objectives are identified for stakeholders.

Relocation of Illegal Squatters

However, there has been concerted effort to relocate over 2500 families from the southwestern Mau forest reserve in order to save some 19,000 ha of forest land. The exercise did generate controversy when it started following recommendations by the Mau Task Force: "Encroachers should be removed from the forests immediately" (Mau Task Force Secretariat 2009, p. 13). The eviction exercise stressed the humane approach in order to ensure peaceful relocation where the squatters are assured of transport, security, food supplies, education, and health services for their families.

There have been other efforts to engage both the government and local capacities in rehabilitation of the Mau catchment.

Efforts by the Government

A report by KFS (2007) reiterates that there has been significant political will to address issues of conservation in the catchment area as demonstrated in the draft Constitution, the Economic Recovery Strategy and Vision 2030. A draft forest policy (2006) is in place, and a new Forests Act (2005) came into effect in February 2007. The key provisions include establishment of the semiautonomous KFS, and an increased role for local communities and other stakeholders in the management of forests. The government has made some conservation efforts:

- Replanting of approximately 7000 ha of forestland in the Mau by the Ministry of Forestry and Wildlife, Interim Coordinating Secretariat (2011).
- The Ministry of State for Defense has started replanting 1000 ha.
- Process to rehabilitate riverine reserves ongoing (WRMA). The Ministry of Environment and Mineral Resources is currently supporting the rehabilitation of the watersheds of Lake Nakuru.

Efforts by the Private Sector

Efforts by the private sector has led to MoUs with the World Wildlife Fund, African Wildlife Foundation, Malaika Ecotourism and Save the Mau Fund, Kenya Wildlife Service, Equity Bank, Nation Media Group, East African Breweries Limited, and the Green Belt Movement. Tree planting has been carried out by Kenya Tourism Board, Serena Hotels, Miss Kenya, Moi University, and Egerton University, among others.

Community Participation

Pro-Mara's conflict reduction through conservation has many facets reaching deeply into the complex historical socioeconomic milieu of the upper Mara. Communities are supported in organizing across ethnic, gender, and age groups in formal arrangements with government to comanage forest and water resources in legally mandated Community Forest Associations and Water Resource User Associations. Pro-Mara also builds capacity of the multi-stakeholder District Peace Committees (DPC) in practical approaches to dispute management and avoidance around land and natural resources. More than 6000 individuals in government and from the Mau community (80% youth) have attended conflict mitigation trainings and meetings.

Most of the indigenous population within the Mau is semi-illiterate and this poses a challenge to raising public and political awareness on international and national biodiversity laws. Furthermore, there has never been a deliberate effort to make this study compulsory in school curriculum: topics geared to improve the availability of information on biodiversity, to transfer knowledge and technology in school libraries and to encourage the creation of specialized courses and training activities in tropical forest taxonomy, ecology, and biodiversity management.

Establishment of Ogiek Council of Elders

The Forest Action Network has an ongoing project in the Mau that aims at creating awareness among the Ogieks on policy and legal issues. This will include sensitizing them on their rights to forest resources. Efforts have been made to document information on the Ogiek's traditional forest management practices, and to organize workshops for different stakeholders of the Mau to enable them come together and work out a plan of action for achieving sustainable forest management. In an attempt to achieve this:

- Two Ogiek workshops to identify candidates for the Ogiek Council of Elders was held on December 18, 2009 and February 5, 2010.
- Consultations with Ogiek communities in all main areas where the Ogiek reside started from March 15–19, 2010.

- Ogiek indigenous Council of Elders was established on April 1, 2010.
- A committee to deal with the Ogiek indigenous community matters was constituted on April 1, 2010.

Mandate of the Ogiek Council of Elders

According to the Interim Secretariat (2011), the mandate of the council of elders for the indigenous community of Ogiek includes and is not limited to

- Assisting in the establishment of an Ogiek Register based on lineages
- Development of proposals for resettling the Ogiek
- Developing proposals involving the Ogiek community in the restoration of the Mau Forest complex
- Developing proposals to support livelihood development in the Ogiek community, as well as traditional Ogiek livelihoods

Pro-Mara activities combine to create genuine hope in Mau communities and in government officials that they are empowered to work together, as they have not before, to conserve their natural resources, while improving livelihoods and mitigating deep-seated conflicts. Such efforts as mentioned above as well as others have led to successful reclamation of vast hectares of land for forest reserves in the Mau.

Extensive encroachments into the gazetted forest areas led to major evictions carried out in 2005 and 2006 by a combined force of KFS, Administration Police, and Kenya Wildlife Service. However, some evictees later returned to some parts of the forests due to lack of monitoring and enforcement by KFS at that time and because of the government's inability to provide them with alternative land. This prompted action by the government and nongovernmental organizations to come up with an institutional framework to be implemented by the Joint Enforcement Unit. The Joint Enforcement Unit was institutionalized on July 28, 2008 to coordinate and implement rules and regulations against illegal activities in the water catchment areas. This led to a lower record of illegal activities including encroachment, logging of trees, and charcoal burning. Timber has been impounded and destroyed in an attempt to secure the Mau.

Efforts by Narok University College

Narok University College (NUC) has been in the forefront in mobilizing resources and the local community in tourism development and promotion, through partnership with other stakeholders. It endeavors to promote maintenance of the natural environment, more efficient use of natural resources and a decrease in waste production. Consequently, NUC offers courses in horticultural science and management, seed science and technology, animal science and management, and human resource management. These programs are geared toward developing local capacities in policymaking, planning, management, and development of their resources in a more sustainable way. NUC has environmental education as a core unit for all undergraduate courses. This is expected to raise student consciousness about conservation efforts.

Recently, the university has tried to conduct community outreach programs in building local capacities and in creating awareness to conserve threatened areas of the Mau. Achieving this delicate balance has been successful through partnering with the local communities and other stakeholders.

Recommendations

Decision makers ought to consider in earnest the need to involve local stakeholders in policy formulation. The formulation of integrated and comprehensive policy reforms geared toward attaining sustainable development is crucial.

Advocacy and Public Awareness

Priority should be given to education and the awareness of the public's role, rights, and responsibilities in conserving and managing forests, including the need to protect the water catchment resources against encroachment, logging of trees, and other deforestation activities.

Curriculum Reform Incorporating Awareness Building

There is need to integrate and make compulsory in the local school curriculum such topics geared to improve the availability of information on biodiversity and transfer of knowledge and technology in school libraries and encourage the creation of specialized courses and training activities in tropical forest taxonomy, ecology, and biodiversity management.

Strengthening Institutional Frameworks

The objective is to monitor physical/environmental changes with a view to counteract the observed changes in order to enhance the potential of the forest. Concerns about global changes, especially those stemming from demands that African forests too shall provide global public goods and services, and regarding environmental protection in particular, are reflected in various international arrangements including treaties and conventions. This new understanding needs to be brought to the attention of policymakers. This calls for a better way of making the case for dry forests at the national, subregional, regional, and global levels.

Participation of Local Stakeholders

Decentralization and devolution of administration and increased emphasis on community participation are key issues in forest management. Authorities should consider the promotion of public participation in planning and decision making so that all stakeholders have ownership of the process of conserving the Mau catchment area and other water resources.

Building Conservation Strategy Partnerships

There is a deliberate need to increase the roles for the private sector in forestry production and processing. An increase in the role of civil society—especially national and international nongovernmental organizations—in influencing forest resource management, particularly through their advocacy role and also through direct involvement in forestry initiatives in supporting community participation will be a big boost in strengthening conservation activities.

Conclusion

The Mau faces problems related to land tenure issues. Policy intervention should ensure not only that participatory forest management is implemented but also secure the property rights of the various stakeholders. The involvement of local institutions at all levels of decision making should be encouraged. All stakeholders including the Ogiek should be represented in decision making concerning the management of the forest and resource use.

Awareness on and advocacy for sustainable forest management should also be considered and where it is already taking place, efforts should be enhanced.

Further policy interventions are needed for the promotion of conservation of forests through sustainable harvesting, forest business, and ecotourism. Building the capacity of forest users, including the provision of technical knowledge in forestry relevant fields such as species enrichment and management regimes, is crucial and should be undertaken in earnest in the area.

Concerted efforts should be made to deal with the underlying causes of deforestation involving all the actors responsible. In Kenya, the Inter-Parties Parliamentary Group is working on a constitutional review and will work on a change of policies to suit the current reality. They intend to accommodate the view of all Kenyans by organizing consultative meetings for the public. Civil society is also creating awareness on conservation and policy issues.

Ecosystem goods and services in the Mau are threatened more than ever before by human activity. Both the government and more particularly those living within the Mau ecosystem are now paying the price for over 30 years of neglect. Neither the remaining indigenous forests nor the forest plantations can sustain the demand for charcoal and timber. This calls for different approaches, including tremendous increase in tree planting on farms.

Success stories with restoration following relocation exist in Kenya. There have been recent successes in both the Mt. Kenya and Aberdare forests. The restoration of the Mau is physically feasible even if it is socially and politically complex, and it is in the national interest that action be taken immediately to avoid irreversible damage to a vital ecosystem. The initiative and long-term commitments must come from the government and the people. For those already living in the forest, they must be made aware of the environmental and socioeconomic impacts and that relocation and resettlement is to their own interest as well as to the interest of the nation.

Policy intervention to support the initiatives of the former Prime Minister must be made in providing technical assistance and facilitating support services aiming to deliver a highly participatory project preparation process, which includes establishment of effective institutional arrangements, monitoring and enforcement, boundary survey and demarcation, preparation of a resettlement framework policy for the Mau, logistics for the relocation of people residing in the forests or critical catchment areas, provision of livelihood support to the people who have been relocated, livelihood development, public awareness and sensitization, rehabilitation of degraded areas, strategic management plans and forest-specific management plans, development of project proposals, and convening of meetings with development partners to secure financial sustainability.

References

Government of Kenya (GoK) and UNEP. 2008. Mau complex and Marmanet forests, environmental and economic contributions. Briefings notes. UN Environment Program. Retrieved from http://www.unep.org/pdf/Mau-Complex_20May08.pdf. Accessed 8/26/14.

Intergovernmental Panel on Climate Change (IPCC). 2002. Climate Change and Biodiversity: IPCC Technical Paper V. New York: UN.

Interim Coordinating Secretariat. 2011. Rehabilitating the water towers towards sustainable development. The case of Mau Complex. Retrieved from http://www.maurestoration.go.ke/index.php/downloads/cat_view/40-presentations. Accessed on 8/26/14.

Joint Enforcement Unit. 2010. Securing forests resources in the Mau forest complex. Retrieved from http://www.maurestoration.go.ke/ … /53-joint-enforcement-unit-1st-progress. Accessed 8/25/14.

Kenya Forest Service (KFS). 2007. Forest law enforcement and governance in Kenya. A paper prepared for the East African community-led regional process in the framework of the Ministerial Declaration, Yaoundé, Cameroon, October 16, 2003 on the Africa Forest Law Enforcement and Governance (AFLEG).

Mau Task Force Secretariat. 2009. *Report of the Prime Minister's Task Force on the Conservation of Mau Forests Complex*, PM's Office, Nairobi.

Nasi, R., D. Brown, D. Wilkie, E. Bennett, C. Tutin, G. van Tol, T. Christophersen. 2008. Conservation and use of wildlife-based resources: The bushmeat crisis. Secretariat of the Convention on Biological Diversity, Montreal, and Center for International Forestry Research (CIFOR), Bogor. Technical Series No. 33, 50pp.

Reconnaissance Flight. 2008. Mau Complex and Marmanet forests, environmental and economic contributions, current state and trends. Retrieved from http://www.unep.org/pdf/Mau-Complex_20May08.pdf. Accessed 8/25/14.

Rehabilitation of the Mau Forest Ecosystem. A project concept prepared by the Interim Coordinating Secretariat, Office of the Prime Minister, on behalf of the Government of Kenya. September 2009. Retrieved from http://www.kws.org/export/sites/kws/info/maurestoration/maupublications/Mau_Forest_Complex_Concept_paper.pdf. Accessed 8/25/14.

Secretariat of the Convention on Biological Diversity. 2009. *Sustainable Forest Management, Biodiversity and Livelihoods: A Good Practice Guide.* Montreal, 47 + iii pages. Retrieved from http://www.cbd.int/development/doc/cbd-good-practice-guide-forestry-booklet-web-en.pdf. Accessed 8/25/14.

Secretariat of the Convention on Biological Diversity. 2009. CBD Program of Work on Forest Biodiversity. Montreal. Retrieved from http://www.cbd.int/decision/cop/?id=7196. Accessed 8/25/14.

Wunder, S. 2008. Necessary conditions for ecosystem services payments. Conference paper. Economics and Conservation in the Tropics—A Strategic Dialogue (January 31–February 1). Retrieved from http://www.rff.org/Documents/08_Tropics_Conference/Tropics_Conference_Papers/Tropics_Conference_Wunder_PES_markets.pdf. Accessed 8/25/14.

Chapter 8

Toward Environmental Sustainability

The Case of the Torgorme Irrigation Project in Ghana

Joseph K. Adjaye and Kwesi Korboe

Contents

Introduction

One challenge confronting our times is environmental sustainability. Environmental preservation is essential for sustainable development and poverty reduction. Yet, environmental degradation and loss continue at an alarming and often an irreversible rate. The main causes of environmental degradation include

- Habitat loss and climate change
- Population growth, migration, and displacement of people caused by political instability
- Land overexploitation induced by increasing poverty
- Environmental damage caused by extractive industries
- Short-sighted development policies
- Lack of effective land management programs

Using the Torgorme Irrigation Project (TIP) in Ghana as a case study and model in sustainable development, this chapter provides a good illustration of how sound participatory management and governance strategies by smallholder farmer organizations and the application of good agricultural standards and protocols in a local irrigation-based project can contribute to environmental sustainability. The study offers recommendations, including the imperative to confront the issue of sustainability within multiple integrative approaches, policy applications and implementation strategies, and ground policies and practices against specificities of local socioecological contexts, and recognizes the concerns of the rural South rather than those of the North.

Sustainable Development

Concerns about environmental preservation in ways that simultaneously promote development have led to the pursuit of "sustainable development," that is, development and maintenance of ecosystem services (natural resources, air, and water quality) at levels that allow future generations access to these resources that do not compromise the needs of the present (Adams 1995; Dryzek 1997). The Brundtland Report defined sustainable development (The World Commission on Environment and Development 1987).

However, in many respects, the 1992 (Rio) UN Conference on Environment and Development, popularly referred to as the Earth Summit, provided the blueprint for environmental sustainability. Unprecedented in the size and scope of its concerns—172 governments and 2400 NGO representatives participated—the overriding issues were the environment and sustainable development. The summit framed economic development in new ways that linked it to the need to halt the destruction of irreplaceable natural resources and the pollution of the planet.

Reaffirming the Stockholm (1972) Declaration of the UN Conference on Human Environment and recognizing the integral and interdependent nature of the earth, the Rio Declaration (1992) issued a global agenda for sustainable development and proclaimed, *inter alia*, that

- Everyone is entitled to a healthy and productive life in harmony with nature.
- The right to development must be fulfilled in ways that equitably meet the developmental and environmental needs of present and future generations.
- To achieve sustainable development, environmental protection shall constitute an integral part of the development process.
- Eradicating poverty is an indispensable requirement for sustainable development, in order to decrease the disparities in standards of living and better meet the demands of the majority of people in the world.
- The special situations and needs of developing countries, particularly the least developed and those most environmentally vulnerable, shall be given special priority.
- In view of their disproportionate contributions to global environmental degradation, developed countries acknowledge the tremendous responsibility that they bear in the international pursuit of sustainable development.

The Declaration also proclaimed that environmental issues are best handled with the participation of all concerned citizens; that women have a role in environmental management and development; that the creativity, ideals, and courage of youth should be mobilized to forge a global partnership in order to achieve sustainable development and ensure a better future for all; and that indigenous people and other local communities have a role in environmental management and development because of their knowledge and traditional practices.

The underlying principle of sustainable development adopted at Rio further incorporated the concept of social justice (Falk et al. 1993, p. 2):

> Equity derives from a concept of social justice. It represents a belief that there are some things which people should have, that there are basic needs that should be fulfilled, that burdens and rewards should not be spread too divergently across the community and that policy should be directed with impartiality, fairness, and justice towards these ends.

During the 1992 summit, the Convention on Biological Diversity (CDB), the UN Framework Convention on Climate Change (UNFCC), the Statement of Forest Principles, and the Convention to Combat Desertification were all adopted along with the Commission on Sustainable Development (CSD). In sum, the

Summit's message underscored the complexity of the problem of environmental sustainability, that poverty as well as excessive consumption by affluent populations place damaging stress on the environment, and that governments should recognize the need to redirect national and international plans and policies to ensure that all economic decisions fully take into account their environmental impact.

Millennium Development Goals

The Earth Summit has influenced all subsequent UN conferences that have examined the relationship between human rights, population, social development, women, and human settlements and the need for environmentally sustainable development. At the 2000 UN Millennium Summit, for instance, leaders from the richer industrialized countries and poorer developing world embraced a vision for a world in which all nations would work in partnership for the betterment of the planet, especially regions inhabited by the most disadvantaged. They committed themselves to a set of targets along a path toward ending extreme poverty worldwide by 2015. To provide a framework by which progress could be measured, this vision was translated into 8 MDGs, 18 targets, and 48 indicators. Collectively, MDGs aim at combating poverty, hunger, disease, illiteracy, environmental degradation, and discrimination against women. In particular, the seventh goal is environmental sustainability, wherein governments were enjoined to "integrate principles of sustainable development into country policies and program [and] reverse the loss of environmental resources" (see Chapter 1 for a discussion of MDGs).

Subsequently, The World Summit on Sustainable Development (WSSD) that took place in Johannesburg in 2002 further placed land reform, environmental sustainability, and social justice at the heart of sustainable development. Then, in 2012, at the third Earth Summit commonly known as Rio + 20, the heads of state of the 192 governments in attendance renewed their commitment to sustainable development and the promotion of a sustainable future. Today, the MDGs have become acceptable reference points for governments, international development organizations, civil society, the scientific community, and social movements working to ensure the sustainability of our earth.

But to what extent have these goals been pursued, and with what success? Some observers might claim that the message put forth by the Earth Summit, MDG Summit, and other international bodies has produced positive results, making eco-efficiency a guiding principle for business and governments alike. Indeed, it has been noted that

- Patterns of production—particularly the production of toxic components, such as lead in gasoline, or poisonous waste—are being scrutinized in a systematic manner by the UN and governments alike.
- Alternative sources of energy are being sought to replace the use of fossil fuels, which are linked to global climate change.

- A new reliance on public transportation systems is being emphasized in order to reduce vehicle emissions, congestion in cities, and the health problems caused by polluted air and smog.
- There is a much greater awareness of and concern over the growing scarcity of water.

However, these are very modest gains. In fact, we continue to suffer environmental degradation and loss as well as environmental change at an alarming rate.

Environmental Change

A further attributable cause of the degradation of our environment is environmental change. The unprecedented scale and alarming rate at which the earth is being transformed by human activities have increasingly raised concerns about the earth's sustainability. One prime source of global environmental change is the ballooning of the human population. UN world population data (http://www.un.org/esa/population) indicate that whereas it took about 150 years (1750–1900) for the world's population to more than triple from 0.7 to about 2.5 billion, it only took 40 years (1950–1990) for the population to double again to 5 billion. And then another 1 billion people were added to the world's population between 1995 and 2008. This unprecedented growth in human population, which has been accompanied by escalated resource consumption and local land-use changes, has placed increasing stress on the ability of biological systems to support human needs (Foley et al. 2005). Consequently, sustainability has been a major guiding principle in environmental policy and decision making undertaken by several international bodies, as noted above. Within the scientific community, the emerging field of land-change science (LCS) has evolved, seeking to promote an understanding of the dynamics of the land system as a coupled human–environment system (CHES) based on the realization of the intertwining of the social and biophysical subsystems of the environment (Turner 2010).

Also in the forefront of the quest for an integrated understanding of environmental change is The Global Land Project (GLP, http://www.globallandproject.org), jointly established by the International Human Dimensions Program on Global Environmental Change (IHDP, http://www.ihdp.org/) and the International Geosphere Biosphere Program (IGBP, http://www.igbp.net/), both promoting LCS for environmental sustainability (Osaki and Braimoh 2010).

Despite all these efforts, environmental sustainability remains an elusive goal in many respects while global poverty is increasing rather than reducing. UN performance reports, for instance, indicate that progress toward the attainment of the MDGs as a whole remains below expectations in Africa. Indeed, as regards economic growth, taking the West African subregion, for example, despite an overall satisfactory performance averaging above 5% over the past few years, growth has not been as strong and sustainable at 7% or above, as required to achieve the MDGs. For the entire subregion, economic growth stood at 3.7% in 2001, then fell to 2.6% in 2002. In 2003 and 2004, the subregion recorded a very good performance at 7.3%. However, this performance could not be sustained and it fell to 5.1% in 2005 before increasing slightly to 6.1% in 2006. The rate fell again in 2007 to 5.1% (ECOWAS 2002–2008). Following the deep global financial crisis and economic recession of the late 2008 and early 2009, the estimated economic growth rate for the subregion was around 4.1% in 2009 (ECA-WA 2010).

Furthermore, according to United Nations Conference on Trade and Development (UNCTAD), poverty estimates show that on average, one person out of two in the least developed countries (mostly Africans) lives on less than US$1 a day and projections show that this number will continue to increase instead of reducing by the 2015 deadline for achieving the MDGs, if current trends persist.

It is these worsening conditions in the developing world, especially among the rural poor, that drove "La Via Compensina," an umbrella organization of indigenous peoples in Africa, Asia, Europe, and the Americas dedicated to promoting global agrarian reform, food sovereignty, and a peasant-based agro-economy to institute a Call to Action to coincide with the 2012 Rio Summit that was held to mark the 20th anniversary of the Earth Summit. Advocates of "La Via Compensina" charged that after 20 years, life has become more difficult for the majority of the planet's inhabitants. The number of hungry people has increased to almost 1 billion, which means that one out of every six human beings is going hungry, women and small farmers being the most affected. Meanwhile, the environment is depleting fast, biodiversity is being destroyed, and water resources are getting scarce and contaminated. They claim, in particular, that the framework of "sustainable development" continues to see peasant agriculture as backwards and responsible for the deterioration of natural resources and the environment.

Intergenerational Equity and Land Sustainability

Interestingly, the guiding principles of groups such as "La Via Compensina" are much akin to those of Africa and other third-world societies where land is the basis of life, providing not only sustenance but also legitimacy to autochthonous claims. For these reasons, societal leaders, including family and lineage elders as well as kings, were traditionally entrusted with custody of land and its embedded resources. These indigenous leaders carried the dual responsibility of ensuring the integrity of these resources from encroachment and alienation, and equity in access. Equity was understood inherently as a right not only to be enjoyed by the present generation but also assured for their progeny. Thus, our forefathers tacitly acknowledged the notions of not only environmental sustainability for future generations but also intergenerational equity. In fact, the Akan and most Ghanaian societies acknowledged the ideal of intergenerational equity on moral/ethical, contractual/usufructuary, and ontological grounds.

Intergenerational equity is premised on the recognition that present decisions can have irreversible consequences on the future, and since the unborn are unable to protect their interests in present decision-making processes, intergenerational equity should be pursued to assure their right to inheritable land resources. It also derives from the recognition that there is complementarity between natural capital (NC), that is, eco-social systems, and human capital (HC), and hence, between people living in a specific time and their culture, skills, knowledge, and institutions. Thus, principles of environmental sustainability were inherent in indigenous land tenure systems.

Equity in access and entitlement to land and its embedded resources is entrenched in international law, for example, the Universal Declaration of Human Rights, which upholds that the "inherent dignity and ... the equal and inalienable rights of all members of the human family is the foundation of freedom, justice and peace in the world," principles that are also entrenched in Ghanaian customary law. Thus, in Western and African legal traditions, there is an implicit contractual vision of a moral obligation for environmental sustainability for future generations (Barrett 1996).

The traditional conception of people's relationship to their environment among the Akan and Ewe of Ghana, for example, was anthropocentric, that is, people valued the environment for its usefulness to humanity, rather than for its own sake; it was human centered. Interestingly, a large segment of thought in contemporary environmental ethics favor this view even though nonanthropocentric voices, that is, love of the environment for its own sake exist in the debate (Buchdahl and Raper 1998). Thus, conceptions of equity and environmental justice that are acknowledged in current international law were recognized under Ghanaian customary and normative systems.

And so were principles of environmental and distributional justice, which were conceived of in a communitarian and utilitarian sense (O'Neill 2000). The Brundtland Report is emphatic on egalitarianism, insisting that "inequality is the planet's main environmental problem" and that sustainability would be futile without efforts to address the problem of global inequality. Indeed, a number of scholars advancing the ethical dimensions of sustainability and international environmental management base their positions on traditional conceptions of justice (Grubb et al. 1992; Anand 2004).

Traditional conceptions of equity were also based on perceptions of the intimate interdependence of humankind and the ecological system, principles that still underlie climate change and global justice today. Equity was a normatively accepted principle based on the acknowledgment that all individuals have a *prima facie* entitlement to the necessities of life. The environment, in terms of its natural resources, constitutes an NC that should be available equitably to all.

Environmental Sustainability

The TIP near Akuse, Ghana was implemented by the Millennium Development Authority (MiDA) under the Millennium Challenge Account (MCA) program with funding from the Millennium Challenge Corporation (MCC), an initiative of the U.S. government. The Government of Ghana, eligible to access funds under this initiative, put together a proposal for funding that aimed at increasing the productivity and business skills of farmers as one of three key objectives toward its goal of poverty reduction via economic growth. As part of its agriculture infrastructure, MiDA is funding the development of 450 ha under the Kpong Left Bank Irrigation Scheme as a start-up for smallholder farmers who have been constituted to form Farmer Based Organizations (FBOs), and medium-sized farmers, out of a total of 2000 ha of land it acquired at Torgorme in the North Tongu District of the Volta Region. About 1000 farmers will eventually be allocated an average of 1 acre of land to farm, with medium-sized farmers being allocated on the average 10 ha each. The TIP is projected to be the largest irrigation development activity under the MCA.

Empowerment of Small-Scale Farmers

To ensure sustainability, a number of interventions were identified and developed such as linking the farmers to Vegpro Ghana Ltd., a subsidiary of Vegpro Kenya Ltd., as an off-taker, providing farmers access to export markets, and contracting a private operator to manage the irrigation scheme. Vegpro Ghana Ltd. has acquired 1070 ha of land adjacent to the scheme for production of high-value vegetables for export to the European Union.

To ensure financial sustainability, farmers and other users of the main canals pay an irrigation services charge (ISC), which comprises operation and maintenance cost, land rent, water rights fee, the Ghana Irrigation Development Authority (GIDA) regulatory fee, and a mandatory fee for equipment replacement set at 5% of the total cost. The ISC per acre per year was initially estimated at GH¢ 209.59 for farmers using the secondary and tertiary canals and GH¢ 157.75 for the anchor farmer, approximately $90 and $71, respectively.

It is worth noting that the adoption of the private–public partnership (PPP) as the strategic approach to managing the scheme was, to a large extent, driven by the goal of promoting the sustainability and profitability of the irrigation scheme. Finally, the strategy of establishing and strengthening of FBOs is a gradual process and will take time. Smallholder farmers will need to adapt quickly from the present almost-subsistence level to a more commercial, market-oriented agriculture. Intensive training of FBOs was undertaken in the initial years to enable them cultivate high-value crops for export as well as to ensure their full participation.

The TIP's overall aims are to enable farmers to cultivate high-value vegetables—primarily baby maize, butternut squash, and chillies—for export;

create job opportunities and a source of income for people in the affected communities and their environs, improve the standard of living of the people in the communities in line with the Government of Ghana's policy of poverty reduction and wealth creation, and improve social infrastructure and amenities in the affected communities. Torgorme, along with Azagornorkope, Fodzoku, Sokope and Nakpoe, are the towns directly affected by the project, while 17 other communities are indirectly benefited.

TIP Management and Local Participation

The Kpong Left Bank Irrigation Scheme's management structure is a model in participatory management. To ensure sustainability of the project, a Scheme Management Entity (SME) was set up under a PPP that is responsible for the operations and management of the project. A seven-member appointed Stakeholders Governing Board (SGB) provides general governance and oversight, made up of two representatives from FBOs, and one representative each from medium-sized farmers, the Ghana Irrigation Development Authority, the district agriculture director of the Ministry of Food and Agriculture, Vegpro, and a representative from the private sector with a legal background, in line with the organization and management manual prepared for the scheme. In addition, a representative of the traditional authorities and the SME serve as honorary (nonvoting) members. The direct stakeholders thus include ACDI-VOCA, MoFA, GIDA, Vegpro Ghana Ltd., Syngenta (a service provider), the North Tongu District Assembly, chiefs and traditional leaders of the traditional areas, FBOs, the SME, and the SGB, along with a number of indirect stakeholders. In addition, a nine-member Torgorme Investment Committee has been formed to oversee the collection, investment, and disbursement of land rent income in the communities on behalf of the Torgorme Traditional Council. This is a useful instrument in diffusing social tensions and ensuring transparency and accountability.

Role of FBOs

The 20 FBOs that have so far been formed and trained are the project beneficiaries. All FBOs have to be registered as cooperatives for the project, with properly constituted internal structures and governance mechanisms to guide the conduct of members and a transparent system of administration, financial management, and record keeping. Some responsibilities of FBOs in the project include ensuring good internal administration and governance, for example, resolving local disputes among members and applying disciplinary actions; keeping records for each farming season; serving as out growers for the anchor farmers; and coordinating with the SME in the collection and payment of irrigation service charges (ISC) and in land allocation, water distribution, and other supportive services offered by the SME. Other major responsibilities relate to managing credit for FBO members where necessary, serving as a link between farmers and anchor/mid-sized farmers, and actively participating in the operation and maintenance of lateral and secondary canals.

TIP and Environmental Sustainability

Environmental Standards Checklist

A checklist was prepared to serve as a guide for farmers and FBOs in the TIP to comply with the environmental standards associated with GlobalGap and other protocols under the arrangement of VGL. Standards and protocols of relevance in the operations of VGL include Tesco Natures Choice (TNC), Fairtrade (FT), and Marks & Spencer Field to Fork. The standards for food, for instance, combine food safety with environmental, health, workers' health, and safety requirements. In short, protocols emphasize environmental preservation, workers' health and well-being, and safety. They function as a self-assessment tool.

Farmers and FBOs use the checklist to verify that they have implemented the recommended practices that are aimed at compliance with environmental standards associated with GlobalGap and other protocols. GlobalGap aims to change the attitudes of management and workers from being purely production oriented to being fully aware of the impact their operations have on consumers, society, and the environment, and requires growers to follow a minimum performance standard with defined criteria intended to stop or mitigate any adverse effects on their production processes.

Good Agricultural Practices

Good agricultural practices also respect the environment and labor legislation as well as the principle of equal pay for all types of labor. The adoption of good agricultural practices makes the production processes benign to the environment, assuring the supply of better-quality products more acceptable to consumers and improving the lots of people who depend on agriculture for their survival and well-being.

Good agricultural practices is the application of available knowledge to the utilization of the natural resource base in a sustainable way for the production of safe, healthy food, and nonfood agricultural products in a humane manner, while achieving economic viability and social stability. As part of its capacity-building plan, the TIP trains farmers and FBOs to adopt the concept of good agricultural practices. The TIP also encourages good soil and water management and conservation practices that favor plant coverage, stimulate biological activity, reduce soil compaction, and nutrient losses, and minimize silting of water bodies and the contamination of adjacent areas. Inadequate management of irrigation and fertigation can cause excessive water and energy consumption, and adversely affect equipment maintenance.

The adoption of correct procedures assures workers' health, satisfactory yields, and environmental preservation. Integrated pest, diseases, and weed management are preferred, utilizing cultural and biological methods whenever possible, instead of chemical methods (pesticides). Good harvest practices contribute to wholesome vegetable produce, favor market acceptance, minimize dissemination of chemical, physical, and biological contaminants, reduce health hazards of workers and consumers, and preserve the environment.

Hygiene, Safety, and Workers' Well-Being

TIP recognizes that it is fundamental to train employees to reduce the risk of chemical, physical, and biological contamination of people, the produce, and the work environment. Observance of the pertinent legislation avoids problems and penalties and assures a healthy workplace. Cleanliness habits and adequate working conditions prevent contamination and reduce the incidence of health problems for personnel and consumers.

Environmental Management

Environmental management in agricultural enterprises is fundamental for the maintenance of soil and water quality, for the conservation of biological resources, and for the quality of life of the local population. The TIP ensures that all activities during all phases of work are performed in accordance with environmental regulations. Compliance with GlobalGap and other environmental standards/protocols is absolutely essential to control microbial risk to ensure good quality produce for the export market, sustain or conserve the natural resource base, and protect human health. Contamination by microbial pathogens can only result from external environmental sources at some point from production to food preparation. The TIP recognizes that the best approach to maintaining wholesome nature and safe consumption of edible horticultural products is to be aware of risks and identify and establish management practices to minimize the chance of external and internal contamination at every step from growing to selling.

Direct and Indirect Benefits of the TIP to Affected Communities

The project has created job opportunities for over 1000 smallholder farmers who cultivate high-value crops for export. Vegpro Ghana Ltd. has also provided employment for about 600 persons in the community in its initial operations. Other jobs that are being created in the communities include tractor operators, hired laborers, factory hands, and security personnel.

Further, commercial vegetable production has brought new job opportunities for women by way of improving their situation within the agriculture and trading sectors. It is envisaged that many women will be employed especially for the packaging of vegetables for export. Also, as more workers from outside settle in the area, industrious women will expand opportunities for catering and trading since there will be an increased demand for food, goods, and services.

In addition, farmers have a regular source of income. Farming activities are more regular and irrigation facilities have been expanded to hundreds of smallholder farmers who are now able to cultivate high-value export crops. Through the activities of Vegpro Ghana Ltd, an anchor investor, and other mid-sized farmers, modern technology for the production and export of vegetables has been transferred to farmers and interested indigenous entrepreneurs to boost the production of vegetables in the country. All these have resulted in improvement in the standard of living in line with Ghana's policy of poverty reduction and wealth creation.

The TIP additionally provides a number of indirect benefits, including improvement of social amenities and infrastructure, opening up of the area to commercial farming, enhancement of financial and nonfinancial credit facilities, increased revenue, and overall expanded investment opportunities to the North Tongu District and adjoining areas.

Critiques

The project has faced a number of challenges with respect to commencement of production by many of the farmers. Although generally recognizing that the project helps in mitigating poverty and creating wealth by way of cultivation of new crops, adoption of new marketing strategies, training, and access to credit, farmers are unhappy about implementation and operational delays as well as the level of compensation they received for their crops and land. The delay in development has resulted in loss of income for the farmers who have not had access to land to produce for markets and their household consumption even though they have received training on the production of high-value vegetables using facilities provided by Vegpro Group with the support of Agribusiness Systems International (ASI) and funding from the Export Development Agricultural Investment Fund.

Recommendations and Conclusion

The issue of environmental sustainability contributes to our understanding of the interface between economic processes, political power, and ecological transformation, and how we should confront the question of sustainability within the context of multiple approaches, policy applications, and implementation strategies.

There is the need for equitable sharing of the costs of global environmental policies between the rich and poor nations (Beckerman and Pasek 2001). Indeed, the developed world should bear a greater responsibility for damaging the environment through high levels of consumption, resource depletion, waste accumulation, global warming, and chemical contamination—all results of affluence, not poverty. The richest industrialized countries should shoulder more of the financial burden of programs relating to land biodiversity conservation.

One should be critical of corporate displacement and exploitation of rural communities, which some view as akin to a new form of imperialism, whereby the problem of sustainable development has assumed strategies by which the dominant North imposes solutions to environmental problems they have created in ways that assure financial benefits to them. Alternatively, global environmental policies are often coercively implemented in the name of conservation, resulting in programs that constrain access to land in rural communities or farmers' ability to eke out a living.

A number of approaches to sustainable development pursued by governments either reinforce or exacerbate rural–urban inequities. Without addressing the concerns of the rural poor, equity will remain merely part of the rhetoric of sustainable development rather than a central concern (Beder 2000). As one third world critic powerfully stated, "The search for sustainable development is closely linked to the solution of problems of inequity that could endanger sustainability and are against the same concept of development" (Padilla 2002, p. 73).

Sustainable development programs should move from technical management approaches to a human-centered agenda that focuses on social justice. Replanting trees, protecting wilderness areas, limiting population growth, and so on is not enough. Policies should confront the underlying principles of inequity. Alternate visions of sustainable development based on practical strategies centered on the needs of the landless and aggrieved local populations and social redistribution of land and natural resources are called for.

Sustainability should be concomitant with a minimum level of equity commitment to the future. In this respect, recognition should be given to intergenerational equity, as argued above. Current, irreversible trends in land use, if unchecked, may seriously harm the right and natural legacy of future generations. Indeed, the struggle to attain environmental sustainability is not only an obligation to the present and future generations but also a counter-hegemonic project of the South against the North for fairness in global resource use (Okereke 2006).

As exemplified by the TIP, programs about sustainability must be grounded against the background of particular socioecological and temporal contexts. It is this context specificity that drives crucial questions of "what exactly is being sustained, at what scale, by and for whom, and using what institutional mechanisms" (Sneddon, 2000, p. 525). It is only when such integrative grounded approaches are applied that creative and appropriate liaisons among academicians, government, policymakers, citizens' groups, and NGOs toward the formulation of effective strategies are enabled. As has been critiqued, "much of ecological economics is embedded within studies of industrialized societies with little leeway for addressing the vastly different historical trajectories and geographic contexts of third-world societies" (Sneddon, 2000, p. 528).

Decentralization and active local participation in the manner of the TIP are prerequisites for the success of sustainable agricultural programs. Equally important for sustainable development are programs that address redistribution of resources. The current inequitable distribution of land and natural resources and exploitative relations of production are at the root of environmental and agrarian problems in Africa. Hence, sustainable development demands the redistribution of land, and one approach is administrative decentralization, which can promote social justice (Botchie 2000).

Indeed, there is the need for land administration reform—not just decentralization and promoting community participation, but fostering responsible social interventions and developing effective linkages between the state, the corporate section, and civil society, creating equitable, accountable, and transparent strategies, and frameworks.

Further, civil society organizations have a role in promoting decentralized management and ensuring transparency in land operations. Yet, some NGOs have been criticized for upholding the positions of the superpowers that maintain existing inequalities (Amanor and Moyo 2008). The collaborative role of chiefs and local organizations is also critical in creating favorable environments not just for foreign investors and international capital, but also for programs that promote sustainable development.

Finally, as demonstrated by the TIP program, integrated approaches are required for the success of sustainable development. More work needs to be done in developing and implementing coherent, holistic, integrative local, national, and paranational policies and approaches that include the following: expanding community educational programs about land use and biodiversity maintenance and conservation; encouraging the participation of local people at all stages in the development of policies involving land use; ensuring that local people share in the benefits of agricultural programs; striking a balance between protected areas (PAs) and ecotourist environmental degradation, which often pays little attention to local needs; safeguarding constitutional protection, sanctions, and enforcement of regulations affecting land access, use, and environmental degradation; and incentivizing and financing transition to sustainable development practices.

Poverty is a complex, multidimensional condition that goes beyond the simple lack of financial resources. It could entail lack of education and skills, poor health, inadequate access to water, and sanitation services. But all too often, a measure of poverty in Africa is food insecurity. Unfortunately, rural poverty is oftentimes a direct consequence of the depletion or misuse of the natural resources upon which previous generations had depended. Conserving, managing, and using natural resources sustainably and equitably is fundamental to actions to eradicate or reduce poverty and achieve sustainable development in Africa. In this regard, the TIP provides a useful model that can be replicated in many parts of the continent.

References

Adams, W. 1995. Sustainable development? In: Johnston, R., Taylor, R., Watts, M. (eds.). *Geographies of Global Change: Remapping the World in the Late Twentieth Century.* Oxford: Blackwell, pp. 354–73.

Amanor, K., Moyo, S. (eds.). 2008. *Land and Sustainable Development in Africa.* London: Zed.

Anand, R. 2004. *International Environmental Justice: A North South Dimension.* Aldershot: Ashgate.

Barrett C. 1996. Fairness, stewardship and sustainable development. *Ecological Economics* 19: 11–17.

Beckerman, W., Pasek, J. 2001. *Justice, Posterity and the Environment.* New York: Oxford University Press.

Beder, S. 2000. Costing the Earth: Equity, sustainable development and environmental economics. *New Zealand Journal of Environmental Law* 4: 227–43.

Botchie, G. 2000. *Rural District Planning in Ghana: A Case Study.* University of Ghana, ISSER. London.

Brown, D. 2004. Environmental ethics and public policy. *Environmental Ethics* 26: 110–12.

Buchdahl, J., Raper, M. 1998. Environmental ethics and sustainable development. *Sustainable Development* 6: 92–98.

Dryzek, J. 1997. *The Politics of the Earth: Environmental Discourses.* New York: Oxford University Press.

Falk, J., Hampton, G., Hodgkinson, A., Parker, K., Rorris, A. 1993. *Social Equity and the Urban Environment.* Report to the Commonwealth Environment Protection Agency. Canberra: AGPS.

Foley, J., DeFries, R., Asner, G., Barford, C., Bonan, G., Carpenter, S., Chapin. F.S. et al. 2005. Global consequences of land use. *Science* 309: 570–73.

Grubb, M., Sebenius, J., Magalhaes, A., Subak, S. 1992. Sharing the Burden. In: Mintzer, I. (ed.). *Confronting Climate Change: Risks, Implications and Responses.* Cambridge: Cambridge University Press.

Okereke, C. 2006. Global environmental sustainability: Intergenerational equity and conceptions of justice in multinational environmental regimes. *Goeforum* 37: 725–38.

O'Neill, O. 2000. *Bounds of Justice.* Cambridge: Cambridge University Press.

Osaki, M., Braimoh, A. (eds.). 2010. Land-use change and environmental sustainability. *Sustainability Science* 5: 5–7.

Padilla, E. 2002. Intergenerational equity and sustainability. *Ecological Economics* 41: 69–83.

Rio Declaration on Environment and Development. 1992. In: Report of the United Nations Conference on the Human Environment, Stockholm, pp. 5–16. New York: United Nations.

Sneddon, C. 2000. Sustainability in ecological economics, ecology and livelihoods: A review. *Progress in Human Geography* 24: 525.

The World Commission on Environment and Development. 1987. *Our Common Future.* New York: United Nations.

Turner, B. 2010. Sustainability and forest transitions in the Southern Yucatan: The land architecture approach. *Land Use Policy* 27 (2): 170–79.

IDENTITY AND GOVERNANCE

IV

Chapter 9

Sub-Nationalist Movements in Africa

Implications for Governance and Sustainable Development

Joshua B. Forrest

Contents

This analysis concerns the recent spread of African sub-nationalist movements (both territorial separatism and full secession) where state structures are marked by growing infrastructure weakness, and then considers governance and sustainable development implications. Much of the literature on Africa either appears in denial about the proliferation of sub-nationalist movements or views them as state enemies requiring demobilization. I contend, however, that these movements represent a ground up effort to reshape political power in unstable areas, aiming for new political authority at the micro-level in the wake of macro-level dysfunction across many rural or marginalized areas.

The governance challenge is to adapt to the spread of these movements that promotes greater political security. Approaches to governance in the wake of the explosive spread of sub-nationalism have emphasized reasserting political and economic control over state territories. I would suggest an approach oriented toward greater political tolerance and inclusion of those movements in a flexible national rule that would portend greater political stability and security as well as economic sustainability (Rothchild 1997). The approach here is consistent with conflict reduction mechanisms developed by O'Leary and Stepan for nations marked by territorially separate communities in regard to their recommendation that progress toward increased security and peacebuilding can only be made through new political frameworks that incorporate territorial autonomy for those self-separated communities (O'Leary 2013).

As for development and sustainability, I suggest that new trade patterns forged as a consequence of these sub-nationalist movements imply a redirection toward localization and regionalization. Constructive economic policies for sustainability ought to favor alternative development strategies that support relatively isolated food and pastoral producers, as well as the increasingly independent markets emerging in peripheral rural areas, with many of those markets linked more to neighboring countries than to the capital cities in their own countries.

Prior to grappling with governance and development challenges, let us first analyze the causes of sub-nationalist rebellion and the factors that have recently generated its spread. My analysis contrasts with three themes in the literature. First, we have the instrumentalization perspective (Chabal 2005), noting the extent to which armed conflicts have proliferated in sub-Saharan Africa in the 1990s–2000s, and suggesting that there are various causes, including overall continent-wide economic decline, associated social alienation, and the formation of predatory rebel groups with economic plunder as a key motive; Africa's marginalization in an increasingly globalized world economy; and the intensification of violence used by neo-patrimonial rulers who have no other political or economic means to prop up their failed states—"the use of disorder as political instrument" (Chabal 2005, p. 7). In support of this, Mehler points out the "conflict-prolonging" factors in Africa—allowing for perpetuation of existing violent conflicts—as including state decline; access by warring parties to oil and other natural resources; and access by rebels to small arms and other weapons available in the global arms trade (Mehler 2005, pp. 99–123).

The second perspective holds that the spate of violence in Africa reflects "new wars" that lack a specific underlying goal or cause, but reflect a quest for power and money by largely amorphous armed actors in the wake of the weakened African nation-state (Duffield 2001; Kaldor 1999). This acknowledges new challenges to state sovereignty and border control, reflecting political and economic pressures associated with globalization, and fiscal weakening of the state domestically. This produced a multiplicity of newly empowered political actors willing to challenge state power but not necessarily aiming to obtain it. The end result is militarization, insecurity, and rebel violence, as armed groups lacking broader goals (other than plunder) continue to proliferate (Boas and Dunn 2007).

The third perspective focuses on "rebels" and "warlords" from a state-centric orientation, acknowledging state decline as responsible for opening the door to rebel proliferation, but also examining ways of restrengthening the state or of transforming rebels who have assumed control of state into nation builders (Reno 2011). This perspective underlines the decline of ideology when examining rebellions in recent years, but insists that states continue to "form the blueprint" for political mobilization, and that the recent spread of localized conflict reflects the changing character of states themselves (Reno 2011). This top-down approach emphasizes that even hardened "warlord and parochial rebels ... reflect the characters of the states that they fight" and ultimately aim to control them (not simply to break free of them) (Reno 2011, p. 30). This presumes the state-supporting system of international politics and global markets are too formidable to be overcome by sub-nationalism (Spears 2010).

My own analysis goes beyond these themes to suggest that the expansion of armed conflict in Africa in the 1990s–2000s reflects the rise of sub-nationalist movements that seek to redress grievances with multiple, long-term historical causes. Illogically configured colonial borders produced a tragic postcolonial legacy juxtaposing a large number of territories misaligned with nation-states they were designed to be part of. While many African local conflicts may lack specific ideologies and seem only to act as self-serving warlord groups or militia, there is a logical, if often indirect, configurative process at work reflecting an ongoing effort to more closely associate local social structure, grassroots economic networks, and existing social units with locally specific historical and geographic logics.

This political restructuring takes one of two forms, either (1) an overt, manifest political mobilization to promote greater territorial autonomy or complete political detachment of a region that is currently part of a nation-state, or (2) "functional separatism," a term I suggest to signify the growing irrelevance of national government authority and increasing trade independence in a given region, with that region developing its own self-sustaining economic strategies and tightening market ties with neighboring states.

In view of the deepening of both processes—overt sub-nationalist rebellion and the functional separatism of a region—governance strategies oriented toward augmenting political stability, improved security, and economic policies encouraging sustainability ought to emphasize tolerance and flexibility toward sub-nationalist movements, while avoiding the construction of an overly regulatory economic framework that might curtail emerging market networks. While an integrated nation-state continues to guide national political leaders, it is now more evident that many African states are weakly rooted, politically and economically, in the nation's social fabric; there was less of a lengthy historical process of nation-state formation in colonial Africa than in other regions (Davidson 1992). This, combined with the real-world dissipation of state-funded social programs and state-managed policy institutions in the 1990s–2000s, explains why state decline opened the door to regional and provincial actors rising up to assert autonomy.

In Africa, such an approach would reflect an understanding of the historical formation of colonial-era nation-states. Here, I refer to the fact that as capital cities were closely connected to Europe, rather than to peripheral regions, the rural countryside was viewed as ripe for economic exploitation—rather than for integration into urban economies. State governments did not emerge organically from local society; as a result, outlying regions often lacked extensive, modern infrastructure links to capital cities and developed their own local markets, often extending into and linking up with nearby nation-states (Bigman 1993; Forrest 2003; MacGaffey 1992). In contemporary Africa's weak and weakening states, this is still the case today and more so than in colonial times. A new governance approach ought to incorporate the meaning of these facts, and accept the new reality by abandoning insistence on territorial integration and state administrative control over all territories within its jurisdictions and would instead accept a wider modicum of regional self-rule and tolerance of unregulated market growth in rural territories (Menkhaus 2006/07).

Many of the peripheral African nation-states are becoming ever more economically self-reliant, while the state's inability (or refusal) to provide economic services to marginalized territories serves as grist for the mill of sub-nationalist mobilization. In many parts of the continent, outlying regions suffer the worst consequences of economic development paralysis and the retraction or dysfunction of provincial government. Economists recognize that 1980s–2000s structural adjustment marked by the withdrawal or diminution of agronomic price supports and government-provided agricultural inputs (such as fertilizer programs and agricultural extension programs) wielded negative impacts on economic development and have worsened economic inequality (Cornia 2005, p. 4). Failure to share wealth more evenly exacerbated regional inequities (Forrest 2004; Ibister 2006). Widening interprovincial differentiation in wealth distribution worsened functional separatism.

In the most marginalized, peripheral territories, citizens are left to fend for themselves (*se débrouiller*): they end up pursuing self-reliance strategies such as intensifying local agronomic and informal marketing activities. Politically, this plays into the ability of activist groups seeking to expand their separatist movements. For example, the secessionist Barotse Freedom Movement of Western Province, Zambia, created in 2011 to struggle for territorial independence on the grounds that the national government decided to abandon its long-postponed promise to provide the Western Province—the country's poorest—with economic development benefits (ZAMBIA 2011).

Such cases are likely to multiply in the wake of the continuing infrastructure, bureaucratic, and fiscal decline of African states, along with their growing inability or unwillingness to integrate outlying territories into nation-wide development processes. In rural zones located far from the center of national military power, people craft their own economies, with political power vested in local authority structures and locally enmeshed sociopolitical networks—recreating self-sustaining economies and authoritative political institutions. Here, development should be reconceptualized to emphasize sustainability of micro-level economic activities oriented toward locally determined capital accumulation processes.

In contrast to these often-isolated rural areas, a small number of marginalized regions benefit from access to lucrative natural resources such as oil, metals, or other resources, with the ability to function, under ideal circumstances, as separate would-be petrostates. Such resources inspire confidence among sub-nationalists in regard to economic self-reliance. Examples include Cabinda (Angola), South Sudan, the Delta region (Nigeria), Cyrenaica in eastern Libya (these four cases are further discussed in the next few pages), and the Anglophone secession movement in northwest and southwest Cameroon. The latter movement emerged out of a sense of discrimination against English speakers and the exploitation of those two provinces' natural resources by the Francophone government (Samah 2010, p. 244). Led by the Southern Cameroons National Council (SCNC), the movement has been fueled by popular awareness that the two Anglophone states provide approximately 70% of Cameroon's production of oil, minerals, and agriculture—but receive only 10% back in return—with the result being that the infrastructure there is notably worse than that in the Francophone states in Cameroon (Samah 2010, p. 253). As with Cabinda, South Sudan, the Delta, and Cyrenaica, western Cameroon holds potential for economic self-sustainability should it become autonomous.

Such resource-privileged redoubts represent exceptional cases. Most peripheral territories do not possess a ready supply of foreign-exchange-producing resources. Instead, their territorial residents have become impoverished and self-reliant, turning toward village-to-village bartering, agronomic, artisanal, and livestock-raising strategies and becoming integrated into the economic and social life-ways of a neighboring nation-state. This functional separatism characterizes rural zones throughout the DRC, including the Kongo region of northern DRC, which has a pro-Kongo political movement—Bundu Dia Kongo—seeking autonomy; local self-administered areas in northern and western Uganda; and many open, poorly patrolled desert areas of the Sahel. Functional separatism is further reflected in a multiplicity of borderlands that operate outside state institutions—between Guinea-Bissau and Senegal, border areas between Mauritania and Mali, Niger and Chad, Niger and Burkina Faso, Chad and the CAR, the CAR and Sudan, northern Uganda and Sudan, and borderland zones surrounding the DRC. These borders offer unmonitored crossings in forests that function as informal mercantile byways, or main routes operating "under the radar" of state officialdom (Forrest 2004).

Thus, in weak states, locally controlled economies are either (a) dominated by agronomic farming, herding, artisanal activities, and forest resource exploitation—such cases represent the majority of weak state rural areas or (b) in possession of unexploited mineral or natural resources providing potential for development once long-term stability is attained. Both represent an opportunity for sustainable development once greater political stability and security are achieved.

Such stability and security are more attainable once we reconceptualize "governance" to allow for new, locally organized, political power structures within territorially oriented communities controlled by sub-nationalists. Most power-sharing efforts in central and eastern Africa have failed to endure, Rwanda, the DRC, Ethiopia, and Angola (Lemarchand 2007, pp. 1–20; Spears 2000, pp. 105–118), because such efforts have presumed continued central state sovereignty. Instead of aiming for agreements that take for granted authoritative state control, and that seek ways of drawing regionally based actors into a centrally controlled power-sharing arrangement, the governance approach advocated here would aim for tolerance of rural-based political authorities—and acceptance of sub-nationalist territorial autonomy (Spears 2000, p. 115). This incorporates reality on the ground into a more modest approach to national governance.

State capacity continues to decline in sub-Saharan Africa, while sub-nationalist movements proliferate. In the 1990s, I was often told that Eritrea represents the one exceptional example of secession in Africa, and that it was not a prelude to a major upsurge of sub-nationalist movements or a stepping stone to more cases of successful secession. Indeed, at that time, few Africanists expected South Sudan to succeed in becoming a new, independent nation. But this is exactly what has taken place, and those two cases have inspired sub-nationalists in other weak states. Such movements include the Tuareg sub-nationalist movement in Mali; the Movement for the Emancipation of the Niger Delta (MEND) in Nigeria; the Movement for the Independence of Cabinda in Angola; Somaliland secessionists (these four movements are further discussed later in this chapter); an Anglophone separatist movement led by the Southern Cameroon's National Council in northwest and southwest Cameroon; the Ogaden Nationalist Liberation movement (Ethiopia); and Movement of Democratic Forces of Casamance (MFDC) in Senegal.

Few of these are likely to secure outright nationhood—but some will, and meanwhile, more and more sub-nationalist movements are gaining control of large territorial swathes. These movements have been growing in size and influence; many sub-Saharan African states have been unable to dampen the sub-nationalist impulse to functionally unify national administrative and economic infrastructures or maintain the prior integration of such infrastructures, much less to craft and sustain marketing linkages throughout their claimed national territories.

Implications for governance and sustainable development are profound. States and leaderships in unstable countries, instead of focusing on confrontation, would be better served to permit sub-nationalist movements a wide berth of administrative authority in the areas those movements already control. This need not be formalized in a redesign of a nation's administrative grid but can be worked out informally with rebel movements, depending on the extent of their territorial control. Newly formed market ties between peripheral economies and neighboring states ought to be allowed to function unimpeded by regulatory bodies. Such a governance and development approach would represent an acknowledgment of the limitations of centralized state power and of the nation-state integrity of Africa's weak states.

The predictable state-centric reaction to sub-nationalism has largely amounted to attempted repression, but a more effective governance approach would emphasize tolerance and negotiation, allowing the possibility of *de facto* near-self-rule in outlying provincial regions in the face of violent defiance. In terms of sustainable development, functional separatism augurs a more pragmatic approach centered on unconventional development strategies that lie outside the norm of standard market, industrial, or agriculturally based approaches. In classical economics, economic growth cannot occur without nation-state integrity, so the first priority would be to strengthen the centralized state. However, in the context of the extensive weakening of state infrastructure, especially in outlying zones, a more promising strategy would favor maximizing opportunities presented by "informal" markets; permitting deregulated exchanges across borderland areas; and allowing leadership groups in rural regions to independently pursue international supports (development aid, health care, agronomic, and veterinary research) that strengthen the crop-growing and pastoral sectors.

Before discussing this, we trace experiences of six of the most noteworthy sub-nationalist movements to dramatize the deepening of sub-nationalist assertion in Africa to make clear the extent of nation-state breakdown, independent political mobilization, rural-based economic activity, and "functional separatism" as critical factors in the generation and proliferation of such movements. This will help to establish the context for reconsidering more effective governance and sustainable development.

South Sudan

South Sudan's metamorphosis into nationhood in 2011—becoming Africa's 54th independent state, and representing the second successful recent sub-nationalist movement (following Eritrea in 1991) to achieve full independence—reflected the culmination of nearly half a century of activism and rebellion, led by the Sudan People's Liberation Movement (SPLM). The declaration of nationhood came 5 months after a February 2011 referendum in which 98.9% of southern Sudanese voted in favor of full independence (Gettleman 2011) and 6 years following a Comprehensive Peace Agreement between the SPLM and Sudan (Khartoum). Often portrayed as a principally Dinka (tribe) or Christian struggle against Muslim or Arab Sudan, the South Sudanese reflect a multiplicity of ethnic, linguistic, and mixed-race identity groups sharing a common territory whose members collectively suffered through a long history of discrimination by northerners (including British colonialists) (Forrest, 2004).

South Sudan benefits economically from access to significant oil deposits. However, this also proved a source of conflict. Political tension between South Sudan and Sudan (Khartoum) emerged within months of the new nation's birth, reflecting disagreements over access to oil fields located near the two countries' border zones, and how exactly to allocate proceeds from oil extracted from South Sudanese deposits and shipped through Sudan's oil pipelines (Garang 2012). These latter issues led to rising tensions between the two countries in late 2011, marked by violent exchanges along the border (especially in oil-rich Upper Nile State) (Garang 2012; Kron 2011)—and then an initial round of cross-border fighting beginning in January 2012 (Reeves 2012). This developed into large-scale warfare by March 2012, with the respective armies focusing on which country would control key oil fields in border states. After heavy fighting, the two parties curtailed large-scale violence in late April 2012. Agreements on oil sharing and border security were signed in September 2012 (Sudan–South Sudan War 2012).

Economic development in South Sudan hinges on oil exports: indeed, 98% of South Sudan's revenue derives from oil. The nearly 1-year delay in oil outflow due to the fighting and disagreement on the oil-sharing formula through the better part of 2012 caused a sharp break in national revenue, setting back the prospects for development (Garang 2012; Raghavan 2014). Profoundly underdeveloped in both agronomy and industrialization, this presents South Sudan with poor economic prospects.

Further, in 2013, internal political discord within the ruling SPLM of South Sudan over how best to deal with neighboring Sudan over the distribution of oil revenues began to magnify. In July 2013, President Kiir dismissed his entire Cabinet—some had opposed appeasing President al-Bashir of Sudan—replacing them with supporters more amenable to deal making with Sudan so as to assure uninterrupted oil flows to both countries (Prunier 2014). Vice President Riek Machar, until that point a defender of Kiir's policies, was dismissed from the government; Machar responded by rounding up soldiers loyal to him and embarking on a civil rebellion against Kiir's government. In November 2013, Sudan had sent a diplomatic mission to Juba, which included President al-Bashir, who sought closer ties with President Kiir, as well as seeking further oil-flow cooperation (Prunier 2014). Machar may have been resistant to Khartoum's out reach. The proto-civil war between Machar's and Kiir's forces in April 2013 proved catastrophic to South Sudan. Major battles took place in key oil-producing states (Blue Nile, Upper Nile, Jonglei, and Unity), with hundreds killed and at least 900,000 displaced, before Kiir's forces won some decisive victories and the two sides agreed to desist by the end of January 2014 (Kulish 2014). However, tensions between government and rebel army factions and between pro-Kiir supporters and pro-Machar political supporters persist and have periodically erupted in serious violence (Kulish 2014); also, local independent militia in Blue Nile and South Kordofan states have added to the unrest, clashing with government troops (Reeves 2014).

Since that time, though, oil pipelines stretching from South Sudanese states to Khartoum have continued to flow without interruption and some have increased in volume. Both countries have benefited from oil revenues (Mcneish 2014). In asserting its hard won and recently achieved political independence while remaining open to compromise with Sudan regarding oil flows, South Sudan may focus more effectively on development in the future. President Kiir's conciliatory political stance toward Sudan to reach an oil deal is perceived by outsiders to reflect Sudan's political machinations within South Sudan and President al-Bashir's successful orchestration in his favor of Juba's internal political affairs (Prunier 2014; Reeves 2012). However, Kiir's cabinet restructuring and peace making can also be seen as an effort to improve his country's security as a newly independent secessionist nation and to work toward the future development of South Sudan. South Sudan has also been seeking to build an oil pipeline to Kenya to avoid dependency on Sudan's port cities for global oil sales, but little progress has been made and in this context deal making with Khartoum can be viewed as crucial to assure South Sudan's future.

South Sudan's half-century road to independent statehood represented a remarkable political achievement, reflecting exceptional tenaciousness and alliance building of a territory-wide sub-nationalist movement. The internal and external challenges for South Sudan remain formidable. But the SPLM has a six-decade long history of overcoming what appear to be insurmountable disadvantages. South Sudan will remain independent. Despite the recent internal political conflagration, ongoing internal political tensions, and structural weakness, its sub-nationalist movement success and new nation status put it in a position to benefit from expanded oil flows. The challenge will be to redirect revenues toward grassroots development.

Somaliland

"Somaliland" is the name ascribed to what had been during the colonial and early postcolonial period the northern region of British-ruled Somalia. Post-independent Somalia descended first into dysfunctional autocracy (1960s–1970s), followed by rapidly declining state capacity (1980s), and then near-total state collapse (as of 1990) (Laitin and Samatar 1987; Lyons and Samatar 1995; Simons 1995). A sub-nationalist movement had been in the process of mobilization for the entire postcolonial period, but had suffered multiple waves of repression from the Somali state. The impact of Somalia's breakdown was to facilitate this sub-nationalist movement in assuming full political control and to govern on its own. Thus, in 1991, "Somaliland" became independent. Beyond political secession, this made it possible for an independent market to develop, and for Somaliland agriculturalists to sell goods locally without concern for confiscation or raids by southern Somali state tax collectors.

For the past two decades, while the remaining stump of the Somali nation-state remains wracked by civil war, sea piracy, and radical Islamic rebels, Somaliland has, in contrast, demonstrated remarkable stability (Jhazbhay 2003, pp. 77–82). Somaliland's political system has a two-chamber elected assembly, three competitive political parties, and an elected president with popular legitimacy, currently President Ahmed Silanyo. Somaliland elections were held in June 2010, and marked by a peaceful transfer of power from former President Hassan Dahir Riyale Kahin (who had taken office in 2002) to Silanyo; an impressive 88% of voters participated (Prunier 2010), a demonstration of the capacity of the new, self-declared Somaliland state.

The most unstable moment in Somaliland's recent history took place in September 2009, when President Kahin feared extensive violence in the capital city of Hargeisa over food price increases. Kahin called upon the armed forces to mobilize troops and consider the suspension of parliament and the upcoming elections. However, this did not take place: the armed forces refused the president's directives, emphasizing the importance of allowing parliament to continue sitting and for the 2010 presidential elections to be held (Prunier 2010).

Somaliland is a stable, autonomous parliamentary democracy, assuring that people benefit from agronomic and pastoral productivity through urban–rural barter trade and a prolific international trade. This is benefiting pastoralists with 1 million live camels, sheep, and goats exported across the Gulf of Aden to the Arab states (Haslam 2013). In addition, because of its location, Somaliland has served as a gateway between East Africa and the Arab world (Haslam 2013). This is a compelling example of how a sub-nationalist movement established and then rapidly expanded trade links with neighboring countries, establishing a multi-sector trade network.

Somaliland represents the next likely candidate for new nation status in Africa. Nonetheless, global powers within the international community largely ignore Somaliland's quest for recognition (Somaliland Another Country in Waiting 2011) while vainly seeking to prop up rump-Somalia's failed state. Somaliland makes clear to sub-nationalists that movement mobilization can culminate in successful self-rule.

Tuareg Sub-Nationalism (Northern Mali)

The pastoral Tuareg people have been engaged in a movement for greater regional autonomy sporadically during the French colonial era and then in earnest from 1963 to the present. Their struggle, fomented by long-term ethnic discrimination by political elites and the Malian government, has included armed resistance with Mali's armed forces often countered with vicious repression (Lecocq 2010). As they expanded their movement, the Tuaregs benefited from crafting a self-sustaining economy based on livestock and also from trade with local agriculturalists and with neighboring Niger, Algeria, and Mauritania. They have also benefited from geographic isolation, a nomadic lifestyle, porous borders, and from worsening Malian state dysfunction.

In the 1990s, the Tuareg movement grew more violent, with a dramatic rise in attacks on Malian army bases. In 2011, the movement embraced secession with formation of the "National Movement for the Liberation of Azawad" (NMLA). While Tuareg rebels had insisted on regional autonomy in past rebellions, NMLA now aimed to establish a fully independent state (Zounmenou 2012). The Malian state had attempted to mollify separatists through decentralization of the northern regions to no effect (Delcroze 2012).

Tuareg rebel strategy was to ambush Malian army caravans or installations and then retreat into the desert (Lecocq 2010). However, in 2010–2011, as Moammar Quadaffi's Libyan regime collapsed, thousands of Tuareg fighters based there returned to northern Mali with stocks of antitank missiles and other advanced weaponry (Leymarie 2012). This, in addition to small arms trade in the Sahel, enabled the NMLA to widen and intensify its offensive missions (Zounmenou 2012). In January and February 2012, the NMLA pushed the Malian army out of at least seven northern Mali towns (Dorrie 2012).

In March 2012, an army garrison in Tessalit was overrun by NMLA (Harding 2012). In early April 2012, rebels took advantage of returning army troops to Bamako in the wake of a military coup d'état. This created the opportunity to widen control of the north: seizing Gao, the largest urban settlement in northern Mali, as well as Kidal and Timbuktu. This represented 2,072,000 square kilometers of Malian territory—65% of Malian territory—that came under rebel control (Leymarie 2012).

The NMLA-led sub-nationalist movement benefited from the functional separatism of northern Mali, as the 900-km border with Mauritania and its 1200-km border with Algeria remain poorly patrolled, helping the NMLA to obtain support and supplies from Mali's neighbors and to deepen trade and economic links more fully with those adjoining states than with Bamako in the south (Leymarie 2012). However, in 2012, the NMLA's dominance over northern Mali was challenged by extremist Muslim rebels. Fire fights broke out between the NMLA and these radical groups. Moreover, their main goals diverged: the NMLA sought secession while Islamists aimed to impose a strict brand of Islam throughout West Africa (Lebovich 2012; Mali Crisis: Key Players 2013).

These differences were suggested because extremists launched a series of attacks into central and southern Mali—in contrast to the Tuareg NMLA, which had set up a defensive posture only in the north (Mali Crisis: Key Players 2013). Islamist military aggression enabled them to control the north-central regions of Kidal, Gao, and Timbuktu (Delcroze 2012). This, in turn, provoked France to send thousands of troops to Mali in January 2013 to support the national government and to oust the Islamists. French attacks proved successful, and the Muslim fringe groups were pushed into the more lightly populated desert areas of the far north of the country before the Europeans began to withdraw (Mali Crisis: Key Players 2013). French troops succeeded in ousting the radical Muslim fighters from central (and some northern) Malian towns, enabling the Malian government to reestablish its control over those areas (and for the French forces to withdraw by April 2013). However, battles between the NMLA and the Malian government resumed in September 2013 (Mali profile 2013), suggesting continuing resilience by the NMLA as a militarily active sub-nationalist rebel group.

The north remains destabilized and economically detached from southern Mali, with northern herders grazing livestock and trading with agriculturalists throughout northern redoubts in self-supporting networks that lack monitoring by the Malian state. Many of these herders and farmers continue to carry on extensive trade relations with food and meat purchasers in Mauritania, Niger, and Algeria, helping to provide income that benefits the movement.

Cabinda (Angola)

Cabinda, with a populace of 600,000, covers a 7250-square-kilometer enclave of Angola physically separated from the mainland by a 60-km wide strip of land possessed by the DRC. The sub-nationalist Cabinda movement, the Front for the Liberation of the Enclave of Cabinda (FLEC), like many others in sub-Saharan Africa, reflects local discontent over a long history of natural resource exploitation and regional discrimination (Ojakorotu 2011). Cabinda accounts for 60% of total oil production (Ojakorotu 2011; Porto 2003). But Cabinda receives little development assistance as compensation. The FLEC was created in 1963 to struggle for independence—first from Portugal, then from Angola once it became independent in 1975 (Forrest 2004). The FLEC now aims for full independence, including seven districts and Cabinda city (Porto 2003).

Between 1979 and the late 1990s, the FLEC's rebel fighting ability increased significantly: the 2000-strong rebel army seized Buco-Zau city and established a presence in Nekuto, Belize, and Miconje. Buco-Zau served as the heart of the FLEC's military stronghold. The FLEC attacked Angolan troops and kidnapped government employees throughout the 1990s (Ojakorotu 2011). In negotiations in the 1990s, the FLEC rejected an autonomous Cabindan province, insisting on independence (Porto 2003).

However, the failure at negotiation led to an intensification of combat between rebels and government forces: in 2002, the government began a serious military drive to rid Cabinda of the FLEC army. By 2003, the FLEC's forces could no longer keep the Angolan army at bay. Angolan troops wiped out the FLEC's fighters (Porto 2003). The FLEC then signed a peace treaty in 2004, wherein it promised to transform itself into a peaceful political party in exchange for Angola promising to accord Cabinda "special status" but still within the framework of a unitary state (Porto 2003). But even so, some FLEC members refused to accept its terms and continued the armed struggle (Angola Signs Deal with Cabindans 2006). In January 2010, the FLEC opened fire on Angolan forces escorting three buses transporting members of Togo's national soccer team. To be sure, repeated waves of repression (including arrests, torture, and killings of dozens of suspected FLEC adherents) by Angolan forces, has weakened the FLEC's military capacity. Nonetheless, the FLEC retains popular support within Cabinda and continues to voice its secessionist aims (Ojakorotu 2011). With its robust oil deposits and natural resources,

Cabinda is well positioned to prove economically viable should the sub-nationalist movement achieve its goals.

Delta Region (Nigeria)

Nigeria's delta region includes the states of Delta, Rivers, Ondo, and Benue (and parts of neighboring states) marked by dense river networks and rich natural resources—including oil. Nigeria has been exploiting oil deposits since the 1970s, allowing international companies to extract oil while desecrating the environment and without the state reinvesting in local development or social programs in the delta region. The Nigerian army has undertaken dozens of repressive counter-insurgency drives attacking or jailing citizens to silence protestors. This led local activist groups and pro-separatist coalitions to mobilize in the 1980s–1990s, along with the formation of a well-armed rebel militia (Forrest 2004).

In 2006, a pro-autonomy confederation of groups and militia emerged, spearheaded by the MEND (Courson 2009, p. 47). MEND-affiliated groups aimed for regional autonomy, expelling Nigerian troops from the Niger delta (Hanson 2007).

Still, there is disagreement among MEND militia about what the movement means by "autonomy": more control over Nigerian political institutions, establishing parallel authority structures, or rejection of Nigerian political institutions and their replacement with indigenous authority structures (Hanson 2007, p. 6)? These differences represent a challenge to the MEND's effectiveness as a region-wide confederation. Its military capacity increased in the 2000s and it destabilized much of Nigeria's delta zone. The potential role of the MEND in a more loosely structured approach to governance appears unlikely, but could grow in viability if internal discord can be healed.

Violent attacks by MEND-affiliated rebels against oil production and military targets produced a disconnect from the rest of the country, while also inflicting considerable damage to the delta region's oil extraction infrastructure (Courson 2009, pp. 16, 21–22, 26). That disconnect is increasingly characterized by functional separatism, as residents have become more self-sufficient and rely on intervillage barter networks and localized village-based food exchanges. A repaired and expanded set of oil producing complexes in the delta would channel an increased percentage of oil profits into the local economy and infrastructure as determined by the coalition of sub-nationalist groups.

Democratic Republic of Congo

As the DRC became increasingly dysfunctional beginning in the 1980s, the nation's infrastructure frayed, creating a political gap between the central state and the localities. Economically, this produced large territorial zones characterized by functional separatism, while politically falling under the control of disparate armed rebel groups (Kisangani 2012). At least 32 armed groups (distinct to particular localities) materialized across the country (Mba Talla 2012).

After forming, the groups eventually dissipated in the wake of factional and local splintering. Indeed, with an ineffective national army and corrupt state institutions devoid of resources, rural areas turned inward in terms of organizational self-reliance, while also cementing closer marketing ties with foreign neighbors (Mba Talla 2012). The net effect has led to an intensification of conflict among the local militia over the control of specific localities, but also the extension of direct, informal (uncontrolled by Kinshasa) economic, and mineral-based trading ties to neighboring Rwanda, Uganda, and Burundi (Kisangani 2012; Mba Talla 2012).

Despite deepening ties with neighboring states and the consequential disarticulation of the Congolese economy, some of the most powerful antigovernment political movements and militia groups, including the single most potent militia in the country, the Mai-Mai of North and South Kivu provinces, aimed for national reunification (Kisangani 2012, p. 137). Militia leaders, when interviewed, made it clear that they were open to the idea of eventually integrating into state organizations—but only if these militia could be certain of retaining their own policy independence while also gaining access to state-controlled resources and powers (Afoaku 2012, p. 162; Mba Talla 2012). This, however, seemed unlikely, as the country remained divided into regions where natural resources, public security, and transportation infrastructure were largely under the control of "parallel institutions," sometimes called "ministries" (Tull 2007), managed by independent armed forces (Kisangani 2012; Mba Talla 2012).

Moreover, in the 2000s, many local militia in North and South Kivu became frustrated by the failure of the Congolese state to follow through with promises to decentralize administrative and fiscal powers. This dramatized the low capacity of the state while exacerbating the already-existing distrust between state and local political actors (Mba Talla 2012; Tull 2007).

Much of the DRC has been functioning as a collection of separate regional and local geographic territories. The fact that rebel leaders abjured sub-nationalist goals does not lessen the reality of functional separatism that is, much of the country was economically disconnected and characterized by autonomous power holding. Localities had separated from the national administrative and economic grid.

Meanwhile, President Yoweri Museveni of Uganda touted integrating eastern Congolese markets into a formal economic alliance with Uganda, Rwanda, and Kenya. Support for Museveni's idea was articulated by French President Nicholas Sarkozy and U.S. Ambassador Herman Cohen, in 2009. Such an unorthodox proposal stands as a dramatic reflection of DRC's failure at national integration and the reality that half the provinces are already more closely tied to the eastern and southern neighboring states than they are to Kinshasa (Kisangani 2012; Mba Talla 2012; Tull 2007). Thus, "economic satellization" of the DRC has taken place as

Uganda and Rwanda have pulled apart the country in terms of exchange circuits (Mba Talla 2012).

Both politically and economically, the rural regions in the eastern portion of the DRC would benefit from a new mode of governance, one more tolerant of the unending variability of political leadership structures and the separate logics of the economies in the outer localities. The broad, multi-country economic alliance proposed by the Ugandan president is forward-thinking creativity that aims to take into account the functional separatism of eastern Congo.

Eastern Libya

A recent manifestation of sub-nationalism took place in post-Gaddafi Libya in March 2012, when a large coalition with "thousands of representatives" from different localities, tribal chiefs, and local militias across the eastern portions of the country declared their intention to assert "semi-autonomy" (Eastern Libyan Leaders Seek Semi-Autonomy 2012). They named their newly declared semi-autonomous territory "Cyrenaica" referring to a territory covering half of Libya (Gabriel Gatehouse 2012). Mobilization of these separatists took place in Benghazi, a city that under Gaddafi was deprived of economic development and oil-derived resources. In 2012, leaders in Benghazi complained the new leaders in Tripoli appeared to be centralizing political power to continue the marginalization of the east (Eastern Libyan leaders).

Sub-nationalists activists held a meeting in March 2012, in Benghazi, in which about 3500 separatists chose members of a "Cyrenaica Provincial Council" as well as an interim leader, Ahmed Zubair al-Senussi. Al-Senussi expressed the hope that the full National Transitional Council of which he was a member would accept greater eastern semiautonomy (Eastern Libyan leaders). Most of eastern Libya is already "effectively composed of many de facto self-governing towns and cities, overseen by a weak central authority" (Alex Warren 2012)—and 80% of Libya's oil reserves are in the east (Keating 2014). Functional separatism explains the rise of a sub-nationalist movement in eastern Libya.

In June 2013, a "General National Congress" was elected in Cyrenaica, which subsequently named a "Transitional Council" that declared Cyrenaica "autonomous" but still "a federal territory within the Libyan state" (Cyrenaica Council). By January 2014, Cyrenaica challenged national government authority, as it attempted to sell eastern-produced oil to overseas buyers. Although Libya's national navy was trying to block oil tankers from entering Benghazi to collect this oil, at least one tanker had made its way through the blockade to Cyrenaica-produced oil (Keating 2014).

These events make clear the Libyan central government's weakness, and how the economic context of functional separatism created favorable conditions for the Cyrenaica sub-nationalists. Moreover, this suggests the potential for independent economic self-sustainability, assuming a political accord can be reached in a loose governance structure tolerant of Cyrenaica's *de facto* neo-sovereignty.

Western Sahara

The Polisario Front, created in 1973 to unify Bedouin tribes and to oppose first Spanish, then Moroccan rule, announced its goal for independence in 1976 (Jensen 2012). The Polisario Front gained support of most Sahrawi (Saharans) and elicited sympathy internationally. Following aerial bombardments carried out by the Moroccan air force in the 1980s, the Sahrawi fled to resettlement camps in Algeria's Tindouf region (Quarante 2012).

Despite a cease fire signed in 1991, political hostilities between the Sahrawi and Moroccans remained acute, and both sides alternated between professing interest in peace agreements and engaging in violence. It became evident that Morocco had no intention of relinquishing political control despite its claims to the contrary (Quarante 2012).

This effort has proven successful in that there are more Moroccan settlers living in the Western Sahara than there are indigenous Sahrawi (200,000 of a total population of 500,000). Many Sahrawi reside in tents in resettlement camps constructed after they had been driven from their homelands by Moroccan army forces (Jensen 2012). The government offers resettlement camp residents cash incentives to abandon camps and return to Saharan cities. But in those cities, the government provides assistance to Moroccan settlers in opening businesses and appoints them to bureaucratic posts, while Sahrawi are restricted to basic hard labor jobs (Quarante 2012).

Such policies have only intensified Saharan resentment and motivate the Polisario to pursue sub-nationalism (Quarante 2012). While the 1991 accord specified that a referendum on self-determination would be held in the Western Sahara, it has not been held (Quarante 2012). Meanwhile, open hostilities between Moroccan settlers and Saharans remain: in October 2010, some 20,000 Saharans set up tents in the desert to peacefully protest Morocco's repressive policies. The Sahrawi called the site "dignity camp." In November, the Moroccan army assaulted the camp, using poison gas and water cannons, followed by troops attacking with truncheons, forcing protestors to dismantle the camp (Quarante 2012).

Despite Morocco's efforts at containment, the borders of the Western Sahara remain porous and "unpoliceable," (Jensen 2012) enabling the Polisario Front to obtain material and arms from outside. It also sustains an informal network of trade and barter links across the Saharan region. Beyond the overt goals of the Front, the functional separatism of the Western Sahara provides an infrastructural context conducive to the movement's continued viability, demonstrating the potential for sustainable development and stability.

First, however, a governance accord needs to be crafted wherein the Polisario is accepted by Morocco as legitimate. Despite occupation of the cities, there remain vast rural redoubts that could serve as a Sahrawi homeland. The Western Sahara conflict cries out for a more peace-oriented, pragmatic governance approach oriented toward the acceptance of Polisario leadership.

Implications for Governance and Sustainable Development

The considerable setbacks and challenges to governance and sustainable development in the weak states of Africa have only been exacerbated and rendered more complex by the rise and spread of sub-nationalist movements and the *de facto* disarticulation of nation-state economies. As movements assert control over ever-widening outlying regions, they make possible a new form of governance, one more grounded in flexible, accommodative arrangements by national states willing to permit movements to control large geographic domains. Such arrangements would have to be worked out by state and sub-nationalist leaders on a case-by-case basis; they would reflect the ground-level reality that, in many cases, sub-nationalists are increasingly able to achieve policy autonomy within their respective territories.

Zartman suggested that "segmentary or geographic neighbors" in discord could potentially agree "to live side by side in peace again" through flexible, informal negotiations (Zartman 2000, p. 223). This is what is suggested here with regard to sub-nationalism: a looser form of governance that generates greater stability and security through acceptance of *de facto* territorial autonomy, managed by independent regional leaderships. Bargaining and flexible political accommodations have long been characteristic of African politics to assure successful precolonial state building, in creating heterogeneous anticolonial political movements, and in achieving stability in the early postcolonial period (Rothchild 1997; Zartman 2000). A new governance perspective embraces this tradition that would search for territorial compromises that open up central state tolerance of sub-nationalist control over peripheral regions.

There is no readymade constitutional model or institutional design that would be applicable to the overwhelming variety of sub-nationalist movements and weak states in contemporary Africa; particular arrangements would have to be worked out informally for each movement. This approach is consistent with historical forms of African conflict management, which emphasize the gradual, flexible, and often-changing details of the negotiation process (Zartman 2000). Menkhaus emphasizes with regard to peacemaking in Somalia and other weak or collapsing contemporary African states that peace agreements are most effective when they reflect "situational, not predetermined" approaches oriented toward a long-term working out of specific accommodations (Menkhaus 2000). The potential for traditional forms of informal peacemaking to work "is strongest at the local and regional levels"

(Menkhaus 2000, p. 197). Considering the ability of rural communities in Somalia in the early-to-mid 2000s to craft their own authority structures at the local level, Menkhaus more generally recommends a "mediated" approach toward state–society relations in Africa based on the central state's acceptance of locally organized self-rule (Menkhaus 2006/07).

These incisive points are consistent with the argument that the pursuit of effective governance in the wake of rising sub-nationalist movements in weak states is to allow them to hold onto already attained territories, and to encourage their leaders to work out informal arrangements with national states so that sustainable security is achieved. The idea that autonomous territorial control over rural regions represents a major threat to nation-state sovereignty should be revisited and therefore national security ought to be replaced by a new mode of governance that accepts *de facto* rural regional autonomy as effective in achieving security and peace. Doing so would help to reattach contemporary African political rule with its "deep historical" antecedents; it suggests a mode of governance based more on a grassroots-oriented *realpolitik* that reflects what is actually happening "on the ground" in fragile and weakening states.

For sustainable development, one of the lessons of state decline is that functional separatism is a consequence of the inability of the central state to regulate markets combined with the ability of rural producers to craft sustainable food growing, handicrafts based, and pastoral local economies. The advantage of sub-nationalist movements is they are closer to the ground than central governments and can encourage farmers and herders toward a more efficient use of land and water resources. Movements would still benefit from external aid, but they may be in a position to make more effective use of such aid by encouraging investment in already-existing, region-specific agronomic, artisanal, livestock trading, and entrepreneurial strengths.

Often, trade links initially established on a local basis eventually extend past national borders and tie peripheral regions to neighboring states rather than to their own nation's capital city. Here we might seize upon a suggestion elaborated in the World Bank 2009 *World Development Report*—to encourage external investment "in cross-country infrastructure to connect regional markets" (World Bank 2009, p. 276). Doing so would bring ancillary trade benefits to subsistence producers in peripheral regions, while adding new value to locally produced agronomic goods. This is not a matter of creating *new* regional market networks, but rather of strengthening *already-existing* informal regional trade links (World Bank 2009). While movements are questing for greater political autonomy, they are also aiming for and in some cases, including Somaliland, are already consolidating more direct ties to international markets. This brings us close to what the World Bank has referred to as "transfrontier regionalism"—which enables rural areas to take advantage of "economic complementarities in bordering regions" (World Bank 2009, p. 279).

In a minority of breakaway cases, including Cabinda (Angola), Cyraenica (eastern Libya), potentially the Delta Region (Nigeria), and South Sudan (with greater political stability), enough high-value accessible natural resources (such as oil) would generate substantial foreign exchange earnings, enough to offer a sub-nationalist movement sufficient income to initiate long-term, sustainable development prospects. In such cases, they can more rapidly and decisively assert their political independence while also generating rising income levels.

Thus, overt sub-nationalism and functional separatism harbor potential for sustainable development, with marketing and transportation linkages based on flexibility and ties between neighboring territories in different countries. This could prove beneficial both to oil-rich regions questing for independence and to those rebellious regions that remain agriculturally self-reliant. Examples include the sub-nationalist movement in the state of Northwest Cameroon, which could be more logically linked to southwestern Nigeria; the persistently rebellious region of Casamance, Senegal, which developed extensive informal economic trading ties with Mauritania, Mali, Guinea-Bissau, and Guinea; and informal livestock trading within and between the mountain zones in parts of Guinea, Mali, Côte d'Ivoire, Burkina Faso, Ghana, Togo, Benin, Niger, and Nigeria. Those livestock networks interconnect Hausa and Mandé cattle traders (among many others) and represent a promising direction for intensified investment.

As a consequence of functional separatism, the standard development approach, presuming state sovereignty and the capacity to engage in meaningful economic planning according to broadly conceived blueprints, is of questionable utility (Ibister 2006). Instead, we underline the need to tailor development programs to the particular economic idiosyncrasies of breakaway regions at the micro-level. Greater regional autonomy regarding investment choices and development strategies, as provided by the achievement of sub-nationalist success, may, in this regard, help to unlock the potential for sustainable development in rural Africa.

A concurrent development strategy that reflects the smaller-scale logic of regional assertion and is oriented toward sustainability over time is to focus on creating social capital across rural regions by building "horizontal linkages" among development stakeholders (Bryant and Kappaz 2005). The focus here is to hone in on already-existing productive activities—such as livestock herding, agronomy, small-scale manufacturing, or tree-product harvesting—and to improve intervillage efficiencies by facilitating transportation and contacts among village associations, trade middlemen, and producer organizations. Intensifying coordination of horizontal economic linkages enables "rural civil society" to make modest strides toward wealth accumulation and toward the generation of economic network-enhancing social capital at the grassroots level (Moore et al. 2005).

Such horizontal linkages can work synergistically with an intensification of political power within each region by the already-mobilized sub-nationalist movement leaders. The aim here would be to encourage them to permit the further consolidation of already-existing ties between food producers and small-scale artisanal or micro-industrial producers in a way that is mutually beneficial (Lanjouw and Stern 2003). Off-farm occupational diversification can generate new small business opportunities and micro-entrepreneurship within rural areas so as to absorb on-farm labor overflow and simultaneously helps to raise rural incomes. Such a development strategy, marked by major increases in the extent of regional-level policy autonomy, has been pursued with considerable success by India, China, Vietnam, Indonesia, Brazil, and Costa Rica (Lanjouw and Stern 2003). The devolution of policy choice facilitated the abilities of provincial leaders to focus on the particular ecological, agricultural, skill-set, and vocational endowments of their particular region (Arkadie and Mallon 2003; Roy and Chatterjee 2006; Weiss 2005).

An approach focused on horizontal micro-linkages can prove to be a successful strategy for sustainable development because of its flexibility—policy options are tailored to local and regional specificities—and because they aim to provide increasing benefits to rural communities dominated by low-income producers (Forrest 2011). Horizontal linkages can contribute to development in functionally autonomous regions insofar as newly empowered regionally based authorities facilitate inter-peasant cooperation and flexible-market opportunities.

Ever-larger portions of the growing number of Africa's weak states are moving toward a significant political reconfiguration, one that reflects the increasing success of sub-nationalist political movements as well as the "functional separatism" of the *de facto* autonomy of vast rural zones. The diversification of regional power holders calls for a new mode of governance, one oriented toward tolerance of multiple nodes of sub-nationalist authority. This, in turn, provides for a new potential for both political security and for sustainable development, given a sufficient reconceptualization of development itself as mandating considerable per-region flexibility and the maximization of micro-level opportunity structures, activities, and local-to-local networks that become increasingly freed up in part due to the upsurge of sub-nationalists.

Those assertions are expanding through ever-greater reaches of rural territory as the infrastructural fragility of a growing number of African states deepens through the course of the second decade of the twenty-first century. In doing so, sub-nationalists are laying the foundation for a new mode of governance, with central state regimes oriented toward significantly greater tolerance of rural regional autonomy. Here, bargaining and negotiation can be emphasized over the more typical turn (back) toward unilateral state-centrism and political repression. Such a governance perspective emphasizes that overall political security, stability, and sustainable economic development in Africa's weak states are likely to be achieved through flexible peacemaking, the tolerance of independent sub-nationalist movements, the acceptance of interregional marketing arrangements that link outer regions with neighboring nations, and the recognition of a broad diversity of on-the-ground regional authority structures.

References

Afoaku, O. 2012. Congo's rebels: Their origins, motivations, and strategies. In Clark, J. (ed.). *The African Stakes of the Congo War*, Chapter 7. New York: Palgrave Publishers, pp. 109–128, 162.

Alex Warren, [Director of Frontier, an international NGO], as quoted in: Eastern Libyan leaders declare autonomy from Libya. 2012. *France 24 International News*, March 7, at: http://www.france24.com/en/20120306-libya-bengazi-cyrenaica-autonomy-federalism. Accessed 8/6/14.

Angola Signs Deal with Cabindans. 2006. BBC News, August 1, at: http://news.bbc.co.uk/2/hi/africa/5236230.stm. Accessed 8/6/14.

Arkadie, B., Mallon, R. 2003. *Vietnam. A Transition Tiger?* Canberra: Asia Pacific Press.

Bigman, L. 1993. *History and Hunger in West Africa.* Westport, CT: Greenwood Press.

Boas, M., Dunn, K.C. (eds.). 2007. *African Guerillas. Raging against the Machine.* Boulder, CO: Lynne Rienner.

Bryant, C., Kappaz, C. 2005. *Reducing Poverty, Building Peace.* Boulder, CO: Kumarian Press.

Chabal, P. 2005. Introduction: Violence, power and rationality: A political analysis of conflict in contemporary Africa. In Chabal, P., Engel, U., Gentili, A. (eds.). *Is Violence Inevitable In Africa?* Netherlands: Brill Publishers, pp. 1–14.

Citation from Cyrenaica Council Head Ahmed Zubair al-Senussi, as quoted in: Mohammed, E. 2013. Cyrenaica declares autonomy, *Magharebia*, June 4, at: http://magharebia.com/en_GB/articles/awi/features/2013/06/04/feature-01. Accessed 8/6/14.

Cornia, G.A. 2005. Inequality, growth, and poverty: On overview of changes the last few decades. In Cornia, G. (ed.). *Inequality, Growth and Poverty in an Era of Liberalization and Globalization*, Chapter 1. Oxford: Oxford University Press.

Courson, E. 2009. Movement for the emancipation of the Niger Delta (MEND): Political marginalization, repression, and petro-insurgency in the Niger Delta. Discussion Paper 47, The Nordic Africa Institute. Uppsala, Sweden.

Davidson, B. 1992. *The Black Man's Burden. Africa and the Curse of the Nation-State.* London: James Currey Publishers.

Delcroze, J. 2012. Effondrement du rêve démocratique au Mali. *Le Monde Diplomatique*, September, p. 9.

Dorrie, P. 2012. Mali's Tuareg rebellion puts region at risk. *World Politics Review*, March 21, at: http://www.worldpoliticsreview.com/articles/11730/malis-tuareg-rebellion-puts-region-at-risk. Accessed 8/6/14.

Duffield, M. 2001. *Global Governance and the New Wars.* London: Zed Books.

Eastern Libyan Leaders Seek Semi-Autonomy. 2012. *Al Jazeera* news network, March 6, at: http://www.aljazeera.com/news/africa/2012/03/201236123841695817.html. Accessed 8/6/14.

Forrest, J. 2003. *Lineages of State Fragility.* Columbus: Ohio University Press.

Forrest, J. 2004. *Subnationalism in Africa: Ethnicity, Alliances, Politics.* Boulder, CO: Lynne Rienner.

Forrest. J. 2011. Development theory, social violence, and conflict resolution: Guinea-Bissau in global context. In Klute, G., Embaló, B. (eds.). *The Problem of Violence: Local Conflict Settlement in Contemporary Africa.* Cologne: Rudiger Köppe Verlag Publishers, pp. 427–433, 439.

Gabriel Gatehouse. 2012. BBC News, March 6, at: http://www.bbc.co.uk/news/world-africa-17271431. Accessed 8/6/14.

Garang, N. 2012. South Sudan puts its army on maximum alert in oil row escalation. *Sudan Tribune*, January 25, at: http://www.sudantribune.com/. Accessed 8/6/14.

Gettleman, J. 2011. Movement's mission is secured: Statehood. *New York Times*, July 9.

Hanson, S. 2007. MEND: The Niger Delta's Umbrella Militant Group, published paper, Council on Foreign Relations, March 22, pp. 3–5.

Harding, A. 2012. Sound and fury: Mali's Tuareg rebels. BBC News, March 13, at: http://www.bbc.co.uk/news/world-africa-17357122. Accessed 8/8/14.

Haslam, N. 2013. Meeting the challenge of promoting pro-poor investment in Somaliland. *The Guardian*, February 5, at: http://www.theguardian.com/global-development-professionals-network/adam-smith-international-partner-zone/adam-smith-international-somaliland-pro-poor-investment. Accessed 8/6/14. http://www.sudantribune.com/Oil-Revenues-Controversy-Sudan-s,41395. Accessed 8/6/14.

Ibister, J. 2006. *Promises Not Kept. Poverty and the Betrayal of Third World Development.* Boulder, CO: Kumarian Press.

Jensen, E. 2012. *Western Sahara. Anatomy of a Stalement?* 2nd ed. Boulder CO: Lynne Rienner Publishers.

Jhazbhay, I. 2003. Somaliland: Africa's best kept secret. *African Security Review* 12 (4): 77–82.

Kaldor, M. 1999. *New and Old Wars*. Cambridge: Polity Press.

Keating, J. 2014. Meet Cyrenaica: The world's newest aspiring (pseudo-) petrostate. *Slate Magazine* [on-line], January 16, at: http://www.slate.com/blogs/the_world_/2014/01/16/meet_cyrenaica_the_world_s_newest_aspiring_pseudo_petrostate.html. Accessed 8/6/14.

Kisangani, E. 2012. *Civil Wars in the Democratic Republic of Congo, 1960–2010.* Boulder, CO: Lynne Rienner Publishers.

Kron, J. 2011. Major humanitarian group leaves a South Sudan region. *New York Times*, November 14.

Kulish, N. 2014. South Sudan's forces clash with rebels. *New York Times*, February 19.

Laitin D., Samatar, S. 1987. *Somalia: Nation in Search of a State*. Boulder, CO: Westview Press.

Lanjouw, P., Stern, N. 2003. Opportunities off the farm as a springboard out of rural poverty. In Fields, G., Pfefferman, G. (eds.). *Pathways Out of Poverty. Private Firms and Economic Mobility in Developing Countries*. Netherlands: Kluwer Publishers, pp. 123–154.

Lebovich, 2012. A. Northern Mali: The politics of ethnicity and locality. *Think Africa Press*, December 7, at: http://thinkafricapress.com/mali/politics-ethnicity-locality-mali-mujao. Accessed 8/6/14.

Lecocq, B. 2010. *Disputed Desert: Decolonisation, Competing Nationalisms, and Tuareg Rebellions in Northern Mali*. Netherlands: Brill Press.

Lemarchand, R. 2007. Consociationalism and power sharing in Africa: Rwanda, Burundi, and the Democratic Republic of the Congo. *African Affairs* 106 (422, January): 1–20.

Leymarie, P. 2012. Comment le Sahel est devenu une poudrière. *Le Monde Diplomatique*, April, pp. 8–9.

Lyons, T., Samatar, A. 1995. *State Collapse, Multilateral Intervention, and Strategies for Political Reconstruction*. Washington, DC: Brookings Institution Press.

MacGaffey, J. 1992. *The Real Economy of Zaire*. Philadelphia, PA: University of Pennsylvania Press.

Mali Crisis: Key Players, 2013. BBC News-Africa, January 24, at: http://www.bbc.co.uk/news/world-africa-17582909. Accessed 8/6/14.

Mali profile. 2013. BBC News, December 27, at: http://www.bbc.com/news/world-africa-13881978. Accessed 8/6/14.

Mba Talla, Modeste Paulin. 2012. Émergence, « fragmégration » et perpétuation des rébellions au Congo-RDC (1990–2010): une politologie des groupes armés. Doctoral thesis. Ottowa: University of Ottowa.

Mcneish, H. 2014. South Sudan Revenue Up. *Agence France-Presse*, January 16, at: http://za.news.yahoo.com/south-sudan-oil-revenue-despite-fighting-khartoum-152316066.html. Accessed 8/6/14.

Mehler, A. 2005. Area studies, the analysis of conflicts and the evaluation of preventive practice in Africa. In Chabal, P., Engel, U., Gentili, A. (eds.). *Is Violence Inevitable in Africa?* Leiden: Brill Publishers, pp. 99–123.

Menkhaus, K. 2000. Traditional conflict management in contemporary Somalia. In Zartman, I. (ed.). *Traditional Cures for Modern Conflicts: African Conflict 'Medicine'*. Boulder, CO: Lynne Rienner Publishers, pp. 183–199.

Menkhaus, K. 2006/07. Governance without Government in Somalia. *International Affairs* 1 (3, Winter) 74–106.

Moore, K., Cissé, S., Touré, A. 2005. Building social infrastructure for sustainable development, In Moore, K. (ed.). *Conflict, Social Capital, and Managing Natural Resources.* Oxford: CABI Publishing, pp. 89–100.

O'Leary, B. 2013. Power-sharing in deeply divided places: An advocate's introduction. In McEvoy, J., O'Leary, B (eds.). *Power-Sharing in Deeply Divided Places.* Philadelphia, PA: University of Pennsylvania Press, pp. 1–65.

Ojakorotu, V. 2011. The paradox of terrorism, armed conflict and natural resources: An analysis of Cabinda in Angola. *Perspectives on Terrorism* 5 (3–4, September): 96–109.

Porto, J. 2003. Cabinda's Year of War. Occasional Paper 77, Institute for Security Studies, August, at: http://www.issafrica.org/pgcontent.php?UID=8195. Accessed 8/6/14.

Prunier, G. 2010. Le Somaliland, une exception africaine. *Le Monde Diplomatique*, October, 6.

Prunier, G. 2014. South Sudan: It all began so well. *Le Monde Diplomatique* [English Edition], February, at: http://mondediplo.com/2014/02/03southsudan. Accessed 8/6/14.

Quarante, O. 2012. Résistance obstinée des Sahraouis. *Le Monde Diplomatique*, February, 18.

Raghavan, S. 2014. With oil at stake, South Sudan's crisis matters. *Washington Post*, January 21.

Reeves, E. 2012. Oil Revenues Controversy. *Sudan Tribune*, January 25, at: http://www.sudantribune.com/spip.php?iframe&page=imprimable&id_article=41395.

Reeves, E. 2014. In the shadow of South Sudan's catastrophe. February 23, at: http://sudanreeves.org/2014/02/23/in-the-shadow-of-south-sudans-catastrophe-khartoums-actions-are-escaping-scrutiny/. Accessed 8/6/14.

Reno, W. 2011. *Warfare in Independent Africa.* Cambridge: Cambridge University Press.

Rothchild, D. 1997. *Managing Ethnic Conflict in Africa: Pressures and Incentives for Cooperation.* Washington, DC: Brookings Institution Press.

Roy, K., Chatterjee, S. 2006. *Readings in World Development. Growth and Development in the Asia Pacific.* Hauppauge, NY: Nova Science Publishers.

Samah, W. 2010. Anglophone minority and the state in Cameroon. In Mbanaso, M., Korea, C. (eds.). *Minorities and the State in Africa.* Amherst, NY: Cambria Press.

Simons, A. 1995. *Networks of Dissolution: Somalia Undone.* Boulder, CO: Westview Press.

Somaliland: Another Country in Waiting. 2011. *The Economist*, January 10, at: http://www.economist.com/blogs/baobab/2011/01/somaliland?zid=304&ah=e5690753dc78ce91909083042ad12e30. Accessed 8/6/14.

Spears, I. 2010. *Civil War in African States. The Search for Security*. Boulder, CO: Lynne Rienner.

Spears, I.S. 2000. Understanding inclusive peace agreements in Africa: The problems of sharing power. *Third World Quarterly* 21 (1): 105–118.

Sudan–South Sudan War. 2012. *War News Updates*, April 30, at: http://warnewsupdates.blogspot.com/2012/04/sudan-south-sudan-war-news-updates_30.html. Accessed 8/6/14.

Tull, D. 2007. The Democratic Republic of Congo: Militarized politics in a failed state. In Boas, M., Dunn, K. C. (eds.). *African Guerillas. Raging against the Machine*. Boulder, CO: Lynne Rienner Publishers, pp. 113–130.

Weiss, J. 2005. *Poverty Targeting in Asia*. Cheltenham, UK: Edward Elgar Publishers.

World Bank. 2009. Winners without borders; Integrating poor countries with world markets. In *World Development Report 2009: Reshaping Economic Geography*. Washington, DC: World Bank Publications.

ZAMBIA: Poverty fuels secession bid by Western Province. 2011. IRIN News [United Nations], January 25, at: http://www.irinnews.org/report.aspx?ReportId=91721. Accessed 8/6/14.

Zartman, I. 2000. Conclusions: Changes in the new order and the place for the old. In Zartman, I. (ed.). *Traditional Cures for Modern Conflicts: African Conflict Medicine*. Boulder, CO: Lynne Rienner Publishers.

Zounmenou, D. 2012. West Africa—The Sahel: Is there a solution to the Tuareg insurgency? Institute for Security Studies, at: http://allafrica.com/stories/201203201295.html. Accessed 8/6/14.

Chapter 10

Identity Politics, Governance, and Development in Africa

John F. Clark

Contents

Introduction

This chapter examines relationships among identity group politics, governance, and development in Africa. It argues, first, that group identities (usually ethnic) are the key to African politics. Where ethnic politics does not prevail, other forms of identity politics associated with race, region, or clan typically dominates African polities. Paradoxically, identity politics is obvious and ubiquitous, yet, most Africanist-political scientists insist that identity is "endogenous to politics," or a function of political processes. Whereas it is true that specific *forms* of identity politics are an outcome of politics, the ontological antecedence of identity politics—as opposed to class or economic-ideology politics—is undeniable in the African context. This reality cannot be ignored in the debates over development in Africa, for development depends upon the "taming" of identity politics. In retrospect, the one-party state model for African governance that predominated between the mid-1960s and 1989 was mainly an effort to control and channel identity politics. Although this effort failed for a number of reasons, the need to limit the negative consequences of identity politics in the interest of development persists. Uncontrolled identity politics have degenerated into civil war in West Africa (Liberia, Sierra Leone, and Côte d'Ivoire), in the Horn of Africa (Ethiopia and Somalia), the Great Lakes (Rwanda, Burundi, and the DRC), and elsewhere in Central and Southern Africa (Angola, Chad, and Congo-Brazzaville). The civil wars in these states impeded the development of them all. African states that have recently enjoyed accelerated development success, such as Botswana (since 1966), Ethiopia (since 1991), Ghana (since 2000), and Uganda (since 1995) have also enjoyed "ethnic peace," or nonviolent competition among ethnic communities. This chapter explores some of the modes of maintaining ethnic peace in African polities.

Undeniably, cleavages in African society since independence have been ethnic, subethnic, regional, and occasionally religious, and African politics has usually revolved around these resulting identity groups. This reality has been most obvious at time when politics is open to competition, but it can also be witnessed when politics is "closed" to competing interest groups. Neither class solidarities nor issue-oriented convictions have yet to have a major impact on Africa politics. The ethnic, or "identity," quality of African politics, in turn, has had a major impact on Africa's prospects for economic development. Often, identity politics has devolved into social conflict or outright civil war. Where it has, economic and social development has generally been put on hold, at best, or fragile economic conditions have deteriorated dramatically, at worst, as in such war-torn states as the Republic of Congo (ROC), the Democratic Republic of Congo (DRC), Liberia, Sierra Leone, and Somalia. Even "low-grade" social violence, such as that experienced by Nigeria since the 1990s, has impeded socioeconomic development. This is not to say that peace among identity communities guarantees economic progress; rather, it is a necessary but insufficient condition for the *possibility* of economic progress. Some of the African states that have established ethnic peace have experienced impressive socioeconomic development (e.g., Botswana, Ghana, and Uganda) over greater or lesser periods of time, while others (e.g., Malawi, Namibia, Tanzania, and Zambia) have had less success. Accordingly, finding a formula for maintaining ethnic peace is, arguably, essential for African development, but not sufficient. Finding such a formula in an era that privileges competitive, multiparty politics is not easy, and often contradicts efforts of Western agents to reinforce political party competition in Africa.

Identity Politics in African States

Identity groups have been the main political constituencies in African politics since independence. This reality is so salient that both professional social scientists and ordinary observers take it for granted (and usually move on quickly to try to make subtler observations about African politics). Yet, observers of Africa take the obvious for granted at their peril: formulas for peace, development, or human rights realization that ignore or deny the fundamental nature of African politics stand little chance of improving the social state of things on the continent. In particular, strategies for African development are unlikely to bear fruit if they deny the necessity of dealing with the identity group contestation—and often violence—that is ubiquitous in Africa.

Identity group politics can take a variety of forms, but "ethnic" politics is the most common. The origins or sources of ethnic contestation in African politics are as obvious as the phenomenon itself: it results from the artificial "lumping" of various ethno-political communities together in the multiethnic states created by European colonial authorities in the two decades after the Berlin Conference of 1885–1886. In the 130 years that have followed, only rapid industrialization, urbanization, and development could have served to mitigate the tensions created by aggregating essentially alien social groups together in common polities, but this was not to be. Even where economic development has been rapid, as in postwar Europe, ethnic identities have only partly been supplanted by class and ideology as bases for social solidarity. Africa has seen impressive urbanization in recent decades, but with scant economic development, and the continent's urban communities have often mirrored the identity configurations of the states in which they are situated, making microcosms of the national social identity spaces.

The ethnic or identity community basis of African politics was first visible in the late colonial period and the early independence period, when political space was briefly open to political competition. In typical instances of late colonial ethnic politics, both ethno-regional and "national" parties, often led by charismatic leaders with transethnic or nationalist aspirations, sprang up to contest power. This was true even when one charismatic figure dominated late colonial politics. Take the two cases of Ghana (Gold Coast) and Congo-Kinshasa, for instance. In the case of Ghana, Kwame Nkrumah was, of course, the great nationalist figure whose Convention People's Party (CPP) would become the country's sole legal party. Yet, we should not forget that other ethnically based parties competed with the CPP when they were permitted to, namely, in the 1954 and 1956 elections. Although the CPP won 71 seats of 104 in each of these elections, ethno-regional parties like the Northern People's Party (representing several northern peoples) and the National Liberation Movement (an Ashanti-dominated break-away party from the CPP) gained significant fractions of the vote. Likewise, in Congo-Kinshasa, Patrice Lumumba was the undisputed nationalist hero. Yet, we should not forget that all the political parties except Lumumba's *Mouvement National Congolais* (MNC) had an ethnic or ethno-regional basis. These included Balubakat (the party of the Luba of Katanga), the Conakat (a regional party for the non-Luba of Katanga), the Abako (a party for the Bakongo people of western Congo), the Cerea (a Kivu-based party), and the (break-away) MNC-Kalonji (eventually, a party dominated by the Luba of Kasai region) (Young 1965). Even the Congo's most prominent Marxist analyst has allowed that, "Except for the MNC-L (that is, MNC-Lumumba wing) and the state-controlled PNP, all these parties were ethnically or regionally based" (Nzongola-Ntalaja 2002: 83). In the free elections of 1960, the vote was divided among these parties, though the MNC-L did win a plurality.

Even the genuinely nationalist parties of the independence era often had some "core" of support among a major ethnic group or region, from which the party leader issued. Lumumba's party, the MNC, for instance, had a regional base in the northern part of eastern Kasai and in the Orientale region, where the party performed particularly well in the 1960 elections. For Jomo Kenyatta's Kenya African National Union (KANU), it was the Kikuyu people; for Félix Houphouet-Boigny's Parti Démocratique du Côte d'Ivoire (PDCI), it was the Baoulé people; and for Agostinho Neto's Movimento Popular de Libertação de Angola (MPLA), it was the Mbundu people of northwestern Angola. In times of crisis, leaders of these parties relied on their core ethnic group for support.

A number of the African states that got independence late, and had to fight for it, developed multiple independence movements, corresponding to large ethno-regional constituencies. Angola is a case in point, hosting as it did the UNITA people party (led by Jonas Savimbi, with an Ovimbundu political base) and the FNLA (led by Holden Roberto, with a Bakongo ethnic base) (Marcum 1969). The ideological pretensions of these parties in the 1970s do not stand up to much scrutiny. Although the MPLA had excellent Marxist credentials, given its origins, we should not forget that UNITA's Savimbi was a protégé of Maoist China before he was the darling of the Reagan administration. Even the FRELIMO party of Mozambique, rightly understood as a creation of *apartheid* South Africa, and sustained by conservative outside forces, was much more of an ethno-regional party, than an ideological party, gaining a large majority of its support from the people of the central-western Manica region (Alexander 1997), Cold War perceptions notwithstanding. Zimbabwe is another example, with ZANU being a Shona-dominated independence party and ZAPU being an Ndebele-dominated grouping.

In states that did not have to fight hard for independence, multiple political parties sprang up representing various ethno-regional groupings, usually without any dominant "nationalist" party. This was the case in many of the French colonies where strong independence movements had not emerged before 1958, but also in some British colonies. Two cases in point are Congo-Brazzaville and Nigeria. In the first case, ethno-regional parties included the Mbochi-dominated MSA party of Jacques Opangault, the Lari-dominated UDDIA party of Fulbert Youlou, and the Vili-dominated PPC of Félix Tchicaya (Bernault 1996). Because no territory-wide party was needed to fight for independence, none emerged, and each large ethno-regional cluster gained its own leader and party. Anglophone Nigeria was not different and indeed less surprising since three *large* (and many smaller) ethnic clusters had even more distinctive political identities in the colonial period. The three parties that emerged were the Northern People's Congress, implanted among the Hausa and Fulani in the North; the National Council of Nigeria and the Cameroons, popular among the Igbo of the southeast; and the Action Group that gained support in all regions, but particularly among the Yoruba in the southwest (Whitaker 1991: 231–233). Electoral results for these three parties in the 1959 legislative elections mirrored the relative demographic weight of these major Nigerian groups (bearing in mind that these represented only 60% of the population.)

Only a very few African states have been dominated by a single ethnic people for long periods, either because of their historical significance, demographic weight, or both. In Burkina Faso, the Mossi people, the inhabitants of a precolonial empire, have dominated the postcolonial Burkinabè state (Otayek 1989). In Ethiopia, the Amharic people have appeared to play a dominant role because of their association with the country's royalty, though it is actually Amhara and Oromo together who have dominated Ethiopia, politically and demographically. Other groups had much less influence until the rise of Meles Zenawi (a Tigray-Tigrinya) in 1991. In southern Africa, the Tswana are the overwhelming identity group of Botswana, so it is hardly surprising that all the country's rulers have come from that group. Meanwhile, Shona-dominated Zimbabwe has only had one independent president (Robert Mugabe, a Shona).

Whereas "ethnic" difference is the relevant social distinction in many African states, (nonclass) identity groups with other labels are more prominent in others. Region is probably the second leading source of identity across Africa as a whole, and there has often been a strong overlap of ethnicity and region. For instance, the Igbo people of Nigeria's dominated the country's southeastern region, which attempted to secede as "Biafra" in 1966. Likewise, the secessionist Katanga region of Congo-Kinshasa was politically dominated by the Lunda people, who were of historic importance there (Bustin 1975). Their leader, Moïse Tshombe, was married to a daughter of the contemporary Lunda emperor. Other ethnic groups in the region were less enthusiastic about secession in 1960. In regions (like northern Ghana or southwestern Congo-Brazzaville) where no one ethnicity is dominant, transethnic regional identities have congealed as political entrepreneurs sought to construct constituencies to support their political ambitions. Even earlier, during the early colonial period, European authorities had (mostly inadvertently) created regional identities in the process of "crystallizing" the spaces delineated by the internal regional borders within colonial states, as in Gabon (Gray 2002, especially 226–227). As is very well documented, ethnic identities were created in a similar fashion through the bureaucratization of colonial rule throughout Africa.

Religion was yet another source of identity politics in the late colonial–early independence periods, either overlapping or competing, but more commonly overlapping. Nigeria and Uganda are obvious cases in point. Most Africanists well appreciate that the practice of Islam in northern Nigeria reinforces the identity difference that the Hausa-Fulani in the north have with their southern compatriots.

The Islamic orientation of the Kano and Sokoto caliphates in the precolonial era and the memory of these political entities serve to further reinforce the northern-Islamic identity difference in Nigeria. In Uganda, the overlap between religion and regional identities is not as clear-cut, but the basic competition among identity groups just before independence is quite obvious. By the time of the 1961 legislative council elections there, three parties had emerged, representing three different identity groups: the Kabaka Yekka, representing the Baganda people who lived in the Buganda region surrounding Uganda's capital of Kampala; the Democratic Party, overwhelmingly supported by Catholics, concentrated in Ankole and the southwestern part of the country generally; and the Uganda People's Congress, overwhelmingly Protestant, and popular in the northern and western parts of the country.

Elsewhere, race was the main source of identity difference among the citizens of some African states, notably in southern Africa and the Sahel. Naturally, as long as there was whites-only rule in South Africa and Rhodesia, the racial cleavages were the ones that mattered in politics. As much as the South Africa's African National Congress (ANC) relished the idea of building a "rainbow coalition" of opposition to *apartheid*, its fundamental orientation was to call for *racial* and not *class* justice. The South African Communist party, with its pretentions to rally people along class lines, was an obvious failure compared to the ANC. Meanwhile, in such Sahelian countries as Mauritania and Sudan, the fundamental cleavage of Arabized-African north versus black African south is undeniable. The practice of slavery of black southerners from these two countries by Arabized northerners is only the most visible and repugnant manifestation of the fundamental racial divide. Insofar as the southerners in each country were not completely repressed, politics has revolved around this racial cleavage, as Sudan's endless civil wars attest.

Identity politics in Rwanda and Burundi were even more salient than in most other African countries, even if scholars have struggled to characterize and appropriately label the two major identity groups. The Hutu and Tutsi identity groups of these two countries are clearly not "ethnic groups" in the normal sense of peoples with their own distinctive traditional territories and languages: in each country, the Hutu and Tutsi speak a common language (Kinyarwanda and Kirundi, respectively), and the representatives of the two groups are greatly interspersed. There are not Hutu or Tutsi "homelands" in either country. Lemarchand (1970) was perhaps most forthright in trying out different labels for the identity groups, testing the labels "caste" and "class," *inter alia*, to describe them. *None* of the generic labels for identity groups used in other countries ultimately quite work to distinguish and name the two groups. Nonetheless, there is no denying this identity difference is the one that matters in both countries, as the episodes of mass killing—and genocide in Rwanda in 1994—clearly attests.

Besides (arguably) Rwanda and Burundi, Africa's other most ethnically homogenous states are Somalia (about 85% Somali) and Botswana (about 80% Tswana). The two countries have of course followed diametrically opposed trajectories in terms of internal social cohesion (and development), the former being Africa's most spectacularly failed state (and society) and the latter being Africa's clearest socioeconomic success story. In terms of identity structures, however, the Somali and the Tswana peoples share something in common: each large ethnic group is divided into *clans* and *subclans*. Just as there is no any agreement (nor can there be) on the number of ethnic groups in any given African country, there is no agreement on the number of clans or subclans in either Somali or Tswana society. Yet, a large majority of people in both societies do identify with specific clans and subclans that play a major role in the structure and variety of social relations, including politics.

Botswana is among a tiny minority of African countries in which identity (clan, in this case) is not readily visible in the party formation or electoral politics of the country, but it is not the only exception. Identity politics has generally been more muted in Southern Africa and in Tanzania, for instance, than in Central or West Africa, where civil wars between or among various identity groups has been common. Because ethnic or identity politics is less visible and less violent, though, it does not mean that it is not quite important to the politics of these countries. For instance, Posner (2005) shows that ethnic politics is crucial in Zambia, even if his main point is more subtle. Among other things, his study demonstrates that Zambians expect members of their political class to distribute patronage according to an ethnic formulation (ibid.: 92–104). Part of the reason for the relatively low profile of ethnic politics in Zambia is because of demographics: the country has a large number of small ethnic groups that have not, for institutional reasons, coalesced into coherent "ethnic clusters." Tanzania, where ethnic politics is also muted, has exhibited a similar pattern of sociodemographic development and ethnic politics. Those who know the country well (e.g., Heilman and Kaiser 2002) are well aware of the growing reality of identity community (religious) politics in Tanzania, not to mention the more obvious tension between Zanzibar and mainland Tanzania.

Strangely, despite the ubiquity of identity politics in Africa, and the large role it plays in both political and developmental outcomes, most political scientists do not put identity politics at the center of their explanations for these outcomes. The reasons are multiple and understandable. First, many of us really wish things were different. Most Africans are suffering much more from the effects of neopatrimonialism and its effects than they are from ethnic, religious, or regional discrimination. Maldistribution of wealth in Africa is shocking, and generation of more wealth, and provision of better social services, seems to be a priority. Socially conscious Africanists really wish that African citizens would come together across *class* lines to insist on better policies that favor growth and a fairer distribution of wealth. Many think and act in terms of devotion of ideas and/or material interests, and project the same values onto others.

Second, to dwell on identity politics runs the risk to have one's name associated with the thoroughly discredited primordialist approach to identity politics. Most of those writing about ethnicity or identity politics in Africa in fact, are writing to demonstrate—once again—that ethnic identities are fluid, artificial, contingent, recently created, socially constructed, and/or products of European colonialism. These arguments are correct, and almost all Africanists have now adopted either an instrumentalist or a constructivist point of view about ethnic and other identities. Yet, correct those these arguments may be, they are often beside the point. With regard to Rwanda, for instance, most professional Africanists understand that the objective basis for a distinction between Hutu and Tutsi is slim indeed: both social groups speak the same language, Kinyarwanda; they have lived together and developed mutual interdependence over many centuries, and often without conflict; individuals from each "group" have intermarried and produced many thousands of "mixed" offspring; there is usually no easy way to tell the difference between a Hutu or a Tutsi based on appearance. Despite the verity of such observations, however, none prevented the mass murder—indeed, attempted genocide—of the Tutsi by a group of fanatic Hutu militants in 1994. Today, nearly everyone, including the Rwandan government, wishes to downplay the "objective" bases for identity difference between the two groups, but there is no gainsaying the depressing truth that the genocide was based on this difference. The fact that the identities are mostly social constructions only underscores the paradox of this terrible situation.

A third reason why Africanists so often downplay the significance of identity politics, even when they take it as a given, is that the *specific form* of identity politics can rarely if ever be foreseen. As Posner (2005) points out, African societies all have *multiple* identity cleavages within them, and one cannot predict which lines of social cleavage will become politically relevant. Although identity politics *itself* is not "endogenous to politics," the specific form of ethnic politics surely is. How do people from a variety of regions come together to vote (and otherwise act) as a group? Why do various small ethnic groups often join forces politically across the lines of larger ethnic clusters? Why is ethnic politics more important in, say, Nigeria and Ethiopia, when the divide between major religious confessions (i.e., Christian vs. Muslim) could just as easily become the main social cleavages? Whereas identity politics itself is a product of culture, specifically of "cultural pluralism" (Young 1976), the specific form of identity politics is surely a product of institutions, as Posner argues so well.

Despite these predilections among Africanist scholars, the reopening of the political space in Africa in the early 1990s again made the primacy of identity politics there undeniable. In retrospect, the one-party state model that dominated African institutional politics from the mid-1960s to 1989, was among other things, an effort to mitigate the effects of intercommunal politics. Many African rulers were explicit about this, even if the one-party model also suited the needs of the personal politics that they practiced. Yoweri Museveni's "no-party" model of politics of the 1990s and early 2000s was the last vestige of the argument in favor of suppressing intercommunal conflict through the limitation of political party activity. Whatever Museveni's actual motives were, there is no denying that the vast majority of political parties that sprang up in Africa following the end of the single-party model were based on identity community constituencies. The parties that served as vehicles for individual ambitions, to the extent that they succeeded, garnered support among specific ethnic, ethno-regional, or other identity groups. The political opening of the 1990s and the nature of the political parties that it produced showed beyond a doubt that the "natural" politics of African society was a contest among identity groups for power. Worse still, the civil conflicts between identity groups in the Central African Republic, Congo-Brazzaville, Congo-Kinshasa, Cote d'Ivoire, Kenya, Liberia, Rwanda, and Sierra Leone all seem related to the identity community politics that followed the end of the one-party state.

Identity Politics and Development

If identity politics is as fundamental to open political competition in Africa as the above analysis suggests, what are the consequences for African development? Unfortunately, it is easy to make a case that underdevelopment and identity politics often form a vicious circle, in which one reinforces the other, as the "conflict trap" of Paul Collier (2007: 17–37) suggests. As Inglehart and Welzel (2005) have demonstrated in their defense of neo-modernization theory, people who have not yet experienced economic development display "traditional values" (rather than "secular-rational values") in their political (including voting) behavior. Poorer and less well educated people have lower levels of trust vis-à-vis "outsiders" than those who are wealthier and better educated. In elections, they generally vote for leaders from their own ethnic groups, and look to those leaders to help them improve their economic circumstances. Such people are less likely to vote on ideological grounds, or on behalf of specific policies that they favor for the general good. Inglehart and Welzel go to great pains to insist that such common values—essentially political culture—*can* change. But political cultures will only begin to change, generationally, once development begins to take hold.

On the other hand, there are multiple reasons to think that *open* identity community politics impedes development, of which two are particularly important. The first is that open politics, in which identity communities are clearly the main participants, seems to increase the level of patronage politics in the polity. When the politics is open, and identity communities claim a share of power, they also claim a share of the wealth. The representatives of various identity communities demand a share of government revenues provided through access to governmental posts. Open politics, inevitably some kind of identity community politics, generally leads to an escalation in levels of corruption (often already high). The politics of Ghana and Nigeria from the 1960s to the 1990s are cases in point. These two states went back and forth between open civilian regimes and closed military regimes. When civilian regimes were in power, they felt very strong pressures to distribute state response to the most visible representatives of various ethno-regional constituencies for personal use. This led to low state performance, and to military coups whose ostensible purpose was to restore effective governance.

If one examines some of the fragmentary data from the 1990s, however, the evidence for this hypothesis is not obviously supported (see Table 10.1). Regimes that remain closed to political competition not only have to provide patronage to opposition groups to maintain a modicum of legitimacy, but also to "buy off" opposition leaders. A comparison between Benin and Togo is instructive here. During the 1990s, Benin was at the forefront of the democratization movement, being one of the first African states to "consolidate" its democratic system with relatively free elections, and to experience two changes of leadership (in 1991 and then again in 1996). Togo, a similarly sized country with many attributes like Benin, including a similar colonial history, remained political closed, with Gnassingbé Eyadema manipulating the elections to remain in power. Yet, the two countries had identical increases in the Human Development Index scores for the 1990–2000 decade. Some regimes that kept their politics closed to ethno-political competition during the 1990s did very well, including Sudan, Uganda, and Ethiopia (not included in Table 10.1, but its average annual rate of growth from 1992 to 2000 was 4.1%). In other cases, there were gradual and controlled political openings, as in countries such as Kenya and Cote d'Ivoire, but these countries fared poorly in terms

Table 10.1 Identity Community Politics in the 1990s

Change in HDI		*Change in HDI*	
Open Politics in 1990s	*1990–2000*	*Closed Politics*	*1990–2000*
Benin	0.040	Cameroon	0.00
Central African Republic	–0.004	Cote d'Ivoire	0.013
Congo-Brazzaville (to 1997)	–0.024	Gabon	0.016
Malawi	0.052	Kenya	–0.013
Mali	0.071	Sudan	0.059
Mozambique	0.045	Swaziland	–0.034
Niger	0.036	Togo	0.040
Zambia	–0.023	Uganda	0.073
Category average	0.024	Average	0.019
African average	0.018		0.018

Source: U.N. Development Program (UNDP: See http://hdr.undp.org/en/data). (No data available for many countries, including Ethiopia, Nigeria, Madagascar, etc.)

of human development improvement. Besides Benin, on the other hand, many states with open electoral competition (generally among identity groups) performed above the African average. These countries included Malawi, Mali, Mozambique, and Niger; of these, only Madagascar was recovering from a civil war situation, and thus starting from an "artificially" low base. Only Zambia and two countries experiencing civil war or unrest—the Congo Republic and the Central African Republic—performed below average.

The other great danger of open (identity community) politics in Africa is civil war. A number of Africa's civil wars of the 1990s can be traced directly back to political openings or for demands for political openings that did not occur. In turn, the insurgents in most of these civil wars were of a distinctive ethnic or regional background; in fact, none of the insurgencies were broadly representative of the populations of the countries whose regimes they fought against. In the first category of cases, civil wars broke out after freely elected rulers did not prove to be democratic in their political behavior, seeking to manipulate elections or close the political space once again after gaining office. The civil wars that broke out in Congo-Brazzaville (1997) and in the Central African Republic (2006) were of this type, and each was clearly associated with disaffected identity groups. The second type of civil war is associated with frustrated demands of identity groups who feel that they are being excluded from power. This type occurs when those in power refuse to organize elections or organize elections that are clearly fraudulent. The civil wars that broke out in Liberia (1989), Rwanda (1990), Somalia (1991), Zaire (1996), Cote d'Ivoire (2002), and Chad (2005) were all animated by insurgent groups from distinctive identity communities different from that of the president and key ruling elites. Each of these conflicts was of course complex and has other dimensions other than the ethnic or identity community dimension. Yet, in each case, the main combatants came from specific ethnic or identity groups with grievances against the ruling regimes. (In some civil wars, like that of Guinea-Bissau in 1998, it is not clear that intercommunal tensions caused the war, though there was tension between President Viera [an ethnic Papel] and the army, dominated by the Balanta group.)

As for the civil wars that had begun long before the era of multipartyism in Africa, those of the 1960s, 1970s, and 1980s, the majority of these, too, were between identity communities. It is noteworthy that the insurgent groups that opposed the Marxist rule of Mengistu Haile Mariam of Ethiopia all had an ethno-regional basis: the Oromo Peoples' Democratic Organization (OPDO), the Amhara National Democratic Movement (ANDM), the South Ethiopian Peoples' Democratic Front (SEPDF), and the Tigrayan Peoples' Liberation Front (TPLF). Insurgents in Angola and Mozambique had an ethno-regional basis, and were defending ethno-regional interests, as much as they were pursuing the ideological agendas with which they were publicly associated.

In other African states, there was civil violence that fell short of civil war. Madagascar has twice experienced civil violence that verged on civil war in 2002 and again in 2009. Kenya saw large-scale intercommunal violence following the disputed elections of December 2007. Many other African countries have experienced intercommunal violence following disputed elections over the past 20 years (as well as some outbreaks of violence that were not identity community-based).

All of these forms of violence clearly impede economic development. As Paul Collier has argued, "Civil war is development in reverse ... Civil war tends to reduce growth by around 2.3% per year, so the typical seven-year civil war leaves a country around 15% poorer than it would have been" (2007: 27). He later claims that the cost of a "typical civil war to the country and its neighbors can be put at around $64 billion" (ibid.: 32). The ways in which civil wars disrupt economic development are obvious: they lead to the deaths of economically productive citizens; they destroy the infrastructure that permits commerce to take place; they divert government funds from capital investments to expenditures on arms; and they serve as a powerful dissuasion to foreign investment, among other negative effects.

Data on the economic performance of African states experiencing civil wars during the 1990s and the 2000s bears out these claims (see Tables 10.2 and 10.3). Data on seven states experiencing long-running civil wars during the 1990s shows that their UNDP Human Development Index (HDI) scores *declined by* an

Table 10.2 Comparison of Development in States with and without Intercommunal Violence in the 1990s[a]

	Change in HDI, States with Civil Wars, 1990–2000	*Average Annual Growth during War*
Burundi	–0.005	–8.2 (1993–2000)
Congo-Brazzaville	–0.024	–2.4 (1993, 1994, 1997, 1999)
D.R. Congo	–0.030 (1995–2000)	–3.9 (1996–2000)
Liberia	–0.01	–21.0 (1990–1996)
Rwanda	–0.015 (1990–1995)	–11.5 (1990–1994)
Sierra Leone	0.011	–4.7 (1991–2000)
Sudan	0.059	4.8 (1990–2000)
Average	–0.014	–6.7
African average	0.018 (1990–2000)	2.4 (1990–1999)

Source: Human Development Report (UNDP: See http://hdr.undp.org/en); World Development Indicators (World Bank: See http://data.worldbank.org/data-catalog/world-development-indicators).

[a] No data for Djibouti, Somalia; low-grade insurgencies, as in Senegal (Casamance) not included.

Table 10.3 Comparison of Development in States with and without Intercommunal Violence in the 2000s[a]

	States with Civil Wars Change in HDI, 2000–2010	*Post- or Pre-War Performance*
Burundi (to 2005)	0.022 (2000–2005)	0.049 (2006–2010)
Liberia (to 2003)	−0.006 (2000–2005)	0.029 (2006–2010)
Sudan (to 2005)	0.026 (2000–2005)	0.025 (2006–2010)
African average (2000–2005)	0.03	
Chad (2005–2010)	0.016 (2006–2010)	0.026 (2000–2005)
African average (2006–2010)	0.03	
C.A.R. (2004–2007)	0.037 (2000–2010)	
Cote d'Ivoire (2002–2007)	0.026 (2000–2010)	
D.R. Congo	0.062 (2000–2010)	
African average (2000–2010)	0.062 (2000–2010)	

Source: Human Development Report (UNDP: See http://hdr.undp.org/en).

[a] No data for Somalia; low-grade insurgencies, such as Tuareg insurgency, not included.

average of 0.014 during the decade, compared to a sub-Saharan African average increase of 0.018. (HDI score is a composite of life expectancy, income levels, and education levels.) While most of sub-Saharan Africa was experiencing modest development, these seven countries experienced decreases in their HDI scores. On average, their GDP figures declined by an average of 6.7% per year during the years that they were at war (despite Sudan's surprising increases, before it began to export large quantities of oil). Meanwhile, the average sub-Saharan African country was experiencing modest GDP growth of 2.4% per annum. Clearly, civil war impoverished the countries that experienced it during the 1990s, though Sudan is an anomaly that begs for explanation.

Data from the countries experiencing civil war between 2000 and 2010 shows a similar pattern. In general, these countries (except Liberia) did experience minor gains in their HDI scores during the decades or half-decades that they experienced civil wars, but they were below the African average. Surprisingly, one country, the Democratic Republic of Congo, did equal the African average for rate of growth in its HDI. How can we explain this anomaly? The answer is that the civil wars that continued to rage in Eastern Congo for most of the decade did not affect large parts of the country. In fact, President Joseph Kabila was gradually bringing peace to some parts of the country. The intensity of the civil wars was diminishing considerably as he negotiated the withdrawal of foreign troops from the country (de Villers 2009). Furthermore, the Congo was virtually at "rock bottom," developmentally speaking, at the beginning of this period, with the lowest rating *in the world.* Although the DRC maintains this dubious distinction, the relative peace and order of the 2000s, especially after elections of 2006, allowed the country to achieve some modest development gains. In general, though, civil wars clearly diminished the developmental gains that African states might have had, compared to their peers, and compared to their own performances before or after civil wars.

Strategies for Managing Identity Politics

Both Western activists and diplomats, and African free-seekers have sought to open the political space in sub-Saharan Africa's 49 different polities over the last 23 years or so. The old argument in favor of a single-party state has been abandoned nearly everywhere. Even Uganda's Museveni agreed to end his country's "no-party" experiment in 2005. In principle, nearly everyone now agrees that multiparty political competition can best promote liberties and human rights, and that the costs and risks of multipartyism are worth the price.

However, the opening of African polities to free political competition has stimulated the creation of political parties based on identity groups, or groups that cohere on account of ethnicity, region, clan, or religion, rather than on the basis of political principles and programs. The political competition based on such parties has brought about political instability, and in a significant number of cases, civil war. In addition to claiming the lives of millions of Africans (particularly in the DRC and in Sudan), these civil wars have retarded the level of development that African might otherwise have achieved. It is true that modest growth returned to Africa in the 1990s, and accelerated during the first decade of the twenty-first century. But these gains came *despite* the outbreak of widespread violence in Africa, not because of it. Rising commodity prices, rapidly increasing Chinese investments, and other forces account for Africa's recent gains.

These conclusions raise the question of how identity community politics in African can be managed. In the long term, one can still hope that identity community politics may be entirely supplanted by something else. Once African societies experience the kind of development that East Asia has known over the past three decades, perhaps the focus of politics in Africa will change. If so, this change will be brought about by a transformation of political culture, as Ingelhart and Welzel have suggested. Perhaps one can observe the beginnings of such a chance in political culture in the wealthier states of Botswana and South Africa already, though this is certainly debatable.

In the short term, the possible socially destructive effects of identity community politics on African societies must be managed. Virtually all African rulers, whether elected in free and fair elections or not, have realized this. Only a few, like Museveni (to 2005), and Mswati III, King of Swaziland, have publicly rejected the ideal of political competition that has so thoroughly captured the imaginations of people across the globe, excepting a majority in East Asia. In Africa, the *ideal* of multiparty political competition has gained complete sway, but the reality of politics in most African countries is one of "electoral authoritarianism" (Schedler 2002). A majority of African rulers now stage regular un-free and unfair elections in which multiple parties participate. They know the multitude of formulas to ensure their re-election, and most of the manipulation takes place well in advance of the electoral event. Millions of Africans have become resigned to such manipulation and in fact take it for granted. As long as their economic lives are improving (as in Ethiopia and Uganda, for instance), they may tacitly accept such manipulation. When economic lives are not improving much, or are getting worse, they may resent it (as in Cote d'Ivoire or Zimbabwe). Only in a few places, such as Benin, Botswana, Ghana, and Senegal, does real political competition seem to be flourishing, while development continues to proceed. Alas, these countries seem to be exceptional.

Focusing both on the general situation and the exceptional cases, two questions arise: What possible formulas exist for introducing real political *choice* (if not competition)? And what is the secret of the success of the apparently exceptional cases? One answer to the first question has recently been suggested by Pierre Englebert (2009). Englebert has dared to raise a possible formula for improving African politics against which a profound consensus exists, both in Africa and in the West: he has suggested that the self-partition (or voluntary partition) of existing African states, and perhaps their recombination into new political entities might be in order (2009: 244–57). Englebert deserves to be celebrated for his willingness to launch a debate about a reasonable idea that both Africans and Westerners have largely shunned for 50 years. If the main ill of African politics is conflict between identity communities trapped inside artificial states, why not let some or all of them have their own polities? To do so would honor the once-cherished ideal of self-determination espoused in the United States from the time of Woodrow Wilson through that of George H.W. Bush (as the Soviet Union disintegrated). It is surely reasonable to ask whether Nigeria, for instance, might be more functional as two or three separate states rather than as one obviously dysfunctional giant.

Yet, Englebert himself has acknowledged some of the great difficulties of unleashing the potentially ferocious animal of devolution. The disruptions in the modest capacities of state bureaucracies built up over decades would be enormous. More to the point, the kind of self-determination of relative homogenous ethnic peoples that Englebert may have in mind would be accomplished only with great violence. The idea of, say, the Bacongo communities of the Republic of Congo, the DRC, and Angola coming together in a common state is far-fetched. The contemporary states in question would all resist such a project ferociously, bringing to bear both ideals of state unity and formidable armed power against it. Nor can one easily imagine the Hausa and Fulani of northern Nigeria ceding all of that country's considerable oil wealth to their southern brethren, surely a demand that those of Delta Nigeria would make. Finally, looking at the cases of Eritrea and South Sudan, the benefits of independence for parts of existing states do not look encouraging. Eritrea has proved to be one of Africa's most rigidly authoritarian states, whereas the interethnic fighting that has already escalated in South Sudan was widely predicted. The latter case raises the obvious question of how far devolution might proceed, given the breath-taking ethnic diversity of the African states.

A more pragmatic—if far from unproblematic—formulation for "developmental African democracies" would be what Arend Lijphart has called the "consensus model of democracy." Lijphart (1999) contrasts the kind of democratic model he has in mind with the highly competitive "Westminster model" of democracy, in which the majority rules, and the losing minority only criticizes, but has no role in governance. Lijphart suggests that (demographic) social circumstances make the Westminster model impractical for some of the multiethnic states of Europe, as well as for Europe as a whole. The two European states he takes as his models are Belgium and Switzerland. Each society is notoriously divided between rather alien identity communities who have historically found it difficult to live together. Yet, each has developed systems of power-sharing (recently, for Belgium!) which have allowed the different identity communities to live peaceably, and also quite *prosperously*, in the same state. More recently (2004), Lijphart has tried to reduce his "consociationalist" agenda down to some basic recommendations for the (political) institutional design of divided societies.

Among Lijphart's (2004) many possible institutional formulas for permitting group representation in the governance process include proportional representation in the legislature; power-sharing within the executive cabinets; stronger judicial reviews that can protect minority rights; the provision for "ceremonial" heads of state, who can remain above the fray of politics, and intervene credibly in intercommunal disputes; and constitutional formulas that allow minority groups to "veto" the proposals of narrow majorities. Each of these ideas is surely fraught with difficulty in Africa, and most of Lijphart thinking is drawn from European examples. But the basic idea of governance by consensus, rather than by narrow majority rule, surely has appeal in African divided states. Such formulas will depend on willing elites, however, who would need to put these ideas into constitutions, and then make them work in practice.

One obvious objection to this kind of formula is that it could threaten to paralyze the policy-making process. Atul Kohli (2004) among others has contrasted the rational, effective policy that "cohesive-capitalist" states (like South Korea) have made with the much less efficacious policies of "fragmented-multiclass states" (like India) and "neopatrimonial states" (like Nigeria). Yet, the multiethnic realities of most African states make the Korean-style model that Kohli endorses incapable of being imitated. The social identities of African citizens may change over the very long term, but in the shorter term, they will remain attached to their communal identities, even as they are forced to continue living with others. This makes the kinds of models advocated by Lijphart the best possibility for nonviolent governance in African states.

Two African states that seem to come close to the "consensus model" of governance that Lijphart advocates are Tanzania and Botswana. The latter of course has a much more economic success than the former. It is endowed with substantial natural mineral resources, and yet it has avoided the infamous resources curse (Gapa 2013). Tanzania has quietly enjoyed some real economic progress, however, since 1995 without sacrificing its vaunted social cohesion. Only in regard to the Zanzibar stand-off has Tanzania experienced some modest intercommunal violence, despite its great ethnic diversity. The country's HDI score has jumped from only 0.364 to 0.466 between 2000 and 2011, far ahead of the African average. It remains to be seen whether Botswana and Tanzania can continue to prosper and also avoid intercommunal conflict when the moment of alternation of power inevitably comes to each country. For the time being, the consensus model of politics seems to be enjoying some positive results in each country.

Conclusion

Politics in almost all African states involves contestation for power among various kinds of identity groups. The specific identity groups that become politically relevant in specific countries depends upon demographics, surely, but just as importantly on how identity is constructed and how elites mobilize identity groups for political purposes. Thus, paradoxically, identity group politics is ubiquitous in Africa, but the groups that become mobilized, and its specific forms, are not inevitable, predetermined, or predictable. The various kinds of identity groups include clans, ethnic groups, regional identity groups, racial groups, and religious communities. Even countries that have been free of overt identity community conflict, like Tanzania and Zambia, experience identity community conflict below the surface, as both locals and country specialists are aware. Only economic and social development will finally subordinate identity community politics to the politics of ideas, contestation over distributional justice, class conflict, and struggles over other social values.

Identity community politics is harmful to development in Africa in two key ways. First, identity community politics requires political regimes of all stripes—openly authoritarian, electoral authoritarian, and democratic—to engage in large-scale patronage of elite representatives of identity communities. Such patronage is a profoundly inefficient way of allocating public resources, reducing funds available for infrastructure, industrial development, and the provision of government services to the public. Patronage practices characteristic of identity community politics represent a significant brake on the possibility of economic development. Second, identity community politics more often leads to violent social and political conflict than other forms of politics. Sometimes, such contestation between or among identity groups can lead to all-out civil war. In the worst cases, violence among identity groups devolves into warlordism and ends in state collapse. By contrast, there are few cases in the world history of class conflict leading to state collapse, violent though such conflicts have often been. Civil war and state collapse, in turn, are essentially "development in reverse." These outcomes set back the painstaking gains achieved on the development front by years or even decades.

These considerations lead us to ask how identity politics in Africa can be managed as we await the economic development that might mute it even further. One set of approaches are essentially institutionalist in nature. Many observers have noted that the kind of majoritarian politics that creates clear winners and losers often tends to exacerbate feelings of grievance and resentment in the "losing" identity communities. Two different but related kinds of institutional solutions to this problem are possible. One is to require that the representatives of all major identity groups reach a consensus on public issues before major policies initiatives are undertaken. The one-party state model that prevailed from the 1960s through the 1980s in Africa embodied this idea, even if it largely failed in practice. A second institutionalist solution—the consociationalist approach—provides each publicly recognized group with specified prerogatives, such as the right to occupy certain constitutional positions of the state. This approach depends upon a prior agreement to the allocation of power positions to certain groups among the key elites. A second approach to managing conflict is essentially culturalist. This approach typically calls for all citizens to subordinate their feelings of group belonging to that of identification with the "national" group, that is, the collective of a given state's citizens. A very different culturalist approach requires citizens to assimilate to a dominant culture, as in Botswana, where the prevailing Tswana ethnicity has effectively assimilated many minority group citizens to their politico-cultural norms. Either set of approaches can only hope to succeed in the presence of patient and sensitive national leaders. Success stories such as that of Ghana reassure us that effective forms of identity group management are possible. Yet, well-intentioned African leaders can hardly be complacent about the challenges that identity group politics pose for development in their countries.

References

Alexander, J. 1997. The local state in post-war Mozambique. *Africa* 67 (1), 1–25.

Bernault, F. 1996. *Démocraties Ambiguës: Congo-Brazzaville, Gabon, 1940–1965*. Paris: Karthala.

Bustin, E. 1975. *Lunda under Belgian Rule: The Politics of Ethnicity*. Lawrence, MA: Harvard University Press.

Collier, P. 2007. *The Bottom Billion*. Oxford: Oxford University Press.

de Villers, G. 2009. République démocratique du Congo De la guerre aux élections: L'ascension de Joseph Kabila et la naissance de la Troisième République (janvier 2001-août 2008). Cahiers Africains 75, 471. Paris: L'Harmattan.

Englebert, P. 2009. *Unity, Sovereignty, and Sorrow*. Boulder, CO: Lynne Rienner.
Gapa, A. 2013. Escaping the Resource Curse: The Sources of Institutional Quality in Botswana. Doctoral dissertation. Florida International University. Miami, FL: FIU Electronic Theses and Dissertations.
Gray, C. 2002. *Colonial Rule and Crisis in Equatorial Africa: Southern Gabon Ca. 1850–1940*. Rochester, NY: Rochester University Press.
Heilman, B., Kaiser, P. 2002. Religion, identity and politics in Tanzania. *Third World Quarterly* 23 (4), 691–709.
Inglehart, R., Welzel, C. 2005. *Modernization, Cultural Change, and Democracy*. Cambridge: Cambridge University Press.
Kohli, A. 2004. *State-Directed Development: Political Power and Industrialization in the Global Periphery*. Cambridge: Cambridge University Press.
Lemarchand, R. 1970. *Rwanda and Burundi*. London: Pall Mall.
Lijphart, A. 1999. *Patterns of Democracy: Government Forms and Performance in Thirty-Six Countries*. New Haven, CT: Yale.
Lijphart, A. 2004. Constitutional design for divided societies. *Journal of Democracy* 15 (2), 96–109.
Marcum, J. 1969. *The Angolan Revolution*, Vol. 1. Cambridge, MA: MIT Press.
Nzongola-Ntalaja, G. 2002. *The Congo: From Leopold to Kabila: A People's History*. London: Zed.
Otayek, R. 1989. Burkina Faso: Between feeble state and total state, the swing continues. In: Cruise, D., Dunn, J., Rathbone, R. eds., *Contemporary West African States*. Cambridge: Cambridge University Press.
Posner, D. 2005. *Institutions and Ethnic Politics in Africa*. Cambridge: Cambridge University Press.
Schedler, A. 2002. Elections without democracy: The menu of manipulation. *Journal of Democracy* 13 (2), 36–50.
Whitaker, C.S. 1991. The Unfinished State of Nigeria. In Sklar, R.L., Whitaker, C.S. (eds.). *African Politics and Problems in Development*. Boulder, CO: Lynne Rienner Publishers, pp. 265–273.
Young, C. 1965. *Politics in the Congo: Decolonization and Independence*. Princeton, NJ: Princeton University Press.
Young, C. 1976. *The Politics of Cultural Pluralism*. Madison, WI: University of Wisconsin Press.

Chapter 11

Religious Movements, Governance, and Development in Africa

William F. S. Miles

Contents

> We are praying for this project to continue.
>
> **—Alfaca, Senegalese herdsman (Bascomb 2012)**

Even more than elsewhere in the developing world, religion in Africa is inextricably tied to the daily struggle to improve material conditions of worshipers and believers. In a region where nearly half the population lives in absolute poverty, any pretence of separation of faith and means is a conceit. Given that economic outcomes are linked to the "goods" of constructive politics and responsive governance ("peace and stability"), religious institutions and movements are drawn into arenas of good governance, conflict mitigation and resolution, and state-administered justice. In Africa, the interplay of religion, development, and governance is not merely intellectually compelling; it is a matter of life and death.

This chapter will adopt three tacks to explore this triple interplay. The first presents an overview of peace-building and conflict mitigation activities. The second examines projects and programs in which faith-based organizations (FBOs) are involved in providing economic and social developmental services. The third, and most "value-added" part of the chapter, examines ongoing, official U.S. Government (USG) efforts to assist and employ FBOs for development, governance, and conflict mitigation in Africa. Special emphasis will be placed on activities supported through the Trans-Sahara Counterterrorism Partnership (TSCTP), where a U.S. security objective is grafted onto other objectives. The chapter questions whether the goal of having religious movements foster good governance, conflict mitigation, and socioeconomic development is undermined when FBOs are used as assets for counterterrorism objectives.

Between the original special issue on religion and development in *World Development* (Goulet 1980; Morris and Adelman 1980; Wilber and Jameson 1980), and the retrospective three decades later in the same journal (Deneulin and Rakodi 2010), scholarship has burgeoned. The literature reflects a consistency in religiosity in the developing world contrasting with fluidity and variability (if not faddism) in development thinking and policy. "Sustainable" is one of many concepts that has become an important qualifying adjective for "development" in policy circles.

From the perspective of most Africans, however, which has a better track record of sustainability: development or religion? Projects or churches? Experts or imams? Political parties or parish priests? This chapter argues that until Western-oriented development specialists—however well meaning—appreciate the comparative advantage religious institutions enjoy over development agencies, efforts to eliminate poverty will be appreciably handicapped. However, that appreciation must be genuine and intrinsic, not strategic and opportunistic.

Data substantiate this argument. On the eve of the millennium (as well as now), 10 of the least-developed nations, according to the UN Human Development Index (HDI), were in sub-Saharan Africa. Of those, six were clustered in West Africa. At the same time, Gallup International released its Millennium Survey. Gallup revealed that, of the six world regions* surveyed, by far the most religious or "faithful" was West Africa.

Correlation, of course, does not equate causation. It is nevertheless remarkable that the region with the lowest levels of life expectancy, literacy, and income (core HDI indicators) is the same one registering the highest levels of religious affiliation, religious service attendance, and personal attachment to the importance of God. This correlation between economic deprivation and spiritual faithfulness

* The other five regions included Latin America, Southeast Asia, Eastern Europe, Western Europe, and North America.

pertains not only to the other least developed nations in Africa, but also to sub-Saharan Africa as well.*

Peace, U.S. Policy, and FBOs

Johnston and Sampson (1994) is the touchstone for discussions of linkages between religion and policymaking, particularly from a peace-building/peace-making perspective. The editors identify religion as the "missing dimension" in the broader foreign policy scheme to promote peace and reconciliation: "spiritually based mediation and conciliation can, under the right circumstances, achieve genuine breakthroughs to peace" (Johnston 1994b, p. 316). Notable, are the chapters highlighting the role of Quakers in ending the Biafran war in Nigeria (Sampson 1994), the evolution of churches during apartheid in South Africa (Johnston 1994a), and religious actors in the struggle for Zimbabwean independence (Kraybill 1994).

In highlighting what they call "transnational religion," Rudolph and Piscatori (1997) paint an otherwise contestable portrait of "fading states." Less disputable is their claim that transnational religion plays an emerging international role to maintain order. In certain cases, transnational religion promotes human stability, development, and solidarity; in others, it fosters interstate conflict. An example is the study by Kane (1997) of contributions the Tijaniyya brotherhood make toward promoting security and stability in West Africa.

Other authors (Haynes 1994, 1998; Toft et al. 2011; Shah et al. 2012) have incorporated religion in their treatment of international relations, drawing attention to religion's potential for conflict mitigation.† Literature on reconciliation in the international arena spans the gamut between religion and politics (Appleby 2000; Torpey 2003, 2006; Daly and Sarkin 2007). For Goldewijk (2007), the contribution of religion to the development of cooperation and international relations lies in the domain of global justice, not just diplomacy and peace negotiations. Global justice provides the nexus between persistent poverty and access to justice.

Since 1990, the U.S. Institute of Peace (USIP) has been tracking the role of religion in conflict; since 2000, it has focused on the role of religion in peace-making, assisting efforts to promote peace between and among the Abrahamic faiths. It has sponsored projects, *inter alia*, in Nigeria and (Southern) Sudan (Smock 2002, 2006).

Concurrent with USIP interest in the relationship between religion, conflict, and peace-making, the U.S. Agency for International Development (USAID) had

* See Pew Research Global Attitudes Project (2008).

† There is another genre of scholarship, which I shall not cite here, that focuses almost entirely on the negative political outcomes of religion in the international arena. Nor shall I rehearse here the fine literature on fundamentalism in international relations and politics.

been quietly increasing its partnership with, or at least support for, overseas FBOs that promote values compatible with U.S. goals. Such state–faith collaboration had generally flown under the radar. According to Clarke (2006, p. 843, invoking Hearn [2002]), "US evangelical and Pentecostal missions in Africa ... are critical to the implementation of [USAID] policy in particular yet effectively function as 'invisible NGOs,' invisible because they have been ignored in the separate literatures on development NGOs and on African Christianity." The election of George W. Bush in 2000 elevated religion to the realm of U.S. policy to an extent not previously seen.

As a born-again Christian and life-long Republican, Bush promoted FBOs to complement, if not supplant, government services in the provision of support networks to socioeconomically troubled Americans. Indeed, until September 11, 2001, the new Office of Faith-Based Community Initiatives (OFBCI) was on track toward becoming the Bush administration's signature policy initiative. The "faith-based" presidency extended to the international arena in addition to the domestic one.

Access to Bush by evangelical leaders with missionary concerns placed African problems squarely on the new administration's foreign policy agenda. One of the earliest of these was the long-standing oppression (some characterized it as genocidal) of southern Sudanese—mostly Christian—by the northern-based—and Islamic—Sudanese government. State Department intermediation played a crucial role in ending the civil war and the negotiated referendum that eventually (after Bush left office) resulted in independence for South Sudan.

The December 2002 Executive Order 13280 creating an OFBCI center in the USAID—a kind of clearinghouse for USG and FBO partnerships—is noteworthy (Clarke 2008, p. 20). This was followed 2 years later by a legal finding by USAID* that NGOs combining humanitarian/development activities with religious ones (e.g., religious instruction, proselytizing, worship) should not be excluded from agency financing, as long as the particular activities financed are nonreligious. By 2009, a full-blown "Toolkit" was produced to illustrate best practices by the USG use of religious organizations to reduce conflict and to promote peace in developing nations (US Agency for International Development [USAID] 2009). The Toolkit was developed by the USAID Office of Conflict Management and Mitigation, itself a unit of the Bureau for Democracy, Conflict, and Humanitarian Assistance. Of the four initiatives in the Toolkit, one—the Interfaith Mediation Centre/Muslim Christian Dialogue Forum—was based in Africa. Known as the "Pastor and the Imam" program of Nigeria, it availed itself of USAID funding to undertake training, peace-building, and media activities. (The pastor, James Wuye, and the imam, Muhammad Ashefa, are two former religiously defined antagonists who came together on their own to found an ecumenical peace-building organization.)

* Participation by Religious Orders in USAID Programs.

President Bush's endorsement of religion in diplomacy and development was unusual for an incumbent President. Like many prominent persons in government and politics, Albright (2006) seems to have "found religion" only after being out of office—as Secretary of State. Albright's reflections on the connection between religion and foreign policy are worthwhile given her experience in government: her chapter on Africa is noteworthy, as illustrated by her visits to and impressions of Nigeria and Sudan.

Now, Rubin (1990) had long ago drawn attention to the "misreading" of religion by U.S. foreign policy makers, and Mead (2006) more recently drew attention to the underappreciated role of evangelicals in foreign policymaking.* But unlike the more academic analyses of foreign policy, Albright cuts to the chase in linking provision of aid to national security interests: "If we want Africans to help in fighting the kind of terrorism that Al-Qaeda practices, we need to assist them in combating the forces that more terrorize them–including disease, a lack of clean water, inadequate schooling, and environmental devastation" (Albright 2006, p. 264). I shall return to the development–terrorism nexus below (pp. 204–206). It is worth quoting Albright a second time—again, in the context of Africa—with respect to Americans' interest in promoting religion abroad: "Faith can provide hope to people who, burdened by the hardships of daily life, might be tempted to despair. Financial contributions—whether from the Middle East or Middle America—can build much-needed schools, clinics, and community centers" (Albright 2006, p. 252).

World Bank Support for Religion's Role in Development

Albright is not the first or only commentator to draw a connection between religion's role with respect to promoting peace and stability and the provision of basic human needs. However, it needed the credibility of a major development player to boost the framing of argument. This occurred in the World Bank's elaboration of, and timetable for achieving, the Millennium Development Goals (MDGs). In the lead-up to that process, the personal rapport between the World Bank President James Wolfensohn and the Archbishop of Canterbury George Carey contributed immensely. An initial step toward institutionalizing the FBO–World Bank relationship occurred in 1998 when the two men cochaired, at Lambeth Palace in London, a meeting with leaders of the world's most widely followed religions. That process gave rise to successive meetings of wider berth, establishment of the World Faiths Development Dialogue (WFDD), and the galvanizing of ecumenical religious organizations (notably the World Council of Religions for Peace and the

* With respect to Africa, Mead highlighted the Bush administration's 67% increase in foreign aid to Africa, especially to combat HIV/AIDS, and its concerted efforts to end war in southern Sudan.

interdenominational Christian "Micah Challenge") to incorporate MDGs in their own objectives. It also resulted in three key World Bank publications.*

The first of these, *Faith in Development,* aims to explicate the ongoing, under-the-radar *Partnership between the World Bank and Churches in Africa* (Belshaw et al. 2001). In their chapters, a combination of African clerics and development workers weigh in on their overlapping perspectives on poverty reduction, gender inequity, AIDS, and as a bridge to the politics of development, conflict and corruption.

Mind, Heart, and Soul in the Fight against Poverty (Marshall and Keough 2004) explicates the World Bank's rationale for partnering with FBOs: the religious basis to the Jubilee 2000 debt relief campaign and rationale for including FBOs in the Poverty Reduction Strategy Paper (PRSP) process. With respect to governance improvement and peace-building, it is worth singling out the treatment in the book's "Peace for God" of the Kacel pi Kuc project for peace in northern Uganda.

Since 1987, the Lord's Resistance Army (LRA)—currently led by the online demon sensation Joseph Kony—has been leading a brutal rebellion against the Ugandan government in Acholiland. Ostensibly to impose the Biblical Ten Commandments, the LRA insurrection has stymied efforts to promote commercial and agricultural development in the area. Kacel pi Kuc ("Together for Peace") is the motto of the Acholi Religious Leaders Peace Initiative (ARLPI), a peace-making group spearheaded by Catholic, Anglican, and Muslim clergymen. ARLPI's goal is to mediate between Ugandan officials and LRA rebels to help resolve the conflict. ARLPI collaboration with the UN Development Programme (UNDP) unlocked funds for peace-building credited with persuading the Sudanese government to suspend support for the LRA.

The World Bank chapter showcases efforts by the Mennonite Central Committee to ameliorate the consequences of violent conflict between the Ugandan government and another northern ethnic group, the Jie. Food, seed supplies, oxen, farm tools, vocational teachers, microloans, and medical assistance (in response to AIDS and Ebola) were all made available to Jie communities, over a 100 of whose villages had been destroyed and thousands of whose families had been displaced.

With the Northern Uganda Social Action Fund, the World Bank involved itself in activities designed to promote peace and reduce poverty. Funds for community development (especially the conflict management and community reconciliation

* Parallel to these World Bank books is that by Tyndale (2006), which includes presentations of Islamic and Christian-based NGOs in Cameroon and a Muslim women's association in Ethiopia. Deneulin and Bano (2009) also invoke African cases in their treatment of religion in development. For a thematic overview of the otherwise "diverse and unconsolidated" literature treating the relationship between religion and development, see Alkire (2006, p. 507). Ver Beek (2000), while invoking some health and agriculture counterexamples from Ghana, Nigeria, and Zambia, documents the general neglect of spirituality and religion in academic and practitioner publications on development throughout the Third World.

components) are being overseen by the United Religions Initiative and the Interfaith Cooperation Circle Initiative of Uganda. In short, the World Bank recognizes that poor people will not raise their incomes unless child soldiers and former rebels are reintegrated into communities, and a mechanism is established for resolving inter-ethnic conflicts.

Development and Faith (Marshall and Van Saanen 2007) fashions itself as a sequel to the 2004 volume, through the prism of the eighth MDG: partnership between the developed and developing nations. Collectively, the volumes showcase the World Bank partnering with Catholic, Protestant, and Muslim organizations to address HIV/AIDS in Mozambique and Uganda, malaria in Mozambique, children's health in Madagascar, reproductive health and waste management in Ghana, underresourced madrasas in East Africa, and female genital cutting in Uganda and (with the assistance of American Jewish World Service) in Senegal. As a formative model, the authors point to the Catholic movement Sant'Egidio. (In the 1970s, Sant'Egidio successfully mediated during Mozambique's civil war between Frelimo and Renamo; since then, it has expanded its works to other countries and broader development objectives.)

Africanists may be surprised by the World Bank's belated acknowledgment of the role of religion in promoting African development. After all, in Africa, missionaries were in the forefront of promoting what today we call "development." Before independence, schools and hospitals throughout the continent were largely missionary enterprises. After independence, these functions were taken over by the state, which saw them as holdovers of colonialism. However, since independence, in most of the continent, the state, and its development projects, has failed. They have failed so often, in fact, that religious institutions and actors have again had to take up the slack.* Today, we refer to them as FBOs instead of "missionaries." But we are talking essentially about the same thing. This is no revelation to scholars who have tracked their activities in, *inter alia*, Ghana (Weiss 2002), Kenya (Hearn 2002), and Zimbabwe (Bornstein 2002). Nor is it new for religious organizations to be involved in peace mediation or postconflict reconciliation: South Africa's Truth and Reconciliation Commission is a prime example.

Interest in the role of religion as a factor for development in predominantly Muslim countries has increased as Islam has captured more of the world's political attention. But long before 9/11, there has been interest in the economic, humanitarian, and transnational actions of informal and formal Islamic organizations throughout Africa. The fostering of trade and commerce through the Tijani and Mouride brotherhoods long ago captured the imagination of scholars such as Behrman (1977), Diop (1981), and O'Brien (1971). Bienen (1983) and Clarke (1979) long ago recognized the importance of Islam for the development of Nigeria. The present author examined the economic implications of the pilgrimage to Mecca

* In those instances where they compromised themselves and collaborated with the regimes for their own institutional welfare, they have had to reinvent themselves (Jennings 2008).

for communities in Niger and Nigeria as well as the reach of transnational Islamic organizations throughout West Africa (Miles 1986, 1990). While Senegal remains the African example par excellence of Islamic networks performing socioeconomic functions (cf. Renders 2002), the sub-Saharan development net now includes as diverse an array of Muslim populations as Cameroon (Salissou 2006; Adama 2007), Chad (Kaag 2007), and South Africa (Sadouni 2007).

Just as the World Bank has belatedly realized the enormous import of religious movements in development in Africa, so has the USG latterly come to perceive a potential linkage between Islam, underdevelopment, and instability on the continent. Its folding of this realization within a regional counterterrorism strategy represents a sensitive development on its own.

Islam, Development, and the Trans-Sahara Counterterrorism Partnership

The TSCTP is a multifaceted, multiyear USG program aimed at defeating terrorist organizations by

- Strengthening regional counterterrorism capabilities
- Enhancing and institutionalizing cooperation among the region's security forces
- Promoting democratic governance
- Discrediting terrorist ideology
- Reinforcing bilateral military ties with the United States

Although the architects of the TSCTP do not spell it out in their above description of the program, the region of their concern—the Sahel and adjoining desert—is overwhelmingly Muslim in population. That U.S. security analysts in the post-9/11 era fixed on the vast "ungoverned spaces" of the "trans-Sahara" as a possible refuge, oasis, or incubator for Al-Qaeda activists or sympathizers may not be all that surprising. That the counterterrorism program strategy should so integrally include USAID will, on the other hand, strike many as counterintuitive. Yet, from the outset, "multifaceted" in this context has meant encompassing a three "D" interagency approach: defense, diplomacy, and development (i.e., the Defense Department, the State Department, and USAID).

In 3D thinking, two of TSCTP's objectives—promoting democratic governance and discrediting terrorist ideology—require developmental programming. In context, "good governance" means enhancing the effective sovereignty of African governments over their physical territory so as to squeeze out the kidnapping-for-ransom operations of Al-Qaeda in the Islamic Maghreb (AQIM). It means creating an economic environment less conducive for potential AQIM recruits: uneducated and unemployed male youth. As for discrediting extremist ideologies, local communication programs shore up moderate voices in inter- and intrafaith dialog fill a rhetorical void that otherwise might be infused with extremist Salafist voices.

In countries such as Burkina Faso, Chad, Mali, Niger, and Nigeria, USAID has accordingly grafted what I call "soft counterterrorist" (Miles 2012) activities onto its traditional mission. For sure, many of those activities (building new schools, providing vocational education) largely complement long-standing development activities. But the elaboration by USAID of analytical models and program guides to address "violent extremism" and "violent Islamic extremism" (Denoeux 2009, Denoeux and Carter 2009) risks distortion, or misunderstanding, of USG developmental intentions vis-à-vis Muslim nations in Africa.

An example of such USAID-funded programming is the Walaikum Project for the Mitigation of Conflicts and Peace Building in Northern Mali. One of Walaikum's objectives is to mobilize and support key local leaders (notables, imams, directors of Koranic schools) in their role as champions of peaceful conflict resolution in communities, communes, and regions. Imams representing Friday mosques in 10 communes of Timbuktu conducted readings of the Koran, preached, and participated in radio debates to promote peace and social harmony messages to the populations.

Walaikum and other peace-building projects could not prevent the 10-month takeover (April 2012–February 2013) of northern Mali (including Timbuktu), first by Tuareg rebels proclaiming an independent Azawad and then by AQIM affiliates who routed them to impose a harsh sharia.* However, Walaikum (or similarly motivated peace-making groups) adapts its messages and strategies in the wake of the stunning Islamist interlude is a subject for future research. The northern Mali episode serves as reminder that governance in the Trans-Sahara carries inextricable religious implications.

A Spirited Caution

As a cautionary note, and in the interest of full normative breadth, it is only proper that a non-monotheistic perspective be invoked. Ellis and Ter Haar (1998, 2004, 2006, 2008) have been reminding Africanists and others that indigenous religious beliefs continue to underlay African society, even among ostensibly monotheistic believers. There is a spirit world that transcends the materialistic basis on which modernist political and economic pretensions rest. This underlying belief in a spirit

* The vigilante-style administration by Ansar al-Din in Mali of what it called sharia is the virtual antithesis of how Islamic law is instrumentalized and adjudicated elsewhere in practice. See, for example, Ibrahim (2012).

world recasts the understanding of development. Spirits give health and impart understanding. Spirits make land fertile and confer prosperity. (Hence, the popularity in Africa of what is called "Prosperity Theology" in the West.) Spirits decide who should govern communities and nations. And spirits determine the outcome of violent conflict, and whether peace shall eventually prevail.

From this perspective, foreign forms of religion—Christianity and Islam—have neglected the spirit world. In addition, the inhabitants of this spirit world need to be either manipulated or appeased. Favorable political and economic outcomes—power, wealth—become a question of proper ministration to the spirits. Democracy and development? These are, from the spirit perspective, superstitious beliefs. Concretely, they have failed to provide either equity or prosperity. Spirits are cultivated for good and evil: religious belief is not an inherent good, be it for development, governance, or conflict reduction.

Where economic pretensions are deceptive or corrupt, indigenous religious beliefs resurge. Particularly in Africa, Ellis and Ter Haar claim, "the development agenda has often disguised the redistribution of power on a vast scale." Invoking no less than Brzezinski (1993), they add that "[d]evelopment [is no less than] a 'coercive utopia' that has been imposed by modern states" (Ellis and Ter Haar 2006, p. 354). Even the World Bank's strategy of providing monetary support to achieve "good governance" is an example of "impos[ing] on Africans a particular view of what is right and wrong," without couching these new norms in indigenous religious terms (Ellis and Ter Haar 2004, p. 148).

Formal, hierarchical Christian and Islamic movements that are officially spiritless (in Ellis and Ter Haar's sense) would not seem to qualify as religious institutions apt to bridge the gap in faith and worldviews between African believers in the spirit world and Western (or Westernized) developmentalists. What is needed, perhaps, is greater recognition of, and organizational support for, groups such as the Union of Believers and Traditionalists of Burkina Faso.* True development includes taking local beliefs seriously, not just as an adjunct or tool for "real" development.

Conclusion

In the West, separation of church and state is a long-standing normative ideal. That it has remained so is in no small measure because citizens there can rely on the state to provide the basic services that guarantee a decent quality of life. Such "services" include the provision of peace and stability. That is not the case in Africa—as the example of short-lived radical Islamist governance in northern Mali attests.

---

* I first encountered a chapter of this organization, locally known as the *Union des Religieux et des Coutoumiers de Burkina*, in Gorom-Gorom, Burkina Faso, on March 9, 2010. In aptly syncretic mode, I was informed that traditionalists (*coutoumiers*) are also Muslim; it was not clear if *all* members of this group of traditionalists also practiced Islam.

In many failed and failing states, governance has fallen, by default, to religious institutions. When religious movements take it upon themselves alone to provide governance, one has the horrific specter of an LRA in Uganda, a Boko Haram in Nigeria, an Al-Shabbab in Somalia, or an Al-Qaeda in the Islamic Maghreb (and affiliate) in Mali. The challenge is for the African state and its external supporters to legitimize peace- and development-oriented religious movements. The challenge is to fully comprehend the religious mindset operating at fundamental levels of African societies.

Tending *only* to souls is a luxury that neither African clergy nor missionary-inspired Western aid donors can afford. The challenge is to responsibly promote religious movements for the purposes of sustainable development and conflict mitigation.

"'Development' is itself a normative ideal and moral cause, and has much in common with faith discourses from which it has traditionally remained aloof," writes Gerard Clarke in the *Journal of International Development* (Clarke 2006, p. 845). On the other hand, Clarke notes that "faith discourses and associated organizations" may often seem "counter-developmental or culturally exotic to secular and technocratic worldviews." Within the context of a small NGO I have founded with my university students that assists two neighboring Muslim villages in Nigeria and Niger (Miles 2009), this latter observation rings loud and true. Two solicitations highlight this disconnect between the worldviews of development and faith-based actors. Typical development assistance runs the gamut from secondary school scholarships to water pump repair tools to goats-for-widows and bull-and-cart projects (see www.neu.edu/abcd).

The first solicitation came from the village's "King of the Blind" and was for a guesthouse for the many inhabitants of the district who had succumbed to trachoma and other sight-destroying maladies common in the region. The "King's" vision for the guesthouse had nothing to do with vocational training or literacy for the visually impaired or any other palliative measures; rather, it was couched entirely within local cultural and religious-based norms of hospitality for strangers and travelers. The second solicitation came from the village "Youth Forum" related to the village cemetery: a fence to keep the animals out of the otherwise unmarked burial area. However, disconnected from mainstream developmental objectives both of the solicitations were, they well reflected the values, priorities, and quotidian concerns of those making the requests. They also revealed incontrovertible cultural disconnects: in the course of realizing the project for the blind, it emerged that their "King" had in mind only blind *men* (Miles 2008).

I close with these two examples to acknowledge the disparate and sometimes inscrutable gulfs that will, from time to time, distance the religiously grounded worldview from the traditionally developmental one. Sustainable development in Africa will require that the religious perspective seriously be taken into account by states and donors. As an aspiration, this is relatively easy to state. To actually incorporate such a perspective, however, may require an outright leap of faith.

References

Adama, H. 2007. Islamic association in Cameroon: Between the Umma and the state. In: B. Soares and O. René (eds.). *Islam and Muslim Politics in Africa*. New York: Palgrave Macmillan.

Albright, M. 2006. *The Mighty and the Almighty. Reflections on America, God, and World Affairs*. New York: Harper Perennial.

Alkire, S. 2006. Religion and development. In: D.A. Clark (ed.). *The Elgar Companion to Development Studies*. Cheltenham, UK: Edward Elgar.

Appleby, R. 2000. *The Ambivalence of the Sacred. Religion, Violence, and Reconciliation*. Lanham, MD: Rowman and Littlefield.

Bascomb, B. 2012. Notes from Senegal. Africa's great green wall of trees. *Living on Earth*. National Public Radio. Available at: www.loe.org/shows/segments.html?programID=12-p13-00013&segmentID=3. Accessed 8/8/14.

Behrman, L.G. 1977. Muslim politics and development in Senegal. *The Journal of Modern African Studies*, 15(2):261–277.

Belshaw, D., R. Calderisi, C. Sugden (eds.). 2001. *Faith in Development*. Washington, DC: World Bank.

Bienen, H. 1983. Religious and economic change in Nigeria. In: J. Finn (ed.). *Global Economics and Religion*. New Brunswick, NJ: Transaction Books.

Bornstein, E. 2002. Developing faith: Theologies of economic development in Zimbabwe. *Journal of Religion in Africa* 32:4–31.

Brzezinski, Z. 1993. *Out of Control: Global Turmoil on the Eve of the Twenty-First Century*. New York: Charles Scribner's Sons.

Clarke, G. 2006. Faith matters: Faith-based organisations, civil society and international development. *Journal of International Development* 18:835–848.

Clarke, G. 2008. Faith-based organizations and international development: An overview. In: G. Clarke and M. Jennings (eds.). *Development, Civil Society and Faith-Based Organizations. Bridging the Sacred and the Secular*. Houndmills, New York: Palgrave Macmillan.

Clarke, G., M. Jennings (eds.). 2008. *Development, Civil Society and Faith-Based Organizations. Bridging the Sacred and the Secular*. Houndmills, New York: Palgrave Macmillan.

Clarke, P. 1979. The religious factor in the development process in Nigeria: A socio-historical analysis. *Genève-Afrique* 17:46–63.

Daly, E., J. Sarkin 2007. *Reconciliation in Divided Societies. Finding Common Ground*. Philadelphia: University of Pennsylvania Press.

Deneulin, S., M. Bano 2009. *Religion in Development. Rewriting the Secular Script*. London: Zed Books.

Deneulin, S., C. Rakodi 2010. Revisiting religion: Development studies thirty years on. *World Development* 39:45–54.

Denoeux, G. 2009. *Guide to the Drivers of Violent Extremism and Terrorism*. Washington, DC: MSI and USAID (February).

Denoeux, G., L. Carter 2009. *Development Assistance and Counter-Extremism: A Guide to Programming*. Washington, DC: MSI and USAID (May).

Diop, M. 1981. Les affaires mourides à Dakar. *Politique Africaine* 1:90–100.

Ellis, S., G. Ter Haar 1998. Religion and politics in sub-Saharan Africa. *Journal of Modern African Studies* 36:175–201.

Ellis, S., G. Ter Haar 2004. *Worlds of Power. Religious Thought and Political Practice in Africa.* New York: Oxford University Press.
Ellis, S., G. Ter Haar 2006. The role of religion in development: Towards a new relationship between the European Union and Africa. *European Journal of Development Research* 18:351–367.
Ellis, S., G. Ter Haar 2008. Africa's religious resurgence and the politics of good and evil. *Current History.* 107(708):180–185.
Goldewijk, B. (ed.). 2007. *Religion, International Relations and Development Cooperation.* Wageningen, The Netherlands: Wageningen Academic.
Goulet, D. 1980. Development experts: The one-eyed giants. *World Development* 39:481–489.
Haynes, J. 1994. *Religion in Third World Politics.* Boulder, CO: Lynne Rienner.
Haynes, J. 1998. *Religion in Global Politics.* London: Longman.
Hearn, H. 2002. The 'invisible' NGO: US evangelical missions in Kenya. *Journal of Religion in Africa* 32:32–61.
Ibrahim, H. 2012. *Practicing Shariah Law. Seven Strategies for Achieving Justice in Shariah Courts.* Chicago, IL: American Bar Association Publishing.
Jennings, M. 2008. The spirit of brotherhood: Christianity and Ujamaa in Tanzania. In: G. Clarke and M. Jennings (eds.). *Development, Civil Society and Faith-Based Organizations. Bridging the Sacred and the Secular.* Houndmills, New York: Palgrave Macmillan.
Johnston, D. 1994a. The churches and apartheid in South Africa. In: D. Johnston and C. Sampson (eds.). *Religion, the Missing Dimension of Statecraft.* New York: Oxford University Press.
Johnston, D. 1994b. Looking ahead: Toward a new paradigm. In: D. Johnston and C. Sampson (eds.). *Religion, the Missing Dimension of Statecraft.* New York: Oxford University Press.
Johnston, D., E. Sampson (eds.). 1994. *Religion, the Missing Dimension of Statecraft.* New York: Oxford University Press.
Kaag, M. 2007. Aid, 'umma', and politics: Transnational Islamic NGOs in Chad. In: B. Soares and R. Otayek (eds.). *Islam and Muslim politics in Africa.* New York: Palgrave Macmillan.
Kane, O. 1997. Muslim missionaries and African states. In: S.H. Rudolph and J. Piscatori (eds.). *Transnational Religion and Fading States.* Boulder, CO: Westview Press.
Kraybill, R. 1994. Transition from Rhodesia to Zimbabwe: The role of religious actors. In: D. Johnston and C. Sampson (eds.). *Religion, the Missing Dimension of Statecraft.* New York: Oxford University Press.
Marshall, K., L. Keough 2004. *Mind, Heart, and Soul in the Fight against Poverty.* Washington, DC: World Bank.
Marshall, K., M. Van Saanen 2007. *Development and Faith. Where Mind, Heart, and Soul Work Together.* Washington, DC: World Bank.
Mead, W. R. 2006. God's country? *Foreign Affairs* 85:5.
Miles, W. 1986. Islam and development in the Western Sahel: Engine or brake? *Journal of the Institute of Muslim Minority Affairs* 7:439–463.
Miles, W. 1990. Islam and development in West Africa. In: J. Okolo and S. Wright (eds.). *West African Regional Cooperation and Development.* Boulder, CO: Westview Press, pp. 215–240.
Miles, W. 2008. The Rabbi's well: A case study in the micropolitics of foreign aid in Muslim West Africa. *African Studies Review* 51:41–57.
Miles, W. 2009. Bulls, goats, and pedagogy: Engaging students in overseas development aid. *PS: Political Science and Politics* 42:181–7.

Miles, W. 2012. Deploying development to counter terrorism: Post-9/11 transformation of U.S. foreign aid to Africa, with special focus on the Sahel. *African Studies Review* 55:27–60.

Morris, C., I. Adelman 1980. The religious factor in economic development. *World Development* 39:491–501.

O'Brien, D. 1971. *The Mourides of Senegal: The Political and Economic Organization of an Islamic Brotherhood.* Oxford: Clarendon Press.

Pew Research Global Attitudes Project. 2008. Chapter 2—Religiosity. Available at: www.pewglobalorg/2008/09/17/chapter-2-religiosity/. Accessed 8/8/14.

Renders, M. 2002. An ambiguous adventure: Muslim organisations and the discourse of development in Senegal. *Journal of Religion in Africa* 32:61–81.

Rubin, B. 1990. Religion and international affairs. *The Washington Quarterly* (Spring). 13(2):51–63.

Rudolph, S., J. Piscatori (eds.). 1997. *Transnational Religion and Fading States*. Boulder, CO: Westview Press.

Sadouni, S. 2007. New religious actors in South Africa: The example of Islamic humanitarianism. In: B. Soares and R. Otayek (eds.). *Islam and Muslim Politics in Africa.* New York: Palgrave Macmillan.

Salissou, I. 2006. Association for environmental conservation and social progress: Sarkan Zoumountsi (Chain of Solidarity). In: W.R. Tyndale (ed.). *Visions of Development. Faith-Based Initiatives.* Aldershot, England: Ashgate.

Sampson, C. 1994. 'To make real the bond between us all': Quaker conciliation during the civil war. In: D. Johnston and C. Sampson (eds.). *Religion, the Missing Dimension of Statecraft.* New York: Oxford University Press.

Shah, T., A. Stepan, M. Toft (eds.). 2012. *Rethinking Religion and World Affairs*. New York: Oxford University Press.

Smock, D. (ed.). 2002. *Interfaith Dialogue and Peacebuilding*. Washington, DC: United States Institute of Peace.

Smock, D. (ed.). 2006. *Religious Contributions to Peacemaking. When Religion Brings Peace, Not War.* Washington, DC: United States Institute of Peace.

Toft, M.D., D. Philpott, T.S. Shah 2011. *God's Century. Resurgent Religion and Global Politics.* New York: W.W. Norton.

Torpey, J. (ed.). 2003. *Politics and the Past. On Repairing Historical Injustices.* Lanham, MD: Rowman and Littlefield.

Torpey, J. (ed.). 2006. *Making Whole What Has Been Smashed. On Reparations Politics.* Cambridge, MA: Harvard University Press.

Tyndale, W. 2006. *Visions of Development. Faith-Based Initiatives.* Aldershot, England: Ashgate.

US Agency for International Development (USAID). 2009. *Religion, Conflict & Peacebuilding: An Introductory Programming Guide.* Washington, DC: USAID.

Ver Beek, K. 2000. Spirituality: A development taboo. *Development in Practice* 10:31–43.

Weiss, H. 2002. Reorganising social welfare among Muslims: Islamic voluntarism and other forms of communal support in Northern Ghana. *Journal of Religion in Africa* 32:83–109.

Wilber, C., K. Jameson 1980. Religious values and social limits to development. *World Development* 39:467–479.

GOVERNANCE AND DEVELOPMENT

V

Chapter 12

Determinants of Subjective Well-Being in Ghana

An Exploratory Micro-Level Study

Isaac Addai, Chris Opoku-Agyeman,
and Sarah Kafui Amanfu

Contents

Introduction

Over the past three decades, social scientists have dedicated a significant amount of scholarly energy to the studying of subjective well-being (SWB) (Andrews and Withey 1976; Campbell et al. 1976). The upswing in scholarly work on SWB is fuelled by a corpus of empirical work, which consistently shows that objective measures of well-being such as per capita income (PCI) do not capture the entire gamut of well-being (Bartolini et al. 2008; Diener and Seligman 2004; Helliwell 2006; Kenny 2005; Putnam 2000). The situation where positive economic growth has been associated with people's negative sense of their well-being has triggered considerable interest in SWB in quality of life studies (see Diener et al. 1999).

SWB seeks to capture noneconomic or nonmaterial dimensions of human life, which are not tapped by objective measures of well-being (Veenhoven 1991). Although definitions vary, SWB is portrayed as a measure that attempts to capture the overall sense of well-being, including happiness and satisfaction with life as a whole and with other domains of life. It is broad and subjective rather than specific and objective (McGillivray and Clark 2006). Psychologists allege that SWB reflects complex judgments of individuals' overall well-being that are based on an integration of self-knowledge regarding many domains of psychological, social, and physical functioning (Diener et al. 1999). The subjective nature of SWB measures has prompted questions about their validity and reliability across cultures. For instance, it has been pointed out that it is not clear whether questions that seek to capture global satisfaction in life and happiness, "taking your life as a whole, would you consider it very happy, somewhat happy or not happy at all?" or if "satisfied in life," is understood in the same way across languages, cultures, and socioeconomic contexts (Wierzbicka 2004) or even how these are interpreted in the same context (Corsin-Jimenez 2007). Despite criticisms, a number of validity, reliability, and comparison studies have confirmed that subjective measures of well-being are comparable to if not better than objective measures of well-being (Kahneman and Krueger 2006). The advantage of using subjective measures of well-being is well articulated by Sarracino (2008, p. 460) as follows:

> Respondent's assessment of their own welfare can highlight factors that are not adequately captured by income measures, including real and perceived insecurity of rewards and incentives systems adapting to structural changes, the state of essential public services (education, health, crime prevention), and norms of fairness and justice.

Background

A review of the literature reveals that almost all the studies on SWB are based on data from developed countries (see Frey and Stutzer 2002 for a detailed review).

With a few exceptions such as Pokimica et al. (2012), Kingdon and Knight (2006, 2007), and Bookwalter and Dalenberg (2004), we know little about SWB in sub-Saharan Africa (SSA). Considering the quality of life challenges facing the region, it stands to reason for objective measures of well-being to be given attention over subjective ones. However, a number of events, ranging from economic reforms, the need for democracy, changes in disease patterns, instability, and levels of poverty, to name a few, taking place in the region make assessment and an understanding of predictors of SWB at the micro-level in the region critical.

First, the success of the prescribed solutions to the region's problems—a free market economic system and democracy—are contingent upon how people perceive their lives. People's subjective assessment of their well-being is found to be an essential prerequisite for successful reform processes and SSA is no exception (Fidrmuc 2000; Hayo 1999). This is because how people feel about their own well-being can boost or undermine the stability of society (Böhnke 2005; Kapitány et al. 2005). In poor countries where survival is always under threat as in SSA, without a positive sense of well-being among the people, economic policy reforms and democratic dispensations are likely to be a mirage. Second, economic and political reforms take time to yield dividends at the micro-level. To avert instability that normally follows reforms in the short term (transitional period), there is a need to develop what is termed propoor policies in the development literature. This is the case in SSA societies where there are no social programs to mitigate negative impacts of austerity measures, which normally form the centerpiece of reforms. For such programs to achieve results, they need to be formulated based on factors molding how people feel about their own well-being. Third, prevailing mental distresses in SSA (Kinyanda et al. 2011) is made worse by increasingly the high incidence of chronic diseases in the region (WHO 2005). In a region where the health infrastructure is not designed to care for people with chronic illness, the care burden falls squarely on family members, particularly women (Akins 2005). The literature shows that the ultimate outcome of the burden of care is mental distress leading to a negative sense of well-being. For instance, in Ghana, studies have found that caring for chronically ill people disrupts marital and family relationships and normally undermines the emotional stability of caregivers (Read et al. 2009) all of which have a direct bearing on the caregivers' mental and physical health. In a region where the etiology of disease continues to be imputed to spirits (Okasha 2002; Twumasi 1975), the high incidence of chronic diseases in SSA tends to be associated with a high level of social rejection of patients and family members (Allotey and Reidpath 2007). Mental stresses that accompany caring for patients with chronic illness are further compounded by poverty (WHO 2005).

Fourth, SWB studies offer the opportunity for policymakers to make comparisons with objective well-being measures and take a decision as to where to put resources to reap maximum results and ensure stability in society (Gurr 1970). Evidence abounds that some people can have good living conditions and at the same time be subjectively dissatisfied (Hayo and Seifert, 2003). SWB analyses might therefore provide policymakers in developing countries with another tool for evaluating policy impact at the micro-level.

Finally, although well-being at the micro-level is an individual responsibility, governments can institute interventions toward the abatement of deprivations. Studies around the globe show that it is possible for some programs to get people out of material and income poverty while keeping them in well-being deprivation (Rojas 2007). A genuine well-being enhancement program needs to be holistic in outlook by liberating people from the claws of material and income poverty and at the same time improving their sense of well-being. Understanding the predictors of SWB is fundamental to designing a holistic well-being-enhancing program (Böhnke 2005). All the above reasons make the assessment of factors influencing SWB at the micro-level, an important area of study in SSA. What we assume we know about factors molding SWB in SSA tends to be based on assumptions and extrapolations from developed countries. However, one would expect that the SWB of people in SSA countries is determined in a different way. The main goal of this chapter is to help fill this gap by exploring factors shaping SWB in one SSA country—Ghana.

Decades of efforts to consolidate economic and democratic reforms in Ghana are transforming the country into a fascinating kaleidoscope of the modern and traditional; the rural and the urban; and the affluent and the impoverished. The challenges to life Ghanaians face range from growing crime, poverty, material deprivations, unemployment, and class distinctions, to name a few (Addai and Pokimica 2012). The country is faced with a situation where positive economic growth and political stability are running in tandem with deterioration in well-being. These and a legion of associated problems have projected themselves in the public psyche with such intensity that many believe the quality of life at the micro-level in the country is waning (Gyimah-Boadi and Mensah 2003). While macro-level indicators of well-being such as gross domestic product (GDP) and gross national income (GNI) are well documented in Ghana (Ghana Statistical Service 2007; World Bank 2011), little is known of how people feel about their own well-being at the micro-level.

This chapter is an attempt to contribute to the growing literature within the social science that is increasingly concerned with factors that contribute to well-being in developing countries, particularly SSA. The analysis is divided into two main sections. The first part reports on the distribution of well-being measures—happiness and satisfaction in life among Ghanaians. The second section explores factors influencing the two measures of SWB under study separately among Ghanaians. It is useful to examine the well-being measures separately for two reasons. First, this approach is likely to give us much more detailed information on people's assessment of their own well-being on each specific SWB measure. Second, such analysis would provide clear insights into the specific measure is to be targeted for intervention purposes. Therefore, findings from this study are likely to yield useful information for governmental and nongovernmental agencies and organizations trying to formulate and implement well-being enhancement programs in the country and other SSA countries. In this study, we utilize data from a World Values Survey.

Data and Measures

We examined predictors of well-being in Ghana by analyzing data from the 2005 to 2008 Wave of World Values Survey. The survey was conducted in several countries and focused on a variety of sociocultural, economic, and political factors. As in other participating countries, the Ghana sample is nationally representative of 1534 men and women aged 16 years and older. The data collection in Ghana occurred between February and April 2007 through face-to-face interviewing of individual respondents selected from households using the Kish Grid. The interviews were conducted in five local languages: Ga, Dagbani, Ewe, Twi, and Hausa. Among other things, the survey collected detailed information about the respondent's views about democracy, their participation in the electoral process, governance, livelihood, well-being, economic concerns, social capital, crime and conflict, and perception about national identities.

In addition to the above, detailed information on the respondents sociodemographic characteristics, including their age, education, place of residence, religious involvement, religiosity, region of residence, ethnic background, and marital status, were also collected. It is the latter questions plus those dealing with well-being that we use in this study. SWB is measured by the self-reported assessment of individuals' own satisfaction and happiness in life. The distribution of self-rated happiness and satisfaction in life will be assessed.

Analytic Techniques

Analysis is carried out at two stages. The first stage uses a nonparametric method (Chi-square) to look at the association between the well-being measures and selected variables. In the second stage, logistic regression equations are used to estimate multivariate models of the odds or the likelihood of a respondent reporting more satisfied life and happiness than worse. The model helps to estimate the predictors of various measures of SWB while simultaneously controlling for other measureable factors associated with well-being. The logistic regression model estimates a linear model in the following form:

$$\ln (pi/(1 - pi)) = b0 + biXi$$

where pi is the estimated probability of a particular event occurring to an individual with a given set of characteristics Xi, b0 is constant that defines the probability pi for an individual with all Xi set to zero, and b is the estimated coefficient.

The ratio pi/(1 − pi) is the odds ratio of respondents with a given set of characteristics reporting better versus worse SWB. The estimate of bi for a particular covariate Xi is interpreted as the difference in the predicted log odds between those who fall within that category of characteristics and who fall within the reference group or who are omitted for those characteristics. If each estimated bi is exponentiated (Exp[bi]), the result can be interpreted as the relative odds of having better SWB for those individuals with characteristic Xi, relative to those individuals in the reference group. All results of multivariate models are given as the exponentiated coefficients. Four significance levels are considered in this study 0.10, 0.05, 0.01, and 0.001.

Dependent Variable

We are cognizant of the debate as to the most appropriate way to measure SWB (see George 1981 for detailed discussion). Whereas some researchers hold a brief for single global measures (Gove et al. 1983; Jackson et al. 1986), others espouse the virtues of domain-specific component measures of well-being (Andrews and McKennell 1980). The well-being literature leans more in favor of the domain-specific measures approach (George 1981, p. 357). However, given that domain-specific measures are absent from our data set, we focus instead on global measures that are found to give comparable results to domain-specific measures.

Generally, two dimensions of global measures of well-being have received considerable scrutiny in the sociological and psychological literature: cognitive and affective (Andrews and McKennell 1980). Affective measures are projected as reflecting spontaneous responses that are assumed to tap into mainly transient assessment and sentiments. On the contrary, indicators of cognitive conditions are thought to capture reflective responses that are based upon implicit comparisons of ideal and real-life circumstances and are assumed to be relatively stable over time (Diener 1984; George 1981). While measures of happiness are projected as indicators of the affective component of well-being, measures of life satisfaction are viewed as capturing the cognitive aspects of well-being. To tap into the affective and cognitive domains of well-being, we analyze happiness and satisfaction in life separately.

Measures of well-being are measured in terms of the respondent's own assessment of his or her life satisfaction and happiness. Answers to "in general how satisfied are you with life" is recoded into a binary measure, with 1 = better (including "much better" and "better") and 0 = worse (combining "same," "worse," and "much worse"). The specific question asked to capture happiness was: taking all things together would you say you are: 1 = very happy to 4 = not all happy. We recoded responses to the original question into: 1 = happy (including very happy and rather happy) and 0 = not happy (including not happy and not happy at all).

Predictor/Independent Variables

To assess the relative importance of various variables in predicting the two measures of well-being, theoretically relevant variables ranging from perceived health status, cultural, demographic, socioeconomic, geographic to social capital variables are utilized in the various multivariate models (Diener et al. 1999). The variables included in the analyses are broadly subsumed under (1) economic factors—relative income and social class, (2) health—self-reported health, (3) geographic—region of residence (north versus south), (4) cultural—ethnicity, religious affiliation, religious involvement, attendance at religious service, and religiosity, (5) social capital—interpersonal trust, institutional trust, civic engagement, freedom of choice, and honesty, and (6) demographic—age, sex, marital status, and education. The average age of the respondents is 33.9 years (Table 12.1).

The distribution of satisfaction in life among the respondents is shown in Figure 12.1.

Generally, it can be said that Ghanaians are satisfied with life. Whereas about 33% of respondents reported being satisfied, approximately 28% indicated being somewhat satisfied with life with only 25% of Ghanaians indicating that they were not satisfied with life at the time of the survey. Figure 12.2 shows that about 55% of Ghanaians reported being very happy and 27% indicated being quite happy. Only 17% and less than 5% of the respondents reported not very happy and not at all happy, respectively.

Comparatively, the data suggest that while the level of happiness among Ghanaians is reasonably high, they are relatively less satisfied with life. The

Table 12.1 Descriptive Statistics for Variables: 2005–2008 Wave of World Values Survey

Variables	*N*	*Range*	*Mean*	*Standard Deviation*
Control Variables				
1. Interpersonal trust[a]	1533	0–7	5.08	1.36
2. Institutional trust[b]	1533	0–4	3.55	0.88
3. Age	1533	16–90	33.86	14.07
4. Civic involvement[c]	1533	0–9	3.29	2.39
5. Community engagement[d]	1533	0–11	4.81	2.38

[a] Interpersonal trust includes trust in relatives, neighbors, friends, and general.
[b] Institutional trust includes trust in government, judiciary, parliament, and police.
[c] Civic involvement includes membership in civil society organizations and their activeness.
[d] Community engagement includes activism, reading news from different sources, and voting in the parliamentary elections.

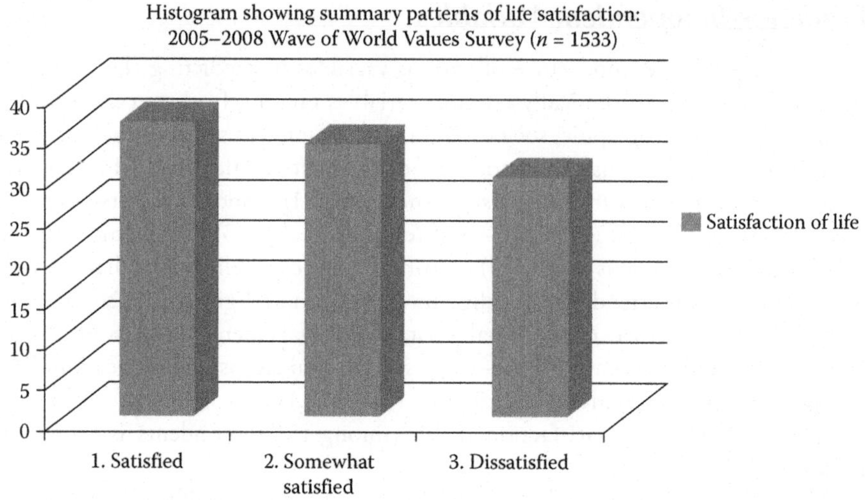

Figure 12.1 Summary characteristics of satisfaction: 2005–2008 Wave of World Values Survey ($n = 1533$).

disparity between affective measure—happiness—and cognitive measure—life satisfaction—may be attributable to the culture of Ghanaians and the socioeconomic realities of life in the country. Ghanaians are generally easygoing people and tend to exude a positive sense of happiness. However, the high sense of hopelessness measured in terms of poverty, unemployment especially among youth

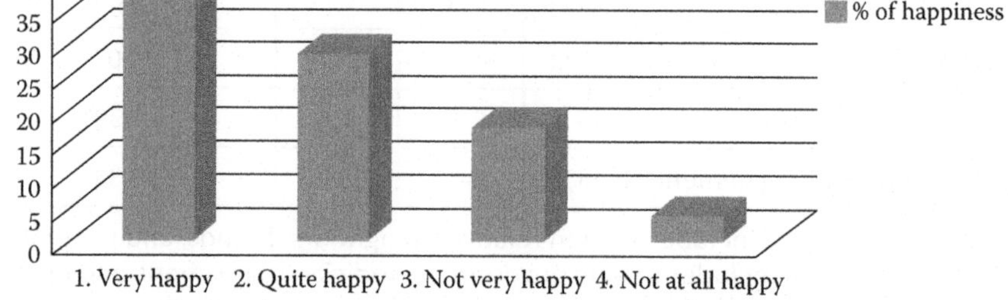

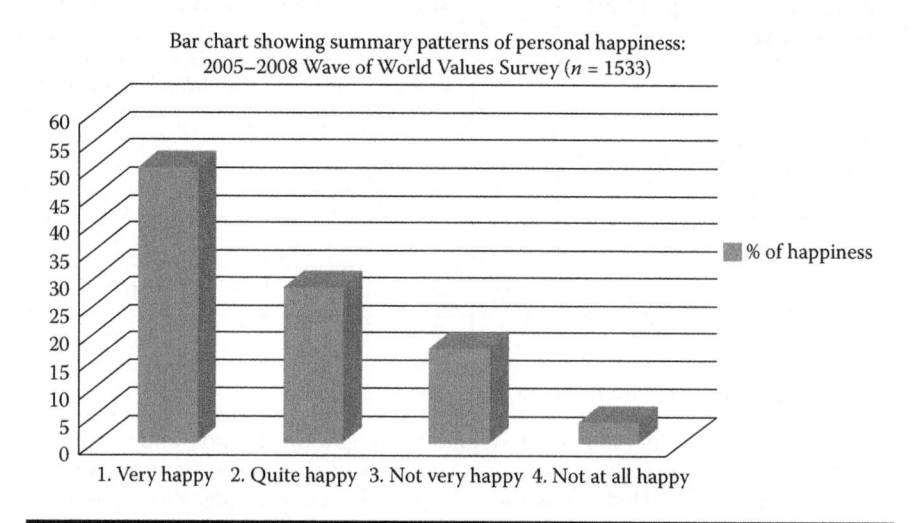

Figure 12.2 Summary characteristics of happiness: 2005–2008 Wave of World Values Survey ($n = 1533$).

and graduates, the high incidence of crime, and material deprivations that have engulfed the country may be undermining people's sense of satisfaction in life.

Bivariate Analysis Results

Table 12.2 displays percentage distribution of happiness and satisfaction in life among Ghanaians by all the variables used in the study except the index ones and age. Ethnicity shows significant association with well-being among Ghanaians ($\chi^2 = 18.883$, $p < 0.001$ and $\chi^2 = 45.515$, $p < 0.001$). Whereas above 60% of Akans reported being happy and satisfied with life, only about 9% of Ga-Adangbes and little above 10% of Ewes reported likewise. For Ghanaians belonging to other ethnic groups, 17% reported being happy and 15% were satisfied with their lives.

With the exception of religiosity, all the religious variables are significantly associated with either one or both measures of well-being under study. For instance, whereas religious affiliation does not show significant association with happiness, it is significantly related to being satisfied in life ($\chi^2 = 16.075$, $p < 0.01$). Whereas above 60% of Ghanaians affiliated with Protestants/Evangelicals reported being happy and satisfied with life, only about 5% of those who belong to the traditional and none religion segment reported being happy and satisfied with life. The percentage distribution of being happy and satisfied with life among Muslims and Catholics were 21% and 14%, respectively. Involvement in religion is significantly associated with both measures of well-being ($\chi^2 = 26.566$, $p < 0.01$ and $\chi^2 = 5.892$, $p < 0.05$). Over 70% of Ghanaians active in religion reported being happy and satisfied with life compared to about 25% of those who are inactive in religion. As expected, attendance at religious service is significantly associated with both being happy and satisfied in life ($\chi^2 = 10.061$, $p < 0.01$ and $\chi^2 = 6.626$, $p < 0.05$). Of the Ghanaians who attended religious service regularly, 45% reported being happy and satisfied with life. Ghanaians who attended religious service once a week and occasionally, 39% and 15%, respectively, reported being happy and satisfied with life.

Relative income is significantly associated with both happiness and life satisfaction ($\chi^2 = 2.647$, $p < 0.001$ and $\chi^2 = 102.970$, $p < 0.001$). Interestingly, the percentage that reported being happy and satisfied in life tends to be higher among Ghanaians in the lower-income category followed by the middle-income category and the last is the upper-income category. There is also a significant association between social class and well-being measures under study ($\chi^2 = 14.617$, $p < 0.05$; $\chi^2 = 50.688$, $p < 0.05$). The distribution of happiness and satisfaction in life among the various social classes show that a higher percentage of the lower class reported happiness and life satisfaction, followed by the middle class, with the upper class coming last. Contrary to expectation, employment status does not show significant association with any of the measures of well-being under study. Social capital variables significantly associate with happiness and satisfaction in life among Ghanaians ($\chi^2 = 2.909$, $p < 0.10$; $\chi^2 = 36.666$, $p < 0.001$; $\chi^2 = 9.925$, $p < 0.01$; and

Table 12.2 Summary Characteristics of Control Variables by Feeling of Happiness and Life Satisfaction: 2005–2008 Wave of World Values Survey

	Personal Happiness		*Satisfaction in Life*		
Control Variables	*Yes*	χ^2 *(df)*	*Yes*	χ^2 *(df)*	*n*
1. Cultural Issues					
Ethnicity					
Akan	61.8%	18.883 (3)****	65.0%	45.515 (3)****	908
Ewe	11.2%		10.0%		184
Ga	9.3%		9.6%		141
Others	17.7%		15.4%		300
Religious Affiliation					
Traditional	4.8%	4.725 (3)	4.7%	16.075 (3)***	82
Catholic	20.5%		20.6%		319
Protestant–Evangelical	60.1%		62.1%		904
Muslim	14.5%		12.5%		228
Religious Involvement					
Active	74.4%	26.566 (2)****	73.2%	5.892 (3)**	1105
Inactive	25.6%		26.8%		428
Religiosity					
Yes	91.9%	2.647 (1)	91.6%	0.170 (1)	133
No	8.1%		8.4%		1400
Attendance at Religious Services					
Regular	45.4%	10.061 (2)***	45.8%	6.626 (2)**	692
Once a week	39.2%		39.2%		582
Occasional	15.4%		15.0%		259
2. Economic Issues					
Relative Income					
Upper	20.9%	2.647 (2)****	22.7%	102.970 (2)****	280
Middle	34.2%		37.1%		485
Lower	45.0%		40.1%		768

(Continued)

Table 12.2 (*Continued*) Summary Characteristics of Control Variables by Feeling of Happiness and Life Satisfaction: 2005–2008 Wave of World Values Survey

	Personal Happiness		*Satisfaction in Life*		
Control Variables	*Yes*	χ^2 *(df)*	*Yes*	χ^2 *(df)*	*n*
Social Class					
Upper class	1.7%	14.617 (3)***	1.8%	50.658 (3)****	23
Middle class	31.2%		33.5%		465
Working class	27.5%		29.7%		402
Lower class	39.6%		35.0%		643
Employment Status					
Yes	58.1%	0.015 (1)	58.7%	0.285 (1)	892
No	41.9%		41.3%		641
3. Social Capital					
Freedom of Choice and Control					
Yes	79.2%	2.909 (1)*	83.2%	36.666 (1)****	1200
No	20.8%		16.8%		333
Honesty					
Yes	41.1%	9.925 (1)***	41.1%	4.639 (1)**	598
No	58.9%		58.9%		935
4. Demographics					
Male					
Yes	51.2%	0.947 (1)	51.2%	0.426 (1)	775
No	48.8%		48.8%		758
Marital Status					
Yes	48.0%	7.309 (1)***	47.5%	5.059 (1)**	763
No	52.0%		52.5%		770
Place of Residence					
North	57.8%	7.376 (1)***	55.7%	0.085 (1)	858
South	42.2%		44.3%		675

(*Continued*)

Table 12.2 (*Continued*) Summary Characteristics of Control Variables by Feeling of Happiness and Life Satisfaction: 2005–2008 Wave of World Values Survey

	Personal Happiness		*Satisfaction in Life*		
Control Variables	*Yes*	*χ^2 (df)*	*Yes*	*χ^2 (df)*	*n*
Education					
No education	14.7%	38.751 (3)****	12.8%	58.518 (3)****	273
Elementary	43.0%		41.1%		642
High school	31.6%		34.3%		468
Postsecondary	10.7%		11.8%		150
Health Status					
Good	86.5%	137.275 (1)****	87.6%	86.072 (1)****	1231
Poor	13.5%		12.4%		302
Sample size ($n = 1533$)					

****$p < 0.001$, ***$p < 0.01$, **$p < 0.05$, *$p < 0.10$.

$\chi^2 = 4.639$, $p < 0.05$). Whereas a higher percentage of Ghanaians who value freedom of choice and control (80%) reported being happy and satisfied with life, only 41% of Ghanaians who value honesty reported being happy and satisfied in life. Contrary to expectation, the data suggest that gender neither associates with happiness nor satisfaction in life. Marital status is negatively related to both measures of well-being among Ghanaians ($\chi^2 = 7.376$, $p < 0.01$; $\chi^2 = 5.059$, $p < 0.05$). Contrary to what the existing literature suggests, a higher percent of Ghanaians who are not married are more satisfied in life and happier (52%) compared to their counterparts who are married (48%).

There is a significant association between place of residence and happiness ($\chi^2 = 7.376$, $p < 0.01$) and satisfaction in life. About 58% of Ghanaians who live in the north part of the country report being happy and 42% of southerners reported being happy. Education is significantly associated with happiness and satisfaction in life ($\chi^2 = 38.751$, $p < 0.001$). While the lower percent of Ghanaians with no formal education reported being happy and satisfied in life, the higher percentage of happiness and satisfaction in life is found among Ghanaians with elementary and high school education. Health status is also significantly related to happiness and satisfaction in life. Whereas about 86% of Ghanaians who reported having better health reported being happy and satisfied in life, only 12% who reported poor health were happy and satisfied with life ($\chi^2 = 137.275$, $p < 0.\ 001$).

Multivariate Analysis

Multivariate logistic regressions were conducted to determine the utility of economic, social capital, religious, geographic, and demographic variables in predicting the likelihood of being happy and satisfied in life among Ghanaians. In the analyses, all the variables were entered using the stepwise method. We found information regarding happiness and satisfaction in life among the respondents.

Happiness

Our research predicts the odds of being happy versus not being happy. The analyses show that cultural variables (ethnicity and religion) are significantly related to well-being—happiness among Ghanaians. The data reveal that having an Akan ethnic background tends to instigate higher odds (Exp[B] = 1.975, $p < 0.05$) of reporting happiness compared to the other Ghanaians. Contrary to expectation, affiliation with the Catholic and Protestant/Evangelical faiths tends to undermine happiness. The probability of reporting happiness tend to be about 47% (Exp[B] = 0.526, $p < 0.10$) and 51% (Exp[B] = 0.490, $p < 0.05$) lower for Ghanaians who are affiliated with Catholic and Protestant/Evangelical faiths, respectively, compared to the reference group. As expected, religious involvement is a significant predictor of happiness. Ghanaians who are actively involved in religion are more than 3 times (Exp[B] = 3.137, $p < 0.001$) likely to report being happy compared to their counterparts who are inactive in religion. Attendance at religious service is also significantly related to happiness. Ghanaians who go to church once a week are approximately 1.5 times (Exp[B] = 1.476, $p < 0.10$) more likely to report being happy compared to those who occasionally attend service. Contrary to expectations, the importance individuals attach to religion that is religiosity is not significantly related to happiness.

As expected in poor countries, Ghanaians who are in the upper- and middle-income brackets are 3.251 times (Exp[B] = 3.251, $p < 0.001$) and about 2.1 times (Exp[B] = 2.069, $p < 0.001$), respectively, more likely to report being happy compared to their counterparts in the lower-income bracket. However, among middle-class Ghanaians, the odds of reporting happiness are approximately 36% lower (Exp[B] = 0.635, $p < 0.05$) in comparison to those who are in the lower class. Community engagement and honesty are the only social capital variables that show significant relationship with happiness among Ghanaians. Ghanaians who are actively engaged in their communities are 1.1 times (Exp[B] = 0.1090, $p < 0.05$) more likely to report being happy compared to the reference group. Likewise, the probability of reporting being happy compared to the reference group among Ghanaians who value honesty are approximately 1.5 times (Exp[B] = 1.486, $p < 0.001$). Interestingly, the likelihood of married Ghanaians reporting being happy are 23% (Exp[B] = 0.771, $p < 0.10$) lower compared to the nonmarried.

Another surprising finding is that the odds of reporting happiness are 45% (Exp[B] = 0.551, $p < 0.001$) lower among Ghanaians who live in the southern part of the country compared to their northern counterparts.

Ghanaians who have elementary education are 45% more likely to report being happy (Exp[B] = 1.445, $p < 0.10$) compared to those who do not have any formal education. The only health-related variable in the equation shows the strongest relative effect on the likelihood of reporting being happy. The likelihood of reporting being happy is 4.4 times (Exp[B] = 4.363, $p < 0.001$) higher among those who perceive their health to be good compared to their counterparts who reported poor health. Together, the predictors accounted for 23% of the variance in happiness.

Satisfaction in Life

Just as in happiness, cultural and religious factors continue to emerge as significant predictors of satisfaction in life. The odds of reporting being satisfied in life are about 65% higher among Akans (Exp[B] = 1.640, $p < 0.01$) in comparison to the reference group. Religious affiliation, involvement, and attendance at service are significant predictors of life satisfaction among Ghanaians. Unlike happiness, being affiliated with the Catholic faith is not significantly related to satisfaction in life. However, affiliation with Protestant/Evangelical faiths continue to show a negative relationship with satisfaction in life (Exp[B] = 0.594, $p < 0.10$). Equally intriguing is the fact that, being affiliated with the Muslim faith shows a positive and significant relationship with satisfaction in life. The odds of reporting being satisfied in life among Muslims are 55% (Exp[B] = 1.553, $p < 0.10$) higher than the reference group. Just as in happiness, the likelihood of reporting being satisfied in life are approximately 56% (Exp[B] = 1.556, $p < 0.10$) higher among Ghanaians who are active in religion in comparison to those who are inactive in their religious organizations. The salience of religion in life satisfaction is reinforced by the fact that attendance at religious service at least once a week tends to instigate higher odds of being satisfied in life (Exp[B] = 1.376, $p < 0.10$).

After the necessary controls, relative income emerged as a significant predictor of satisfaction in life. The probability of reporting being satisfied in life are 2.6 times (Exp[B] = 2.617, $p < 0.001$) and approximately 2.1 times (Exp[B] = 2.083, $p < 0.001$) higher among Ghanaians belonging to the upper and middle class, respectively, compared to the lower class. Likewise, compared to Ghanaians in the lower class, the working class are 56% (Exp[B] = 1.564, $p < 0.01$) more likely to report being satisfied with life. The data reaffirm the potency of social capital variables in molding life satisfaction. For instance, the likelihood of reporting being satisfied with life tends to be higher for Ghanaians who engage in community activities (Exp[B] = 1.095, $p < 0.05$) and those who favor freedom of choice and control in one's life (Exp[B] = 2.090, $p < 001$). Another variable that significantly predict well-being—satisfaction in life is how Ghanaians assess their own health—self-rated health. Ghanaians who rate their own health good 2.6 times (Exp[B] = 2.611, $p < 0.001$) more likely to report being satisfied in life. All in all, 21% of variance in satisfaction in life is explained by the variables included in this study.

Findings and Discussion

In the present study, we attempted to elucidate factors predicting two measures of well-being—happiness and satisfaction in life at the micro-level in Ghana. Our bivariate and multivariate results indicate that ethnicity is an important predictor of well-being among Ghanaians. For Akans, ethnicity plays a vital role in their well-being. Similar findings have been reported by Addai and Pokimica (2010) in an earlier study about ethnicity and economic well-being in Ghana. The Akans' higher odds of reporting happiness and satisfaction in life may be attributable to the relative advantage position the group enjoys in terms of access to social amenities and economic opportunities. Another possible reason may be due to the social organization of the group. The Akans practice the matrilineal kinship system, which is noted for its strong kin network and support. This group tends to put the welfare of all extended family members at the center of family affairs. Except for religiosity, all the religious measures in the study are significant predictors of well-being among Ghanaians. Generally, religion is assumed to influence well-being through various ways: by providing members a sense of belonging and serving as a source of social support, providing meaning and purpose to individuals' lives, and encouraging people to lead healthier lifestyles (Ellison et al. 1989). Religious affiliation is both a blessing and a curse as far as happiness and satisfaction in life are concerned among Ghanaians. Interestingly, with the exception of the Muslim faith, all the global religious faiths (Catholic and Protestant/Evangelical) tend to undermine happiness and satisfaction in life in comparison to the indigenous and nonreligious among Ghanaians. Similar findings have been reported in earlier studies based on data from Ghana (Pokimica et al. 2012).

The data show that involvement and attendance at service are positively related to well-being, even with the effects of numerous demographic, socioeconomic factors, denominational affiliation, and personal religiosity held constant. The importance of religious involvement and service attendance in predicting well-being indicates that among Ghanaians it is engagement in activities of particular religious groups that contribute to well-being and not just affiliation. In Ghanaian society, the strong relationship between religious engagement and well-being may be explained in the context of the important role religion is assuming in the country. Owing to the failure of government to meet the needs of the population coupled with breakdown of traditional family structure, churches are gradually emerging as the most reliable source of social support and well-being. Churches are providing schools, hospitals, orphanages, universities, insurance and credit facilities, and funeral services to their members. Increasingly, they are providing institutional settings and regular opportunities for social interaction between people of like minds and similar values that transcend family and ethnicity. Religious involvement has therefore emerged as the most important medium of nurturing friendship and social networks with a direct bearing on the social and economic well-being of Ghanaians.

Religiosity is neither related to happiness nor to satisfaction in life at both bivariate and multivariate levels of analyses. This casts doubt on the general hypothesis that personal religiosity buffers the effect of stress in the Ghanaian context. Nonetheless, a note of caution is in order here. These insignificant findings may reflect limited variation in religiosity variables. Background diagnostic of the variable (not shown here) shows that the large majority of the respondents rated themselves "very religious" leading to the possibly inaccurate result. Research using more discriminating and detailed indicators of religiosity could yield different results. Data lend credence to the assertion that the richer members of a society are generally happier than their poorer counterparts. The general proposition in mainstream economics is that, other things being equal, more income will increase welfare through access to more and superior goods and services, better health, quality education and the like (McGillivray 2004). Also, an increase in relative income is expected to induce improvement in standards of living, and consumption norms may change, which may cause material aspirations to shoot upward (Easterlin 1974, p. 116). Thus, people will judge their well-being based on whether their income allows them to fulfill their material aspirations. This is more likely to be the case in poor countries like Ghana. The link between income and well-being needs to be made with caution as studies have established that at a certain point, a higher income may not necessarily increase happiness and satisfaction in life (Graham and Pettinato 2002). One interesting finding in this study is the positive relationship between working class background and satisfaction in life. The rationale behind this finding may be contested in the context of the aspiration theory (Hayo and Seifert 2003). The economic and political transformations in Ghana may have resulted in high aspirations for the working class. Despite the challenges in the country, the working class may be hopeful of their future and sense improvement in their lives. Social capital captured by community engagement shows a positive relationship with well-being. Ghanaians active in communities signing petitions, joining boycotts, attending peaceful demonstrations, reading newspapers, books, using e-mail, talking to friends, and who voted in the recent parliamentary elections show higher odds of reporting happiness and satisfaction in life. The relationship between social capital measures and well-being reported in this study may be suggestive that the increase in relational goods as suggested by Putnam (2000) is an important force when it comes to how Ghanaians appraise their own happiness and satisfaction in life.

That interpersonal and institutional trust, and civic involvement do not show up as significant predictors of either satisfaction in life or happiness is somewhat puzzling, especially in light of findings that identify these as important determinants of

SWB (Becchetti et al. 2008). Considering the documented evidence of the salience of marriage, trust, and education in well-being studies, the fact that these variables barely register as predictors of happiness and are not significantly related to satisfaction in life is problematic and calls for more study.

The analyses cogently confirm that the strongest predictor of well-being—happiness and satisfaction in life—seems to be how individuals perceive their own health. This finding has been collaborated in earlier studies (Helliwell and Putnam 2004). The relative strength of this variable could suggest that health does actually have an intrinsic value. It may serve as means to other ends such as a good job, a happy marriage, and others. However, the causal relationship between well-being and health is not straightforward as it is possible the people who are happy and satisfied in life pursue healthier lifestyles and vice versa.

Conclusion and Policy Implications

Governments have always been preoccupied with policies and programs that promote a better life and improve the quality of life of citizens. This is more urgent in SSA where the perils of poverty, the HIV/AIDS epidemic, and the increasing prevalence of chronic diseases pose real threats to well-being at the micro-level. Despite the fact that an individuals' well-being is highly shaped by what transpires around them, research implicates individual attributes in molding well-being, particularly how they feel about their own lives (Diener et al. 1999). With few exceptions, studies on determinants of SWB are virtually nonexistent in SSA. To fill this vacuum, we made it our purpose in this chapter to assess the factors molding happiness and satisfaction or SWB at the micro-level. This study presents cross-sectional evidence of a significant association between cultural, economic, social capital, health variables and happiness, and life satisfaction among Ghanaians. The findings from this study need to be taken with caution due to some limitations. First, methodologically, the cross-sectional nature of the data limits one's ability to assess trends and establish causation between the two well-being measures and the factors included in the study. Second, availability of more domain aspects variables of well-being would have shed more light on predictors of SWB. Third, having data on physical health such as morbidity and functional limitation variables would have shed more light on our understanding of which aspect of health is germane to well-being. Finally, the data also limits our ability to probe the relative importance of internal and external variables in shaping well-being in Ghana. Despite these limitations, there are some important findings with policy implications.

The study shows that after decades of economic and political transformation, ethnicity continues to be a significant determinant of well-being at the micro-level. The observed relationship between ethnicity and SWB in Ghana is an important finding that demands further research. If studies can give credence to the social organization hypothesis about the association between ethnicity and SWB as suggested here, then policymakers can harness such cultural assets for the stability of the country. Since the Akans form the majority of the population in the country, this is an important finding that merits attention in welfare policy formulation and implementation.

The study confirms that religion is a potent force in how Ghanaians perceive their well-being. Religion can be a blessing and a curse as far as well-being is concerned. Whereas affiliation with certain religious groups undermines well-being, some instigates higher well-being. Any program that tries to promote well-being needs to pay attention to this variable. Well-being promotion programs specific to certain religious groups may be a step in the right direction. The fact that religious involvement and attendance at service are positively related to well-being, makes investing more resources in promoting religious engagement a vital well-being promotion strategy in Ghana. However, to fully reap the dividends of religion for well-being, researchers need to make sure that they adequately capture the ways different aspects of religion work independently as well as interact to affect well-being. So many aspects of religion do not easily lend themselves to quantification; as a result, any study that seeks to capture this factor needs to employ qualitative and quantitative methods. Such an approach would help reduce the risk of reductionism error that tends to characterize most studies on religion.

Salience of self-rated health status in predicting well-being indicates that, if policymakers' objective is improving well-being, they should focus on making health a priority. This has implications for research and public policy. For policymakers, the clear message is that there cannot be any meaningful enhancement in well-being without paying attention to how Ghanaians gauge their own health status. Therefore, studies on factors influencing self-rated health in the country may help in the formulation of well-being promotion programs. Equally, the charge for government is to commit resources to the health needs of the people.

The significance of social capital measures: community engagement, freedom, and control in predicting well-being suggest that social capital is a valuable asset that demands serious consideration in Ghana's well-being strategies. Since the extent to which Ghanaians have trust in the nation's institutions as a proxy for the perceived quality of governance does not seem to be a significant predictor of well-being, we could assume that this mechanism is simply not plausible in the Ghanaian context. This might be because people feel they have been consistently disappointed with institutions so that they have become immune to what is going on in the country. They may have mentally eliminated this variable from their well-being "equation." Equally, interpersonal trust did not emerge as a significant predictor of well-being. Findings are not consistent with an earlier study that found trust to be a significant predictor of material deprivation among Ghanaians (Addai and Pokimica 2012).

If we take Ghana to be somewhat representative of the SSA region as a whole, we can conclude that the determinants of SWB at the micro-level might well be a bit different for this region than for the much more heavily researched Western world. More empirical work clearly needs to be done in this region if we wish to better understand SWB. However, this study vividly confirms that the promotion of well-being in SSA and especially among Ghanaians will require a multidimensional approach. Boosting relative income is important but equally critical is creating an environment where the middle class can achieve their dreams and minimize frustrations that always serve as springboard for instability in poor countries. Equally, cultural and social capital variables need to be accorded serious attention in any well-being promotion effort. The virtue of cultural and social capital factors in well-being promotion is that they would require very limited financial resources.

References

Addai, I., Pokimica, J. 2010. Ethnicity and economic well-being: The case of Ghana. *Social Indicators Research* 99(3): 487–510.

Addai, I., Pokimica, J. 2012. An exploratory study of trust and material hardship in Ghana. *Social Indicators Research* 109(3): 413–438.

Aikins, A.D.G. 2005. Healer-shopping in Africa: New evidence from a rural urban qualitative study of Ghanaian diabetes experiences. *British Medical Journal* 331: 737.

Allotey, P., Reidpath, D. 2007. Epilepsy, culture, identity and wellbeing. *Journal of Health Psychology* 12(3): 431–443.

Andrews F., McKennell, A. 1980. Measures of self-reported well-being: Their affective, cognitive, and other components. *Social Indicators Research* 8(2): 127–155.

Andrews, F., Withey, S. 1976. *Social Indicators of Well-Being.* New York: Plenum.

Bartolini, S., Bilancini, E., Pugno, M. 2008. *American Declines of Social Capital and Happiness: Is There Any Linkage?* Mimeo: University of Siena.

Becchetti, L., Pelloni, A., Rossetti, F. 2008. Relational goods, sociability, and happiness. *Kyklos* 61: 343–363.

Böhnke, P. 2005. First European quality of life survey: Life satisfaction, happiness, and sense of belonging. European Foundation for the Improvement of Living and Working Conditions. Retrieved from www.eurofound.eu.int/areas/qualityoflife/equls.htm. Accessed 9/11/05.

Böhnke, P. 2007. Feeling left out: Patterns of social integration and exclusion. In: Alber, J., Fahey, T., Saraceno, C. (eds.). *Handbook of Quality of Life in the Enlarged European Union.* London: Routledge, pp. 304–324.

Bookwalter, J., Dalenberg, D. 2004. Subjective well-being and household factors in South Africa. *Social Indicators Research* 65: 333–353.

Campbell, A., Converse, S., Rodgers, W. 1976. *The Quality of American Life.* New York: Russell Sage Foundation.

Corsin-Jimenez, A. 2007. *Culture and Well-Being: Anthropological Approaches to Freedom and Political Ethics.* UK: Pluto Press.

Diener, E. 1984. Subjective well-being. *Psychological Bulletin* 95(3): 542–575.

Diener, E., Seligman, E. 2004. Beyond money: Toward an economy of wellbeing. *Psychological Science in the Public Interest* 5(1): 1–31.

Diener, E., Suh, E., Lucas, R., Smith, H. 1999. Subjective well-being: Three decades of progress. *Psychological Bulletin* 125(2): 276–302.

Easterlin, R. 1974. Does economic growth improve the human lot? Some empirical evidence. In: P. David and M. Reder (eds.). *Nations and Households in Economic Growth: Essays in Honor of Moses Abramovitz*. New York: Academic Press, Inc.

Ellison, C., Gay, D., Glass, T. 1989. Does religious commitment contribute to individual life satisfaction? *Social Forces* 68: 100–123.

Fidrmuc, J. 2000. Political support for reforms: Economics of voting in transition countries. *European Economic Review* 44: 1491–1513.

Frey, B., Stutzer, A. 2002. *Happiness and Economics: How the Economy and Institutions Affect Well-Being*. Princeton, NJ: Princeton University Press.

George, L. 1981. Subjective well-being: Conceptual and methodological issues. In: Eisdorfer, C. (ed.). *Annual Review of Gerontology and Geriatrics*. New York: Springer, pp. 345–382.

Ghana Statistical Service. 2007. *Pattern and Trends of Poverty in Ghana 1991–2006*. Accra: Ghana Statistical Service.

Gove, W., Hughes, M., Style, C. 1983. Does marriage have positive effects on the psychological well-being of the individual? *Journal of Health and Social Behavior* 24: 122–131.

Graham, C., Pettinato, S. 2002. Frustrated achievers: Winners, losers and subjective well-being in new market economies. *The Journal of Development Studies* 38(4): 100–140.

Gurr, T. 1970. *Why Men Rebel*. Princeton, NJ: Princeton University Press.

Gyimah-Boadi, E., Mensah, K.A.A. 2003. The growth of democracy in Ghana despite economic dissatisfaction: A power alternation bonus? Afrobarometer Working Paper No. 28.

Hayo, B. 1999. Micro and macro determinants of public support for economic reforms in Eastern Europe. ZEI Working Paper 25. University of Bonn.

Hayo, B., Seifert, W. 2003. Subjective economic well-being in Eastern Europe. *Journal of Economic Psychology* 24: 329–348.

Helliwell, J. 2006. Well-being, social capital and public policy: What's new? *The Economic Journal* 116: 34–45. Royal Economic Society.

Helliwell, J., Putnam, R. 2004. The social context of well-being. *Philosophical Transactions of the Royal Society B: Biological Sciences* 359(1449): 1435–1446.

Jackson, J., Chatters, L., Neighbors, H. 1986. The subjective life quality of black Americans. In: Andrews, F. (ed.). *Research on the Quality of Life*. Ann Arbor: University of Michigan Institute for Social Research, pp. 193–213.

Kahneman, D., Krueger, B. 2006. Developments in the measurement of subjective-being. *Journal of Economic Perspectives* 20(1): 3–24.

Kapitány, B., Kovacs, K., Krieger, H. 2005. *Working and Living in an Enlarged Europe*. European Foundation for the Improvement of Living and Working Conditions, Luxembourg. Available at: www.eurofound.eu.int/living/qual_life. Accessed 8/8/14.

Kenny, C. 2005. Does development make you happy? Subjective well-being and economic growth in developing countries. *Social Indicators Research* 73: 199–219.

Kingdon, G., Knight, J. 2006. Subjective well-being poverty versus income poverty and capabilities poverty? *Journal of Development Studies* 42(7): 1199–1224.

Kingdon, G., Knight, J. 2007. Community, comparisons and subjective wellbeing in a divided society. *Journal of Economic Behavior and Organization* 64: 69–90.

Kinyanda, E., Waswa, L., Baisley, K, Maher, D. 2011. Prevalence of severe mental distress and its correlates in a population-based study in rural south-west Uganda. *BMC Psychiatry* 11: 97.

McGillivray, M. 2004. Towards a measure of non-economic national well-being achievements. ESRC Research Group on Well-Being in Developing Countries. Available at: http://www.wellbdev.org.uk/news/hanse-papers.htm. Accessed 8/8/14.

McGillivray, M., Clark, M. 2006. Human well-being: Concepts and measures. In: McGillivray, M., Clarke, M. (eds.). *Understanding Human Well-Being.* Basingstoke: Palgrave Macmillan.

Okasha, A. 2002. Mental health in Africa: The role of The WPA. *World Psychiatry* 1(1): 32–35.

Pokimica, J., Addai, I., Takyi, B. 2012. Religion & subjective well-being in Ghana. *Social Indicators Research* 106(1): 61–79.

Putnam, R. 2000. *Bowling Alone. The Collapse and Revival of American Community.* New York: Simon & Schuster.

Read, U., Adiibokah, E., Nyame, S. 2009. Local suffering and the global discourse of mental health and human rights: An ethnographic study of responses to mental illness in rural Ghana. *Globalization and Health* 5: 13.

Rojas, M. 2007. The complexity of well-being: A life-satisfaction conception and a domains-of-life approach. In: Gough, I., McGregor, A. (eds.). *Researching in Developing Countries.* Cambridge: Cambridge University Press.

Sarracino, F. 2008. Subjective well-being in low income countries: Positional, relational and social capital components. *Studie Note di Economia Anno XIII* 3: 449–477.

Twumasi, P. A. 1975. *Medical Systems in Ghana: A Study in Medical Sociology.* Tema: Ghana Publishing Corporation.

Veenhoven, R. 1991. Is happiness relative? *Social Indicators Research* 24: 1–34.

Wierzbicka, A. 2004. Happiness in cross-linguistic and cross-cultural perspective. *Dædalus Spring* 133(2): 34–43.

World Bank. 2011. *World Development Indicators 2011.* Washington: World Bank Publications.

World Health Organization. 2005. *Preventing Chronic Disease. A Vital Investment.* Geneva: WHO.

Chapter 13

Developing Hearts and Land

A Case Study of Reconciliation, Governance, and Development in Rwanda

Zachary A. Karazsia

Contents

Introduction

We live two decades removed from the twentieth century's most rapidly executed genocide. In 1994, the small East African state of Rwanda descended into chaos. Scholars estimate between 500,000 and 800,000 Tutsis and moderate Hutus were slain in a period of 100 days. It is circulated that another 100,000–200,000 people have died from the concurrent civil war (estimates vary). In the years since the genocide, Rwanda has faced multiple challenges in achieving reconciliation, economic development, and sustainable peace. Attaining sustainable peace between warring ethnic groups once blood has been spilled is difficult under normal circumstances. For Rwanda, this task is magnified by the brutality of genocidaires.

Less than 24 hours following the assassination of the Hutu president Juvénal Habyarimana, genocidaires were conspiring to eradicate Tutsis throughout Rwanda. On the morning of April 7, 1994, Dr. Clement Kayishema, a former *prefet* or governor, encouraged Tutsis in Kibuye to seek shelter in the stadium or parish. Kayishema ordered gendarmes to be stationed near these locations and to instruct fleeing Tutsis to seek safety here. After 10 days and tens of thousands of Tutsis flocking to these locations, Kayishema ordered the killing of the Tutsis and personally fired the first shot (Rakiya and de Waal 1995, p. 132). The genocidaires were not restricted to government officials. They included businessmen like Edouvard Bandetse who burned civilians alive in a marketplace on April 7, teachers like Silas Karangwa and Jonas Kategekimana, soldiers such as Emmanuel A. Ubuyiremuye, judges such as Francois Karekezi, peasants like Godefroid Kanyankoze and Egide Gatamezo, veterinarians such as Jean-Bapiste Maninaho, and finally students like Frederic Ngabonziza and Gilbert Fils Kalibwende (Rakiya and de Waal 1995, pp. 138–159). The genocide was not committed solely by the state. As shown, the genocidaires were from every walk of life. Considering this fact, how best can the government of Rwanda achieve good governance, economic development, and ultimately sustainable peace?

This chapter defines sustainable peace as a period of years in which a return to violent ethnic conflict, including civil war, genocide, pogroms, or mass violence directed against any national or subnational group, is significantly diminished, and intergroup conflict is arbitrated through political institutions in place of violence. Achieving sustainable peace between the Hutu and Tutsi will prove difficult given the magnitude of the genocide. Other mechanisms are required to achieve this outcome, including sustainable development and good governance. How has the Rwandan government achieved peace and economic prosperity since the genocide?

In this chapter, I explore the codependency of reconciliation and economic development as necessary mechanisms in achieving good governance and sustainable peace in postgenocide Rwanda. The chapter begins with the methodology employed for analysis, a brief history of Rwanda from 1912 to 1973, a mini-case study of Juvénal Habyarimana's rule under which Rwanda experienced economic development, then turns to postgenocide leadership by Bizimungu and Kagame, and concludes with final thoughts on Rwanda's developmental path.

Methodology

This chapter examines a model of conflict mitigation that combines reconciliation and economic development as codependent in realizing sustainable peace and development. I employ process tracing tools to unravel the impact of reconciliation and economic development. The focus is on Habyarimana's influence over ethnic tensions and development from 1973 to 1990 and governance under Presidents Pasteur Bizimungu and Paul Kagame from 1994 to the present. This chapter examines the history of stability and development under Habyarimana as comparative analysis for governance issues in postgenocide Rwanda. Three indicators of reconciliation are investigated: developing a sense of *security* in society, bridging an intergroup *trust deficit*, and creating a *new social contract* between the government and citizenry.

Throughout early independence, isolated incidents of killings and massacres of Tutsis were present culminating in the 1963 pogrom. From 1973 to 1990, during the Habyarimana regime, no massacres of Tutsis were reported (OAU 2000, p. 22). While there was no sincere effort to reconcile Tutsi and Hutu hatreds during this time, Tutsis were able to reside in specific spheres, typically of noninfluence, without widespread fear of physical injury. This chapter compares broad-spectrum reconciliation, governance, and development in postgenocide Rwanda (1994–present) to the policy of political stability in exchange for economic prosperity during the Habyarimana regimes. World Bank development indicators are used to quantify development. These indicators provide a baseline for assessing Rwanda's development progress, particularly since genocide. In validating my hypothesis of codependency, we should expect to see correlations between reconciliation efforts and economic development and note that the absence of one of these variables weakens the probability of achieving sustainable peace and development.

Rwanda: A Case Study in Sustained Peace

To overcome ethnic conflict, we must understand the complexity of intergroup histories and their perspectives. Practitioners of peace must abolish the notion that *your* truth is not *my* truth and *your* existence threatens *my* existence. Ethnic conflict and subsequent reconciliation must address the structural challenges facing ethnic rivalries, weaken hardened identities, and create new intergroup commonalities to develop relationships in forming reconciliation (Lederach 1997, p. 23).

There are conflicting histories regarding ethnic hostilities and intergroup dynamics in Rwanda. Some argue ethnic tensions existed prior to German and Belgian colonial rule. Others challenge this assertion and contend colonizers created ethnic hostilities through elevating the Tutsi over the Hutu in socioeconomic and political prominence. Some level of ethnic tensions was present in Ruanda–Urundi, the German unified colonial name for Rwanda and Burundi, and these tensions were heightened under colonial rule. The cycle of ethnic violence is a self-reinforcing mechanism. Once blood has been spilled at the hands of ethnic conflict, reducing tensions becomes exponentially more difficult.

A Prelude to Genocide: Brief History from 1912 to 1973

There are three identifiable ethnic groups located in Rwanda: the Twa, the Hutu, and the Tutsi. The Twa were the first inhabitants of the Rwandan territory (Rakiya and de Waal 1995, p. 2). The Twa are traditionally considered to be hunter gatherers and pottery makers (Uvin 1997, p. 92). Following the Twa was the Hutu. The Hutu population was historically agriculturalists and emigrated from Central Africa. The final ethnic group to enter Rwanda was the Tutsi in the fifteenth and sixteenth centuries whose occupation predominantly included cattle rearing (ibid.). Following the German surrender in the First World War, Belgium acquired control over Ruanda–Urundi. The colonizers and local elites propagated already permeating racist perceptions attached to each ethnicity, which were initially invented by “missionaries, explorers, and early anthropologists” (OAU 2000, p. 11). While the perception of incongruous ethnies persisted, the ethnies shared the same language, Kinyarwanda; they shared religious beliefs; and the Tutsi and Hutu were geographically intermixed, and some intermarriage occurred (approximately 25% of Rwandans shared a Tutsi and Hutu great-grandparent) (OAU 2000, p. 10).

In 1912, a rebellion against the Tutsis’ attempt to govern the state was supported by harsh resistance from the northern Hutus (Rakiya and de Waal 1995, p. 6). The rebellion was defeated and the northern Hutus were made subordinate to Tutsi kings, solidifying Tutsi hegemony for the next 60 years. The dominance of Tutsi kings with colonial support generated grievance in many Hutu communities. This grievance led to the “Bahutu Manifesto” of 1957. The nine drafters of the manifesto were young males, educated, seeking Western privileges of opportunity and employment. From 1932 to 1957, Tutsis were three quarters of the student population in the city of Butare, 95% of the civil service personnel, 43 of 45 chiefs, and 549 of 559 subchiefs. The monopoly of the Tutsis over the Hutus during these decades fueled grievance within Hutu families. The “Bahutu Manifesto” refers to “dual-colonizers,” the Belgians and the Tutsis when discussing the monopoly over state apparatus. The Tutsi monopoly of the state was replaced with Hutu monopoly from independence until the genocide. The same grievance remained, yet the ethnies switched proverbial locations in their perception of fairness and equity. One difference in monopolizing the state under Hutu dominance was the violence directed against Tutsis on a large scale, which was unseen in previous periods. For reconciliation to last, the state must address this grievance and integrate both ethnies into a cohabitant peaceful society.

On July 1, 1962, Rwanda gained its independence from its colonial rulers (Prunier 1995, p. 54). Later that year, on December 21, 1963, Tutsi exiles launched attacks into Rwanda from their bases in Burundi (Rakiya and de Waal 1995, p. 12). The rebels reached the outskirts of Kigali, the capital city, and due to inadequate military supplies, poor military planning, and a lack of cohesion, the rebels were repelled. As the rebels were defeated, an estimated 10,000–12,000 Tutsis were massacred and 20 prominent Tutsi politicians were killed (the politicians were targeted for their political prominence) between December 1963 and January 1964 (ibid.). Throughout the remainder of the decade, the Kayibanda government—Grégoire Kayibanda was the first elected Hutu president of Rwanda—continued to neglect its duties in establishing reconciliation and in drawing to a close this intergroup conflict resulting in bloodshed between the ethnies. During the 1960s, the Tutsis were beginning to be referred to as *inyenzi* or cockroaches (Prunier 1995, p. 54). This dehumanization of the Tutsis would prove critical nearly three decades later in the development and execution of the twentieth century's most rapidly executed genocide. The dehumanization of the Tutsi ethny over 30 years strongly permeated the national discourse and intergroup dialog. It is clear from 1961 to 1994 that the Hutu regimes would not seek a broad-spectrum reconciliation among indigenous ethnies but a core–peripheral relationship.

The Habyarimana Years: 1973–1990

Security, Governance, and Economic Development

In the final months of the Kayibanda government, tensions began to rise between the northern and southern Hutu elites. These tensions centered on power politics in the regime with particular interests in rent-seeking behaviors. With the increasing intensity of internal power struggles, the Kayibanda government showed signs of cracking. On July 5, 1973, the cracks reached a point of critical mass and Major General Juvénal Habyarimana, took power in a bloodless coup d'état. Following the coup by Habyarimana, ethnic tensions subsided. Initially, Habyarimana was welcomed by Hutus and Tutsis for bringing stability to the country. For the first 17 years of the Habyarimana regime, there were no massacres of the Tutsi (OAU 2000, p. 22). This is a significant distinction between parsing Habyarimana's strategy of political stability from the present government's strategy of reconciliation, good governance, and economic development. For the first 17 years of the Habyarimana regime, Tutsis were relatively safe from massacre and an element of security and stability was provided. During this time period, Tutsis were still referred to as *inyenzi* or cockroaches and were excluded from the political process. In many aspects of society, quotas were placed on their participation. Despite these exclusionary policies and vitriol, which are not conducive to reconciliation and intergroup cooperation, the physical safety of Tutsis in Rwanda was pragmatically secured through Habyarimana's policy of stability. Governance was conditioned on the ability of the Tutsis to submit to Habyarimana's rule and in exchange they received a minimum level of security in place of state-directed violence. Throughout the Habyarimana regime, Tutsis were largely excluded from the army officer corps, and Hutu officers were expected to avoid marrying Tutsi women. Without a representation in the national military, Tutsis could not feel physically secure; but the policy of ethnic violence was replaced with a policy of ethnic tolerance in exchange for returns in economic development.

One of President Habyarimana's goals was to elevate Rwanda to a position of importance in Africa. Throughout this period, Habyarimana attempted to bring foreign direct investment (FDI) in and elevate Rwanda to a regional position of power. FDI as a percent of GDP grew throughout the beginning of the Habyarimana regime and began to decline as global commodity prices fell in the mid-1980s. The decline in the price of coffee, tea, and tin particularly affected Rwandan exports and the Rwandan macroeconomy. Increased revenues from foreign investment point to increased levels of political and economic security. FDI is one indicator of Habyarimana's stability policy because it directly assesses the level of stability within Rwanda, as perceived by outside actors. With respect to foreign investment, stability of the state and security are two central indicators that investors monitor. Political stability in exchange for economic opportunities helped Habyarimana in the subsiding of ethnic tensions from 1973 to 1990. As FDI gauges business perceptions of Rwanda, the GDP per capita provides a real estimate of Rwanda's economic development. When Rwanda gained its independence in 1962, the GDP per capita was $41 USD; when Habyarimana took power in 1973, the GDP per capita had risen to $71 USD (World Bank; see Figure 13.1). The GDP per capita quadrupled by the end of Habyarimana's first 17 years in office (circa 1990) and by the conclusion of his stability policy, to $353 USD. With the quadrupling of income per capita in little under three decades, it is clear Rwanda was making significant strides in economic development, most of which had taken place during the relatively "peaceful" years of the Habyarimana regime 1973–1990. Tutsi safety was traded for returns in economic development or conditionally secured by the government. Furthermore, there were no major challenges to Habyarimana's regime and he retained political control. This informal policy ended with the outbreak of civil war in 1990.

For Rwanda to rise out of poverty, investment proved and will continue to prove essential. Saving finances investment, in part, whether these savings come from international institutions, the government, or domestic households. There is a correlation between diminished gross domestic savings and ethnic violence in Rwanda. The 1963 pogrom and the mid-1980s saw declines in commodity prices (coffee, tea, and tin), and most notably during the 1990–1993 civil war and the 1994 genocide. However, during the early years of Habyarimana rule, a correlation

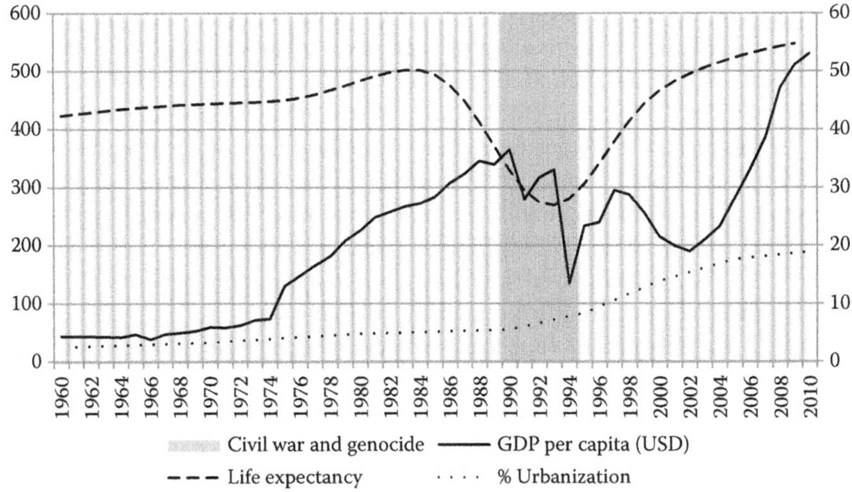

Figure 13.1 Economic development indicators.

existed between the increased safety of the Tutsis and the minimization of violent ethnic tensions coupled with an increase in the gross domestic savings rate (see Figure 13.2). This trade-off of nonviolence between Hutu and Tutsi contributed to efficiency and economic development. As the Tutsis felt more secure on a daily basis, they could begin to contribute to the economic productivity of the state, when permitted to do so.

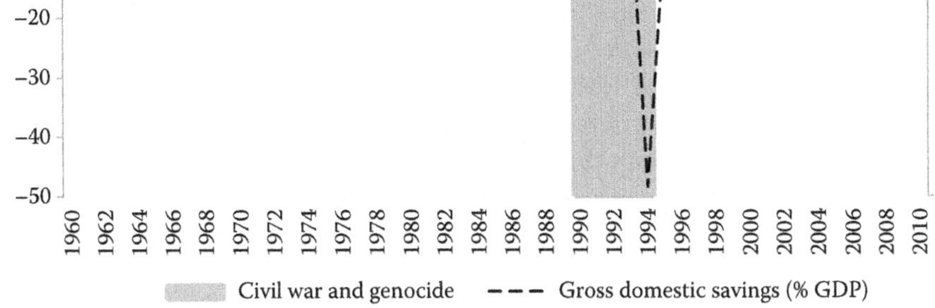

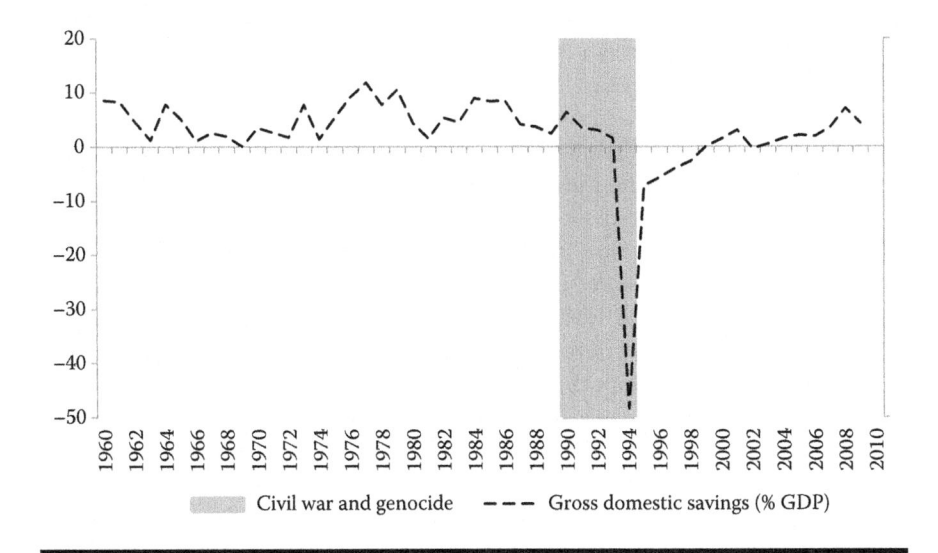

Figure 13.2 Gross domestic savings rate.

Modern economic growth is defined as achieving high per capita growth rates, increased economic productivity, and some level of urbanization in society. As people move from rural communities to urban centers, modern economic growth is often witnessed in the macroeconomy. When urbanization occurs, it is usually a by-product of the industrialization or modern development processes. The transformation to an urban society is one sign of modern economic development. Throughout this temporal period, we see migration to urban centers with 3.7% of residents urbanized in 1973 and 5.4% at the beginning of the civil war (World Bank 2014). Rwanda remains a largely rural society with only one-fifth (19.4%) of the population residing in urban centers by 2012 (ibid.).

There is a correlation between economic development in the 1960s to mid-1980s and greater life expectancy, and this begins to decline as commodity prices fall and conflict ensues in the early 1990s. Until the collapse of commodity exports in the mid-1980s Habyarimana's stability policy of security in exchange for economic prosperity remained. After the decline in economic development, cracks began to emerge in this informal policy. Another indicator of population health is the infant mortality rate. In Rwanda infant mortality rose throughout the 1960s, 1970s, and began to decline in the 1980s. The infant mortality rate increased during the civil war and subsequent genocide; but began a rapid decline in its aftermath. This tells us that while life expectancy was increasing and overall economic development was improving, some segments of the population were continuing to face privation.

Trust and Reconciliation

When a government engages in reconciliation it must address the trust deficit of opposing ethnies. Throughout the Habyarimana years there are several trust deficits worth noting. There was a trust deficit between the Hutu-led government and the Tutsis. The Tutsi population could not engage in establishing trust between the government under Habyarimana because of several factors. The Tutsis were excluded from political discourse, socioeconomic participation, and the military. The Tutsis had ethnic quotas placed on their involvement in the formal sectors of the economy. When there are limitations placed on an ethnic group, particularly a minority ethny, the element of trust becomes severely diminished. To reconcile the Hutu and Tutsi in Rwanda, reestablishing trust must be at the core of any reconciliation program. During the Habyarimana government, establishing trust between Hutu and Tutsi was not a priority but the focus was on only in securing safety as it buttresses economic development.

Lederach (1997) contends reconciliation is rooted in building relationships between individuals and ethnies in society. Habyarimana ignored all aspects of reconciliation. Instead, Habyarimana engaged in a policy of conditioned stability that allowed for the stabilization of the regime and society for the purpose of achieving economic development. During 1973–1990, little was done to build positive relationships. Throughout this time, the Tutsis continued to be referred to as *inyenzi*, discrimination was rampant, and the Tutsis were excluded from positions of power. Habyarimana's *Mouvement républicain national pour la démocratie et le développement* (MRND) political party was the singular political party allowed by law in the electoral process. MRND did not establish relationships with the Tutsis. In fact, it was exclusionary and marginalized the Tutsis. Developing hearts and minds of the ethnies is just as important as developing the land and the business community. This interpersonal reconciliation was avoided and discouraged under the Hutu governments of Kayibanda and Habyarimana.

A New Social Contract

Establishing a social contract is fundamental to integrating Hutus and Tutsis into a cohabitant peaceful society. There needs to be a perception where each ethny understands the new social contract (e.g., all ethnies being equal under the law, living in intergroup safety, and able to freely participate in the democratic process). Under the Habyarimana regime, there was a conditional social contract wherein the Tutsis were excluded from the political structures of society in exchange for nonviolence and pseudosafety. This social contract was upheld for most of the Habyarimana regime. The contract was broken with the 1990 invasion by the Rwandan Patriotic Front (RPF), a Tutsi-led political and military force seeking regime change.

As development wavered in the mid-1980s, so did Habyarimana's grasp of state security and development. Tensions between both Hutu and Tutsi ethnies, including the respective elites, continued to increase. Also, we begin to see equivocation from Habyarimana on this conditional contract. Beginning in 1990, there was a return to violence against the Tutsis. Other factors cannot be ruled out as having caused this divergence and slowdown in economic development but it is worth noting that throughout Rwandan history from the late 1950s to the early 2010s, when economic development was booming, reconciliation becomes more effective (or codependent in achieving a level of peace in society). Reconciliation is a tool that needs to be started in the short run following violent conflict and extended into the long run. Economic development is needed for sustainability in the medium to long run. Development subdues tensions and limits the avenues by which opportunistic leaders can pit ethnic groups against each other.

The Habyarimana Years: 1990–1994

In the final years of the Habyarimana government, stability was eliminated. Scholars have argued Habyarimana was more moderate in leadership than other senior Hutus. This was tautologically proven following Habyarimana's assassination on April 6, 1994 with the Hutu interim government initiating plans to eradicate Tutsis in Kigali and quickly spreading throughout the country, which resulted in the twentieth century's most swiftly executed genocide. Prior to the 1990 invasion by the RPF, ethnic tensions were on the rise and reconciliation between Hutu and Tutsi was increasingly unlikely. On October 1, 1990, the RPF, who were the descendants of Tutsi refugees that fled to Uganda during the 1960s, invaded from the north seeking regime change (OAU 2000, p. 34). Three years into the RPF invasion, 1.3 million, mostly Hutus, were internally displaced and forced to reside in settlement camps located in the center of the country (OAU 2000, p. 37). The internally displaced persons coupled with Hutu propaganda concerning the rebels and population inside Rwanda led to a fertile ground for the raising of Hutu militias, namely, the Interahamwe. The Interahamwe would prove fundamental in executing the genocide along with the presidential guard, military, and coerced and willing participant civilians.

In retaliation for the RPF invasion, the government rounded up and arrested some 8000 Tutsis and several Hutus in Kigali (ibid.). Many of the arrested were forced into the national stadium in Kigali for questioning. Some were held for months on end. The implied social contract established by Habyarimana was eliminated and ethnic tensions escalated and violence ensued. Throughout the civil war, several massacres and pogroms of Tutsis were reported, particularly the vicious pogrom of 300 Tutsis in 1992 in southern Rwanda (ibid.). After the October 1, 1990 invasion, both rhetorical dehumanization and physical violence against the Tutsi were present and intensified throughout society. This period of physical violence and dehumanization would be a precursor to genocide.

Countless scholars have published work on the causes and consequences of the 1994 Rwandan genocide (Gourevitch 1998; Mamdani 2001; Prunier 1995; Straus 2006; Uvin 1997; Valentino 2004). This chapter examines reconciliation and economic development as codependent in achieving sustainable peace and good governance. Throughout the final 5 years of the Habyarimana regime, no efforts were made to maintain the stability social pact between domestic ethnies in exchange for returns in economic development.

The Bizumungu and Kagame Years: 1994–Present

Lederach's (1997) book *Building Peace* provides, in part, some of the underlying assumptions of peacemaking in postconflict Rwanda for this chapter. It is useful to explore the Bizimungu and Kagame government's reconciliation and economic development years through five developmental categories with some suggested time spans. *Crisis management* actions that transpire in 0–1 year following the conclusion of violent conflict. *Stabilization* approaches to maintain government functionality, rule of law, and security, which occurs in 1–3 years removed from conflict. *Institutional reform* occupies the 3–10-year window with large foundational alterations (inter alia reforming civil service diversity demographics would be considered a foundational alteration that incorporates both Hutu and Tutsi) toward sustainable peace. *Structural transformation* occurs in the 10–30-year time period following violent conflict and integrates many of the reconciliation and economic development indicators in achieving sustainable peace.

Crisis Management (0–1 Years)

On July 19, 1994, the new RPF-led government assumed power in Kigali, bringing an end to the Rwandan genocide (Prunier 1995, p. 299). The RPF were fighting with the old Habyarimana regime for 4 years prior to the formation of their new government. The 1990–1993 civil war resulted in the 1993 Arusha Peace Agreement. The assassination of Juvénal Habyarimana on April 6, 1993 ignited the Rwandan genocide. In the aftermath of the genocide, the Rwandan infrastructure, sociopolitical identity, and business sectors lay in ruin. Rwanda's roads were destroyed during the civil war. Some Tutsi families lost between 40 and 60 members during the genocide (OAU 2000, p. 165). Human capital, productivity, and knowledge were lost to the countless genocidaires. The GDP per capita declined from $325 USD in 1993 to a meager $132 USD in 1994 (see Figure 13.1). Gross domestic savings declined by 49% in 1994 alone, resulting in persistent negative gross domestic savings rates until the end of the decade. FDI plummeted. The population size and annual growth rate severely contracted in both size and magnitude. Life expectancy was on the decline since 1984 with the average Rwandan expecting to live 50 years and reaching an all-time low in 1993 with a life expectancy of 27 years (shockingly, 1994 saw a life expectancy of 28 years despite the genocide). During the genocide, approximately 150,000 homes, mostly Tutsi were destroyed in the fighting (ibid.). Within 1 year's time, over 2 million refugees were reported in Burundi, Tanzania, Uganda, and Zaire (currently the Democratic Republic of Congo). Of the roughly 2.1 million refugees outside Rwanda's contiguous borders, 1.245 million resided in eastern Zaire, specifically in the cities of Goma, Bukavu, and Uvira (OAU 2000, p. 193). These situations notwithstanding the amount of mass trauma endured by Rwandan society after having suffered through the twentieth century's most swiftly executed and arguably most intimidatingly carried out genocide was incalculable.

The new Rwandan President Pasteur Bizumungu and his vice president and minister of defense Major General Paul Kagame were keen to ensure they did not suffer a similar fate as Habyarimana's government from foreign refugees (meaning the RPF was once a refugee force turned rebel movement that toppled the government in 1994). Second, related to the previous dilemma, along with refugees residing close to Rwanda's borders and within thousands of meters in some cases, so too were former combatants and genocidaires who escaped the RPF and fled to Zaire. Genocidaires quickly manipulated and threatened their way into controlling food and medical supplies to the refugee camps, thus having a two-pronged effect. First, establishing a continual supply of food and medicine to their fighters and second, establishing a hierarchy within the refugee camps. This created pseudoautonomous societies within eastern Zaire controlled by genocidaires. Rwanda was to eventually face this problem with two large-scale invasions culminating in the collapse of the Mobutu government in the late 1990s.

In an attempt to address the trust deficit, the RPF initially selected Pasteur Bizumungu as president and Paul Kagame assumed the positions of vice president and minister of defense. Bizumungu was a Hutu and Kagame a Tutsi descendent from the diaspora in Uganda. Bizumungu joined the RPF for the 1990 invasion after his brother who held the rank of colonel was assassinated (OAU 2000, p. 246). The government of national unity was based on the MRND-RPF style of government described in the Arusha Accords. The Hutu population was represented in the government as a percentage of the total population. However, some concerns began to permeate society with the worry of a shadow or "parallel" government of RPF leaders pulling the strings. In 1995, 11 months after the swearing in of the new government, chief of staff to the Hutu Prime Minister J.D. Ntakirutimana resigned. This led to the Prime Minister Faustin Twagiramungu's resignation with an additional four Hutu cabinet members following shortly thereafter (OAU 2000, p. 167). This was a major blow to the government of national unity.

With the RPF victory over the Rwandan Armed Forces (FAR) and the Interahamwe (the former being the military under Habyarimana) and the ending of the genocide, the new government abolished the use of ethnicity in formal society and has since emphasized the national nonethnic identity of being a *Rwandan* over Hutu, Tutsi, or Twa.

Stabilization (1–3 Years)

By 1995, only one year removed from the genocide, the government began hearings for 35,000 imprisoned Hutus accused of participating as genocidaires (OAU 2000, p. 181). The hearings were immediately suspended because of the financial burden to the state. These hearings would be replaced by Gacaca courts in the years to come. The international community through a UN Security Council resolution approved the establishment of an International Criminal Tribunal for Rwanda (ICTR) in November 1994. After the genocide, in all of Rwanda, there were five judges and 50 practicing lawyers (OAU 2000, p. 175). Twenty-five months after the end of the genocide in August 1996, there were 120,000 prisons awaiting trial (OAU 2000, p. 183). At this point, a meager 1.25% of prisoners were tried by the domestic courts. According to the *International Panel on Eminent Personalities,* a commission of the Organization of African Unity (OAU), interviews conducted with some prosecutors yielded the acknowledgment that up to 15%–20% of detained persons may be innocent and/or political rivals of the RPF (ibid.). Establishing trust between the government of national unity and the broader Hutu population, comprising around 85%, is fundamental in achieving reconciliation, economic development, and sustainable peace.

Bridging the trust deficit has proven difficult in the postgenocide era. In 1996, 2 years after the end of the genocide, 15 of 22 chiefs of ministerial staff, 16 out of 19 permanent secretaries, six of 11 *prefets,* 90% of judges being trained, 95% of faculty at the national university in Butare, and 80% of the country's burgomasters were

RPF Tutsi (OAU 2000, p. 167). This is significant in terms of intergroup trust inter alia a sense of security.

Institutional Reform (3–10 Years)

Within 4 years of the genocide, the number of detained prisoners related to crimes committed in the genocide rose to 130,000 (OAU 2000, p. 178). Throughout the institutional reform period, Rwanda has attempted to make security, trust, anticorruption, and intergroup acceptance central pillars of its governance strategy. However, Rwanda has faced many challenges. In 1999, 45,000–60,000 households were headed by children who were under the age of 18; this includes 300,000 children who lived in these households (OAU 2000, p. 170). Having a high volume of children essentially parenting and running households creates several development, psychological, and reconciliation problems.

In 2001, Rwanda unveiled a new flag and national anthem seeking to strengthen reconciliation and national unity. These symbolic moves were aimed at diverging Rwanda from previous symbols of tension and ethnic hatred. In addition, in 2001, Rwanda began to utilize the cultural tradition of Gacaca courts in bringing justice to detained genocidaires. Gacaca courts are a local communal-based court system where the judges are elected locally. Prisoners must go before these local courts and recount their crimes and recant their actions. Gacaca courts have typically been reserved for lower-level offenders (e.g., categories 2 and 3 offenses). According to Chakravarty (2006), category 1 crimes are reserved for the International Criminal Tribunal for Rwanda (ICTR) although tensions exist between the ICTR and the government. These are the genocidaires who participated in the planning, organizing of weapons, and execution of the genocide. Categories 2 and 3 are reserved for the vast majority of defendants who will be tried through the Gacaca court system in Rwanda by Rwandans.

Throughout the second half of the twentieth century up to July 1994, the RFAR under Hutu governments were used to segregate, arrest, and harass indigenous ethnic populations specifically targeting the Tutsi. Following the genocide, the Rwandan Defense Forces (RDF) now comprised the lion share of the military, which for the most part were former RPF soldiers. In this situation, having the military swap from Hutu dominant to RPF dominant led to increasing concerns from the population on security. The new government actively engaged this issue by stationing RDF forces throughout urban and rural centers in Rwanda; trying to show the population that the RDF was here for peace and security, not for harassment or suppression. In 2004, under the direction of president Paul Kagame, Rwanda began its participation in the African Union–UN peacekeeping mission in Darfur, Sudan. On August 15, 140 RDF soldiers arrived in Darfur to begin Rwanda's peacekeeping mission, which is aimed at protecting civilians from massacre and genocide (The Guardian, 2004). In addition to showing the international community that Rwanda's new military was used to protect civilians, the RDF annually conducts operations that directly assist locals through infrastructure construction, tree planting, and training seminars. These actions have directly contributed to the positive perception of the RDF in Rwandan society and have helped to bridge the trust deficit.

Structural Transformation in Society (10–30 Years)

The government had originally postponed elections scheduled for 1994 for 5 years following the genocide (OAU 2000, p. 170). After 5 years ended, in 1999, the government postponed the elections for an additional 4 years. In 2003, the government held elections. At the time, Paul Kagame ran for his first elected term of office and won (Kagame became interim president following the resignation of Bizimungu in 2000). Kagame served as the president of Rwanda for 7 years, and sought re-election in 2010. Kagame is limited by the constitution to two terms, which conclude in 2017. According to Freedom House, which tracks political rights, civil liberties, and the freedom of the press globally, Rwanda held a "Not Free" rating during the 2010 election cycle (Freedom House 2010). By virtue of the 2003 constitution, the president is bestowed significant authority. Some of the powers of the presidency include the power to declare war under Article 136, powers of instituting a state of emergency under Article 137, and that he/she shall nominate, appoint, and remove the prime minister according to Article 116 (Government of Rwanda 2003). Since election, the government has faced criticism over press freedoms and in its control of the state. These tensions are highlighted by Mahmood Mamdani (Mamdani 1998, p. 6):

> After 1994, the Tutsi want justice above all else, and the Hutu [want] democracy above all else. The minority fears democracy. The majority fears justice. The minority fears that democracy is a mask for finishing an unfinished genocide. The majority fears that demand for justice is a minority ploy to usurp power forever.

Mamdani may have simplified this dichotomy between Hutu and Tutsi but the illustration highlights important perspectives. Establishing a government of national unity, incorporating democracy, bridging the trust deficit, providing security to all residents regardless of ethnicity, and restoring justice to Rwanda through the prosecution of genocidaires and igniting economic growth and economic development are all priorities in postconflict Rwanda. Choosing a top priority is a monumentally difficult task wrought with fear and uncertainty. Rwanda has yet to reach 30 years of sustainable peace, and analysis of this final category remains premature.

Conclusion

To move beyond the events of 1994 requires a deep understanding of the complex causal mechanisms that led to the twentieth century's most swiftly executed genocide. Understanding how teachers, students, businesspersons, veterinarians, soldiers, and government officials could perpetrate genocide against their neighbors is fundamental in securing a path forward. Sustainable peace and good governance requires more than the absence of ethnic conflict. It requires government action to bridge ethnic divides, local initiatives to overcome years of ethnic dehumanization, and organic and dynamic processes of reconciliation aimed at establishing new relationships within society. Security, trust, and societal norms (or social contracts) are three indicators of reconciliation. The Government of Rwanda has delivered security through integration programs for ex-combatants, security sector reforms, anticorruption measures, and in strengthening the rule of law. Intergroup distrust has been reduced since its height in 1994. Moreover, sincere efforts are made to reconcile ethnic hostilities through incentivizing reconciliation.

Memorials remember the victims but survivors carry the burden. Reconciliation remains elusive in the absence of economic prosperity. The economy is the engine that fuels society that provides hopes and dreams of advancement. Effective reconciliation builds upon this foundational element to secure peace. In the 20 years since the genocide, Rwanda has made great strides in economic development, implementing good governance measures, rooting out corruption, and in sustaining interethnic peace. Critics of the government argue that Rwanda is receding toward more authoritarian policies, yet the achievements of economic development over the past two decades cannot be ignored.

In 1994, Rwanda reported a low GDP per capita of $132. By 2012, Rwanda's GDP per capita increased fivefold to $620 (World Bank). A remarkable feat for a country that witnessed more than 10% of its population murdered two decades earlier. Similarly, life expectancy in 1994 was 28 years for the average Rwandan. In 2012, this rose to 63 years. FDI (as a percent of GDP) rose from 0.0001% in 1994, meaning practically no FDI was present, to 2.25% in 2012. This relative increase in FDI demonstrates an understanding by investors that Rwanda has progressed in security, handling of corruption, enforcement of the rule of law, and overall good governance measures. The infant mortality rate among children under 5 years old decreased fivefold between 1994 and 2012. Across a wide array of economic development indicators, Rwanda has made leaps and bounds. The economic development in Rwanda is remarkable considering the extent of mass trauma experienced two decades earlier.

In comparing the progress Rwanda has made over the two dominant periods—Habyarimana and Kagame—we see vastly different outcomes. During Habyarimana's rule, a strategy that traded political stability in the short run for sustained economic growth in the medium run moved the needle on many economic development indicators circa 1973–1990. Under Kagame's leadership, Rwanda has achieved far greater accomplishments in economic development, good governance, security, and in sustaining interethny peace. Sustainable peace requires more than short-term measures of stability; it requires consolidated reconciliation efforts between ethnies built in conjunction with economic development. Economic development brings more than higher wages and foreign investment. Economic development dampens ethnic conflict through collective benefits of economic security and interdependence. Reconciliation buttresses development with social benefits of cooperation and security. Neither component can operate independently. Achieving lasting sustainable peace requires both the development of the land and reconciliation to develop the heart.

Acknowledgments

I am very grateful to Louis A. Picard, Terry F. Buss, Macrina Lelei, reviewers at Taylor & Francis, and particularly Taylor Seybolt for their helpful comments and criticisms of this chapter.

References

Chakravarty, A. 2006. Gacaca courts in Rwanda: Explaining divisions within the human rights community. *Yale Journal of International Affairs* (Winter|Spring) 1(2): 132–145.

Freedom House. 2010. Available at: http://www.freedomhouse.org/report/freedom-world/2010/rwanda. Accessed 8/8/14.

Gourevitch, P. 1998. *We Wish to Inform You That Tomorrow We Will Be Killed with Our Families: Stories from Rwanda.* New York: Farrar, Straus, and Giroux.

Government of Rwanda. 2003. Constitution of the Republic of Rwanda. Available at: http://rwandahope.com/constitution.pdf.

Lederach, J. 1997. *Building Peace: Sustainable Reconciliation in Divided Societies.* Washington, DC: The United States Institute of Peace.

Mamdani, M. 1998. When does a settler become a native? Reflections of the colonial roots of citizenship in Equatorial and South Africa. Inaugural Lecture. New Series, No. 208. South Africa: University of Cape Town. Available at: http://citizenshiprightsinafrica.org/docs/mamdani%201998%20inaugural%20lecture.pdf.

Mamdani, M. 2001. *When Victims Become Killers: Colonialism, Nativism, and the Genocide in Rwanda.* Princeton, NJ: Princeton University Press.

Organization of African Unity. 2000. International Panel of Eminent Personalities to Investigate the 1994 Genocide in Rwanda and the Surrounding Events: Special report. Addis Ababa.

Prunier, G. 1995. *The Rwandan Crisis: History of a Genocide.* New York: Columbia University Press.

Rakiya, O., de Waal, A. 1995. *Rwanda: Death, Despair and Defiance.* London: African Rights.

Straus, S. 2006. *The Order of Genocide.* Ithaca, NY: Cornell University Press.

The Guardian. 2004. Rwandan force lands in Darfur. Available at: http://www.guardian.co.uk/world/2004/aug/16/sudan.

Uvin, P. 1997. Prejudice, crisis and genocide in Rwanda. *African Studies Review* 40(2): 91–115.

Valentino, B. 2004. *Final Solutions: Mass Killing and Genocide in the 20th Century.* Ithaca, NY: Cornell University Press.

World Bank. 2014. Available at: http://data.worldbank.org/. Accessed 8/8/14.

Chapter 14

Violence, Development, and Democracy in South Africa

Elke Zuern

Contents

> "Strengthening legitimate institutions and governance to provide citizen security, justice, and jobs is crucial to break cycles of violence."*
>
> "What rights are you talking about, we do not have rights, none of us have rights. I mean if we did have rights, we would be treated with more respect. ...This democracy of theirs ends with the vote [*democracy e ya bona efella ka go vota*]."†

* World Bank (2011, p. 2).

† Mr Ntobong, cited in Khunou (2002, p. 69).

Violence undermines development. Statistically, high levels of violence and low levels of human development tend to go together. The World Bank has drawn attention to the human, social, and economic developmental consequences of violence identifying improved state capacity as a central means of lessening violence and improving consequences for development (2011). While it is important to document the impact of violence upon societies, it is equally important to understand that the causal relationship between violence and development cannot be reduced to the negative consequences of violence upon state-led development plans. Development, however defined, is an interactive process that relies not just on effective planning but also on citizen engagement and support. Far too often, solutions are conceived as requiring stronger states and more efficient planning, thereby neglecting or even negating citizen input. The consequences of such actions, as will be demonstrated below, can be disastrous.

First, development offered by nonaccountable but strong state institutions has itself, at times, triggered violence. Enhancing state capacity without addressing democratic accountability will not address this problem. Second, state responses to the perceived threat of violence from the general population can also undermine prospects for democracy and development. As states try to promote stability and shore up their institutions against threats, they risk insulating their institutions from popular input. Echoing Huntington's (1968) *Political Order in Changing Societies* thesis, the WB argues "grievances can escalate into acute demands for change—and the risks of violent conflict—in countries where political, social, or economic change lags behind expectations" (Huntington 1968, p. 5) These demands for change can alternatively be viewed as threats to the stability of the state or opportunities for government to engage popular concerns to improve the prospects for both democratic governance and sustainable development.

South Africa offers a challenging mix of such opportunities that have frequently been presented as threats by leading government officials. The country has a long history of popular protest, which waned briefly in the first years after the formal end of apartheid in 1994 only to increase again from 1999 (Ballard et al. 2006; Desai 2002; Gibson 2006). At the same time, government leaders have repeatedly referred to their state as a "developmental state" working to promote a "better life for all" (ANC 1994; Mbeki 2006). Elected politicians have understandably wanted to demonstrate relatively quick progress after the end of apartheid to convince citizens that the new regime would be inclusive, competent, and able to tackle the stark inequalities created by colonialism and apartheid. Access to free basic maternal and infant health care was relatively quickly rolled out, but reforming the health system, and other key sectors including education and policing, has proved to be much more difficult (Von Holdt 2010). Jay Naidoo, the former minister coordinating the country's initial Reconstruction and Development Program (RDP) later reflected on the country's overall development goals: "There was a need for tradeoffs on timing and the maintenance of social consensus to manage the mismatch between the aspirational goals of the Reconstruction and Development Program, the macro and fiscal framework to pay for them, and the institutional capacity to implement them" (WB 2011, p. 115). Within a few short years of the end of apartheid, the government moved from the inclusive RDP to the much more technocratically driven neo-liberal Growth, Employment, and Redistribution Program (GEAR) in 1996. GEAR was not based on democratic input but designed to address fiscal concerns despite popular resistance. Only a few years after the introduction of GEAR, popular protest reached new postapartheid highs.

Ideally, development and freedom would neatly work together (Sen 1999). Improvements after the institution of democratic regimes would be demonstrated by dramatic increases in human development indicators. This unfortunately has not been the case for South Africa. It is difficult to overstate the incredible challenges faced by South Africans in the aftermath of apartheid. The measured language of the United Nations Development Program (UNDP) stressed the severity of the economic and social crisis: "The first democratically elected government in South Africa inherited apartheid policies and institutions that had resulted in a stagnant economy, an exceptional level of poverty, inequalities in income and wealth and extremely skewed access to basic services, natural resources and employment" (2003, p. 12). South Africa's Human Development score compiled from three indices—life expectancy, educational attainment, and gross domestic product—reached its highest level in 1995 after slowly rising over the previous decade under apartheid. After 1995, instead of continuing to rise, it dropped precipitously. By 2005 it had declined to a low not seen since the 1980s, before slowly rising again.* South Africa's postapartheid statistical downturn is due to the impact of HIV/AIDS. But, the degree to which the epidemic spread and the general lack of adequate treatment is indicative of far-reaching challenges beyond the health care sector.

Despite some per capita growth, the distribution of income has remained incredibly skewed against the poor. South Africa's Gini coefficient is among the highest in the world and has not declined since the end of apartheid.† When we consider former apartheid racial classifications, the overwhelming majority of whites remain in the highest expenditure quintile (83%), while less than 8% of black Africans belong to this wealthy group (Statistics South Africa 2008, p. 8).‡ Unemployment has also risen in the postapartheid period. Under the expanded definition, which

---

* http://hdr.undp.org/en/data/trends/

† The South African government reported a Gini coefficient of 64.0 in 1995, rising to 68.0 in 2000, and again to 69.0 in 2005. (Presidency 2009, p. 25). In 2011, it reported a score of 70 (National Planning Commission 2011, p. 3). The UN calculated a coefficient of 59.6 in 1995, which increased to 63.5 in 2001 (UNDP 2003, p. 43) and decreased to 57.8 in 2007 (UNDP 2009, p. 197).

‡ In order to track changes since the end of apartheid, statistics are still gathered according to apartheid era racial classifications. Instead of state-assigned classifications, respondents are now asked to self-identify. The categories are white, "colored," Indian/Asian, African (referring to black Africans).

includes frustrated job seekers among the unemployed, unemployment rose from 29.3% in 1995 to 42.1% in 2003 (UNDP 2003, p. 20) and remained over 40% in 2013 (*Economist* 2013). Under the narrower definition, which includes only those who actively looked for work in the 4 weeks prior to the survey, South Africa's unemployment rate in the second quarter of 2014 was a stark 25.5%.* Poverty remains overwhelmingly black, almost exclusively so among the poorest. In the poorest quintile of households, 95% are Africans. Members of this segment of the population struggle to feed their families, allocating more than half of their total expenditure just to food. At the other end of the scale, almost 50% of the wealthiest 20% of households are white (Martins 2007).

Developmental State and Democracy

South Africa's political leaders have repeatedly offered the developmental state as the solution to the country's challenges. In a speech to the National Assembly, former President Thabo Mbeki quoted Amartya Sen's *Development as Freedom* to underline the central importance of the creation of a developmental state for South Africa's future (2006) and the country's current president, Jacob Zuma, made headlines by championing the developmental state to bring about a transformation in health and education as well as in the fight against crime. (*Mail and Guardian* Nov. 29, 2008) In late 2011, the National Planning Commission (an advisory body) released its *National Development Plan* designed to eliminate poverty and reduce inequality by 2030. In it, the authors lay out the shortcomings of the current state of development in South Africa and work to chart a new course. They underline the danger of not doing so: "Persistently high levels of poverty will prompt social instability, leading to a rise in populist politics and demands for short-term measures that lead to further tension and decline" (2011, p. 4). Their argument is poverty and weak state institutions lead to increased conflict and violence.

The plan offers innovative proposals and seeks to engage South Africa's citizens, but it continues to follow the state-centric conviction that the best way to improve development efforts is solely to improve state capacity. It fails to consider the dangers of a lack of democratic accountability to ordinary citizens.† While sectoral capacity is essential to the implementation of development programs following a defined plan, improving capacity does not necessarily improve opportunities for citizen engagement and input into the planning and prioritizing of local development projects. The planners seek to increase participation in existing development projects and reduce corruption, but they do not address the question of who defines local priorities and how ordinary citizens might participate in that process. Development planners are concerned with accountability within government but provide no

* http://www.statssa.gov.za

† Interestingly, the word "democracy" never appears in the development plan.

solutions to the stark challenge of accountability between government officers and ordinary citizens. This is particularly problematic given the well-documented weakness of accountability in most of South Africa's local governments. The level of government closest to the people in many of the poorest areas has repeatedly failed to respond to citizen petitions and requests for information, to develop transparent processes and to engage communities in democratic processes. Lack of accountability has led to repeated protests, at times violent.

To understand the prospects for conflict and violence and its connection to development, we need to consider the state of democracy. South Africa is a "dominant-party democracy"; the governing African National Congress (ANC) has achieved repeated and overwhelming victories in national, provincial, and local elections.* Although the ANC's ascension to power has occurred through popular support rather than intimidation or fraud, the danger in any system marked by repeated single-party success is that it will lead to reduced checks on the power of the winner and fewer opportunities for opposing ideas, arguments, and policies. Such party dominance has allowed for both developmental and authoritarian politics (Evans 2001; Wade 1992; Woo-Cumings 1999). Either or both are possible; neither will necessarily follow great electoral success.

Under Thabo Mbeki's leadership, the ANC took on the great challenges of postapartheid governance. To do so, it centralized power within the government and the party and suppressed dissent within both. The centralizing drive of the ANC government was closely tied to the desire to improve poor service delivery and to transform all levels of government. In order to address the fragmentation of the state and to "streamline" administrative and financial systems, the office of the president was strengthened, and numerous oversight positions staffed by loyal political appointees of the president were created. In his analysis of these reforms, Anthony Butler argues: "New oversight and co-ordination mechanisms, and the highly centralized formal structure of the core executive, are understandable reactions to the provincial incapacities in policy design and implementation" (2000, p. 198). He adds, however, that Mbeki also demonstrated a clear unwillingness to allow those provinces and cities that had the capacity to address challenges to take control of their own reform processes. As Mbeki centralized authority in the executive, forums for transformation that were designed to encourage broad participation increasingly gave way to top-down and technocratic approaches to governance (Gevisser 2007; Heller 2000; Lodge 1999).

South Africa's closed-list proportional representation system works to strengthen the power of party leaders since the leading figures in each party have extensive control over party members of parliament, undermining constituent representation in the system as a whole (Mattes and Thiel 1998, p. 105). At the local level,

---

* Dominant-party democracy is commonly defined as one characterized by "electoral dominance for a prolonged and uninterrupted period, dominance in the formation of governments, and dominance in determining the public agenda" (Giliomee 1998, p. 128).

the participatory demands of the domestic antiapartheid movement are reflected in the formal institutions of the state, but the implementation of these ideals is weak. First, the Constitution of the Republic of South Africa (1996) stresses the importance of participation by stipulating that local government should "encourage the involvement of communities and community organizations in the matters of local government" (Chapter 7, Sec. 152, 1.e.). Second, the Local Municipal Structures Act (1998) goes even further by calling for the creation of community-staffed ward committees "to enhance participatory democracy in local government" (Chapter 4, Pt. 4, 72.3). These ward committees were meant to institutionalize the best of participatory democracy achieved by the local level organizations during the anti-apartheid struggle.

Makgane Thobejane, in the Johannesburg City Manager's office, argued: "The new system of local government actually emphasizes organs of people's power by talking about the establishment of ward committees. So right from the ward level there will be a mechanism of representation … so it becomes a regulated kind of participatory democracy" (Thobejane, interview, January 22, 2001). Despite the creation of these new institutions, many activists have argued that there is no "real" democracy at the level of local government.* Popular surveys have consistently demonstrated the highest levels of citizen dissatisfaction with local rather than provincial or national government (Afrobarometer 2009; Mattes et al. 2000; Taylor and Mattes 1998).† The Municipal Demarcation Board appointed by President Mbeki, the national ministry responsible for local government, politicians across the political spectrum, local activists, and the media have repeatedly expressed concern over the state of local government, describing it as unresponsive, inefficient, ineffective, and often corrupt.

Within local government, councilors across party lines have described the ward committees as mechanisms for the government and the ruling party to disseminate information to residents (Gomati, interview, January 25, 2001; Moepi, interview, July 16, 2002) rather than forums in which residents could raise their concerns to their elected representatives.‡ Some have gone so far as to describe ward committees as "just an advisory body" (Moedi, interview, July 19, 2002) or even a "farce" (Fuchs, interview, July 16, 2002). Studies conducted in municipalities across the country have demonstrated that the ward committee system simply does not

* Activists echoed complaints frequently heard from township residents since the mid-1990s. One resident of a poor area of Soweto noted: "[Our] councilor doesn't want educated people. He wants to tell people what to do. This leads to disputes" (Kaizer Twala, interview. July 21, 1997).

† In Afrobarometer's 2008 survey, 64% of respondents noted that local councilors "never" or "only sometimes" "try their best to listen to what people like you have to say." Again, 64% said local council is "very badly" or "fairly badly" following procedures "allowing citizens like yourself to participate in council's decisions" (Afrobarometer 2009).

‡ One councilor described the ward committee as her "eyes and ears" (Bapela, interview. January 26, 2001).

provide a mechanism for constituents to hold their councilors to account (Bénit-Gbaffou 2008; Piper and Deacon 2008; Raga and Taylor 2005). Even when ward councilors make efforts to represent their constituents' concerns, their powers are limited by the centralization of policy making dominated by the ANC.* A government report investigating the state of local government reported: "In practice sector departments hardly ever consult or involve ward councilors in plans and projects" (RSA, Cooperative Governance and Traditional Affairs 2009, p. 15).

South Africa's Resurgent Movements

Democracy in South Africa brought all adult citizens the right to vote, but at the same time that political and civil rights expanded, envisaged socioeconomic rights contracted (Zuern 2011). A politics of cost recovery was introduced reducing subsidies and requiring consumers, even in desperately poor communities, to pay close to the full cost of services such as electricity and water.† Banks and municipalities were able to quickly evict poor residents from their homes after relatively short periods of nonpayment and low arrears. At the same time, democracy reshaped expectations for claim making and for popular contention. All South Africans were now expected to play their formal role in the electoral process by turning out to vote. Their newly elected representatives would then chart a course for development. When citizens sought to challenge decisions, large or small, they were to employ legal processes, to work through formal institutions, and to be patient. More radical demands, it was argued, needed to be deferred in order for democracy and development to take hold. But the legacies of the past could not be undone overnight. As many grew increasingly desperate as a result of the government's economic policies and frustrated by feelings of political marginalization, South Africa saw a resurgence of social-movement activity. The movements challenged government policies, but they also confronted structures of power that they defined as antidemocratic.

State leaders responded by defining the movements themselves as antidemocratic and a threat to the new regime. The unfolding debate over the role of social movements in new democracies reflects two broad sets of concerns. On one hand, those working within newly democratized state institutions point to the threats that movements may pose and suggest the need to reduce political and economic instability by restraining protest. On the other hand, social-movement activists

* Some councilors have apparently been quite honest with their constituents as to whom they expect will hold them to account for their actions. "The last councilor, when as the residents we call him, he will just tell you: 'No, I have never been elected by you, the residents. I have been elected by the ANC'" (Bozo, interview. January 23, 2001). The councilor in question was elected via the proportional representation list, not as a ward councilor.

† Cost recovery forms a central pillar of the World Bank's discourse of adjustment and good governance (Abrahamsen 2001).

argue that governments use the fear of instability as an excuse to repress valid claims and thereby undermine popular representation, critical debate, and democracy itself. These concerns tug at the roots of the struggle for democracy. What was the struggle actually for? Have these ends been achieved or thwarted? Should the struggle continue? These questions become all the more difficult when the new leaders of the democratic state are the same people who participated in and often led the struggle against authoritarian rule.

In the case of South Africa, ANC leaders had once encouraged wide-ranging protests and even "ungovernability" in the townships in order to bring down the apartheid state. Once in government, they raised concerns that protests might undermine their intended restructuring and reform of state institutions. Protest, they argued, could cause instability in the markets and provoke capital flight. In seeking to address these fears, they strongly encouraged their allies in the struggle against apartheid such as the South African National Civic Organization (SANCO), which is comprised of community organizations, to support their policies and their power. As local organizations became frustrated with these attempts to influence their actions, they considered when and how they might press their demands more forcefully to their former comrades, who now seemed too busy with the business of the state and private business ventures to receive the petitions of poor communities. SANCO which once represented the largest numbers of ordinary township residents lost support as it blindly endorsed all ANC policies. New organizations, more critical of the government and its policies, gained prominence.

As popular organizing in poor townships once again increased in the late 1990s and protesters took to the streets, many South Africans feared the specter of unrest. Recent history seemed to suggest that demands for change and violence went hand in hand, but it is important to note that different mechanisms are at work in creating violence during protest actions (Klopp and Zuern 2007). On one hand, the fear of protesters tends to assume that it is protesters who initiate violence by throwing stones or burning property. Protest actions can also provide opportunities for criminal violence. Continuing high rates of criminal violence in South Africa (Shaw 2002) have prompted arguments to restrict civil liberties to assist in the policing of crime.* On the other, the police are poorly trained, underresourced, and overstretched, and as a result they often fall back on authoritarian policing practices whether in response to an armed robbery or a rowdy public protest (Leggett 2005; Marks and Wood 2010). This has led to a high rate of deaths as a result of police actions including innocent bystanders shot by the police (Bruce 2005; *Economist* June 23, 2012). The majority of protest actions in South Africa since the end of

* In Alexandra, one civic leader who had helped turn in a few minor criminals explained the dangers of doing so as alleged criminals, even if apprehended by the police, were often quickly back on the street. "[Then he] comes back to you then next day and points a finger at you. You find yourself in a situation where you don't know what you have to do next time, if you find a criminal" (Langa, interview. June 19, 1997).

apartheid have been peaceful, but protest and the threat of violence by the police or protesters are tied together in the popular consciousness. Since 2010, a number of protest actions have led to violence (Alexander 2012; Lavery 2012).

The centralization of state policymaking, the demand for unity within the dominant party, the weakness of opposition political parties, and the shortcomings of local government authorities weakened key formal avenues of interest representation for the poor majority. As a result, by the end of the 1990s, some of the loudest voices representing the concerns of the country's marginalized citizens came from the extra-institutional protest actions of social movements and community organizations. Movements such as Abahlali baseMjondolo ("the people who live in shacks", AbM), the Soweto Electricity Crisis Committee (SECC), the Landless People's Movement (LPM), and the Western Cape Anti-Eviction Campaign (WCAEC) (Ballard et al. 2006; Bond 2006; Gibson 2006; Pithouse 2008; Zikode 2006) received substantial local and international press attention for their demands ranging from access to clean water and electricity to land reform and redistribution. Their actions publicized citizens' socioeconomic claims and the state's responses to them as they employed a range of tactics including both legal and illegal actions.

Movements such as AbM, the SECC, LPM, and WCAEC, which challenged the government's privatization policies, were consistently demonized by government and much of the popular press. They engaged in actions including marches and petitions as well as the reconnection of disconnected electricity, the occupation of vacant land, and the reinstatement of people evicted from their homes. These latter actions led to violence between protesters and police or private security companies who came to forcibly remove them. While supporters of the activists pointed to the excessive force employed by the police, ANC leaders labeled these movements a direct threat to democracy.

Need to Create "Damage"

The WCAEC, the SECC, and other organizations such as AbM work to draw attention to the dire circumstances of a large population of people struggling to make ends meet. Although not all members of the communities they claim to represent necessarily agree with the methods or broader goals of the movements (Sinwell 2009), their presence does press the state to respond. The government's response to these new movements has ranged from verbal attempts to delegitimize and marginalize them to physical acts of intimidation and repression. When ANC activists have directly addressed the demands of the movements, it has been largely to engage in the politics of blame: to suggest that others aside from the government are responsible for the problems that the movements cite, to argue that the movements themselves offer no credible solution to the problems, and to restate the argument that current government policies offer the best solutions. The ANC has also employed its ally, SANCO, hoping that it might be able to draw support away from more radical actors to reinforce the state's policies and power. This approach has met with mixed success.

Despite its rhetoric as a revolutionary social movement and representative of South Africa's poor, SANCO has supported the logic of credit-control measures even when this means widespread electricity disconnections and the installation of water-flow restrictors. SANCO has therefore worked to support a neoliberal framework of governance in which certain citizenship rights become contingent upon access to financial resources and support for the broader economic system. One civic leader in the Vaal summed up this perspective in stark terms: "We need to protect [the consumer] as SANCO, but you protect a consumer who is obedient" (Lehoko, interview, June 9, 2004). As residents in Soweto became increasingly desperate and angry, SANCO continued to lose support, and groups such as the SECC, which took a more radical approach, gained in popularity. SANCO's response to this challenge was to leverage its position by threatening mass action in an attempt to upstage the SECC (SAPA, June 7, 2001) while simultaneously presenting itself as a credible negotiating partner with ESKOM, the electricity utility. In 2002 SANCO participated in negotiations with ESKOM and government representatives, which led to an agreement that residents with faulty meters would pay a flat fee of R120 ($16) per month until their meters were repaired (SAPA, April 26, 2002). Civic leaders strategically drew attention to these agreements to try to convince community residents that SANCO rather than the SECC would find a solution to their problems (Sugar Monnakgotla, interview, July 15, 2002). Despite the weakness of its local branches, SANCO sought to assert itself as the primary broker between township residents and state actors.

SANCO's greatest triumph came in May 2003. ESKOM and the Ministry of Public Enterprises (headed by Jeff Radebe, a recent member of SANCO's National Executive Committee) along with the Human Rights Commission and SANCO came to an agreement to write off R1.39 billion ($190 million) in Johannesburg electricity arrears. Although this write-off was clearly in response to the influence of movements such as the SECC, SANCO rather than the SECC was included in the negotiations. SANCO presented itself as the public representative of the poor and was given at least formal credit for the write-off. A supporter of the SECC campaign wrote: "All but moribund 12 months ago, SANCO has suddenly come to life with resources and influence from political heavyweights in national government, determined, it would seem, to counter the growing influence—and anti-neoliberalism—of SECC ..." (McDonald 2003).

A SANCO leader summed up SANCO's strategy regarding challenges faced from groups such as SECC and the ways it employed its relationship with the government.

> Credit goes to SANCO.... As a civic movement we grab those people that support Trevor [Ngwane of the SECC], look at their issues, and

> actually change them. We can strategize.... Let the credit come to SANCO, and then SANCO will take the credit back to government. It is quite a nice ballgame.... Whilst now we confront, they deliver. The credit goes to SANCO. You take the credit back to government. You call a mass meeting, address the people, and say government has delivered.... That is how you deal with it. You actually strategically try to isolate them [SECC and others]. (Anonymous Gauteng SANCO leader, interview, January 2004)

From the perspective of the SECC, Trevor Ngwane argued:

> Earlier they [the government] responded by calling us agitators, criminals, or denying that we exist. Now they are acknowledging our existence. Now they are vicious and clever; they are gonna smash people, but they are clever enough to acknowledge that there are such organizations. They might not publicly say there is the SECC, but you can see it from their strategies that they are kind of adapting. (Ngwane, interview, July 19, 2002)

SANCO presented itself to local communities as a problem solver that could employ its relationship with the government to address residents' concerns. This argument, however, deliberately ignores the role that the SECC had played. Without pressure from the SECC and massive nonpayment, ESKOM would never have offered such a large write-off. In contrast to SANCO's claimed success in Soweto, where the SECC mobilized, it failed in Tshwane, where there was no group like the SECC. In Tshwane SANCO leaders also participated in a series of negotiations with the metropolitan government council, but the council refused SANCO's request to write off outstanding arrears, arguing that effective credit-control measures were already in place (SAPA, May 12, 2003). Without popular pressure, which at times led to violence, government representatives saw no reason to address citizen's demands.

SANCO leaders in Tshwane learned from their mistakes. They began to innovate by employing some of the tactics used by groups such as the SECC. In Tshwane, regional SANCO leaders realized that they could not rely on their alliance with the ANC to maintain their relevance. They needed to reach out to local communities and work to draw attention to their concerns. They learned from the actions of the SECC that institutional politics were not enough to garner the government's attention and demand some form of change. Local leaders in Tshwane repeatedly argued that it was necessary to demonstrate their capacity for protest and even the potential to cause "damage" (suggesting damage to property or broader violence) to draw attention to their concerns. One leader argued: "I believed in our branches in SANCO actually creating damage so that the ANC can run to us ... The ANC will keep despising you if you are not acting. That's why we go there and stop the [government development] project completely" (Anonymous SANCO Tshwane leader, interview, January 2004). He continued to explain that he would claim ignorance when ANC leaders asked him why local community members from his organization stopped the projects, but would offer to mediate between community members and government. In this way, he could maintain his presumed "innocence" to present the organization's demands to ANC officials, even while continuing to encourage activists on the ground to act to frustrate government leaders.

Regional leaders openly acknowledged the contradictions of their actions but noted that this was simply the most effective way of bringing about change.

> When you are a leader and you have followers, they wouldn't necessarily do things like [engaging in the destruction of property] without informing you. They would actually want your approval... And you wouldn't say to them: "Look, invade the land." You would just say to them: "Comrade, you are a leader. Do what has to be done. Take a decision and implement."... (Anonymous SANCO Tshwane leader, interview, January 2004)

SANCO leaders in Tshwane therefore navigated a careful line of supporting popular community demands and condoning and even encouraging the tactics employed by the so-called antisystem movements such as the SECC. At the same time, they presented themselves as reliable negotiators with local government authorities. SANCO could potentially capture the power of a locally based social movement by encouraging protest and the threat of damage and harnessing that influence by employing its politically connected national structure.

Actions of SANCO Tshwane and arguments of its leaders underscore the crucial role that movements such as the SECC and the threat of violence play in South Africa's new democracy. They raise voices that are otherwise not heard in the corridors of power by making it impossible for those living far from the poor townships to ignore their demands. The fact that SANCO needed to employ the methods of South Africa's radical movements also underlines the simple truth that these demands are not being addressed via formal institutional channels, even for those with connections to government.

Service Delivery and Democracy

Significant pressure for the enforcement and expansion of economic as well as political rights has come from outside the formal institutions of the state. It has also changed the way those institutions operate. The 2004 national government elections took place amid great social movement mobilization demanding that government pay more attention to the needs of the poor. In response government budgets allocated increased funding to infrastructural investment, public works programs, and social welfare (Habib and Valodia 2006, p. 248). Seekings reported: "Expenditure on social assistance almost doubled from about 2 percent of GDP in 1994 (and 2000) to about 3.5 percent in 2005" (2007, p. 19). Although such grants did not address the central demands of movements such as the WCAEC and the SECC for the right to housing and basic services, they did allow the ANC government to argue that it was engaging in pro-poor policy reform and that it was responding to popular inputs for development. Government officials repeatedly argued that this increase in spending was not a result of increased social mobilization but rather part of a long-term plan. There is, however, a strong correlation, between the resurgence of pro-poor movements and the increased allocation of government funding to many of the concerns to which the movements drew national and international attention.

During his time in office, President Mbeki centralized power in the executive and demonized movements that challenged his economic policies. The president's undermining of political contestation was not confined to those he labeled as anti-system but spread to his opponents on a wide range of issues. As he attempted to maintain control of the state and defend his policy decisions, he removed members of government who defied him (Feinstein 2007) and aggressively protected his supporters against all critics. As a result, he lost the support of much of his key constituency: the intelligentsia and the urban middle and upper-middle classes (Gevisser 2007), and his approval ratings dropped precipitously in 2007, leading up to the ANC party elections.* This shift was a product of several factors, but most importantly, the sense that Mbeki was defying popularly accepted and expected democratic norms (Habib 2008).

Mbeki's shortcomings opened the door for South Africa's embattled Jacob Zuma† to become the leader of the ANC and then the president of the country. Zuma's first few months in office were hardly quiet. In July and August, the so-called service delivery protests spread to several townships across the country. By the end of August, the number of such protests in 2009 had significantly exceeded those of the past few years, including 2005, a year of widespread protests (RSA, Cooperative Governance and Traditional Affairs 2009, p. 12). Thandakukhanya, outside Piet Retief in Mpumalanga province, was the site of one of the first large protests after Zuma became president. Several residents who had previously met as the Committee of 13, formed to address concerns over the allocation of housing, joined with other community members to elect the 30-member Concerned Group. In a memorandum sent to the provincial premier, David Mabuza, the group stated its purpose: "to request the office of the premier to facilitate an urgent investigation

* In December 2006, 53% of those polled believed Mbeki was doing a "good job"; in June 2007, this number was basically unchanged at 54%. By September 2007, only 40% approved of the job Mbeki was doing. Disapproval ratings rose more steadily from 31% to 36% to 48% over the same period as fewer people were unsure about how they felt about Mbeki (Angus Reid Global Monitor 2007).

† This occurred despite corruption charges and an earlier rape trial in which Zuma was acquitted.

to our local Mkhondo municipality in connection with the following high rate of alleged corruption happening within the municipality" (reproduced in Sinwell et al. 2009, p. 9–11). The memorandum detailed residents' concerns and demands including the call for more-transparent and accountable local government. It made specific requests for the minutes of municipal committee meetings, a clear accounting of the use of funds allocated from national and provincial government, the qualifications of administrative hires, and the procedures regarding the allocation of houses and the determination of rates to be paid by residents.

Echoing many previous civic and other movement demands, the memorandum called for "proper consultation in terms of resource distribution and infrastructure" and recommended that local councilors be suspended pending the outcome of investigations.* The demands made in this memorandum reflected those submitted in a previous memorandum delivered to the local town hall and sent to the premier. On June 22, the Concerned Group met with the premier and asked that the local councilors be suspended. Premier David Mabuza promised to come to the area for an open forum the following Sunday to respond to the community's concerns. On the agreed upon date, the Premier failed to visit the township, but sent representatives to meet with community members (Sinwell et al. 2009, p. 2). In July, residents staged another march during which some protesters burned tires and blocked roads. Cars belonging to the municipality, a health clinic, and a public library were burned; two protesters were killed, reportedly by police and security forces (*Times*, December 26, 2009).

Similar demands not just for "service delivery" but most importantly for government accountability were repeated in townships across the country. In Thokoza and Diepsloot in Gauteng, Khayelitsha in the Western Cape, Duncan Village in the Eastern Cape, and elsewhere, citizens took to the streets. As the protests grew, two areas received the greatest media attention: Siyathemba and Sakhile, both in Mpumalanga. Protests in the Siyathemba township outside Balfour began with a march to the local municipal offices. When the municipality failed to respond, a community meeting was held, but clashes erupted between the police and residents after the police fired rubber bullets and teargas in an attempt to disperse the crowd (Sinwell et al. 2009, p. 5). Some protesters also blocked roads and looted foreign-owned shops. In response to the protests and the destruction that ensued, President Zuma surprised residents by briefly visiting the township and promising to listen to their concerns.

In Sakhile, described as a "battlefield" by the local press (*Sowetan*, October 14, 2009), residents promised to continue their protests, including the barricading of

* In order to address any accusations that they were motivated by opposition parties or the quest for local government offices, the memorandum to the premier argued that the group's members were also members of the ANC: "We are in no position to be elected as councilors and we are mostly working, but cannot sit and fold our arms while the municipality is misusing the rate payers' money" (reproduced in Sinwell et al. 2009).

roads and the burning of government buildings, until the president also came to resolve their issues (*Mail and Guardian*, October 15, 2009). The Sakhile township residents demanded the "right to elect their own representatives," instead of ANC party structures determining candidates for local office, and called for an inquiry into alleged corruption. The protests and the police response led to significant destruction of property and the injury of at least 14 people (*Mail and Guardian*, October 16, 2009). Although President Zuma did not visit Sakhile, ANC officials did come to the area and, in a surprise move, fired the municipal mayor and her entire committee just days ahead of a presidential meeting with all the country's mayors and municipal managers (*Sunday Independent*, October 25, 2009, p. 1). The lesson, it seems, is that violence works.

Violence, Civility, and Development

Although the protests drew important attention to the demands for accountable government, most were able to attract attention only by blocking roads and destroying property and through the corresponding police responses, which included rubber bullets and teargas. The news media ran pictures of burning tire blockades, damaged public buildings, and police taking aim at protesters. This immediately raised the question of the "civility" or "civicness" of the protesters. How could protesters destroy public buildings when they claimed to be agitating for better public-service delivery? How could protesters press for more-responsible government when they were proving to be irresponsible themselves? Minister in the presidency Trevor Manuel in a talk at the Graduate School of Public and Development Management in Johannesburg condemned the protesters' actions arguing that a behavioral change was necessary for development (October 26, 2009).

This argument that citizens must be more civil and must work to support state-based initiatives has long been employed to challenge the legitimacy of popular demands. It suggests that the public should defer to the expertise of technocrats and policy makers. It also deliberately ignores the question as to what opportunities ordinary citizens have at their disposal for participation and engagement with their elected representatives. In its review of four protests, the Center for Sociological Research at the University of Johannesburg found that each protest "only occurred after unsuccessful attempts by community members to engage with local authorities over issues of failed service delivery" (Sinwell et al. 2009, p. 1). Arguments concerning the need for behavioral change to allow for development to take root ignore the demands of the protesters for democratic accountability. Instead, they frame citizens' actions as merely "service-delivery protests" that might be addressed with minimal infrastructural improvements.

In these cases, residents first sought to employ institutional routes to petition government, but government actors failed to engage their requests by meeting with local residents, listening to their concerns, and working to address them. In each case, protest actions began with organized nonviolent marches. Those that later turned to violence tended to do so as a product of interactions with local authorities, particularly the police. Trevor Manuel's arguments concerning the need for a certain degree of popular civility in order for democracy to function echoes the arguments of civil society analysts such as Robert Putnam (2000). While this argument may be convenient for a government minister seeking to institute his model of development, it is based upon a misunderstanding of how democracy is established and deepened. Democracy is generally not the product of good behavior but rather of protracted struggles that often meet with great resistance from those who seek to defend their privilege (Foweraker and Landman 1997, 243).

Zhekele Maya, a member of the Dipaliseng Youth Forum in Balfour, summed up the importance of social mobilization arguing that "protest is a democratic right" in South Africa today, but it only became a right "through a culture of defiance" (Center for Sociological Research workshop, October 30, 2009). Ideally, residents' questions and concerns would be addressed by an effective public administration overseen by accountable elected officials, but every study of local government in South Africa, both by government and nongovernmental actors, has repeatedly demonstrated that this is often not the case. In this context, the discourse of civility suggests that citizens should accept a lack of accountability when their petitions are ignored and government offices offer no response to residents' questions and concerns. But, it is exactly the perceived "uncivil" actions that draw attention to claims for democracy and development that are easily sidelined when presented via institutional means.

Data from the Minister of Police demonstrate the continuing high rate of protest in South Africa (Alexander 2012). Police statistics also show a high rate of unrest incidents versus peaceful gatherings. In the year from April 1, 2011, there were an average of 3.2 such incidents recorded by the police per day. The majority of these unrest incidents are reported to be related to service delivery.* As local governments in many areas of the country continue to suffer from a lack of accountability and allegations of corruption, citizens in some areas are organizing to demand change. When petitions and peaceful protests do not garner a response, unrest often occurs. This is a product of police and security force actions, of a changing strategy by some activists wishing to draw attention to their communities, and of opportunistic action by some seeking economic or political gain.

The so-called "service delivery" protests, like the social movement protests that preceded them, will not be addressed by increases in state capacity and delivery alone. While protesters do demand services, they are also expressing their discontent with a system that denies them opportunities to offer input

---

* In 2010, the Minister of Police reported an average of 500 participants in peaceful gatherings and an average of 4000 in unrest incidents for 2008/2009. Similar figures were not given for the most recent year (Alexander 2012).

into development processes or to hold their local representatives to account. The increased violence at these protests is not a product of a weak state but rather of police who receive instructions to act forcibly against protesters and protesters who often feel the only way to attract attention to their concerns is to engage in sufficient destruction to warrant a front page photograph in the daily newspapers. There is no doubt that such violence is detrimental to development in the short-run. But, it is important to also note that the protests are a response to the means by which development is envisioned by the state—a nontransparent, noninclusive approach designed by officials, however well meaning, who local community members argue they cannot even reach to engage. The solution is not merely a new development plan but also the creation of a more democratic and accountable regime.

References

Abrahamsen, R. 2001. Development policy and the democratic peace in sub-Saharan Africa. *Conflict, Security & Development* 1(3): 79–103.

Afrobarometer. 2009. Summary of Results, Round 4 Afrobarometer Survey in South Africa. Available at: http://www.afrobarometer.org. Accessed 8/5/2014.

Alexander, P. 2012. A massive rebellion of the poor. *Mail and Guardian* April 13. Available at: http://mg.co.za/article/2012-04-13-a-massive-rebellion-of-the-poor.

ANC. 1994. Election Manifesto. http://www.anc.org.za/show.php?id=262 Accessed 8/5/2014.

Angus Reid Global Monitor. 2007. Available at: http://angusreid.org/.

Ballard, R., Habib, A., Valoodia, I. eds. 2006. *Voices of Protest: Social Movements in Post-Apartheid South Africa.* Durban: University of KwaZulu-Natal Press.

Bénit-Gbaffou, C. 2008. Are practices of local participation sidelining the institutional participatory channels? *Transformation* 66/67:1–33.

Bond, P. 2006. Johannesburg's resurgent social movements. In: *Challenging Hegemony: Social Movements and the Quest for a New Humanism in Post-Apartheid South Africa*, ed. N. Gibson, 103–28. Trenton: Africa World Press.

Bruce, D. 2005. Interpreting the body count: South African statistics on lethal police violence. *South African Review of Sociology* 36.2:141–59.

Butler, A. 2000. Is South Africa heading towards authoritarian rule? Instability myths and expectations traps in a new democracy. *Politikon* 27.2:189–205.

Desai, A. 2002. *We Are the Poors: Community Struggles in Post-Apartheid South Africa.* New York: Monthly Review Press.

Evans, P. 2001. *Embedded Autonomy: States and Industrial Transformation.* Princeton, NJ: Princeton University Press.

Feinstein, A. 2007. *After the Party: A Personal and Political Journey inside the ANC.* Johannesburg: Jonathan Ball.

Foweraker, J., Landman, T. 1997. *Citizenship Rights and Social Movements: A Comparative and Statistical Analysis.* Oxford: Oxford University Press.

Gevisser, M. 2007. *Thabo Mbeki: The Dream Deferred.* Johannesburg: Jonathan Ball.

Gibson, N. ed. 2006. *Challenging Hegemony: Social Movements and the Quest for a New Humanism in Post-Apartheid South Africa.* Trenton, NJ: Africa World Press.

Giliomee, H.B. 1998. South Africa's emerging dominant-party regime. *Journal of Democracy* 9(4): 128–142.

Habib, A. 2008. Substantive uncertainty: South Africa's democracy becomes dynamic. *African Analyst* 3.2:79–98.

Habib, A., Valodia, I. 2006. Reconstructing a social movement in an era of globalization: A case study of COSATU. In: *Voices of Protest: Social Movements in Post-Apartheid South Africa*, eds. Ballard, R., Habib, A., Valodia, I. 225–53. Durban: University of KwaZulu-Natal Press.

Heller, P. 2000. 'Technocratic creep' threatens local government reform. *Synopsis* 4.1:1–2, 12.

Huntington, S. 1968. *Political Order in Changing Societies*. New Haven, CT: Yale University Press.

Khunou, G. 2002. 'Massive cutoffs' cost recovery and electricity service in diepkloof, soweto. In: *Cost Recovery and the Crisis of Service Delivery*, eds. McDonald, D., Pape, J. 61–80. Cape Town: HSRC Press.

Klopp, J., Zuern, E. 2007. The politics of violence in democratization. *Comparative Politics* 39.2:127–46.

Lavery, J. 2012. Protest and political participation in South Africa: Time trends and characteristics of protesters. *Afrobarometer Briefing Paper* No. 102, May 2012.

Leggett, T. 2005. Just another miracle: A decade of crime and justice in democratic South Africa. *Social Research* 72.3:581–604.

Lodge, T. 1999. Policy process within the African national congress and the tripartite alliance. *Politikon: South African Journal of Political Studies* 26.1:5–32.

Marks, M., Wood, J. 2010. South African policing at a crossroads: The case for 'minimal' and 'minimalist' public police. *Theoretical Criminology* 14.3:311–29.

Martins, J. 2007. Household budgets as a social indicator of poverty and inequality in South Africa. *Social Indicators Research* 81:203–21.

Mattes, R., Davids, Y., Africa, C. 2000. Views of democracy in South Africa and the region: Trends and comparisons. *Afrobarometer* Working Paper 8. Available at: http://www.afrobarometer.org. Accessed 8/5/2014.

Mattes, R., Thiel, H. 1998. Consolidation and public opinion in South Africa. *Journal of Democracy* 9.1:95–110.

Mbeki, T. Address of the President of South Africa, Thabo Mbeki, on the occasion of the Budget Vote of the Presidency. National Assembly, Cape Town, June 7, 2006.

McDonald, D. 2003. More carrot, less stick. *Mail and Guardian*, May 26, 2003.

National Planning Commission. 2011. *National Development Plan*, November 11.

Piper, L., Deacon, R. 2008. Party politics, elite accountability and public participation: Ward committee politics in the Msunduzi municipality. *Transformation* 66/67:61–82.

Pithouse, R. 2008. A politics of the poor: Shack Dwellers' struggles in Durban. *Journal of Asian and African Studies* 43 1:63–94.

Presidency. 2009. *Development Indicators 2009*. Pretoria: Republic of South Africa.

Putnam, R. 2000. *Bowling Alone: The Collapse and Revival of American Community*. New York: Simon & Schuster.

Raga, K., Taylor, J. 2005. An overview of the ward committee system: A case study of the Nelson Mandela municipality. *Politeia* 24.2:244–54.

Republic of South Africa (RSA), Cooperative Governance and Traditional Affairs. 2009. State of Local Government in South Africa. http://www.polity.org.za. Accessed 8/5/2014.

Seekings, J. 2007. *Poverty and Inequality after Apartheid*. Centre for Social Science Research Working Paper 200. Cape Town: Centre for Social Science Research.

Sen, A. 1999. *Development as Freedom*. Oxford: Oxford University Press.

Shaw, M. 2002. *Crime and Policing in Post-Apartheid South Africa: Transforming under Fire*. Bloomington, IL: Indiana University Press.

Sinwell, L. 2009. Participatory spaces and the Alexandra Vukuzenzele crisis committee (AVCC). *Social Dynamics* 35.2:436–49.

Sinwell, L., Kirchner, J., Khumalo, K., Manda, O., Pfaffe, P., Phokela, C., Runciman, C. 2009. *Service Delivery Protests: Findings from Quick Response Research on Four Hot Spots—Piet Retief, Balfour, Thokoza, Diepsloot*. Johannesburg: Centre for Sociological Research.

Taylor, H., Mattes, R. 1998. *Public Evaluations of and Demands on Local Government*. Idasa Public Opinion Service POS Report 3. Cape Town: Institute for Democracy in South Africa.

UN Development Program (UNDP). 2009. *Human Development Report*. New York: Palgrave.

United Nations Development Program (UNDP). 2003. South Africa Human Development Report—The Challenge of Sustainable Development: Unlocking People's Creativity. http://tinyurl.com/y9xvsrj. Accessed 8/5/2014.

Von Holdt, K. 2010. Nationalism, bureaucracy and the developmental state: The South African case. *South African Review of Sociology* 41.1:4–27.

Wade, R. 1992. *Governing the Market*. Princeton, NJ: Princeton University Press.

Woo-Cumings, M., ed. 1999. *The Developmental State*. Ithaca, NY: Cornell University Press.

World Bank. 2011. *World Development Report 2011: Conflict, Security and Development*. Washington, DC: The World Bank.

Zikode, S. 2006. The third force. *Journal of Asian and African Studies* 41.1/2: 185–189.

Zuern, E. 2011. *The Politics of Necessity: Community Organizing and Democracy in South Africa*. Madison, WI: University of Wisconsin Press.

Chapter 15

Evaluating Governance Programs

Donors and Political Parties in Morocco

Barry Ames, Louis A. Picard, and Miguel Cabrera

Contents

Political Trends and Recent Developments

Governability and Good Governance

International donors often refer to governability and good governance as the ways parties contribute to effective democratic decision making regardless of election results. Political parties contribute through support for an open policy process, promotion of human rights, and willingness to work for consensus and compromise in advancing policy.

This chapter focuses on political change in Morocco, assessing the role of political parties and their potential evolution in a regime that can be described as "competitive authoritarian." However, good governance should also be related to the substance and implementation of decisions and to that extent good governance is different from democratic processes.

Do political parties compromise and build coalitions that yield policy advances favorable to all supportive members? In Morocco this question is difficult to evaluate. A given cabinet can be composed of members of four to six parties. However, although many parties work together in government, it is difficult to talk about policy compromises in the context of Moroccan politics.

We argue in this book that good governance is the missing link between human security and sustainable economic development and explain the finding here that Morocco has poor governance. However its human rights record and economic development are both rising. Morocco's governance system, like that of many African and Middle Eastern countries is a work in progress. We find Aili Mari Tripp's term, "hybrid regime"—that promotes certain human rights but at the same time curtails other elements of participation—appropriate in understanding Morocco. Morocco illustrates the complexity of defining a relationship between governance and socioeconomic development but suggests that "competitive authoritarianism" or "hybrid regimes" need to be accounted for in the role human security plays as an intervening variable in the move toward sustainable development.

Moroccan Case

Policies implemented by the Moroccan government are not the result of a negotiation process between different parties in the cabinet. Rather, parties implement the program of the throne. Hence, the "governmental coalition" appears as a top-down imposition from the king, rather than a free decision by the parties to come together. The same cannot be said about the *kutla*—a coalition of traditional parties emerging from the independence movement (Istiqlal, USFP, PPS). These parties formed a democratic bloc that opposed the regime between the 1960s and 1990s, sometimes calling for a boycott of elections organized under Hassan II. However, with the cooptation of these parties by the monarchy through the *alternance* government, the *kutla* lost much of its meaning.

In spite of these *ad hoc* coalitions, parties in the cabinet do not work together in Parliament, often splitting on key votes.* Despite appearances, policy coalitions play only a very limited role. This reality may change in the near future. In fact, if the creation of poles of parties along ideological lines finally materializes, coalitions may become more stable, and policy compromises may further democratic governability.

Does the opposition play a constructive role, or does it oppose all the laws and reforms the Government wants to pass? The Party of Authenticity and Modernity (PAM) is considered to be an opposition party because it does not participate in the cabinet. But the PAM always votes for governmental projects and supports the economic and political modernization put forward by the monarchy. As the PAM is led by a close friend of the king, and some consider it an opposition party merely to preserve a democratic façade.†

Moroccan governance is not democratic. Still, governability is not Morocco's main problem. Although parties play a minimal role in governance, governability is ensured by the king (and the general respect by citizens of the monarchy) and by the technocratic advisors surrounding him. The king decides the orientation of policies implemented (e.g., regional development), and supervises their implementation. The impression of Moroccans is the king gets things done while parties are corrupt and inefficient.

Freedom House characterizes Morocco as "partly free" (Freedom House 2010b).‡ Elections are held regularly, and there is no clear evidence of electoral fraud. Still, the monarchy can influence electoral results by gerrymandering or excluding certain political forces. Hence, the electoral process cannot be considered free and fair. The main limitation to democracy is the predominant role played by the monarch (a monarch enjoying widespread support in the population) and corresponding lack of autonomy of parliament and government.

---

* Interview with Fanida Oubnaissa (USFP), Rabat, May, 2010.

† Interview with Omar Bendourou, Rabat, May, 2010.

‡ The Polity IV project defines Morocco as an *autocracy* with a score of −4 in 2012. The Polity IV scores go from −10 to +10. The established threshold to be considered a democracy is a score of 6.

Over the past 20 years, Morocco has experienced a period of continued liberalization that has created effective party strengthening. During most of the Hassan II era (1961–1999), Morocco's regime was clearly authoritarian.* The king used different strategies to limit the role of opposition parties, including the creation of "administration parties" loyal to the monarchy (UC, RNI, MP), the modification of electoral rules, and electoral fraud. The reign of Hassan II was marked by opposition and by heavy-handed government responses to criticism and opposition.

Repression and human rights abuses were high during the so-called "years of lead" between the 1960s and 1980s (Storm 2007). In the 1990s, Morocco's poor human rights record eroded the country's international reputation, forcing Hassan II to start a process of liberalization. This process has been described as "a process of controlled, well-managed change that maintains social peace while promoting economic development" (Maddy-Weitzman 1996). Liberalization was sustained by a series of constitutional reforms that provided more powers to the parliament and allowed direct election of members of the lower chamber of parliament (Gershovich 2008).

The assent to power of Mohammed VI in 1999 signaled a break with the past and an acceleration of reforms. Elections became more transparent, and they are now held at regular intervals. Respect for public freedoms and civil liberties also improved. The king released thousands of political prisoners and allowed exiled political leaders to return. In 2004, the king formed the Equity and Reconciliation Commission (Vermeren) to investigate human rights abuses committed during the "years of lead" (White 2008).

Another aspect of the new era has been Morocco's modernization, including in the political arena. Mohammed VI has committed to improving the status of women, and has reformed the family code (*Moudawana*). Under the reformed code, women are no longer subject to the guardianship of a male; they have the right to divorce; and the minimum age for marriage is set at 18 (it was formerly 15 for women) (Wuerth 2005). The king decreed a law obliging political parties to be more internally democratic and more open to participation by youth and women. In a society where Islamic fundamentalism is a minority current, the king's leadership appears to be welcomed by the majority.

Despite these positive early steps, Mohammed VI and his close advisors (the *Makhzen*)† still dominate the political system. Political institutions continue to be weak. The monarchy uses exorbitant fines and libel suits to restrict freedom of the press. Moroccan authorities shut down a leading independent news magazine (*Le Journal Hebdomadaire*) because it could not pay its fines. Liberalization has so far fallen short of full democratization (Freedom House 2010a).

* For a discussion of the Hassan period see Entelis (1989). Pennell (2000) provides a good one volume history of Morocco.

† Sometimes referred to in English as "the Throne."

Decentralization is another recent political trend. In an attempt to achieve economic decentralization and also to confirm the country's claims to the disputed Western Sahara, King Mohammed has named an advisory committee on expanding regionalization. Regionalization, however, is not devolution of political power but rather administrative deconcentration as a means of furthering economic and social development.*

Socioeconomic Context

While reforms are unlikely to eventuate in strong regional governments with active participation by political parties, it is possible that regionalization will open new space for party activity related to local development projects. The political system's evolution is tied to the country's socioeconomic context. This section considers ethnic divisions (the Berber question), the role of Islam in politics, and the social and economic situation since Mohammed VI assumed power. We analyze how these issues affect the party system.

Although the majority of Moroccans are Arabs, the Berbers (or Amazigh) represent 30%. Berbers are spread out in rural areas: the Rif Mountains, Middle, High, and Anti-Atlas, and southern Souss Valley, as well as Morocco's major cities. However, according to Willis (2008, p. 227) "there were no meaningful political distinctions between Arab and Berber speakers" until the 1980s.

The unwillingness of Morocco's Amazighs to organize politically resulted from the alliance formed between the monarchy and Berber notables after independence. Berber speakers came to dominate the *Mouvement Populaire* (MP), one of the parties close to the monarchy. This strategic move allowed the monarchy to co-opt the Amazighs.

The MP has always been the "party of the Berbers" rather than the "Berber party." This party does not have a Berber agenda centered on the socioeconomic and cultural interests of the Amazighs. Rather, the MP closely follows the king's program. This is as true today as it was 30 years ago.

The MP obtains most of its votes in areas populated by Berbers, and remains an administration party following the monarchy. Over the past 20 years, however, many Berber cultural associations were formed, taking advantage of political liberalization. The monarchy has made concessions to demands of these associations. For instance, the Royal Institute for Amazigh Culture (IRCAM) was created in 2001. Concessions defused ethnic tensions and reinforced the monarchy/Berber alliance (Howe 2005, 171–196; Willis 2008).

It seems unlikely Berbers will press the regime for their own political party to pursue an Amazigh agenda. Moreover, there is little concern about conflict between Berbers and Arabs, since both share the Islamic faith.

---

* Interview with Miloudа Hazeb (PAM), Rabat, May 2010.

Islam in politics is critical from a domestic and international perspective (Cohen and Jaidi 2006). The rise of a moderate Islamist party, the Justice and Development Party (PJD), in the last decade has sparked a great deal of attention. Some consider that it is only a matter of time before Morocco becomes an Islamist regime (Beau and Graciet 2006). However, the threat has been overstated. First, there is an historical factor: unlike other countries in the Maghreb, in Morocco independence did not arrive through a secular movement that downplayed Islam. Hence, there is no feeling of culpability that could lead Moroccans to vote for an Islamist party. More importantly, Moroccans favor a more moderate reading of Islam influenced by the Maliki school.*

The country is moving into a social and economic opening. Most Moroccans are satisfied with this modernization and do not want radicalization.† The king has a religious role, considered in the constitution as the "commander of the faithful." The religious symbolism of the king has served as a barrier against radical Islam. According to Marvine Howe (2005, 124), Mohammed VI has "always preached an Islam of moderation and dialogue." For instance, in the reform of the *Moudawana*, the King broke the stalemate between the civil society groups pushing for reforms and Islamists opposing changes to the status of women, by providing clear support for the reform.‡

Nonetheless, Islam in Moroccan politics and society is becoming more important. The Islamic movement can be divided into two organizations: the radical Justice and Charity Movement and the moderate PJD. The Justice and Charity Movement is active at the grassroots but remains at the sidelines of the political arena. The PJD was seen as threatening by the regime, but its development was blocked for several years due to its own failures and the intervention of the *Makhzen* (the throne). This includes gerrymandering, and the creation of the PAM, a new pro-monarchy party. However, the PJD became the main governmental party after the last elections in 2011. Prime Minister Abdelilah Benkirane and several members of cabinet are PJD. The PJD's rise and its impact on the system will be discussed.

The last issue is Morocco's socioeconomic situation. Economics have fluctuated since Morocco's independence. According to Maghraoui (2001) "because agriculture remains the engine of the economy, dry seasons spell disaster for the entire economy.... Economic growth rates fluctuate dramatically as a result of climatic changes." However, the economy has improved since 2000.

* This is slightly changing as Wahhabism becomes more influential among younger generations, especially as a response to what they perceive as an aggressive intervention of the United States in the Muslim world. For instance, some practices associated with a literal interpretation of Islam that were uncommon a generation ago (e.g., the use of the headscarf) are now becoming widespread (interview with Latifa Jbabdi, Rabat, May 2010).

† Note that the World Values Survey, which does survey in Morocco, did not ask its usual question about confidence in institutions about the king.

‡ Interview with Hassan Benadi (Secretary General of PAM), May 2010, Rabat.

GDP per capita was stable between 1990 and 2000, but has considerably increased since. Similarly, GDP growth fluctuated during the 1990s but with uninterrupted growth after 2000. This related to good crops due to good weather conditions. More importantly, however, this improvement was due to a series of structural reforms initiated under the late Hassan II and accelerated after Mohammed VI came to power. These reforms include removal of trade barriers, liberalization of the financial sector, and modernization and privatization of the public sector.

Economic reforms have reinforced Morocco's external position and contributed to stabilized prices. As a result of these changes, Morocco has become a more attractive destination for foreign direct investments (Boukhalef 2005; Vermeren 2009). The country also signed a free trade agreement with the United States and reinforced ties with the European Union by obtaining "advanced status." Morocco tops the list of partners that have benefited from the EU's financial support as part of neighborhood assistance.*

However, despite economic improvement, Morocco is still suffering from a social crisis. Poverty remains high in the rural areas and in the slums of the big cities (especially Casablanca). There were 2.8 million poor in 2008. The problems are especially acute for young people. A significant number of young Moroccans do not finish school, and many are illiterate. In 2006, 30% of young Moroccans were unemployed (Vermeren 2009) and many more were underemployed. They are underqualified for employment, and have difficulty integrating into the formal economy.

Many young Moroccans hold a university degree but are also unemployed. They have organized a movement (*mouvement des diplômés chômeurs*) to protest against this grim situation, and they often hold public demonstrations in Rabat and other cities. Young unemployed Moroccans were among the players in the *Mouvement du 20-Février* which led mass demonstrations against the regime demanding reforms during the "Arab Spring."

Institutional Context

In this section, institutions that shape the evolution of Morocco's party system will be examined. We will consider, in turn, the executive and legislative power and their implications with regard to political party development.

Executive Power

The political system places power in the executive branch. In spite of liberalization, the king and his advisors (the *Makhzen*) are dominant. This was evident in the

* This increased cooperation with the United States and the European Union builds momentum for an increased political and economic liberalization of the regime, since Morocco is bound to be more sensitive to the demands of these external actors.

1996 Constitution, which upheld the secular and sacred power of the monarch by declaring him "commander of the faithful" and the symbol and the guarantor of the Moroccan nation.

The constitutional reform of 2011 introduced important political and symbolic limits to the power of the king. On the one hand, the king abandoned his constitutional "sacredness." On the other, the new constitution obliges the king to choose a prime minister exclusively from the party that wins legislative elections. These are important concessions, made to defuse civil society unrest. However, the king remains the predominant player in the political system. Analysis of the new constitution by Ahmed Benchemsi (2012, 62) suggests that: "Morocco has a parliament elected by the people, but the king can still block any law he dislikes. He alone convenes, presides over, and sets the agenda for the council of ministers—a body whose approval is needed before parliament can even consider a bill. Also, he alone appoints and dismisses the secretary-general of the government, an official who can block laws at any stage (including after parliament approves them) by subjecting them to a 'review' process that many bills have entered but never left. Add to this that Article 42 gives the king the personal privilege of issuing laws by royal decree—which is in fact how most laws get made." The king also has the constitutional right to dissolve parliament by direct decree (Article 51).

A comparison of the roles bestowed to the king and the prime minister confirms the preeminent position of the monarch. The prime minister (now called "chief of government") and the king share appointment powers, but while the king has the right to appoint governors, ambassadors, the central-bank chairman, high-security officials, and "executives of strategic public enterprises and establishments" (Article 49); the chief of government only has the right to appoint lower-ranked public servants (Article 91). In a similar vein, the chief of government is allowed to "propose" ministers for nomination but the king does not have to accept these propositions and he retains the power to appoint and dismiss ministers at will (Benchemsi 2012).

Legislature

The Moroccan legislature is composed of two chambers: the chamber of counselors and the chamber of representatives. In the chamber of counselors, 270 members are elected by indirect vote to serve nine-year terms. Members are elected indirectly by local councils, professional organizations, and labor unions. One-third of the members are renewed every three years.

In the chamber of representatives, 325 members are elected for a five-year term, 295 elected in multiseat constituencies and 30 in national lists consisting only of women. Consistent with the "divide and rule" strategy of the postindependence monarchy, the electoral system historically has increased party-system fragmentation.

In 2002, the monarchy changed the single-member district system into a PR system. Ninety-five multimember districts have two to five seats each, with a complex "remainder system" allocating seats. This system makes it hard for any party to obtain more than one seat in any district. Hence, a substantial share of the votes cast for the most popular parties—mainly the PJD—are "wasted." Some analysts argue the current electoral system is not sustainable and may result in intense forms of protests unless the system becomes more representative (McFaul and Cofman Wittes 2008).

PR systems are more representative than majoritarian systems: minorities achieve representation in PR but are shut out in a winner-take-all system. But fragmented systems dilute and blur the responsibility of each party such that citizens have difficulty holding the government accountable. Knowing they cannot be held accountable, parties represent citizen interests less effectively.

Party System Context

The monarchy's postindependence strategy can be described as "divide and rule." To weaken the two major parties emerging from independence (Istiqlal and UNFP, the Independence Party and the National Union of Popular Forces), the Monarchy encouraged creation of other parties loyal to it: the MP, UC (Constitutional Union), and RNI (National Grouping of Independents). The barriers for entry for new parties were set low, and the electoral system favored small over large parties (Storm 2007). Quarrels among leaders and differences in attitudes toward the regime contributed to party-system fragmentation.

Leadership squabbles relate to obstacles that new leaders face in reaching leadership positions, typically in the hands of old cadres, especially in the older parties. In most parties, leadership positions appear to be lifelong sinecures. Differences in attitudes toward the regime are evident in former leftist opposition parties (USFP and PPS, the socialist Union of Populist Forces and the Progress and Socialism Party). After four decades in opposition, these parties finally joined the *alternance* government in 1998. In exchange, they accepted the political rules of the game and the preeminence of the king.

Multipartyism existing today results from historical factors. If we take the 2002, 2007, and 2011 elections as indicators of the numbers of parties, there are six big parties obtaining between 22% and 8% of the votes (USFP, Istiqlal, RNI, PJD, MP, PAM). Numerous minor parties obtain between 2% and 5% of the votes (see Table 15.1). In sum, the party system is highly fractured.

Political Islam is one of the greatest challenges facing Moroccan political leadership. A moderate Islamist party, the PJD, emerged in the last decade as a powerful force. The PJD accepts the monarchy's legitimacy and is willing to play the electoral game. Moreover, the PJD is characterized as the most internally democratic party and one of the political organizations most open to young people (McFauland and Cofman Wittes 2008). These factors have enhanced the credibility and popularity of the PJD, as well as its image of moderation. The PJD first ran (under the name Constitutional Movement for Popular Democracy) in the 1997 elections, winning

Table 15.1 The Results of the Legislative Elections (2002, 2007, and 2011)

2002 Election		
Party	*% (of Valid Votes)*	*Seats*
Socialist Union of Popular Forces (USFP)	15.38	50
Istiqlal Party (IP)	14.77	48
Party of Justice and Development (PJD)	12.92	42
National Rally of Independents (RNI)	12.62	41
Popular Movement (MP)	8.31	27
National Popular Movement (MNP)	5.54	18
Constitutional Union (UC)	4.92	16
Democratic Forces Front (FFD)	3.69	12
National Democratic Party (PND)	3.69	12
Party of Progress and Socialism (PPS)	3.38	11
Democratic Union (UD)	3.08	10
Social Democratic Movement (MDS)	2.15	7
Democratic Socialist Party (PSD)	1.85	6
Democratic Party for Independence (PDI)	0.62	2
Others	7.08	23
2007 Election		
Party	*% (of Valid Votes)*	*Seats*
Independence Party/Istiqlal Party (IP)	10.67	52
Party of Justice and Development (PJD)	10.92	46
National Rally of Independents (RNI)	9.65	41
Popular Movement (MP)	9.21	41
Socialist Union of Popular Forces (USFP)	8.82	38
Constitutional Union (UC)	7.23	27
Party of Progress and Socialism (PPS)	5.35	17
PND–Al Ahd Union	5.5	14
Front of Democratic Forces (FFD)	4.49	9

(Continued)

Table 15.1 (*Continued*) The Results of the Legislative Elections (2002, 2007, and 2011)

Party	*% (of Valid Votes)*	*Seats*
Democratic and Social Movement (MDS)	3.7	9
PADS–CNI–PSU Union	3.2	6
Labor Party (PT)	3.0	5
Environment and Development Party (PED)	2.9	5
Party of Renewal and Equity (PRE)	1.8	4
Others	13.2	14
2011 Election		
Party	*% (of Valid Votes)*	*Seats*
Party of Justice and Development (PJD)	22.8	107
Istiqlal Party (IP)	11.9	60
National Rally of Independents (RNI)	11.3	52
Authenticity and Modernity Party (PAM)	11.1	47
Socialist Union of Popular Forces (USFP)	8.6	39
Popular Movement (MP)	7.5	32
Constitutional Union (UC)	5.8	23
Party of Progress and Socialism (PPS)	5.7	18
Labor party (PT)	2.3	4
Environment and Development Party (PED)	2.3	2
Democratic and Social Movement (MDS)	1.7	2
Others	9.0	9

nine seats. In 2002 the party obtained 12.92% of the votes and 42 seats, and in 2007 it obtained 10.92% of the votes and 46 seats.

In spite of its moderate image and its acceptance of the rules of the game (McFauland and Cofman Wittes 2008), before the last election many rival political actors described the PJD as a threat to modernization. They feared the PJD would radicalize when it came to power.* The PJD's electoral victory and the appointment of its leader Abdelilah Benkirane as prime minister proved these fears to be

* Interview with Hassan Benadi (Secretary General of PAM), May 2010, Rabat.

unfounded. Although the PJD attempted some "Islamic" reforms (e.g., higher taxes on alcohol and a ban on betting advertisements on television), it remains moderate. Party leaders want to convince the *Makhzen* that they do not want a radical change. In a revealing statement made to the Spanish newspaper *El País* soon after becoming chief of government, Benkirane pointed out that "in Morocco the chief of government has power, but the king is the supreme owner of that power. The king intervenes in the decisions of the chief of government and can appoint whoever he wants as a personal advisor. (…) We are not a parliamentary monarchy and Moroccans do not want to change this. (…) In our country, there is no difference between the church and the palace. The two institutions are reunited in one person: the king" (El País 2012).

Another recent development is the formation of the PAM in 2008. The PAM was created by Fouad El Himma, former interior minister and counselor to the king. It involved the merger of five smaller parties. Many elected representatives from major parties switched to the PAM. Although it did not participate in the 2007 elections, the PAM became the largest player in the legislature. In 2009, the party won the most votes, 22%, in the municipal elections, but its share declined in 2011 to 11.1%.

Some have described the PAM as a new "palace party," created with support from the king to block the PJD (Boubekeur 2008). The PAM has a loose ideology of modernization, in contrast with the conservative ideology of the moderate Islamist party. The president of the PAM national council holds that this new party is very different from the administration parties of the past, and that the king is not directly behind PAM.* The creation of the PAM may have reduced the number of parties in Morocco. The king appears to favor a "rationalization" of the party system, including a reduction in the number of parties and the emergence of four party poles: a left pole (USFP, PPS), a center pole (UC, MP, RNI, PAM), a right pole (Istiqlal), and the PJD. Although this reorganization seems to be favored by the *Makhzen*, it is far from sure whether these poles of parties will emerge. As Szmolka (2010, 17) puts it, "even though party unification as a way of combating fragmentation is constantly present in Moroccan political discourse, especially from the left wing, very few mergers have taken place."

Any reorganization must involve negotiations among the elites of all parties, though some are better off with the status quo. Moreover, some members of *kutla* (e.g., the PPS) prefer to remain within the traditional alliance than to move to a new pole organized around ideological lines, in which they will be weaker.†

---

* Interview with Hassan Benadi (president of the National Council of the PAM), Rabat, May 2010.

† Interview with Mohammed Nabil Benabdallah (Secretary General of the PPS), Rabat, May 2010.

Moroccan Political Parties through the Lens of Party Development Goals

Accountability, Representation, and Participation

Well-functioning democracies are representative, closely linked to the participation of citizens in the public sphere, and the accountability of elected leaders.

For parties to be accountable, they must elaborate coherent, stable programs and transmit their ideas to voters. In Morocco, political parties' programs are vague. Parliamentary elections are "not about putting competing political projects or societal options before the voters in order to let them choose among them" (Tozy 2008, p. 37). Consider the view of Mohammed Boutaleb, a leader of MP, during the campaign before the 2007 legislative elections. When asked what differentiated MP from other parties, Boutaleb replied, "first, the MP seeks to perpetuate and enrich the dignity of the Moroccan citizen, and, second, what makes us different is our simplicity" (*Le Matin du Sahara*, August 28, 2007). Most Moroccan parties share this ideological fuzziness.

The lack of programmatic coherence stems from the election of local notables to run as legislative candidates. Politics is personalized around political figures. These notables are not attached to party programs. However, programmatic vagueness is due to the domination of the political system by the king and his close advisors (the *Makhzen*).

Parties lack incentives to develop programs, because they do not have policy prerogatives to legislate or implement programs. Institutions created by the monarchy "compete" with parties to implement policies preferred by the *Makhzen*. For instance, the Royal Foundation (a quasi-nongovernmental organization) created by Mohammed VI provides social services to persons working in education and to their families. The National Human Development Initiative (INDH), launched in 2005 under the initiative of the king, has led to more than 15,000 development projects benefitting some 4 million people.

These parallel institutions undermine the capacity of parties in government or in opposition to influence policy. Cabinet ministers lack autonomy in implementing party programs. When they join the cabinet, ministers are aware that they will implement the government's program rather than their platform.* Political parties face a difficult dilemma: if they participate in the government, they are co-opted by the king; if they do not participate they become isolated.

There are many obstacles to accountability and representation in Morocco. As the symbol of the unity of the nation and the religious leader of Morocco, the king can be said to represent Moroccan citizens. The king, however, is by definition unaccountable since he cannot be removed even if citizens are dissatisfied with government policies. The nature of the Moroccan regime also makes it very difficult for

* Interview with the Minister of Social Development, Nouzha Skalli, May 2010, Rabat.

citizens to hold leaders from political parties accountable. Because political parties lack coherent programs and cannot implement their policy proposals, citizens lack clear bases on which to judge their actions. Moreover, there are so many political parties present in the parliament and in the government (more than 20 parties in the parliament and four different parties in the cabinet) that no party can credibly take responsibility. Similarly, the large array of choices dilutes responsibility and accountability.

Regardless of the choices open to voters, parties are unaccountable unless their organizational, campaign, and legislative activities are transparent. Transparency requires mechanisms for informing citizens about party activities. All political parties have their own newspapers, but circulation is limited. Media with broader circulation tend to focus more on the king's activities than on party work. For example, the newspaper with the largest circulation in the country (*Le Matin du Sahara*) is very close to the throne, and its first three or four pages are always devoted to the king.

Party activity in the government or parliament often goes unnoticed. Another obstacle to transparency is lack of information on party legislative activity. Because there are no roll call data, it is difficult for the press and civil society organizations to be informed.

Given this lack of accountability, citizen disenchantment with the political system is not surprising. This is evident in a recent series of official or semi-official polls. According to a 2004 poll that accompanied the *Rapport du Cinquantenaire*,* only 10% of Moroccans think about becoming party members, and less than half can distinguish between the "right" and the "left." More than two-thirds are unable to locate themselves in the political arena. Similarly, citizens base political expectations on a moral rather than partisan basis. For 91% of the population, the only thing that matters in a politician is *ma'qoul* (serious work, integrity, transparency). Another poll, conducted in 2007, before the elections, confirmed this picture:† 73% were uninterested in politics (Vermeren 2009).

Disenchantment with politics and political parties has reduced citizen engagement. According to the *Daba 2007* poll, only 3% of Moroccans are affiliated with a political party. More troubling, turnout in legislative elections has decreased considerably (see Table 15.2). Voter turnout has also decreased since the early 1990s. Whereas over 62% of registered voters turned out in 1993, just 45.4% turned out in 2011. This is confirmed by the increasing percentage of invalid votes.

If the low levels of political participation in Morocco are undeniable, the high level of participation in civil society associations is equally remarkable

* Report of the 50th Anniversary of Moroccan Independence. The poll was conducted with a representative sample of 1000 persons between September and October, 2004, under the direction of Hassan Rachik, Rahma Bourquia, Abdellatif Bencherifa, and Mohammed Tozy.

† Representative poll with a sample of 1200 persons conducted in July 2007, by the semi-official organization Daba 2007.

Table 15.2 Voter Turnout in Legislative Elections

Year	*Population*	*Registration*	*Voting Age Population*	*Total Vote*	*Invalid Votes (%)*	*VAP Turnout (%)*	*Voter Turnout (%)*
2011	31,968,361	13,475,435	21,356,831	6,117,847	NA	28.65	45.40
2007	33,241,259	15,462,362	20,555,314	5,721,074	19	27.83	37.00
2002	30,645,305	13,884,467	17,923,815	7,165,206	17.10	39.98	51.61
1997	28,024,000	12,790,631	14,852,810	7,456,996	14.60	50.21	58.30
1993	26,069,000	11,398,987	13,816,570	7,153,211	13	51.77	62.75

Source: IDEA Voter Turnout Database.

Note: VAP turnout is defined as the percentage of the voting age population that actually voted. Voter turnout is defined as the percentage of the registered voters that actually voted.

(Khrouz 2008; Sater 2007).* During the "years of lead" (between the 1950s and the early 1990s), NGOs and civil society activists were repressed or manipulated by other actors in the system. The liberalization process started during the last years of Hassan II and accelerated when Mohammed VI assumed the throne. This liberalization process was a way of "coping with the complex swirl of cross-pressures created by advancing economic and technological globalization, shifting demographics, grinding poverty and inequality, a rising awareness of human rights (including those of women and ethnic minorities), the threat of terrorist violence, and the emergence of political Islam" (Khrouz 2008, p. 42). The new atmosphere of freedom after three decades of repression led to an explosion of civil society groups both at the national and at the local level. Morocco has today one of the most dynamic civil societies in the region, with almost 40,000 NGOs.

Active participation of women's movements and human rights NGOs in the reform of the family code (*Moudawana*) shows that the blossoming of civil society can directly impact government policies.† *Moudawana* reform was the first priority of women's movements since the 1980s. The sweeping changes to the family law implemented in 2004 were largely a result of civil society activism (Khrouz 2008).‡

National NGOs are also active in human rights and good governance. Many civil society groups, such as the Moroccan Human Rights Organization (OMDH), work to increase respect for human rights and to mobilize public opinion. The Equity and Reconciliation Commission (Vermeren) created by Mohammed VI in 2004 to investigate the excesses of the "years of lead" has relied on the work done by these civil society organizations (Khrouz 2008). After being outlawed for many years, Transparency Maroc (linked to Transparency International) got official recognition in 1998 (Sater 2007).

Civil society organizations are present at the local level. In an effort to reduce its budget deficit, the Moroccan state retreated from its welfare functions in the 1970s. Since the 1980s, civil society organizations were created at the local level to address some of the problems (poverty, illiteracy, disease) left behind by the retreat of the state. These organizations are linked to parties, trade unions, universities, and local governments. NGOs contribute to local development. Civil society associations often work on literacy efforts, microloans, and support to cultural activities at the same time.

---

* This is not entirely surprising. When citizens cannot get essential services through formal political institutions (i.e., political parties) they set up parallel institutions to provide these services.

† The intervention of the king was determinant to impose the reform despite the opposition of the PJD, but the role of women's movements was key to put this issue in the policy agenda.

‡ Interview with Latifa Jbabdi (former president of the NGO Women's Action Union [UAF] and current USFP deputy), May 2010, Rabat. See also Naciri (1998).

Stable and Peaceful Contestation

Stable and peaceful contestation refers to the goal of developing a healthy competition among parties, a competition based on policies rather than personalities. It also implies that parties develop roots in society such that some voters shift their support in response to policy positions but volatility is limited.

The political and party context does not create the conditions for programmatic competition among parties. The king is the predominant player in the political system. Political parties lack incentives to design detailed platforms because they know they will end up implementing the program of the monarch. "Low-quality" political competition also results from the very short time parties have to campaign before elections.

Political parties cannot begin campaigning until two weeks before the elections. Two weeks is hardly enough to communicate a party platform, so elections focus on personalities. This is especially true outside urban areas. Local and regional political leaders tend to come from the elites of the districts in which they run and prefer to cultivate personal rather than party links.* Some local councilors, for example, recognize that they can easily switch to another party because voters are attached to them.†

Given the electoral system and the intervention of the *Makhzen* before elections, it is almost an "iron law" of Moroccan politics that no party can obtain more than 25% of the vote (see Table 15.1).‡ As a result, no party dominates nationally.§ Szmolka (2010) calculated the effective number of electoral parties, using Rae's electoral fractionalization index, for three legislative elections in Morocco. Table 15.3 confirms that the system is competitive and fragmented.

This extreme though shallow competitiveness provides incentives to create new political parties. The creation of a new political organization may be rational: even parties with very little popular support have a realistic chance of winning seats in the legislature, especially if their bases of support are concentrated.¶ For example, the Democratic Party for Independence (PDI) obtained two seats in the legislature in the 2002 elections despite a very low score at the national level (0.62%). The Party of Renewal and Equity (PRE), created in 2002, won four seats in the legislature in the 2007 elections despite only obtaining 1.8% of the votes.

---

* Interview with Abdellah Boussif (journalist, member of the Central Committee of RNI), Rabat, May 2010.

† Interview with Rashid Ben Mehdi (municipal councilor from FD in the Tangier region), Tangier, May 2010.

‡ Interview with Nadir El Moumni (political science professor at Mohammed V University), Rabat, May 2010.

§ Of course, this competitiveness is artificial because it is linked to the "divide and rule" strategy of the monarchy started under Hassan II and perpetuated by an electoral system that favors small parties. It is difficult to predict what would happen under more democratic conditions.

¶ The minimum needed to win a seat in Parliament is 3% of the vote in local constituencies.

Table 15.3 Electoral Fragmentation in the 1997, 2002, and 2007 Elections

	1997 Election	*2002 Election*	*2007 Election*
Parties competing in the elections	16	26	35 and 13 independent lists
Parties gaining legislative representation	15	22	23 and 5 independent lists
Rae's electoral fractionalization index	0.908	0.936	0.933
Effective number of electoral parties	10.8	15.6	15.0

Source: Adapted from Szmolka, I. 2010. *Journal of North African Studies 15*(1), 13–37.

Creation of new parties is facilitated by low entry barriers created by the 2004 party law. To become a political party, an organization needs 300 founding member signatures from at least half of the regions plus holding of a congress of 500 persons. There are no financial requirements, so these conditions are relatively easy to satisfy.

Creation of new parties makes stable competition among established parties impossible. For example, the 10 parties created between 1997 and 2002 accounted for 45.5% of the total number of legislative seats (Szmolka 2010). New parties often lack strong roots in Moroccan society. But the constant emergence and relative success of new parties also makes it clear that citizens are not tied to established parties: for example, formed in 2008, the PAM obtained the highest score in the municipal elections one year later.

Rule of Law and Fair and Honest Elections

Democracy demands that parties compete for the public offices they seek in fair and honest elections. Good governance, as viewed by donors, looks for an approximation of democratic processes but often sees transitional democracies with the characteristics of authoritarian, the so-called hybrid regimes (Tripp 2010). Transitional democracies gain credibility when votes are counted fairly and losers graciously accept defeats. This section considers: (1) limiting undue influence on the electoral results, (2) oversight of the electoral process, and (3) development and adherence to laws governing campaign and party finance.

Does the monarchy exert undue influence on the electoral process, thereby affecting the outcome of the elections? Accession to the throne by Mohammed VI has opened a new era and marked a clear break with the past. Under Hassan II, legislative elections were held at the King's discretion, and electoral fraud was widespread to ensure results acceptable to the monarch and the *Makhzen*. The new approach to elections is a cornerstone of Mohammed VI's strategy to modernize and democratize.

Legislative elections are now held at regular intervals. The first elections were held in 2002, the second in 2007, and the third in 2011. In the last legislative elections the administration increased voter registration and turnout. For example, in 2003 the publicist Noureddine Ayouch (a man close to the palace) created *Daba 2007* ("2007, it's now!") to mobilize the electorate.

Finally, the monarchy appears to have renounced large-scale electoral fraud. The 2007 elections were seen as the freest and fairest in history (Vermeren 2009). The 2011 elections were held in the shadow of the Arab Spring and followed the ratification of a new, more democratic constitution. The PJD won a plurality of votes and nominated the prime minister in a coalition government.

Despite these steps toward democratization, the *Makhzen* continues to influence electoral results by other, more discreet, means. First, the electoral system adopted in 2002 ensures that seats are evenly distributed, regardless of who wins the largest share of the vote. Second, the ministry of the interior modifies district boundaries before each election. Gerrymandering intends to hurt the electoral performance of the PJD. Because the PJD is stronger in urban areas, rural zones surrounding big cities were added to urban districts, affecting performance.* Casablanca is a good example: although it contained 12.4% of registered voters in 2007, Greater Casablanca sent only 7.8% of the elected deputies.

The state reserves the right to recognize political parties. The *Makhzen* did not authorize creation of a Berber party in 2007, nor did it allow a more radical Islamist party in 2008. The administration did not authorize the participation of the PJD in 40% of the districts in 2002. Elections are no longer marked by widespread electoral fraud, but the monarchy still has many discreet ways of influencing the process and results (Vermeren 2009).

In 2007 and 2011, national and international observers were allowed to observe the electoral process. In both occasions, electoral observers concluded that the elections were reasonably free and fair. Still, absence of a neutral, nonpartisan electoral court may pose a serious obstacle to oversight. Allegations of campaign rule violations were presented to the ministry of justice through the ministry of the interior. As these two institutions are closely linked to the *Makhzen*, they cannot ensure reliable monitoring of elections.

Party Organization and Technical Capacity

A developed party system requires organized and technically capable political parties that can organize outreach, represent and mobilize voters in different regions, analyze and implement policy, raise funds, oversee their own bureaucracies and run election campaigns. This section assesses the technical capacity of political parties in internal communication, internal party democracy, and staffing.

* Interview with Idriss Touijer (USAID), Rabat, May 2010.

Very poor internal communication is the most important organizational weakness of parties. Some analysts describe political parties as Jacobin because the center decides the party program and has very weak ties with local branches. Councilors at the municipal level work exclusively on local issues and do not base their actions on broader party programs. Given this disconnection local branches cannot contribute at the national level, even when they are successful at addressing local problems.*

The disconnection above is reflected in the limited number of party offices (and their poor staffing) at the regional and local level. Having functioning offices is essential. Regional offices can channel citizen demands to the center (political bureaus) and information about party activities and resources to the public. Parties do not have an institutionalized presence regionally. If they exist, offices are only open during election time. The PJD is the sole exception. It holds meetings every week at the level of the *arrondissement* (district).†

A party that is internally democratic is inclusive of women and youth. A party also allows constituents or activists a considerable role in candidate or leadership choice and in platform development. Moroccan parties have been reluctant to incorporate women and youth, especially in leadership. The current modernization process desired by Mohammed VI appears to have shaken some old practices, but change is slow. The willingness of the king to modernize and democratize led to adoption of a new party law imposed by *dahir* (decree) in 2006. According to the preamble, the goal is to "lead to an institutional and political modernization, and to consolidate the modernist democratic process in our country." According to Article 22, statutes of parties must set a proportional number of youth and women that will be part of party leadership.

The law is not very demanding, because it fails to indicate what this number should be. Still, it was seen as a step forward by women and youth involved in politics. To comply with the law, parties have aimed in their statutes to reach between 10% and 30% of women and youth in the leadership. However, parties have fallen short of their goals. According to Nadir El Moumni, one of the reasons for failure is that youth and women tend to be locked into youth and women sections, disconnected from the political bureaus.‡ The main barrier to the participation of youth in leadership is the resistance of old cadres of established parties. The incorporation of women into the parties is difficult, because women often do not have the skills and the expertise to participate in politics, especially at the municipal level. Many women are illiterate and unused to speaking in public, thus creating obstacles to their participation.§

* Interview with Abderrahim Manar Slimi (political science professor at Mohammed V University), Rabat, May 2010.

† Interview with Adnan Maiz (municipal councilor from PJD in the Tangier region), Tangier, May 2010.

‡ Interview with Nadir El Moumni (political science professor at Mohammed V University), Rabat, May 2010.

§ Interview with Zahra Chagaf (deputy from MP), Rabat, May 2010.

Many party leaders feel the need to develop a party bureaucracy with full-time employees, but they argue that the lack of resources makes it impossible.* This is true regionally and locally. According to a PJD councilor, "lack of salaries hurts party development because [local councilors] can't work full time."

The organizational problem is also felt by parties in their parliamentary work. The foreign affairs committee in the parliament has 30 members but only 3 staffers, and these possess little experience in foreign affairs and lack fluency in French.† Overall, the legislature has a low level of organizational capacity, and there is little capacity for policy analysis as a part of the legislative process.

Political Change and Strategic Alternatives

Liberalization versus Democratization

Political scientists often distinguish between *liberalization* and *democratization.* Liberalization is the process of redefining and extending rights. It is a process making effective rights protecting individuals and social groups from arbitrary acts of the state. Liberalization typically includes habeas corpus, freedom of speech, due process, freedom of the press, and so on. Extending these rights lowers the costs of expression and multiplies the likelihood that others will express themselves.

Democratization is citizenship. It means that people have rights to equal treatment, and it puts obligations on the ruled. Many institutions have come to be called democratic. Always, however, there is the secret ballot, universal suffrage, and regular elections. Sometimes, but not always and not necessarily, democratization includes judicial review. At its core, democratization means accountability.

Liberalization and democracy are naturally related. Although the interval between liberalization and the development of representative institutions is extremely variable, liberalization always occurs first. People begin to express themselves; the regime allows the expression; more people take up their right to express themselves, and the process becomes irreversible. And this experience of liberalization, in the United States, Europe, and much of Latin America, seems inevitably to lead to democratization, though the democracies that result may be representative, with strong checks and balances and clear lines of accountability, or plebiscitary, with a strong executive free to govern until the next election.‡ Moreover, democratization has come to seem intrinsically intertwined with a free-market economy and with the protection of property rights.

On the basis of our earlier discussion, it can be argued that it is clear that political parties can contribute both to democratization and to good governance. But Morocco's

---

* Interview with Mohammed El Habti (USFP), Rabat, May 2010.

† Interview with Mbarka Bouaida (RNI deputy), Rabat, May 2010.

‡ Here, plebiscitary democracy is synonymous with O'Donnell's (1994) concept of "delegative democracy."

political parties remain weak, both organizationally and programmatically; they continue to be internally oligarchical, and they are largely without policy-making authority. The problem, however, is one of reciprocal causation: party weakness contributes to the absence of policy authority, and the absence of policy authority denies parties the incentives to strengthen themselves. Political parties in Morocco are representative of the transitional characteristics we have identified in hybrid regimes.

National-level party support programs, programs focused on overall party development, tend to be expensive. Their potential benefits, at least in terms of measurable improvements in accountability, participation, representation, and governability, are likely to be very limited until (or if) the king gives parties more authority (e.g., by reducing the number of sovereign ministries). Only if that condition is met can parties consolidate and appeal to more distinct electorates.* Of course, supporting parties could help them prepare for future liberalization, and such support has some diffuse impacts such as affording donor agencies access both currently and for the future. That said, while good governance is a goal in Morocco, at least among some political elites, it is less clear that the country can move much beyond the hybrid status defined here in an evolutionary process. Further, the Moroccan case, illustrates the limits of the movement toward good governance even as it suggests that the linkage between governance and sustainability (and human security) are real.

Morocco is not likely to move in the direction of a strong parliament model, that is, toward a British- or European-style system of parliamentary government (what the British call "responsible government") in which the executive is fully dependent upon holding a parliamentary majority in the legislature. Not only is external pressure for a strong parliament model unlikely, but evidence from other countries in North Africa and the Middle East (Lebanon, Jordan, Iraq, and Palestine) suggests Islamic nationalist parties will consistently be a very strong bloc in such a government. The PJD, of course, is already the largest political party in parliament. Full parliamentary government could be very unstable or even hegemonic if an Islamic political movement were to gain strength.

Presidential Monarchy

Given the absence of political will, either among Moroccan political parties or among other Moroccan political elites, to move toward a parliamentary model, where lies Morocco's political future and how does this relate to Moroccan hopes for a more sustainable model of development? We think a "presidential monarchy," a variant of the French model, is more likely than the British system of responsible government.† Such a presidential monarchy would be based on a kind of

* Consolidation does not mean reducing to as few as two or three parties, but it does mean reducing in the direction of the three to four poles that Moroccan observers predict, with each pole having some rough ideological distinctiveness.

† The classic discussion of French politics is Ehrmann's *Politics in France*.

"presidential" executive headed by the monarch, but without the elections defining the French presidency. In this scenario, the monarch would enjoy strong but not unlimited power along the lines of the current French presidency, with a weak premier and parliament (but requiring a parliamentary majority to govern, as in "co-habitation"). A likely Middle Eastern model for Morocco is Jordan, where the king has a more defined constitutional role, a role in which, for example, two-thirds of the legislature can override the king's veto. This scenario assumes a further consolidation of political parties in the near future. Such a consolidation of political parties seems reasonably probable. Two potential mobilizing political movements, the PJD and (perhaps) the PAM, have carved out significant influence in Moroccan politics. Their gains will reduce fragmentation at the expense of small parties. In the current parliament, seven major political parties hold 80% of the seats, and there has been a similar consolidation in the last local government elections. These levels of fragmentation are not outside the norm for proportional representation systems (Hamzawy 2007).

Role of Donor Support

Within this development scenario, is there a place for international support of political parties? Our diagnosis suggests a cautious affirmative answer. First, political party support shows that the donor community is committed to the process of political change in North Africa in the wake of the North African spring. Second, party support recognizes and supports the incremental changes currently occurring in Morocco. And finally, support for political party development affirms that even without a full democratic government, political parties play an important role in civic life and in the institutionalization of politics. Parties carry out constituency work, mobilize members for policy debate, and help keep bureaucratic officials accountable, even if they do all these things poorly. Overall, parties play indispensable roles in the social, economic and political life of Morocco (Cherkaoui and Ali 2007; Hursh 2010).

Support for political parties is another way of recognizing that liberalization precedes full democratization, that transition to democratization is one of indeterminate length, and parties play a role in transitioning to a democratic, open access order.

An Integrated Approach to Party Assistance

Consolidation of Donor Efforts

We have found in this research that current support for political parties is based upon iterative and often non-incremental programs. Breadth rather than depth is the most appropriate way to describe the current program, and a recent evaluation found current efforts to be widely scattered and largely unconnected. Their impact is difficult to judge, as little systematic assessment was built into their design.

Suppose there is little significant change in national-level political institutions over the next five to ten years. Political parties remain weak and largely unconsolidated; political reform stalls, and there are no significant institutional changes in the country in the near or medium term.* And suppose the international community accepts the idea that continued stability is more important than the exertion of pressure on Morocco (and its executive institutions) to move toward democracy. Given this scenario, continued small, unconsolidated activities do no harm and may do some good if only in terms of good public relations within Morocco.

The argument here suggests, however, that because the actors themselves are uncertain as to the pace and direction of political change in Morocco, and because their actions are mutually interdependent, there is considerable scope for political party assistance. It is precisely the ambivalence and open-endedness of the tactics of the king and party leaders that justifies a well-conceived party assistance strategy.

Integration of Civil Society, Political Parties, and Local Officials

We urge consolidation of assistance programs. Political parties do not function in a vacuum, in isolation from other parts of the political process. Instead, parties operate with civil society groups, interest associations, and public officials, and they function at local, regional, and national levels. *There needs to be a better integrated, sustained, targeted, and planned intervention by the international community to support political party development as part of a broad strategy supporting democratic and institutionalized governance in Morocco.* Programs supporting the rule of law, improving media discussions of party programs and issues, and strengthening anti-corruption efforts involving prosecutors and courts are all part of maintaining a liberal climate while awaiting the maturation of the "doorstep" conditions discussed above.

As we pointed out earlier, real change (such as the reform of the family code) has occurred in Morocco when civil society raises issues, political parties respond, and negotiations occur among elected officials.† From the perspective of political change, the goal is to strengthen all these political actors simultaneously. Since it is impossible to do this all over the country, we recommend targeting political party

* See Maghraoui (2001), for discussions of this continuing debate. And see Willis (2002) for a pessimistic view perspective on institutional reform.

† The reform of the *Moudawana* was introduced in the agenda by civil society groups and was then debated by political parties in Congress. This eventually led to a stalemate between progressive parties favoring the reform (e.g., UFSP) and more conservative parties—mainly the PJD—opposing the reform. Eventually, the intervention of the king broke this gridlock.

assistance on a few well-chosen communities in the 75,000–150,000 population range. These communities could become examples followed by other communities, and they could become models for support by other donors.

Local-Level Party Organizational Development in Selected Policy Areas

The core of this option is political party mobilization (in councils and via civil society). The activity focuses on local-level communication, anticorruption efforts, and local government/civil society activities in such policy areas as health, school maintenance, and microlevel finance for social development. Civil society organizations that could be involved alongside local political parties might include Transparency Maroc (*vis-à-vis* corruption), women's rights groups, neighborhood associations (especially on sustainable development), locally elected officials and their party groupings, and the media and private sector.

This kind of program is difficult to implement. It focuses on party goals in government and on relationships with civil society rather than political processes themselves. It requires coordination between donors (and its venders and grantees) and other donors and members of the international community. Such a program would require serious evaluation, follow-up, and dissemination.

National-Level Programs

The first option is to continue the programs currently in place. International donors do implement a portfolio of activities largely at the national level, with some regional activities. These activities include training and related support activities for female party members and, more generally, for younger party supporters, those under 40 years of age. These activities garner stories and pictures in the newspapers and other media. Even their short-term impact is difficult to measure in the absence of serious evaluation.

If the donor community wishes to provide token support for political parties as stabilizing entities, a case can be made for continuing party support grants within the present framework for another few years. A better strategy would be to target a small national-level program on the parliament, with the goal of helping parties become more responsible actors and thus more reliable partners for the king should he pursue a democratic opening. We would focus on this program because organizational and capacity issues currently block even willing and active members of parliament from engaging in policy-making activities with the executive branch.

Though we believe that focused national-level efforts to support political party development should wait on a clearer future for Morocco constitutionally and institutionally, two potential areas of focus at the national level should be considered, including (1) the development of a political leadership program related to specific policy areas, and (2) support for the operation of a legislative budget office providing policy research for parliamentary debates.

Support for Party Work in Parliament

Assuming some movement toward more active party-centered policy debate and parliamentary control of the executive, assistance could focus on supporting the operations of the parliamentary party in the national legislature, especially on the development of professional staff in parliament. Support for a legislative budget and/or research office would help empower parties or clusters of parties.

Strategy in a Nutshell

In sum, we see a two-track strategy in thinking about political party development. The focus on local-level activities—a program targeting party, civil society, and elected officials—is the basis of our strategic recommendation. Donor coordination is central, since a single donor can manage only a small portion of these integrated activities. If it becomes clear that political parties are showing progress toward consolidation and that Morocco is moving toward institutional norms in terms of executive leadership (before or after 2012), then a national-level program merits serious consideration.

The second track, a more national-level approach that recognizes the overall argument of the book and of this chapter is that good governance is the missing link between human security and sustainable economic development and the finding here that Morocco does not yet have an evolving good governance program even though it has the elements of a human rights regime. Our findings here suggest that its human rights record and economic development are both on the rise.

Morocco's governance system, like that of many countries in Africa and the Middle East is a work in progress. We reiterate our recognition of Aili Mari Tripp's term, "hybrid regime" (regimes that both promote certain human rights but at the same time curtail other elements of participation) assists in our understanding the Moroccan case study.

Morocco illustrates the complexity of defining a relationship between governance and socioeconomic development, but suggests that "competitive authoritarianism" or "hybrid regimes" need to be accounted for in discussions of the role human security plays as an intervening variable in the move toward sustainable development.

Through the Moroccan case study, and the North African dilemmas in the wake of the North African spring, we recognize the role of good governance and human security and sustainable development, understanding the move from a transitional governance system to one which locks in human rights and political participation is part of a complex social and political change process.

Acknowledgment

Support for this research came from the U.S. Agency for International Development to the Department of Political Science, University of Pittsburgh.

References

Beau, N., Graciet, C. 2006. *Quand le Maroc sera islamiste*. Paris: Editions La Découverte.

Benchemsi, A. 2012. Morocco: Outfoxing the opposition. *Journal of Democracy 23*(1), 57–69.

Boubekeur, A. 2008. *Morocco: The Emergence of a New Palace Party*. Washington, DC: Carnegie Middle East Center.

Boukhalef, A. 2005. Croissance économique au Maroc: Inquiétude de la Banque Mondiale. *Le Matin*, August 14.

Cherkaoui, M. and Ali, D.B. 2007. The political economy of growth in Morocco. *The Quarterly Review of Economic and Finance* 46(5): 741–761.

El País. 2012. El día que Argelia quiera, la cuestión del Sáhara se resolverá. *El País* May 20.

Freedom House. 2010a. *Free Speech under Attack in Morocco*. Washington, DC: Freedom House.

Freedom House. 2010b. *Freedom in the World Report 2010*. Washington, DC: Freedom House.

Gershovich, M. 2008. *Democratization in Morocco: Political Transition of a North African Kingdom*. Washington, DC: The Middle East Institute.

Hamzawy, A. 2007. The 2007 Moroccan Parliamentary Elections Results and Implications. Carnegie Endowment for International Peace. Available at: http://carnegieendowment.org/files/moroccan_parliamentary_elections_final.pdf.

Howe, M. 2005. *Morocco: The Islamist Awakening and Other Challenges*. Oxford: Oxford University Press.

Hursh, J. 2010. Moving toward democracy in Morocco? *Air and Space Power Journal: Africa/Francophonie* 64.

Khrouz, D. 2008. A dynamic civil society. *Journal of Democracy 19*(1), 42–49.

Maddy-Weitzman, B. 1996. The Islamic challenge in North Africa. *Terrorism and Political Violence* 8(2): 171–188.

Maghraoui, A. 2001. Monarchy and political reform in Morocco. *Journal of Democracy 12*(1), 74–86.

McFaul, M., Cofman Wittes, T. 2008. The limits of limited reform. *Journal of Democracy 19*(1), 19–33.

Naciri, R. 1998. The Women's Movement and Political Discourse in Morocco. UN Research Institute for Social Development. Occasional paper 8. Switzerland: UNDP.

Sater, J. 2007. The consolidation and mobilization of civil society under the 'new system' (1993–2002). In *Civil Society and Political Change in Morocco*. New York: Routledge.

Storm, L. 2007. *Democratization in Morocco: The Political Elite and Struggles for Power in the Post-independence State*. New York: Routledge.

Szmolka, I. 2010. Party system fragmentation in Morocco. *Journal of North African Studies 15*(1), 13–37.

Tozy, M. 2008. Islamists, technocrats, and the palace. *Journal of Democracy 19*(1), 34–41.

Tripp, A. 2010. *Museveni's Uganda: Paradoxes of Power in a Hybrid Regime.* Boulder, CO: Lynne Rienner.

Vermeren, P. 2009. *Le Maroc de Mohammed VI.* Paris: La Découverte.

White, G. 2008. The 'End of the Era of Leniency' in Morocco. In Y.H. Zoubir and H. Amirah-Fernández (eds.). *North Africa: Politics, Region, and the Limits of Transformation.* London: Routledge.

Willis, M. 2008. The politics of Berber (Amazigh) identity: Algeria and Morocco compared. In Y. Zoubir and H. Amirah-Fernández. (eds.). *North Africa: Politics, Region, and the Limits of Transformation.* New York: Routledge.

Wuerth, O. 2005. The reform of the Moudawana. *Hawwa 3*(3), 309–333.

Chapter 16

Fiscal Responsibility, Sustainability, and Governance

Local Government Financing in South Africa

Thomas Mogale and Louis A. Picard

Contents

Introduction

A successful local government is vital for the stability and economic success of developing countries in Africa. South Africa illustrates the importance of governance. Post-1994 South Africa emerged from a highly fragmented intergovernmental fiscal relations system based on the ethnic homelands and African townships but within a unitary and highly centralized local government system. The postapartheid government tried to move to a radically decentralized fiscal system. Given the historical and geographical diversities of 283 newly established local government structures, fiscal decentralization raised a new set of questions of how national government could achieve horizontal and vertical equity.

From 1995 in line with the newly approved constitution, local government was significantly restructured in South Africa. New pieces of legislation, including the Municipal Systems Act (2000) and the Municipal Finance Management Act (2003) were enacted to give effect to the decentralization mandate implied in the constitution (i.e., autonomous but interdependent status)—thereby introducing far-reaching changes to existing intergovernmental relationships between local governments and other spheres of government. The focus was on the way local government planned and executed their functions, used their resources, raised revenue, and managed their finances.

This chapter (using material from Picard and Mogale, 2014) seeks to explore the conceptual basis of fiscal decentralization and how it influences the restructuring of governmental functions and finances between national and subnational structures, especially at the local government level in South Africa. It furthermore outlines and explains South African legislative and policy measures enacted since 1994 to underpin governmental restructuring and to facilitate the functioning of the new intergovernmental fiscal relations system. This chapter is exploratory rather than definitive, suggesting fiscal responsibility is one of a set of governance indicators often neglected by students of African governance.

Given geographical and historical economic imbalances between subnational structures (vertical) and among structures at same levels (horizontal) the chapter poses the questions, what powers and functions are assigned to which subnational structures? How are inherent differences in the capacities and needs among them to be mediated and adjusted? What are the revenue streams of different substructures and how are the imbalances between expected revenues and expenditures resolved? Using publicly available local government performance data, audited financial statements and personal interviews as preliminary indicators, the chapter concludes by noting several issues which could pose serious threats to the long-term sustainability of local governments in South Africa.

We focus on questions of relevance to specific institutional and fiscal restructuring of the national government, provincial structures, and local governments in South Africa. This explores the theory to derive basic principles and practical considerations taken into account in the initial restructuring of the country' governmental functions and finances, and attempts to assess these against 17 years' experience of implementation of intergovernmental fiscal changes in a developing country context. Additionally, it raises questions about fiscal sustainability and how this has been attended to.

Although the pace of institutional and legislative change in South Africa has in recent years slowed down, many developments are underway to address local government sustainability challenges. Using local government performance reports, audited financial statements and personal interviews, the authors identify several issues that pose serious questions to the sustainability of local government.

We see a connection made between intergovernmental fiscal relations and the two core themes of this book, namely governance and sustainable development. Our premise is that governance is influenced by fiscal intergovernmental relations, a link which is not always made. Further, because local government is linked to service delivery, its performance is closely related to sustainable social development.

Based on these experiences and a growing literature on intergovernmental fiscal relations, the chapter suggests first, that in developing country contexts like those in South Africa, attention must be paid to both the macro- and microeconomic circumstances of provinces (intermediary government) as well as those constituting local government structures. Second, while lessons may be drawn from 17 years of implementation of an intergovernmental fiscal relations system these should be treated with caution given the country's relatively short history of constitutional transformation and limitations in reliable data sets. Third, fiscal responsibilities and local government financing lessons drawn from South Africa may be of limited general applicability to other sub-Saharan African countries.

While fiscal decentralization has in recent years received the attention of developing countries, we are mindful that much of the growing intergovernmental fiscal relations literature and experiences are derived from industrialized countries where the evolution of constitutions and government structures have been going on for many years (Fukasaku and de Mello 1999). Yet, Bahl and Smoke (2003) are sanguine about this and suggest that South Africa is likely a case that many governments and students of fiscal decentralization will follow closely since there have been some noticeable successes in problematic areas of reform. Yet, for South Africa, the state of intergovernmental fiscal relations and fiscal sustainability of government substructures are at a critical debating point which spawns doubts and viability questions about the provinces and the future of local government districts.

This chapter is organized around four intergovernmental fiscal relations questions that must be answered with respect to theory-based principles juxtaposed against implementation experiences derived from South Africa in the past 17 years:

1. What are the legislative and policy basis for local government?
2. Which powers and functions are assigned to which subnational structures?
3. What are the revenue streams of different substructures and how are the imbalances between revenues and expenditures resolved?
4. Given geographic and historical economic imbalances between subnational structures (vertical) and among structures themselves (horizontal), how are the differences in capacities and needs adjusted?

Fiscal Decentralization: The Role of National Substructures

The theory of fiscal decentralization identifies three functions for governments: macroeconomic stabilization, income distribution, and resource allocation (Oates 1972). The theory ascribes macroeconomic stabilization and income distribution responsibilities to the national government, while assigning a significant role to subnational government to allocating resources. According to fiscal decentralization theory, macroeconomic stabilization and income distribution responsibilities are assigned to national government, stabilization being usually considered inherently national in nature, apart from the fact that subnational structures lack the macroeconomic wherewithal to carry out such policies. The confluence of these factors makes incentives to decentralize by national elites problematic.

With respect to income distribution, the dominant view in public finance literature is that income redistribution should be a mainly national competence and, deems unwise efforts by local government to achieve redress as this will most likely result in unfair outcomes (Prud'homme 1995a). It is argued further that decentralized income redistribution is likely to be self-defeating especially if one takes into account that measures to foster income redistribution, say by heavily taxing the rich and giving high benefits to the poor may result in the outmigration of the rich to lightly taxed regions and an influx of the poor from low performing to high performing jurisdictions. The massive movement from the Eastern Cape to the Western Cape in South Africa over the past 20 years illustrates this problem.

In a counterveiling argument, Sewell (1996) has noticed distributive policies that have taken place at decentralized levels without prejudicing economic growth and social justice objectives. For instance, some regulatory policies assigned to subnational authorities in South Africa, such as land use and rent controls, have generated profound distributional implications. Public health care, primary education, water supply, housing, and electricity supply assigned at subnational levels have yielded important redistributional results. In poorer countries such services are often the only mechanism for income distribution.

The fiscal decentralization model assigns a significant role to subnational governments in terms of resource allocation. Accordingly, the model holds that in a democratic society decentralizing resource allocation to structures closest to the people will result in a more appropriate match of demands and supply for local level public goods (Oates 1972). Because provincial and local governments are closer to the public and, because at least in theory democratic societies are participatory in planning development, it is claimed that these structures are better placed to identify local communities' needs and to determine the appropriate level and quality of services (Rondinelli et al. 1989).

However, a few critical comments about federal and even devolved fiscal theory are in order. Generalizability of assumptions underpinning fiscal decentralization is subject to a serious challenge when applied to developing country contexts. Prud'homme (1995a) for instance, questioned their relevance by highlighting perception differentials of what a development priority is for developing countries. He argued that for them, it might not be about differentiating gradations in tastes and preferences between jurisdictions of national substructures but rather meeting basic needs. He challenges the model assumption by suggesting that in developing country contexts communities in subnational jurisdictions do not always express preferences through voting. That this is true in industrialized countries does not foreordain similar outcomes in newly independent and developing societies.

In newly democratized countries such as South Africa, where the legacy of apartheid is still fresh in people's minds, where land and labor markets do not function properly and democratic values are still in infancy, it may be unrealistic to assume that people can vote purely on government performance, move easily between jurisdictions or make their voices heard through the political process. Prud'homme asserted further that, even where elected officials wanted to fulfil their mandates from voters, they cannot because of gross mismatch between available resources and promised expenditures. Therefore, local representatives in developing countries lack incentives to keep promises.

Local government bureaucrats in many developing countries are, he argues, often unresponsive, poorly motivated and poorly qualified, and might have reasons to pursue their own agenda rather than the agenda of their superiors. This argument is supported by the observation in South Africa that national government is likely to attract better qualified people, partly because it offers higher salaries and partly because it can offer better careers, with greater diversity of tasks, more possibilities for promotion, and longer view of issues.

In summary, the assignment of functions between levels of government is a complex exercise. In many countries it has opened up responsibility-sharing between national government and subnational jurisdictions. However, without the necessary transparency and an appropriate regulatory framework, there can be no accountability. South Africa in the late 1990s provided an example: national government and provinces had joint responsibility for health and education, but the exact responsibilities were not clearly spelt out. The result is that provinces received transfers to fund these services but could use them for other purposes, knowing well that the national government would intervene to provide the needed service.

There are two elements of governmental provision of services at play here. One is the assignment of functions; the other is the process of carrying out those functions. While the element of assignment is complex it may be much less complex than the task of implementation, which is a function of bureaucratic incentives, resource availability and personal interests. While the focus here is on the former, we do not suggest that the latter issue is any less important.

Overarching Legislative and Policy Frameworks of the Fiscal System

The pre-1994 the South African fiscal and financing system mirrored the rigid, centralized, and hierarchical apartheid structural architecture and operationally was characterized by a nontransparent allocative arrangement to white, colored, Indian and African local authorities.* The system of financing local government was largely overridden by ideological considerations and rooted in the desire to reinforce racial separation and to preserve white local government privilege rather than pursue efficiency and equity considerations.

Fiscal arrangements and allocations were neither formula based in the sense that they ignored demographic and socio-economic criteria of South African communities nor were they predictable for intended beneficiaries on a year-to-year basis. The fiscal system was arbitrary and not formula based even though it consistently and disproportionately favored white local municipalities both in funding and provision of services. The existing tax base naturally concentrated within the geographic space of the jurisdiction of established white municipalities, was heavily fragmented and displayed no predictable pattern on a year-to-year basis.

The post-1994 policy and legislative framework for intergovernmental relations by contrast was premised on a radical transformation agenda of funding, financial allocation, and management to a new provincial and municipal dispensation. As a result, South Africa's intergovernmental fiscal and financing system is designed to support the functioning of the three spheres of government—national, nine provincial, and 283 local governments in line with their constitutionally enshrined and defined competencies. The basic point of departure is that finance should follow functions allocated to sub-national structures. The spheres and concomitant functions are specified in the country's Constitution; namely, national, provincial, and local—with each sphere provided sufficient funds to fulfil its mandate.

The interdependencies of the three spheres is held by a labyrinth of legislative and institutional measures that grant national government legislative authority of the republic in its totality, provinces responsibilities and a measure of concurrency over school education, health, social grants (social services), housing, provincial roads, and agriculture. As regards local government, the Constitution distinguishes three categories of local government—metropolitan, local, and district. Section 175 specifies functions of local government as the provision of services such as water, sanitation, transport, electricity, housing, and security.

Sentiments on the new intergovernmental fiscal relations dispensation were felt in crafting the Constitution. The Constitution assigned powers and functions to the three spheres of government while setting up an equitable system of financing for them. According to Fjeldstad (2011), this is equivalent to the allocation of

* See Figure 16.1 where the thickness of the lines illustrate the urban and white bias to the fiscal system.

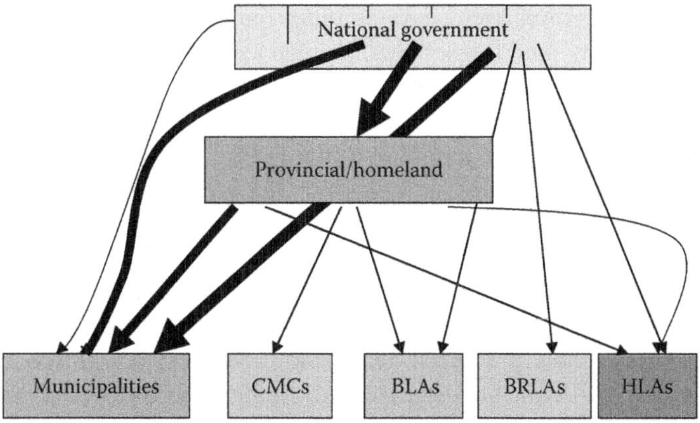

Figure 16.1 Income transfers. CMCS, cape municipal councils; BLAs, black local authorities; BRLAs, black rural local authorities; HLAs, homeland local authorities.

responsibility and authority for public sector decisions among the several different power centers (see Figure 16.2).

The Constitution promulgated in 1996 and implemented in 1997 enjoined the national government to enact legislation that would outline the structure and role of national sub-structures, prescribe how these should be structured, and give guidance as to how they should be managed and governed. In this respect, Section 215 of the Constitution prescribes, "provincial and municipal budgets and budgetary

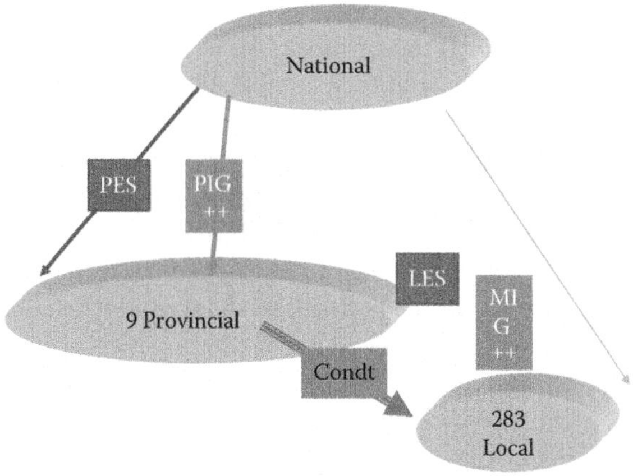

Figure 16.2 Intergovernmental grants. PES, provincial equitable share grants; PIGs, provincial infrastructure grants; LES, local government equitable share grants; LIGs, local government Infrastructure grants; Condt, conduit (e.g., passed through provincial to local government).

processes promote transparency, accountability and the effective financial management of the economy" and further, that national legislation be enacted to lay down the form that all government budgets across the three spheres should take and, that they disclose their sources of revenue and how their proposed expenditure would comply with national legislation and priorities.

The Constitution vested the legislative making function within "parliaments" of democratically elected representatives in the three spheres of government. The national parliament is responsible for the development of policy and provides guidelines toward implementation. In keeping with this, Chapter 13 of the Constitution, prescribes that the national parliament enacts national legislation pertaining to how provincial and local government should be structured and function. As a result between 1998 and 2005, parliament had passed and enacted numerous finance and fiscal related legislations and regulations that included:

- Intergovernmental Fiscal Relations Act
- Provincial Tax Regulation Process Act
- Borrowing Powers of Provincial Government Act
- Public Finance Management Act (PFMA)
- Municipal Finance Management Act (MFMA)
- Financial and Fiscal Commission Act
- Local Government Property Rates Act
- Local Government Powers and Functions (Act)
  - Annual Budget Acts of Parliament
  - Annual Division of Revenue—Explanatory memorandum and extensive tables
- National and Provincial Appropriation Act
- Tax legislation (Taxation and Revenue Laws Amendment Acts)

The constitution highlighted the distinctiveness yet interrelatedness of the three spheres of government. Section 151 of the Constitution accentuates the important position covering the entire country with wall-to-wall municipal structures. The provincial parliaments and local government councils are vested with executive and legislative authority and at the political level are run by democratically elected councils and accountable officials.

Municipalities are granted the right to govern on local affairs autonomously subject to national and provincial legislation. Picard (2005) asserts that as a result of poor understanding of the principles of separation of the party and the government by members of the ruling party, a degree of autonomy from central government in political, administrative and fiscal decision making is compromised. In addition, though South Africa is legally and politically a unitary state, the country still has a highly centralized policy control mediated by uneven patterns of implementation caused by inefficiencies, corruption, and limited fiscal resources.

Legislative Basis for Financial Management

Section 214 (a–j) of the Constitution requires that an annual Division of Revenue Act be enacted by parliament with the requirement that the revenue sharing mechanism be implemented to account for expenditure needs of spheres of government in addition to which it must take into account their fiscal capacity. Unfortunately, illustrating this process is difficult since in practice capturing revenue collection in South Africa is still a challenge. Partly as a result of the above and the need to strengthen coordination and integrated development systems, the Intergovernmental Relations Act (Act No. 97, 1997) was enacted to promote co-operation between the three spheres on fiscal, budgetary and financial matters, to prescribe a process for the determination of an equitable sharing and allocation of revenue raised nationally. The Public Finance Management Act (Act No. 1, 1999) (PFMA), (as amended by Act No. 29) applies to national and provincial government structures and hence renders void the need for each province to have separate legislation on fiscal responsibility.

Primarily, PFMA meant to give effect to the provisions of Sections 213 and 215 of the Constitution for the national and provincial spheres of government by modernizing the system of financial management in the public sector and to enable and hold accountable public sector managers. Further, PFMA was to ensure that relevant and good quality financial information about national and provincial spheres is provided and to eliminate waste and corruption.

PFMA was also designed to catalyze the optimal utilization of limited government resources for the purposes of promoting service delivery. PFMA adopted a new approach to South African financial management whose strength was the focus on outputs and responsibilities rather than the rule-driven approach of the previous Exchequer Acts. The Act formed part of a broader strategy to improve financial management in the public sector across national and provincial spheres.

The introduction of this new approach raised questions of how consistency in fiscal responsibility objectives was to be achieved between the provinces and between the various national government departments. In all these questions the principles of uniformity and precedence of national economic policy was invoked. Structurally, Section 154 of the Constitution reinforced the principle of co-operative governance by enjoining the national and provincial governments to support and strengthen the capacity of municipalities to manage their own affairs, to exercise their powers and to perform their functions.

The Intergovernmental Relations Framework Act (Act No. 13, 2005) was enacted to provide for the establishment of structures and institutions to foster intergovernmental relations and promote cooperative governance. Once established, the structures could facilitate coordination in the implementation of policy and legislation between national, provincial, and local government and all organs of the state. Furthermore, the Act is meant to promote coherent government and the effective provision of services, monitor implementation of policy and legislation, and realize national priorities. Most important areas covered by the legislation included service delivery, public accountability, coordination and integration, effective implementation, and dispute resolutions.

Section 215, Subsection 1 of the Constitution prescribes the nature of national, provincial and municipal budgets and that budgetary processes need to be structured in a manner that promotes transparency, accountability and the effective financial management of the local economy.

Yet another seminal piece in the municipal financial management jigsaw puzzle is the Municipal Finance Management Act (Act No. 56, 2003). MFMA is to local government what PFMA is to provinces and national structures. It marked a major turning point in municipal financial management and was enacted to bring into effect the modernization of budgeting and financial management practices, and a sound financial governance framework that clarified and separated roles and responsibilities of key municipal functionaries.

MFMA is comprehensive in its sweep and most importantly is spearheaded by the National Treasury. By enforcing MFMA and issuing regular financial regulations, the National Treasury is able to bring in a raft of fiscal and financial reforms which focused on new budget processes which are linked to integrated development planning (IDP). New accounting standards and formats (GAMAP* and GRAP†) were introduced to set out a framework of the accounting standards that were to be applied by municipalities in South Africa in preparation of annual financial statements. Accompanying these reforms was the establishment of audit committees and other internal controls, improvements to procurement and supply management systems, performance measurement reporting, and staff competency levels. In theory, MFMA was meant to empower various stakeholders to perform municipal financial management roles.

MFMA informs on the national, provincial, and municipal budgets, to determine when national and provincial budgets must be tabled and, that budgets in each sphere of government show the sources of revenue and the way in which proposed expenditure will comply with national legislation. Accordingly, budgets in each sphere of government must contain estimates of revenue and expenditure, differentiating between capital and current expenditure; proposals for financing any anticipated deficit for the period to which they apply and, an indication of intentions regarding borrowing and other forms of public liability that will increase public debt during the ensuing year.

Assignment and Division of Revenue

Existing literature suggests a lack of uniform agreement among policy makers about which taxes should be assigned to which level of government (Musgrave

* GAMAP = Generally Accepted Municipal Accounting Practices.

† GRAP = Generally Recognized Accounting Practice.

1983; Oates 1993). Bahl (1996) cites principles for consideration when decisions below are taken:

- Subnational government structures should be assigned taxes whose burdens fall within their jurisdiction,
- Subnational government structures such as local governments should not levy taxes that cause businesses to adopt tax avoidance and hence inefficient measures of doing business. Such inefficient methods, he argues, may have the effect of harming local economy, and that,
- Local governments should not levy taxes that impose heavy administrative and compliance costs.

The South African Intergovernmental Fiscal Relations is premised on the following characteristics:

- Different spheres must be able to meet their constitutional mandate (Section 154, 156[1], 155[7], and 125[3]):
- Equitable and fair
  - Transparent
  - Simple
  - Predictable and stable
  - Address income and expenditure gaps
  - Poverty targeted
  - Correct incentives
  - Based on official and credible data

The government relies on a variety of instruments and sources for raising revenues, including direct or indirect taxes, general or specific taxes, corporate or personal taxes. Provinces themselves have very low revenue raising capacity and previous estimates suggest that they can only raise approximately 3% of their own revenue whilst the remaining 97% is derived from national transfers or grants. Local government on the other hand and partly in theory has significant revenue raising capacity, mostly from own sources such levies and charges from water, electricity, refuse removal, housing infrastructure, and municipal roads. However, disparities in revenue raising capacity among municipalities vary significantly, from urban metropolitan municipalities such as Johannesburg and Cape Town raising over 95% of own revenue to poor rural municipalities averaging 30% to as low as 10% from own sources.

As regards revenue assignment, the following arrangement applies to the three spheres with national government keeping custody of the four biggest taxes: personal income tax, corporate tax, VAT, and fuel levy. Provinces can impose taxes as prescribed in the constitution, with the largest revenue sources currently being motor-car license fees, duties on casinos, wagering, gambling, lotteries, and racing. Municipalities have property taxes and surcharge on electricity, water, and sanitation.

Any gaps between expenditure requirements and revenue in both subnational governments are filled by Central Government grants including

- Equitable share
- Conditional grants
- Nonconditional grants
  - Conditional and other grants mainly used for infrastructure backlogs, national priority programs, and spill-over effects

How to Manage Vertical and Horizontal Imbalances

Although the fiscal decentralization literature has yet to come up with an ideal system of tax assignment between national and subnational structures, a set of commonly agreed principles has been identified. The case for centralizing revenue collection to the national sphere is built on equalization and macroeconomic considerations. The case is made for decentralization on local government level on efficiency considerations (Fjeldstad 2001). The main consideration, however, is how government balances these things out. For transitional societies, the question of the local government's capacity to administer taxes at local level is likely to weigh in quite heavily when decisions around this matter are taken. It is pointless to assign taxing powers to local jurisdictions in the likelihood that they would not accurately assess and collect such taxes.

South Africa appears, as have many transitional societies, to have succumbed to the temptation of designing a system that perpetuates a mismatch between revenue generation and expenditure functions that led to the highly publicized incidences of provincial and local governments' excessively large expenditure functions and unfunded mandates. As has previously been mentioned most revenue raising tax bases such as corporate tax, VAT, and personal income taxes have remained with the national government. Yet, many expenditure functions at subnational government exceed available revenues sources—a phenomenon referred to as "vertical imbalance."

The majority of the 283 municipalities in South Africa are in this situation and are heavily dependent on national transfers and conditional grants from the National Treasury to fill the vertical fiscal gap. For instance, in 1990, South Africa's local government share of total public expenditure amounted to 20.7%, with tax revenue equal to 5.5%. In 1997, the figures had risen to 49.8%, of a tax revenue that had fallen to 5.3% of total tax revenue collected. The figures reveal an increasingly growing gap between expenditure and revenue generation over the years and a potentially growing dependence of subnational governments on national government transfers. Added to that is the Constitutional mandate which requires local government to promote social and economic development, forcing local government to put money aside for the creation of an environment suitable for local and foreign investment.

Though several but fairly sophisticated sharing arrangements of reducing financial imbalances between national and subnational structures have been developed and implemented through, for instance, revenue sharing and grants, in practice, none of the methods have thus far managed to arrest the escalating fiscal gap whilst meeting growing local level service delivery expectations.

Whilst revenue sharing according to a predetermined formula might be like a general purpose unconditional block grant, it does not address the problem of horizontal imbalances, that is, imbalances between rural and urban municipalities, between metropolitan areas and districts and the implications for demographic movements. The general rule of thumb in these cases is that flexibility should be exercised in sharing arrangements to allow subnational structures to build contingencies to deal with problems generated by their unique circumstances.

Apart from revenue sharing mechanisms to reducing financial imbalances between national and subnational structures, South Africa's Financial and Fiscal Commission (FFC) recommended the use of an intergovernmental system of grants; that is, unconditional, conditional, and equalization*. Examples of unconditional grants include provincial and local government equitable shares, and conditional grants include provincial and local government infrastructure grants, for example, PIG and MIG. South Africa uses a formula-based form of unconditional grant, referred to as equitable share.

The Constitution in Section 214 requires a legislation providing for equity be passed by parliament only after the provincial governments, organized local government (SALGA) and the FFC have been consulted, and any recommendations of the Commission have been considered, and must take into account, the national interest; consideration of national debt and other national obligations, and so on. In the fiscal decentralization literature, equity is associated with the principle that taxation be fair, certain, convenient, and efficient. Musgrave (1973, 211), argues that: "Everyone agrees that the tax system should be equitable, that is, that each taxpayer should contribute his' fair share to the cost of government. But there is no such agreement about how the term 'fair share' should be defined." However, the literature agrees that there are two main approaches that can be taken: the so-called "benefit" principle and the "ability-to-pay" principle. This is where choice comes into play.

Conclusion

One major concern coming out of this preliminary overview of the conceptual and empirical literature reviewed above on intergovernmental fiscal relations is that there needs to be a nuanced approach adopted when determining the sources

* Equalization is about raising the capacity of local governments to provide "national standards" level of goods and services.

of revenue and the capacities of the subnational structures. While accountability measures are in place, enforcement measures must be in place to ensure that the subnational structures are not only accountable but that they must be seen to be accountable for what they do with allocated resources.

The question of how intergovernmental systems are arranged suggests they be approached with sensitivity to historic and socioeconomic circumstances applicable to a specific country, and this needs to be done consistently with the achievement of relevant policy objectives. As a departure point, South Africa's initial conditions from which the intergovernmental fiscal relations system is built is consistent with its history, and the system in place in part reflects the politically negotiated process preceding it. Broadly, such objectives must be consistent with overall goals supportive to fiscal decentralization, inclusive of macroeconomic stabilization, income distribution, and allocation of resources.

To reiterate: while we see this chapter as exploratory, we believe it draws a connection with linkages between intergovernmental fiscal relations and the book's two core themes, namely governance and sustainable development. Our premise is good governance is influenced by fiscal intergovernmental relations, a link which is not always made. Our suggestion is that because fiscal analysis is difficult, it may be the neglected component of the governance literature, and an important part of the link back to sustainability.

In South Africa, from a historical and nation building perspective, fiscal issues are part of the need to achieving redress from the legacy of apartheid and to achieving regional balance. As has been recognized in the past 17 years (since 1996), these have often generated conflicts between spheres of governments and between communities within the same jurisdictions. Also, given that the South African intergovernmental fiscal relations system followed from a negotiated process, greater recognition must be given to crafting intergovernmental fiscal relations policies that recognize political constraints facing policymakers, such as the strengths of provinces and groups within those provinces in carrying out political decisions.

Concrete fiscal analysis can help us better understand these processes and allows policy makers to enforce aggregate fiscal discipline in the sense that, for instance, budgets be respected (like all laws) and that fiscal aggregates stay within set limits. Further, the system is designed to foster the principle of allocative efficiency in resource allocation which would be in line with set national and local government priorities. In other words, good programs get more and vice versa. A further objective of the system is the promotion of operational efficiency which promotes the delivery of more developmental outputs for less resource outlays.

References

Bahl, R. 1996. Fiscal decentralisation: Lessons for South Africa. In: *Restructuring the State and Intergovernmental Fiscal Relations in South Africa.* Johannesburg: Friederich-Ebert-Stiftung.

Bahl, R., Smoke, P. 2003. Restructuring local government finance in developing countries: Lessons from South Africa. *Studies in Fiscal Federalism and State-Local Finance.* Cheltenham, UK: Edward Elgar Publishing.

Fjeldstad, O. 2001. Taxation, coercion and donors. Local government tax enforcement in Tanzania. *The Journal of Modern African Studies* 39(2), 289–306.

Fjeldstad, O. 2011. Taxation and state-building in Africa: The role of civil society. *Chr. Michelsen Institute & International Centre for Tax and Development.* At: http://www.eleicoes2009.cip.org.mz/cipdoc%5C75_Taxation%20and%20state%20building%20in%20Africa%20-%20the%20role%20of%20civil%20society.pdf. Accessed 8/07/14

Fukasaku, K., De Mello, L. (eds.). 1999. *Fiscal Decentralization in Emerging Economies. Governance Issues.* Paris: Development Centre of the OECD. At: (http://www.oecdbookshop.org/oecd/display.asp?sf1=identifiers&st1=411999061P1). Accessed at: 8/7/14.

Musgrave, R. 1973. *Public Finance in Theory and Practice.* New York: McGraw-Hill.

Musgrave, R. 1983. Who should tax, where, and what? In: *Tax Assignment in Federal Countries.* McLure, C. ed. Canberra: Centre for Research on Federal Financial Relations, ANU Press: 2–19.

Oates, W. 1972. *Fiscal Federalism.* New York: Harcourt Brace Jovanovich.

Oates, W. 1993. Fiscal decentralisation and economic development. *National Tax Journal* 46 (1), 237–243.

Picard, L. 2005. *The State of the State: Institutional Transformation, Capacity and Political Change in South Africa.* Johannesburg: Wits University Press.

Picard, L., Mogale, T. 2014. *The Limits of Democratic Governance in South Africa: Centralized Power vs. Local Needs.* Boulder, CO: Lynne Rienner.

Prud'homme, R. 1995a. Assignment of expenditures and of taxes between levels of government for the Republic of South Africa. Unpublished.

Prud'homme, R.1995b. The dangers of decentralization. *The World Bank Research Observer* 10(2), 201–220.

Rondinelli, D., McCullough, J., Johnson, R. 1989. Analyzing decentralization policies in developing countries: A political-economy approach. *Development and Change* 20(1), 57–87.

Sewell, D. 1996. The dangers of decentralization' according to Prud'homme: Some further aspects. *World Bank Research Observer* 11(1, February), 143–150.

CONCLUSION VI

Chapter 17

Governance and Development in Africa

Taylor B. Seybolt

Contents

Introduction

The central idea of this book is that the proper goal for progress on the African continent is *sustainable human development* and that *good governance* is required to achieve this goal. Sustainable policies and actions meet current needs without compromising the ability to meet future needs. Human development seeks economic growth in the context of equal opportunity and social justice. It is concerned with the well-being and rights of a country's citizens just as much as the growth of standard national economic indicators. Good governance is a process of political rule that is participatory, transparent, inclusive, responsive, and guided by the rule of law. In the absence of good governance, countries are unlikely to have the building blocks of sustainable human development, such as strong education systems, healthcare infrastructure, and resistance to corruption.

Sustainable human development is a diversified, bottom-up enterprise that stands in sharp contrast to the hierarchical approach followed by the major development institutions (the International Monetary Fund and the World Bank) and foreign development assistance agencies (e.g., USAID) that focus on financial goals and national economic measures. In the words of the then Secretary-General of the United Nations, Kofi Annan, "without the people being the driving force of development, which (good) governance espouses, development can hardly take place and if it does, it cannot be sustainable" (UNDP 1997, p. 19). The problem is particularly acute in countries with weak governing institutions that have difficulty providing public goods.

This book tries to strike a balance between recognizing the need to bring politics back into development programs and understanding the limitations of political institutions in weak states. To that end, it looks at the challenges of development through a human security lens and identifies the ways that good governing practices at local and national levels can meet many of those challenges. The following pages articulate the main themes that have emerged, summarize the findings of the chapters, and offer a few closing remarks.

Themes

Former Speaker of the U.S. House of Representatives, Thomas "Tip" O'Neil, famously said, "All politics is local." The phrase is widely understood to mean that people care most about the mundane, every-day aspects of their lives, not about esoteric national policies. A successful leader must attend to the local needs of his constituents first and then turn his attention to higher level, more abstract issues of national governance. It is only a slight exaggeration to say that all development assistance is political, from which it follows that all development is local. It is easy to overplay the point, but like all good aphorisms, O'Neil's words encourage us to think about things we take for granted. In the current discussion, they lead us to consider the context, structure, and processes of development assistance.

The political context of development aid is a core theme of the book. Although they often deny it, donor governments seek to promote their political interests through development assistance. Bilaterally, they provide aid to allies but not to adversaries; through multinational organizations most governments promote economic liberalism. Recipient governments view development assistance as a valuable policy instrument that enables them to pursue preferred projects and, in worst-case situations, feeds corruption.

A second theme is the structure of recipient governments, differentiating between national, subnational, and local offices. Most development aid is directed to the national government while local government is frequently ignored. A national focus makes sense from the perspective of traditional state-centric models of economic development. From the sustainable human development perspective, local governance is crucial and aid that bypasses the substate and local levels of government misses an opportunity, at best. This book's chapter authors repeatedly demonstrate, in multiple counties and with reference to numerous development problems, that sustainable development is rooted in local-level involvement.

The third theme builds on the national-local distinction but it concerns agency and processes, with the main difference lying between processes that are top-down and those that are bottom-up. Development projects are far more likely to be sustainable if they have the support of local leaders and the people they are intended to help. People live locally. Sustainable development needs participatory and accountable governing processes that seek input from the bottom-up. This is not the way most development assistance has been designed or implemented in the past. The contributions to this book suggest that it should be a much bigger part of development programs in the future.

Chapter Summaries

The introductory chapter, by Picard and Lelei, sets out the puzzle of sustainable development in Africa and articulates the core idea of the volume. An initial surge in economic growth during the immediate postcolonial period was followed by stagnation across most of the continent, prompting considerable efforts by wealthier countries and international financial institutions to stimulate the national economies of African states. Despite the attention, for decades sub-Saharan Africa had the world's lowest economic growth rate. Now many African countries have a higher rate of economic expansion than the rest of the world. Nonetheless, a number of countries on the continent continue to lag behind and the successes are endangered by political unrest and unmet needs for human security. Picard and Lelei ask why the development history is so varied and inconsistent. As a prelude to the essays that follow, they argue the quality of governance is the key intervening variable between economic assistance and sustainable human development.

In Chapter 2, Belasco, Buss, and Picard establish the historical background of the sustainable human development model of economic assistance, and ask about aid donors' priorities in the current African context. They trace great swings in the theory and practice of development aid, from the early 1900s, when limited assistance was provided by private and religious philanthropies, to the enormous and politically motivated U.S. government-funded reconstruction efforts in the post-World War II period, concentrated in Europe and Japan. After they recovered from the war, European and Asian governments emulated the practice of bilateral development programs in African countries. Disillusionment set in during the 1970s in reaction to the perceived failure of aid to improve economic performance. In response, in the 1980s the World Bank and bilateral donors began to emphasize long-term programs to provide for the basic needs of the population for the building blocks of economic success, such as universal basic education, public health, and consultation with the recipients of aid. In short order, and amidst disagreement about the reasons why billions of dollars of aid had failed to lift underdeveloped countries out of poverty, the initial turn to a human development approach was overtaken by top-down structural adjustment programs, implemented through the World Bank and the International Monetary Fund, that focused on national debt reduction. To lessen their debt burdens, African countries were forced to cut back their spending on social programs, leaving large portions of their populations without access to the basic building blocks of productive economic activity. In the 1990s, the pendulum began to swing back toward the human development perspective with the UN Development Program's influential Human Development Index providing an annual record of performance that harks back to the concept of basic needs.

The Millennium Development Goals (MDGs)—a quintessential human development approach—can be understood as part of the history of ever-shifting models of development aid. The eight goals are to eradicate extreme poverty and hunger; achieve universal primary education; promote gender equality and empower women; reduce child mortality; improve maternal health; combate HIV/AIDS, malaria and other diseases; ensure environmental sustainability; and develop a global partnership for development. As the ambitious 15-year multinational program to lift the world's most destitute people out of extreme poverty comes to an end in 2015, with mixed results, the correct balance of top-down large-scale projects and community-based, people-centered programs remains elusive. Belasco, Buss, and Picard observe a disjuncture between many countries' embrace of the MDGs in principle and their bilateral aid programs that are driven by political interests, particularly in the so-called fragile states where stability in the age of terrorism is considered more important than poverty alleviation. Rather than ignore or try to minimize the political nature of development aid, the most effective analytical response is to adopt a concept of political involvement that sheds light on the reasons for higher economic achievement in some African countries than in others. The concept of good governance brings into the discussion the key factors of accountability, rule of law, equal opportunity, political pluralism, and respect for civil liberties.

In Chapter 3, Belasco, Buss, and Picard examine how aid and governance individually and jointly affect human development. Using indicators of income, educational attainment, and health, adopted from the UN Development Program's Human Development Index, Belasco, Buss, and Picard, test the proposition that the effect of economic aid on human development is filtered through the quality of governance. Their analysis of data from 150 countries found that aid directed to health programs, in combination with certain institutions of good governance (namely, voice and accountability), led over time to higher scores on the human development index. Importantly, health aid was also found to have a negative relationship with human development in countries that have low voice and accountability ratings. Somewhat surprisingly, they found no such relationship between education aid, good or bad governance, and human development. They conclude that either the human development index is not adequately capturing education aid (a methodological problem) or education aid is not implemented in a way that helps human development (a policy problem).

Bucki et al., continue the investigation of foreign aid goals and practices in Chapter 4 by turning our attention to the policies of governments that are trying to raise their countries out of poverty. They ask why some countries have been more successful than others in achieving the targets set forth in the MDGs. They test the idea that a country's ability to imbed the MDGs in their World Bank Poverty Reduction Strategy Papers (PSRP) is a key determinant, on the grounds that those papers are a major mechanism for requesting foreign aid. Investigation of all 59 countries that submitted strategy papers "failed to expose a set of explanatory factors that might help countries and policymakers improve MDG goal attainment using PRSPs as a vehicle" (Chapter 4, p. 89).

If the process of developing poverty reduction strategy papers appears not to have a consistent impact, the institutions of governance do make a difference. Capshaw and Bassichis, in Chapter 5, turn our attention to a core function of the state that is not often considered by development specialists: to provide stability and safety. Unfortunately, the agents of protection—the armed forces and police—often undermine social cohesion and the potential for development in African countries through their corruption and capricious use of power. Good governance characteristics of accountability, adherence to the rule of law, and respect for civil rights require military organizations "that are professional, trustworthy, representative of the people, and controlled by civilian institutions" (Chapter 5, p. 94). Helping to create professional military organizations is one of the main objectives of the U.S. Africa Command (AFRICOM). As such, AFRICOM plays an important role in the long-term effort to create sustainable development and promote human security on the continent. Capshaw and Bassichis detail the process of strategic assessment that is integral to the regional military command's self-evaluation and its interaction with African militaries.

Section III investigates "Sustainable Development Challenges" in three chapters by African scholars. Their contributions shift the focus from macrolevel foreign aid debates to national and local-level challenges posed by the tension between economic development and environmental changes. In Chapter 6, Mutunga starkly lays out the problem of population growth in sub-Saharan Africa: three-fifths of the countries are projected to at least double in population size by 2050 and Africa is the only continent that is expected to see overall population increases in the twenty-second century. The linkages between population growth, economic well-being, climate change, and resilience to natural disasters are sobering. The continent's population growth rate is likely to far outstrip economic growth, leaving the majority of people in poverty. Mutunga argues that population growth leads to increased greenhouse gas emissions. Those gases, in turn, lead to changes in long-term weather patterns and intensified short-term weather events that affect food security, potable water availability, disease contagion, and human migration. Impoverished communities have very limited capacity to absorb the effects of such changes.

He concludes there is a need for governments to prioritize public health, fertility, and population programs as a route to sustainable development. To succeed, they need help to "improve technical capacity in program design, research, and application of research to decision-making processes" (Chapter 6, p. 119). Mutunga's contribution is very much in the bottom-up, participatory human development camp.

Chacha also adopts a participatory, local-level development perspective as he describes a reforestation project in Kenya. The Mau forest in the Rift Valley—a crucial watershed for the region—is subject to "a relentless onslaught from illegal loggers and land-grabbing farmers" (Chapter 7, p. 123) that for the most part has been ignored, and sometimes abetted, by national level politicians. If sustainability means meeting current needs without diminishing the ability to meet future needs, then this current practice is not at all sustainable. Local councils of elders and community-based nongovernmental organizations recognize that the Mau forest is indispensible and have taken on pivotal roles to educate forest communities and support conservation efforts. Chacha advocates bottom-up, local-national partnerships to restore the Mau forest and the water it holds. There can be no sustainable development if there is no coordinated effort to govern "the commons."

Adjaye and Korboe continue the theme of local-level governance as a route to sustainable development in their case study of an irrigation project in Ghana. The project illustrates how participatory management and governance strategies by smallholder farmer organizations can contribute to environmental sustainability. Adjaye and Korboe introduce the case study with an historical overview of human development from 1972 to the present, noting the importance of social justice based on the participation of all concerned citizens. Although they lament, "environmental sustainability remains an elusive goal in many respects while global poverty is increasing" (Chapter 8, p. 137), they present the Ghanaian irrigation project as an effective and optimistic counterexample. The most important of several factors is the management role the project gives to local organizations representing small-time farmers. The positive economic and environmental outcomes lead the authors to recommend that future development projects should "confront the issue of sustainability within multiple integrative approaches...; ground policies and practices against specificities of local socio-ecological contexts; and recognizes the concerns of the rural South rather than those of the North" (Chapter 8, p. 134).

Having established the importance of local-level governance for the success of sustainable development, Section IV consists of three chapters that consider the challenges of local leadership in countries where identity politics often cause conflict among neighboring communities. Forrest, in Chapter 9, is more sanguine than most observers about the growing number of subnational movements in weak states that seek regional autonomy or outright secession. Instead of seeing the movements as threats to be defeated, he contends "these movements represent a ground-up effort to re-shape political power in unstable areas, aiming for new political authority at the micro-level in the wake of macro-level dysfunction across many rural or marginalized areas." Subnational movements do want to change the power structures but it is "functional separatism" that promotes political security and economic development in places where instability is the norm. Review of eight autonomous regions in Africa, leads Forrest to conclude that changes in the local governance structure, if accompanied by political tolerance and inclusivity, create new trade patterns that are directed locally and regionally, instead of being exploitatively linked to export routes. The appropriate development model in these circumstances is to build horizontal linkages among rural communities. "Horizontal linkages can contribute to development in functionally autonomous regions insofar as newly-empowered regionally-based authorities facilitate inter-peasant cooperation and flexible-market opportunities" (Chapter 9, p. 170).

Clark takes up the debate by arguing, "uncontrolled identity politics has degenerated into civil war" and impeded economic development in many parts of Africa. The countries that have maintained peace between ethnic groups have enjoyed economic growth. Therefore, "development depends on the 'taming' of identity politics" (Chapter 10, p. 176). This goal is at odds, he notes, with Western countries' promotion of competitive, multiparty politics since most political parties are built around ethnic identity groups. One potential solution, Clark suggests, is allow the devolution or partition of existing states. However, he foresees chaos and conflict if such a policy were adopted and he quickly rejects the idea that Forrest views as potentially viable. He prefers the consociational democracy model, although he recognizes it is more applicable to small European countries where it was developed. Clark concludes by flipping the question of how governance can promote sustainable development. "Only economic and social development will finally subordinate identity community politics to the politics of ideas, contestation over distributional justice, class conflict, and struggles over other social values" (Chapter 10, p. 191).

Miles begins Chapter 11 with the provocative statement, "In Africa, the interplay of religion, development, and governance is not merely intellectually compelling; it is a matter of life and death" (Chapter 11, p. 196). Through discussion of the actions of a number of African and non-African faith-based organizations (FBOs), he demonstrates their central role in conflict resolution and sustained social and economic development. Big international donors like USAID and the World Bank support many of the FBOs. With financial support come the strategic political interests of the donors and, consequently, the potential to undermine sustainable development. In particular, Miles is concerned that recent U.S. government use of FBOs in counterterrorism efforts undermines those organizations' goals of good governance, conflict mitigation, and socioeconomic development. "The challenge," he writes, "is to responsibly promote religious movements for the purposes of sustainable development and conflict mitigation" (Chapter 11, p. 205).

Section V, titled "Governance and Development," consists of five case studies that explore the ability (and inability, on occasion) of several governance models to unravel the Gordian knot of sustainable human development in the context of contentious politics. In Greek mythology, the Gordian knot famously had no visible loose end from which to begin untying it. The first 11 chapters of this edited volume identify several possible places to start, but none necessarily lead to success and some of them work in opposition to each other, potentially making the knot tighter. Does one find the loose end of the knot in top-down structural adjustment policies and external assistance to infrastructural development programs? Or is the solution to be found in bottom-up, community-based human development models? What are the most appropriate ways for local-level approaches to minimize the disruptive effects of ethnic and religious identity politics? Is it useful to see sub-state factionalism and religious movements as offering opportunities for sustainable development (and peace), or are ethnicity and religion the reasons why people fight (and ruin economies)?

Addai and colleagues, in Chapter 12, argue that objective material conditions are not as important as people's subjective assessment of their well-being, defined as "the overall sense of [material and non-material domains], including happiness and satisfaction in life as a whole" (Chapter 12, p. 212). Subjective well-being takes into account perceptions of security, fairness, and justice. These factors are important determinants of social stability when governments try to implement economic reforms. Using data from the World Values Survey in 2007, the authors study Ghana "where positive economic growth and political stability are running in tandem with deterioration in well-being" (Chapter 12, p. 214). They find Ghanaians' sense of well-being to be positively correlated most strongly with personal health, followed by ethnic and religious identity, wealth, and community engagement. There is not a significant correlation in their data with interpersonal or institutional trust, nor with civic engagement. With the caveat that their data is not as fine-grained or reliable as they would like, Addai and his coauthors conclude, "cultural and social capital variables need to be accorded serious attention" (Chapter 12, p. 229).

A sense of justice is essential to achieving economic development, which in turn is necessary for good governance and sustained peace in postgenocide Rwanda, according to Karazsia in Chapter 13. Rwanda has experienced rapid economic growth during the two decades since the genocide, which helps to dampen ethnic conflict, but the country must continue to work toward reconciliation if it is to continue on the path of recovery. In contrast to the preceding chapter's study of Ghana, he finds a sense of personal security, interpersonal trust, and "a new social contract" between government and the people to be crucial building blocks of reconciliation. Karazsia's and Addai's opposing findings on trust could be due to several considerations, most likely among them are methodological differences—a statistical snapshot in Ghana and historical process tracing in Rwanda—and the extraordinary circumstance of genocidal violence in one country but not the other.

"Violence undermines development." So begins Zuern's chapter in which she argues development "is an interactive process that relies not just on effective [state-led] planning but also on citizen engagement and support" (Chapter 14, p. 250). She contends that the World Bank and other international donors too often see the answer to the negative impact of violence on state-led development projects as requiring more state involvement and stronger state institutions, "thereby neglecting or even negating citizen input," (Chapter 14, p. 250) with potentially disastrous consequences. Like Forrest, Zuern sees opportunity where others see threat. Popular demands for change are an occasion for government to engage the population, increase democratic governance, and promote sustainable development. In postapartheid South Africa, the people faced severe political, economical, and social crises, which the government has sought to resolve by creating a "developmental state." The approach focuses on strengthening state capacity at the cost of neglecting citizen engagement in setting priorities and making no provision for government accountability to the people who are the supposed beneficiaries. That undemocratic combination has led to sometimes-violent street protests that endanger development objectives.

Ames, Picard, and Cabrera, in Chapter 15, write about development in Morocco's "competitive authoritarian" system, making the point that good governance does not consist of democratic processes alone but also includes the substance and implementation of decisions. The country's political system—led by the king and consisting of political parties that lack organizational capacity and coherent ideational platforms—is unaccountable to the people who have become disenchanted with the government and therefore do not participate in the political system. The authors argue that sustainable development requires "the international community to support political party development as part of a broad strategy supporting democratic and institutionalized governance in Morocco" (Chapter 15, p. 292). At first, this position appears to oppose Zuern's findings in South Africa on the dangers of development programs that aim to strengthen the state. Ames et al., however, point out that Moroccans frequently and actively participate in national and local civil society groups and political parties are responsive to those groups. To enhance this mechanism of government accountability, they call for strengthening the structure and process of governance by engaging political and civil society actors at the local level, accompanied by limited and focused efforts to support party capacity at the national level.

The final chapter in the book's section on governance and development is an exploration by Mogale and Picard of fiscal decentralization as a mechanism for restructuring the functions of national and local governing bodies. Like Zuern, they locate their study in South Africa and find reason to be concerned about the sustainability of subnational and local governing structures. Echoing a theme that carries through many of the chapters, they suggest "because local government is linked to service delivery," poorly functioning local government institutions detract from development goals (Chapter 16, p. 299). They trace fiscal reforms since 1994, showing that the national government "still has a highly centralized policy control mediated by uneven patterns of implementation caused by inefficiencies, corruption and limited fiscal resources" (Chapter 16, p. 304). The imbalance is most noticeable in the mismatch between revenue and expenditures at the provincial and local levels, leading to budget shortfalls and dependence of local governments on national financial assistance, which moves accountability for implementation of policies out of the local sphere.

Closing Remarks

The interdependence of political stability and economic development is widely recognized, but debates continue about the nature of the relationship. This book seeks to move the discussion in a new direction. It adopts a human security perspective and in so doing it naturally takes people rather than states as the point of reference. As the target date for achieving the MDGs passes, much progress has been made but extreme poverty continues to haunt hundreds of millions of people around the world, many of them in Africa. If the goal is to lift people out of poverty, then normal everyday people have to be integrated into the processes that set development priorities, monitor progress, and hold responsible parties to account. Sustainable human development needs local agents to have a strong voice and that requires governing processes that are participatory, equitable, accountable, and responsive.

Reference

UNDP. 1997. *Governance for Sustainable Development Conference.* New York, July 28–30. New York: UNDP.

Index

A

B

C

D